iGuerilla

iGuerilla

Reshaping the Face of War
in the 21st Century

by
John Sutherland

H P c

History Publishing Company
Palisades, New York

Copyright © 2015 by Sutherland, John R., III.

LCCN: 2015941182
ISBN: 9781940773100 (QP)
ISBN: 9781933909706 (e-book)
SAN: 850-5942

iGuerilla : reshaping the face of war in the 21st century / by John
Sutherland. -- Palisades, New York : History Publishing Company,
[2015]

pages ; cm.

ISBN: 978-1-940773-10-0
Includes bibliographical references and index.
Summary: iGuerilla traces the history of warfare from the Roman
wars with the Huns, Goths and the many barbarian hordes, to the
present wars with Hamas, Hizbollah, ISIS, Al Qaeda and other
emerging Jihadist organizations. It explains the differences between
the Sunni and the Shia segments of the Muslim world, and outlines
their objectives and how they intend to achieve them, including the
use of social media to recruit, propagandize and organize. It also
illustrates how Western states can deal with and defeat the Jihadists
by containing them, as was done to the Communist threat in the
Cold War.--Publisher.

1. Military history. 2. Military history, Modern. 3. War--
History. 4. Security, International. 5. Jihad. 6. Terrorism--
Religious aspects--Islam. 7. Violence--Religious aspects--Islam. 8.
Islamic fundamentalism. 9. Foreign enlistment. I. Title.

HV6431 .S88 2015
363.325--dc23   1505

Published in the United States of America by
History Publishing Company, LLC
Palisades, New York

For the Love of my Life—Lisa.

Thanks for believing in me and driving me towards completion.

And our Kids Beth, Hannah, Kai, Shea for keeping me humble.

On April 19, 2013, as the hammer dropped on the Brothers Tsarnaev, my boss asked for my opinion; *'are these guys lone wolves infected with jihad fever or are they in the terrorist network?'* They're networked, I said. Believe it or not, lone wolves are as scarce as hen's teeth in the Internet Age. Self-radicalization of anyone other than a madman or a tragic survivor is exceptional. Radicalization usually requires external influence – a mentor/enabler.

Consider the *In Cold Blood* murderers of the Holcomb, Kansas, *Clutter* family. *Richard 'Dick' Hickock* planned a caper to plunder an imaginary safe while urging his compatriot, *Perry Smith*, to leave no witnesses. They found a full house and an empty safe. Actually there was no safe at all. Perry dutifully fulfilled the role drummed into his head by Dick by killing Mr. and Mrs. Clutter and two of their four children who had the misfortune of being home at the time of the failed robbery. It's doubtful that Perry could, or would, have massacred the Clutter family without Dick's hectoring influence. That's how it works.

The World Wide Web is crawling with hate mongering mentors. These digital demagogues spew virtual vitriol to any anxious acolytes willing to listen via Blogs, YouTube videos, Facebook posts, Twitter, and numerous other social media outlets. They *inspire* their targets with impossible utopian visions. Then they *incite* them to hate the enemies blocking the utopian vision. Then they *suggest* ways and means to punish the enemies. Then they sit back and watch the carnage unfold without exposing themselves to hazard. The agitators agitate and utopia is deferred; awaiting more blood sacrifices.

The *Boston Bombers* are the most recent examples of wiki-warriors. They struck using relatively low cost, commonly available commercial materials, to spread high visibility mayhem. They didn't need a military industrial complex or elaborate labs.

Dzhokhar and Tamerlan Tsarnaev's pressure cooker schematics can be found online in Al Qaeda's *Inspire* Magazine. The components are easy enough to acquire and shape. They didn't need to be affiliated with a terrorist group although they probably were. They didn't need their own ideology or motivation – it was down-loadable online in the form of an Australian hate merchant Imam. Everything they needed was online. The Tsarnaev's are likely homegrown, self-tasking, virtual volunteers, reruited by an agent of an *official* terrorist network. They're not lone wolves; they're pawns.

Wiki-warriors need not form their own ideas or chose who to hate or how to hurt them. They need not decide when or where to hit the enemy or how to maximize media coverage. Everything the aspiring *'terrorvangelist'*[1] could want is online and affordable. Modern mass killers don't need 007's 'M' to motivate or 'Q' to equip; all they need is a Netbook and a credit card.

---

[1] *Terror and Consent: The Wars for the Twenty-first Century* by Philip Bobbitt, Knopf, April 2008

Adapt and Innovate or Capitulate to Caliphate

TABLE OF CONTENTS

FOREWORD

Through the 1990s, the defense establishments of Western nations gave low priority to the threats posed by armed groups that employed guerilla and terrorist tactics. Although those threats were expanding, they were regarded as minor—discrete problems rather than an interconnected global phenomenon. After Al Qaeda's mass murder attacks of September 11, 2001, counterterrorism became a major focus of the United States and its allies. Later, in the wake of successful military operations to unseat regimes in Afghanistan and Iraq, the U.S. military and its partners confronted nascent insurgencies that gained strength over time. Insurgent organizations entered into alliances of convenience with terrorist and criminal organizations.

The United States and its partners were slow to adapt to the shifting characters of the conflicts in Afghanistan and Iraq, but eventually crafted strategies and applied resources to reverse rapidly deteriorating security situations. However, by 2014, a failure to consolidate military gains politically combined with the effects of a growing civil war in Syria and the subversion of the Iraqi government and security forces by Iranian backed militias led to a return of large scale communal violence in Iraq, the collapse of Iraqi security forces, and the establishment of a terrorist pseudo-state in portions of Syria and Iraq. In Afghanistan, a reinforced international security effort from 2010 to 2014 and the expansion of Afghan forces arrested the resurgence of Taliban groups. It remains to be seen if the collapse of security in Iraq has convinced the U.S. and partners to stay engaged in Afghanistan to harden the state against the regenerative capacity of those groups across the border in Pakistan. The security challenges in Syria, Iraq, and Afghanistan are not aberrational. As John Sutherland reveals in this important book, the iGuerilla problem, armed groups empowered by globalization, information-based technologies, sophisticated networked organization, and state weakness, represent a grave threat to international security.

Sutherland reveals how iGuerillas—those who possess a medieval vision use modern technology and a sophisticated campaign of subversion—use espionage, and propaganda to pursue that vision. These groups thrive in weak states and chaotic security conditions, conditions that they foster by undermining or co-opting governance. They manipulate the law and democratic principles. They employ violence asymmetrically, using the gruesome and indiscriminate murder of innocent people as a tactic to perpetuate conflict and establish control of populations through fear and intimidation. They establish clandestine infrastructure for communications, finance, logistics, and intelligence. And iGuerillas are increasingly adept at using social and traditional media for recruitment and to effect popular perception and international opinion.

The need to craft and implement a comprehensive response to this threat is growing. Sutherland anticipates how terrorist and insurgent organizations will acquire, develop, and apply more dangerous capabilities in the future. These groups are no longer limited to remote areas of the globe. They operate within and across state boundaries, across geographical regions and, sometimes, globally. Many of these groups already possess military and informational capabilities previously associated only with nation states. By describing these groups in detail, Sutherland has laid the foundation for an international response to the grave threat modern guerillas pose to all civilized peoples. Strategy must begin with an understanding of the enemy. Most citizens of the nations engaged militarily in Afghanistan, however, would have difficulty even naming the main enemy organizations against which their soldiers, alongside Afghan security forces, are fighting (i.e. the Haqqani network, Hizb-Islami-Gulbuddin, and the Quetta Shura Taliban).

Without an understanding of the enemy, it is difficult to appreciate what is at stake and how to respond. And failure to understand the enemy can produce strategies that are inadequate and inflexible. The ability to craft and execute an effective strategy against iGuerillas is increasingly vital to national and international security. As Henry Kissinger observed in his book *World Order*, we may be "facing a period in which forces beyond the restraints of any order determine the future." Sutherland has provided readers with a valuable resource for engaging a subject vital to securing our societies from an increasingly complex and dangerous threat.

H.R. McMaster

INTRODUCTION

Next

¡Guerilla

"We have slain a large dragon, but we live now in a jungle filled with a bewildering variety of poisonous snakes. And in many ways, the dragon was easier to keep track of."
—James Woolsey

In 1941 the Japanese Empire sent a Naval Task Force to attack the U.S. Pacific Fleet at Pearl Harbor, Hawaii. The Task Force consisted of 6 aircraft carriers, 2 battleships, 2 heavy cruisers, 1 light cruiser, 9 destroyers, 8 tankers, 23 fleet submarines, 5 midget submarines, and 414 aircraft. The sailors and airmen were recruited, trained and equipped by one of the world's Great Powers at the time. It took years of training to prepare them for their mission. On December 7th they attacked and sank 18 ships, killed 2,402 people and wounded another 1,139. It was the first direct attack on American soil in the 20th Century. It also prompted America's entry into World War II.

Sixty years later on September 11th, 2001, 19 Islamists hijacked four commercial airliners, two 757s and two 767s, to use as guided missiles to attack America. The hijackers were recruited by a stateless terror group. They were armed with box cutters and some had flight simulator training. Two planes were crashed into two World Trade Center Towers in NYC; a third crashed into the Pentagon in Washington DC; and the fourth crashed in Pennsylvania after the passengers resisted the hijackers. It was probably headed for the White House or the Capital. The attacks killed 2,996 people; caused 10 billion dollars damage; prompted the grounding of all civil aviation; caused a stock market crash; and triggered two wars—all for a half million dollars or less.

Al Qaeda's 9-11 terrorists weren't the first iGuerillas; nor were they the most innovative or imaginative. They were just the first to achieve large scale success by killing thousands, causing billions of dollars of damage, and capturing the attention of world media for months. I argue that the first iGuerillas emerged in, of all places, Japan. They were a millenarian cult, like Al Qaeda, led by a charismatic leader, like Usama Bin Laden, motivated by an apocalyptic vision, like the restoration of the Caliphate. They were Aum Shinrikyo (Supreme Truth) led by Shoko Asahara. In 1993, they launched a biological attack by releasing Anthrax over Tokyo. It failed because they used a vaccine strain harmless to healthy people. Other than an unpleasant stench in the air, there was no sign of the attack. They also tried to release hydrogen cyanide into a public ventilation system that also failed due to a faulty detonator. Their first success came in 1995 when they released sarin gas in the Tokyo subway system that killed a dozen people, sickened some 5,000 plus and left hundreds with lingering side effects.

Aum and AQ's web warriors and tech terrorists were inspired, empowered and enabled by a new world order that gave them access to technology, information and travel. The path to the iGuerilla goes through three 20th Century wars (two hot and one cold) that dramatically decreased state control of information, technology, trade and movement. The resulting democratization of power debilitated the state and allowed the stateless to achieve state-like destructive capacity while avoiding state-like accountability. While terrorists grew more powerful by exploiting information and technology; states grew more vulnerable given their over-reliance on the same information and technology to run their infrastructure. This is the great information age asymmetry. Tech systems that replace redundancy with efficiency are cheap and easy to attack and result in catastrophic results. The attacker is more capable and the defender is more vulnerable.

Before we look at 21st Century iGuerilla, we have to look at the 20th Century that made him.

The 20th Century was brutal. The first half featured two World Wars separated by the Great Depression and the second half featured the Cold War. According to historian and author Niall Ferguson, the two World Wars were actually one long war. He's right.

The Long War spanned 31 years like its 17th Century predecessor; the Thirty Years War. Both changed Europe and the world. The 17th Century version ended sectarian war in Europe and formalized the sovereign state under the Treaty of Westphalia. The 20th Century version ended the Great Power multipolar world and ushered in the cold war that lasted until the final decade of the Century. Its end led to the great unraveling of the 350 year old Westphalia world order.

THE LONG WAR

Round One. Part one of the long war began in 1903 with the Ilinden-Preobrazhenierevolt against the Ottoman Caliphate. As the Balkans pulled away from the Caliphate they drew near the Europe creating a new competitive hot zone which inspired full scale war by 1914. As expected, none of the Great Powers could win alone so teams formed; the Central Powers against the Allies. The whole thing ended in exhaustion in 1918.

Great Britain, France, Germany, Russia, Austria-Hungary, and the Ottoman Empire entered this round as Great Powers; only Great Britain and France remained so at the end. Germany and Russia collapsed and fell into chaos; Austria-Hungary was dismantled and the Ottoman Empire was stripped and secularized. The Romanov, Hohenzollern, Hapsburg, and Ottoman dynasties fell leaving only the Windsor House standing.

The war weary Great Powers, under the depression, realigned and picked new governments. Winner Britain maintained the status quo while France went socialist. Newly arrived Great Powers Italy and Japan, slighted at Versailles, ditched their partners in search of New Rome and the Asian Co-prosperity Sphere. Losers Germany and Russia swapped Royals for Dictators loyal to ideals over titles.

The United States moved up to Great Power status with its tide turning entry into the Great War followed by its roaring 20's economy. The Soviet Union rejoined the Great Powers and won a global fan base by transforming Imperial Russia into a fairy tale workers Utopia; a vision made more appealing given the Great Depression.

Round one of the long war left the volatile, multi-polar, Great

Power world order in place; only the names had changed.

Round Two. Round Two got under way with the Japanese in Manchuria in 1931, Italy in Ethiopia in 1935, the Spanish Civil War and the Germans in the Rhineland in 1936. Versailles inspired revanchism, helped turn small wars into world war in 1939 when the Nazis and Soviets carved up Poland to retake land lost by the Kaiser's Germany and the Tsar's Russia.

The Soviets plundered Finland while the Nazis conquered France and blitzed Britain. Japan hit the U.S. while up to its eyeballs in China, Burma and India. The second half was worse than the first. All sides learned the lessons of the first war and had studiously improved their equipment, training, and tactics. The lesson learned from Versailles was not to lose so no one accepted defeat.

While the Great Powers wore each other out in the first half, they beat each other to death in the second. Europe was reduced to rubble; Japan was in flames; China was embroiled in Civil War and everyone else was broke. Great Britain, France, Germany, the Soviet Union, Italy, Japan and the United States entered round two as Great Powers. When the dust settled; only America and the Soviet Union were left. The Soviets had the world's largest army but the Americans had transcontinental bombers and nukes.

The old world order was gone. There were no more Great Powers vying for Imperial dominance in a multipolar world. The world's fate was tied to two Super Powers vying for ideological dominance in a bipolar world haunted by the specter of nuclear holocaust.

COLD WAR

Closing Act. The second half of the 20th Century was dominated by the Super Power standoff between two states; the United States of America (USA) and the Union of Soviet Socialist Republics (USSR). The Americans championed participatory democracy and free market capitalism while the Soviets championed dictatorship of the proletariat and command economy communism. They were about as opposite as they could be.

The Super Powers were so named given their record in WWII.

They fielded the world's largest and most powerful armies, air forces, and navies. They also had nuclear bombs, missiles, and submarines. Clearly, neither state nor the world could survive a direct confrontation between these mighty powers—thus the war would be a Cold War.

But the Cold War was cold in more ways than one. It froze the potential of head to head confrontation between the Super Powers but it also froze all the traditional motives for war. Everyone had to side with the East or West and had to clear their actions lest an errant provocation spark a nuclear exchange. The ethno-sectarian, irredentist and revanchist tensions over faith, blood and land were shelved in deference to the secular ideological struggle between communist authoritarianism and capitalist democracy.

The Cold War ebbed and flowed between tense moments like the Cuban Missile Crises and hopeful moments like the Apollo-Soyuz mission. All in all, the conflict itself was indecisive; it was the combined effects of socialist economic failure coupled with the one-two punch of perestroika and glasnost that exposed the rickety foundations of Soviet Communism. On December 1991 the Hammer and Sickle was lowered form the Kremlin flagpole for the last time and the Russian Federation Tricolor was raised in its place. An exodus of the nations previously chained to the Soviet Union followed throughout 1992.

The era after communism dawned with hopes for the end of history; mankind finally united behind liberal democracy and free market economics.

HYPER POWER

And Then There Was One. In January 1993 William Jefferson Clinton took office as America's first post-Cold War President. It was a time of optimism and high hopes embodied by his foreign policy of Engagement and Enlargement. America would engage the world's newly freed states and enlarge the family of democracies. The old world order based on the bipolar standoff between the Superpowers was over. In its place was the seemingly more stable, unipolar, Hyperpower, new world order. The United States was the reluctant draftee responsible for global security.

Positive Developments. The world seemed to be a safer place. NATO grew by adding former Warsaw Pact Satellites to the alliance and Russia was neither able nor willing to stop the shift. Localized blood-baths in remote corners of the globe such as Rwanda, Somalia, and Sudan burned but none of them threatened to trigger a Super Power clash. Europe and most of the rest of the world reduced defense spending to cash in on the Peace Dividend. The specter of nuclear war dissipated drastically as Russia and the United States reduced their nuclear stockpiles. The resolution of the Cold War was seen by some as the end of History as the world rallied around liberal democracy.

- *Pax Americana.* In the post-Cold War world war era, war and peace were pursued on American terms. Operations Desert Shield, Storm and Provide Comfort were U.S. led interventions in the oil rich Middle East that would not have been possible during the Cold War. In fact, Saddam Hussein's invasion of Kuwait wouldn't have been possible either. Events that would have triggered a nuclear standoff a decade earlier now prompted hyper-power resolution. While global peace didn't break out, neither did the threat of global war. Global tensions and conflicts remained local and contained. We had entered a period of localized conflicts that would not provoke a general war among Great or Super Powers. Pax Americana resembled Pax Romana and Britannia where the world's dominant power guaranteed relative peace.
- *Globalization.* Another benefit of the post-Cold War thaw was the opening of the world. The barriers between the pro Soviet camp and the pro American camp came down literally and figuratively with the Berlin Wall. The former Soviet satellites were free to travel, trade, and communicate with the west. Open borders and nearly unrestricted travel, free trade and global communications exploded—legal and illicit.
- *Internet Revolution.* One of the leading drivers of the expansion of global trade and communications was the explosive growth, accessibility, and increasingly collaborative nature of the Internet. The World Wide Web was finally worldwide. Government restrictions on access and content faded as powerful social media tools expanded.

- Amazon went online in 1995 (Customer base of 30M+)
- BLOGS (1997 / 2009) (~ 240M)
- Face Book used for organization and collaboration (2004) (1.1B)
- Flickr for images (2004) (87M))
- YouTube for clips (2005) (1B/Mo)
- Twitter for micro blog and proliferation of links(2006) (218M)

- *Negative Developments.* Weapons Proliferation was the immediate problem as the remnants of the Red Army were liquidated and nuclear, chemical and biological weapons expertise hit the open market. Former Soviet scientists and rogue nuclear experts, like Pakistan's AQ Khan, cashed in on the global hunt for weapons of mass destruction in the emergent weapons bazaar. The buyers were wannabe regional powers like Libya and Iran and non-state terrorists like Al Qaeda. The U.S. and its allies scrambled to contain the hemorrhaging of such destructive technologies but plenty of leakage occurred in the chaotic years following the Soviet collapse. The sharing and proliferation of lethal capabilities was exasperated by the unleashing of the age old tensions of ethnic nationalism, sectarianism, and revisionism: blood, faith and land.
- *Nationalism.* A nation is a large body of people from the same ethnic family who usually share a common territorial origin, language, history, culture, and religion. They are conscious of their identity and unity and seek a government of their own. The long war was sparked by an ethnic nationalist struggle between the Serbs and Austro-Hungarians. Nationalist passions repressed during the Cold War were violently unleashed after it. European tribalism began to make a comeback during the Soviet Union's slow decline which began during the Soviet invasion of Afghanistan. With the fall of the Soviet Empire, it erupted. First came the exodus from 'the prison of nations' as the former Soviet Republics declared their independence. Next came the violent breakup of Yugoslavia along ethnic lines followed by the amicable breakup of Czechoslovakia. The peoples of the world were

aroused and seeking self-rule in their historic homelands making the 90's the decade of the Nationalist Awakening.

- *Sectarianism.* Sectarianism refers to faith with a sect being a body of people who adhere to a particular religious faith or denomination that is defined by strict qualifications for membership. Faith based wars dominated history for centuries and played a part in part one of the long war. In particular, the Caliphate defined the Islamic world from the 600's to the early 1900's until the dissolution of the Ottoman Empire by the Turks. Islamists, who seek the restoration of the Caliphate under Sharia Law, chafed under post Ottoman dictators but their desires were also suppressed by the Cold War. The loosening of bipolar restraints unshackled the Islamist pursuit for the reunification of the Islamic world. The world's Muslim states weren't going to lead the charge as rulers retrenched. The task was left to non-state actors who had joined in Islamic resistance movements in Chechnya, Bosnia-Herzegovina, Afghanistan and throughout Asia. Sunni terrorist groups, in particular, popped up like mushrooms. Al Qaeda, which started as a mujahedeen group in Afghanistan, saw the victory over the Godless Super Power Soviets as a divine mandate to restore Muslim global dominance. On September 11th, 2001, they took their divine writ to a new level by attacking the other super power; the United States. Within a year Islamist terrorism would engulf the world and the decade would end with the beginning of the Arab Spring/Islamist Winter. The 2000's would be the decade of the *Islamist Awakening.*
- *Revisionism.* Political revisionism is the desire to depart from the generally accepted practice of the times in order to amend or correct the situation. Revisionist states seek their return to relevance. Germany and Italy were the revisionist states of the 20's and 30's. Russia and China are the revisionist states of the 2010's. China has pressed its claims, mostly unsubstantiated, throughout the Pacific and the South China Sea at the expense of Vietnam, Japan, and the Philippines to name a few. Russia has invaded Georgia, stripping it of Abkhazia and South Ossetia which are now autonomous republics of Georgia; Russian protectorates.

The Ukraine followed as Crimea was annexed outright with Lugansk and Donetsk locked in a Russian backed civil war. Moldova and the Baltic States are also feeling the heat. Russia and China are seeking the end of uni-polarity in favor of Great Power multipolarity. Russia would dominate Eurasia, China would dominate Asia and the Pacific, and the U.S. would dominate the West. Their theoretical tools are revanchism, the state policy of retaking lands previously lost under duress such as the Ukraine for Russia, and Taiwan for China and Irredentism the state policy of acquiring another country's territory as justified by cultural, historic or ethnic reasons such as the Crimea for Russia and a number of Pacific island chains for China. The 2010's will be the decade of the *Great Power Awakening*.

- *Multipolarity?* The positive developments are reinforcing the negative developments making for a challenging 21st century. Instead of a lone hyper power, we may well see a future with three Great Powers (U.S., Russia, China), a few regional hegemons (Brazil, South Africa, Iran, India) and a half dozen stateless micro powers (ISIL, AQAN, Taliban) with the gap between top and bottom narrowing all the time. In many ways, 2014 looks more like 1914.

iGuerilla. In the wake of the fall of Saddam Hussein a new type of insurgent emerged in the bowels of Iraq. Gone were the Che Guevara, low tech, guerilla bands stalking the hinterlands toting vintage AK47's and pineapple grenades; replaced by something altogether different— more lethal and frightening.

The new age insurgent tote cell phones and lap tops; his tools are anything but vintage. They organize on Facebook, communicate on Twitter, propagandize on YouTube, recruit on blogs and equip themselves with state of the art consumer technology that's re-tasked for destruction. Unlike the Guerilla Che, the iGuerilla Zarqawi didn't have to pull off spectacular attacks in the defended heart of an enemy stronghold to get attention. Zarqawi simply kidnapped an American aid worker and made a horrific video. With his hostage kneeling before him, he read his manifesto then he decapitated him; on film. The bloody spectacle was posted on YouTube where it was sure to go viral in the Internet age. People the world over logged in to see the gruesome terror vision exhibition like motorists rubbernecking at a roadside accident. Abu Musab Zarqawi and Al Qaeda in Iraq were on the map.

The ready for primetime graphic violence of the Berg beheading was tailored made for the visually oriented information age millennials. Why such barbarism? The answer to that highlights another aspect of the iGuerilla.

iGuerilla's use modern technology but are motivated by ancient goals. Che's Cold War guerillas were driven by a secular utopian ideology designed to unite the workers of the world under the red banner of communism. They meant to transform the existing order and replace it with a 'brave new world'. Zarqawi's iGuerillas are driven by a sectarian dystopian ideology designed to subjugate the un-believers of the world under the black banner of Islamism. They mean to destroy the existing order and replace it with a resurrected medieval Caliphate.

iGuerillas use progressive means in pursuit of regressive ends resulting in an exponentially more dangerous and lethal threat. His modern tools give him a destructive capacity that rivals many states. Internet media exploitation gives him global access to the disaffected and asocial. His religious motives are non-negotiable and his license to kill is sanctioned by Allah. His call for a primal society appeals to the cynics tired of political compromise. His pitiless mind is uncluttered by modern sensibilities and he unambiguously states what he wants and he goes after it. He is barbarous and yet is a tech savvy denizen of the modern world. He's a schizophrenic cross between Attila the Hun and Mark Zuckerburg. He uses the best of the present to resurrect the worst of the past.

The Islamist iGuerilla claims to be a victim of imperialism while seeking to impose imperialism. He has one foot in an unjust present and the other in a glamorized past. For him, there is no doubt filled navel gazing; no cultural self-loathing; and no revisionist past. Instead there is triumphalism; a sense of inevitability and confidence that appeals to a legion of 'rebels without a cause'. Add the incessant barrage of jihad video "warnography" and you have a witch's brew that is barbarizing the Middle East while inspiring rogue state copy cats. The iGuerilla Dark Ages have spread to the Levant, North Africa, Arabia and East Asia and has been imitated in Georgia, Ukraine and the South China Sea.

- An Australian recruit and his son hold up heads of decapitated Syrian soldiers
- American and British hostages are beheaded on camera in Syria
- Christians are stoned in Mosul and Iraqi troops are lined up and shot
- Yazidi women are sold in sex slave markets
- Al Houthi insurgents crucify Yemeni soldiers
- Palestinian collaborators are shot in the street before a crowd
- Boko Haram terrorists slaughter 59 students at a boarding school in Nigeria
- Al Qaeda in the Maghreb kidnap and kill French hostages in Algeria
- A Malaysian airliner is shot down by Astroturf separatists in Ukraine killing 298

Al Qaeda in Iraq (AQI), the premier iGuerillas, took the new wave up several notches after they fled the Anbar Awakening and U.S. Surge in Iraq for the Syrian Civil War. AQI became the Islamic State of Iraq and the Levant (ISIL). The brutality that failed them in Al Anbar made them heroes in the all or nothing Syrian conflict. With each battlefield victory, they earned Islamist recruits and inherited Syrian military gear. Their stock rose with the U.S. withdrawal from Iraq followed by the anti-Sunni crackdown led by Iranian toady Nouri Al Maliki. The result for ISIL was a flood of trained Iraqi soldiers.

Almost overnight, ISIL went from iGuerilla band to iGuerilla Army. On 29 June 2014, ISIL took the unprecedented next step by declaring itself a state. They claimed to be the mythical Caliphate itself with their leader, Abu Bakr al-Baghdadi, as Caliph. All Muslims were historically compelled to support the "Islamic State". As expected, the Islamic State recognizes no borders and aspires to reclaim the ancient Caliphate from Spain to India and the Balkans to North Africa. All this is just a prelude to the inevitable establishment of the global Caliphate ruled by Sharia and worshipping Allah alone.

The Islamic State mimics the iGuerilla tactic of declaring ungovernable spaces as mini-states, statelets and city states that defy international conventions and the Westphalian global security model. Like the infamous pirate state of Tortuga, these statelets become rogue safe havens used as attack launch pads against the surrounding states. Their willful rejection of international law allows them to execute any atrocity or crime with impunity.

The process of declaring autonomy without international consent has spread to non-Islamist aggressors like the Russian backed faux separatists in Transnistria, South Ossetia, Abkhazia, Crimea, Luhansk and Donetsk and by China in the Senkaku and Paracel Islands. This is the ultimate expression of a New Dark Age: unchecked aggression in pursuit of uncompromising sectarian and nationalist goals.

The iGuerilla has accelerated the process with the innovative exploitation of modern technology coupled with adaptive tactics, techniques and procedures that are learned and proliferated on the World Wide Web. We will explore: the rise of the iGuerilla, his methods and their growing influence on states.

The iGuerilla has been on the march since his first breakthrough. There was 9-11 in 2001; the Moscow theater attack in 2002; the Madrid bombings in 2004; the London bombing in 2005; Hezbollah's rocket war in 2006;Lashkar-e-Taiba's Mumbai attack in 2008; the Maersk Alabama in 2009; Arab Spring kickoff in 2010; the Syrian Civil War in 2011; Mali in 2012; the Boston Marathon bombing in 2013; and the Islamic State's Caliphate in 2014. We could add Israel's Operation Cast Lead 2009 and Protective Edge 2014. The latter uncovered a network of tunnels and a nefarious plan by Hamas to use those tunnels to blow up grade schooners, insert kidnappers, and unleash raiders in a Palestinian Tet that aspired to kill thousands.

Stateless exploitation of Information, technology, the web, global travel and "Lawfare" the use of law as a component of warfare to delay tactical and strategic procedure, will accelerate and keep the pressure on. The civilized world will struggle to develop affordable and effective responses to what the iGuerilla's are doing now while also trying to anticipate what they will do next.

In this book we'll explore the confluence of three major trends that led to the rise of the iGuerilla; the reawakening of nationalism and sectarianism; the information revolution, and globalism. The fourth trend, revisionism, will not be covered in depth since the resurgence of Russia and the assertion of China are big but not closely related topics.

We'll explore how iGuerilla's exploit the three major post-Cold War trends to make their local causes go viral. We'll see how they use the web to recruit, radicalize, and eventually task jihadists. We'll see how social media is used to distribute propaganda and finance operations. We'll see how global markets enable weapons acquisition and development and, perhaps most importantly, we'll see how iGuerillas collaborate, share lessons learned and proliferate successful terror tactics.

As important as it is to understand where they are now, we must also try to determine where they might be headed in the future. How will Moore's Law and Carlson's Curve effect weapons of mass destruction (WMD) development in the years ahead. What does the future hold in store? What capabilities will the iGuerilla develop in terms of cyber, nuclear, chemical and biological warfare? When will they get drones, robotics, and nanotechnology and what will they do with it? Will mass disruption be even more effective than mass destruction? We'll discuss:

- The rise of ideologically unconstrained transnational state threats and their alternately governed regions that erode state control and the impact of diplomacy.
- How the emergence of global communications through the Internet allows the stateless threat to transcend state control of information and enables learning and dissemination of information, enhances recruiting and facilitates the proliferation of propaganda.
- How access to advanced weaponry and the proliferation of weapons of mass destruction couples with the exploitation of consumer technology to makes borders less defensible.
- How decreased restrictions on movement between states and open borders have allowed local threats to go global.

- How Western values coupled with liberal national and international laws have been used as tools known as Lawfare.
- How global trade, global currency exchange, and the energy market are increasingly outside state control, empowering stateless threats.
- How stateless threats co-op political instability and how rogue and aggressor states are emulating their success.

We can't know it all but we can trace the trajectory to develop a concept of how the iGuerilla will shape 21st Century Warfare.

PROLOGUE

"The future ain't what it used to be."
—Yogi Berra

> pro·gres·sive (pr?-gr?s'?v) adjective - Moving forward;
> advancing.
> re·gres·sion (r?-gr?sh'?n) noun - Reversion; retrogression;
> relapse to a less perfect or
> developed state

Wiki-War gets its name from the online encyclopedia that drove Britannica's into extinction. Wikipedia was the first of its kind, getting input from anyone with expert knowledge and the willingness to share. The old model of collecting esoteric authors to write about esoteric topics was gone. Gone too was the door to door salesman, the new cyber version is online and free. Anyone can contribute and anyone can learn. You trade off a higher incidence of error for broader coverage and instant access. Serious researchers don't quote Wikipedia but they go there first to get the lay of the land.

Wiki-War is like Wikipedia: anyone can contribute and anyone can get access. There are no screeners of barriers—its point click conflict. The Internet bestows 'wikiness' by globalizing information that used to be either guarded by the state or was the purview os a few criminal masterminds. Today, you don't need chemistry degree or a jihadist friend to figure out how to build a fertilizer bomb; all you need is a laptop and a Starbucks with free Internet.

This new ease of knowledge acquisition bypasses the discipline of invention. The 'user' simply employs the acquired information without responsibility. He uses progressive techniques in pursuit of regressive goals. Wiki-warriors are making wholesale mayhem collaborative, cheap, and accessible. Anonymous miscreants are able to pursue mass disruption or destruction.

Sectarian motivation makes extreme Wiki-war even more attractive. War-like attacks are more likely to come from sectarian fanatics cloaked in non-state anonymity. In the old days, it took Imperial Japan or Nazi Germany to attack a major western city. They wouldn't get away with it either since they were identifiable and accountable. Today's wiki-warriors can attack New York, Moscow or Mumbai and get away with it.

In the radical sectarian world progression, or moving forward, coexists with regression, moving backwards. The secular dictators of the past have been supplanted by the Sheikh and fake Jihadi, the militant militiaman, and the apocalyptic cultist of Wiki-World.

The Three Laws of Wiki-War

Moore's Law - a hypothesis that postulates that processor speed will double every 18 months thus spurring exponential increases in computer processing and capability.[2]

Carlson's Curves – Moore's Law applied to biotechnology; it postulates that biotechnology makes exponential leaps forward while becoming progressively less expensive.[3]

Metcalf's Law – the value of a telecommunications network is proportional to the square of the number of connected users of the system.[4]

Enemy States
Stateless Enemies
User-friendly conflict
Come as you are combat
Global Warfare version 2.0

---

[2]http://www.intel.com/technology/mooreslaw/ - In 1965, Intel co-founder Gordon Moore predicted that the number of transistors on a chip would double every two years. Intel kept pace for nearly 40 years.

[3]*The Pace and Proliferation of Biological Technologies* by Rob Carlson,
http://www.kurzweilai.net/meme/frame.html?main=/articles/art0614.html - Carlson's Curves mirrored Moore's Law, applied to Bio Technology; the capability will increase

[4]http://www-ec.njit.edu/~robertso/infosci/metcalf.html
The Fundamentals of Information Science

"The greatest impact of this information age is that it makes the global masses aware of their inadequacy."
—**Ralph Peters** [5]

Laws in Motion:
- Home Box Office debuts in 1972
- CNN debuts in 1980
- Harvard Graphics becomes the first presentation program in 1986
- The first formal PowerPoint presentation is delivered in 1992
- Fox Network News debuts in 1996
- Facebook debuted as Facemash in 2003; by 2011 Facebook has roughly 800 million subscribers
- Three former PayPal employees debut YouTube in 2005
- Twitter is a microblogging service that was launched in July 2006: it has over 140 million active users as of 2012

Generations.   The interval of time between the birth of parents and the birth of their offspring is defined as a generation. This is usually defined as approximately 30 years.   Social scientists explain the behavior patterns of generations by studying the customs and events of their time.

1978.   When I began this project in 2008 my initial question was, *"Where were we thirty years ago?"* [6] Leonid Brezhnev was the General Secretary of a seemingly omnipotent Soviet Union and Jimmy Carter was President of a faltering United States.   The Shah ruled Iran and Ahmad Hassan al-Bakr was president of Iraq.   Afghanistan was a Soviet satellite and Osama Bin Laden was an obscure scion of a wealthy Saudi businessman and the world geopolitical system was based on the secular Westphalian model.

Global affairs were dominated by the bipolar *'Cold War'* between

---

[5]Ralph Peters is an outstanding contemporary strategist with a multitude of informative and insightful books such as *Beyond Baghdad* and *Wars of Blood and Faith* among many others.

[6]Martin Gilbert's *A History of the Twentieth Century Volume Three: 1952-1999* is an excellent resource for contemporary history.

the United States and Soviet Russia. The world aligned with one or the other of the superpowers by necessity. The North Atlantic Treaty Organization (NATO) and the Warsaw Pact held center stage, Poland was a satellite while the Ukraine and Georgia were part of the USSR proper.

Yugoslavia and Czechoslovakia were states. Bosnians, Serbs, Croats, Slovaks, and Kosovar's were anachronistic relics of European tribalism and Islamism was unheard of outside of Egypt. The only Muslim terrorists were secular Palestinian hijackers. In 1978 there were no nukes in Pakistan or India.

Global passions were held in check by the threat of nuclear escalation as was amply demonstrated during the Cuban Missile Crises and the '73 Arab Israeli War. Mutually assured destruction regulated global conflict.[7] Wars like WWII were obsolete. Atomic wars fought by super powers were the wave of the future. The threat of imminent destruction inhibited all other potential forms of global conflict. Local struggles remained local; they were not allowed to spread.

Laptop computers, Net-books, the Internet, CD's, DVD's, thumb-drives, Blueray, and biotechnology either didn't exist or weren't accessible to the masses. There was no Hotmail, g-mail, chat-rooms, blogs, Yahoo, Google, Flickr, or eBay. There was no HLN, MSNBC, CNN, or FNC. Flat-screen TV's, cell phones, GPS, and DNA sequencing were the stuff of Star Trek, The Twilight Zone and sci fi novels.

In 1978, there were only 200,000 personal computers sold for a total of $500 million. Shipments of floppy disks reached 270,000 and Microsoft recorded its first $1 million year. Radio Shack shipped 100,000 TRS-80 computers while deliveries of Commodore computers reached 25,000 and Apple II reached 20,000. Atari's Pong was the cutting edge of computer games and cordless phones were theoretical. News was largely restricted to 30-minute broadcasts on one of the three networks or from newspapers.[8]

---

[7] See Bernard Brodie's *Strategy in the Missile Age* for a detailed discussion of Cold war strategy.

[8] CNN's Video Almanac online at
http://www.cnn.com/resources/video.almanac/ provided a full review of the history of the cable news network.

Only soldiers, diplomats, and political junkies knew what was going on in the global backwaters like Georgia, Afghanistan, Pakistan, or Somalia. Travel outside ones homeland was limited to jet setters and government officials.

Utopians, nihilists and apocryphal miscreants were isolated in their own myopic little worlds. They resorted to occasional violent local outbursts that were as alarming as they were irrelevant. They operated alone or in small groups, cults, or cells. The 'nut-jobs' were self-contained and were incapable of spreading their paranoia given their lack of access to anything more than local outlets. Jim Jones and Yasser Arafat could whip up some support but they couldn't go 'viral'. Global outrage was rare even in the aftermath of the '72 Munich Olympics.

Today's angry men are not limited to petty crime or obscure backwater movements in petty third world states. Modern guerillas can go online and form networks of like-minded individuals or join ones already in existence. Whether you are a utopian, a nihilist, or a secular humanist or sectarian theocrat, a political ideologue or a criminal...it makes no difference. If you search long enough and hard enough you can form, join, or find a posse of likeminded malcontents and you can develop the capacity to kill any number of people. Once they meet in cyberspace, anything is possible.

This phenomenon has been accelerated by globalization and accessible high level technology.[9] The 'barbarians at the gate' are no longer Goths and Huns—today they are Islamists and Drug Lords. They are not tied to states though they may derive succor from them. Al Qaeda (AQ), Lebanese Hizballah (LH), Earth Liberation Front (ELF), and Somali Pirates are autonomous though they can and will form coalitions with states where possible thus generating hybrid warfare. Today's barbarians are marauders whose prosperity is based chaos. They are opportunist exploiting declining state influence.

I don't propose to offer any new revelations. I propose to offer a description of what's happening accompanied by a few ideas about why it's happening and how we might respond. All that I know for sure is...that the times, they are a changing...

---

[9]For a brilliant exposition of the nexus of globalization and terrorism, see *Terror and Consent: The Wars for the Twenty-First Century* by P. Bobbitt

21st Century
Progressive Regression

Terrorists
Militias
Pirates
Arms Dealers
Drug Traffickers
Hacktivists
and
Rogue States

ACRONYMS

AAB - Abdallah Azzam Brigades (*Terror Group*)
AAD - Ansar al-Dine (*Terror Group*)
AAI - Ansar al-Islam (*Terror Group*)
AAMB - Al-Aqsa Martyrs Brigade (*Terror Group*)
AASLT - Air Assault
ABN - Airborne
AH - Al Houthi
ALOC - Air Line of Communications
ANF - al-Nusrah Front (*Terror Group*)
ANO - Abu Nidal Organization (*Terror Group*)
AO - Area of Operations
AOI - Army of Islam (*Terror Group*)
AOR - Arear of Responsibility
APOD - Air Point of Departure
APOE - Air Point of Embarkation
AQ - al-Qaeda (*Terror Group*)
AQAN - Al Qaeda and Associated Network
AQAP - Al Qaeda in the Arabian Peninsula
AQAP - al-Qaeda in the Arabian Peninsula (*Terror Group*)
AQI - Al Qaeda in Iraq
AQIM - Al Qaeda in the Maghreb
AQIM - al-Qaeda in the Islamic Maghreb (*Terror Group*)
AS - al-Shabaab (*Terror Group*)
ASG - Abu Sayyaf Group (*Terror Group*)
AUM - Aum Shinrikyo (*Terror Group*)
BH - Boko Haram (*Terror Group*)
C2 - Command and Control
CNA - Computer Network Attack
CCMD - Combatant Command
CENTCOM - Central Command
CIA - Central Intelligence Agency
CJCS - Chairman of the Joint Chiefs of Staff
CND - Computer Network Defense

COIN - Counterinsurgency
CONOP - Concept of Operations
CONPLAN - Contingency Plan
CONUS - Continental United States
CW - Conventional Warfare
DEA - Drug Enforcement Administration
DHS - Department of Homeland Security
DIA - Defense Intelligence Agency
DOD - Department of Defense
DOJ - Department of Justice
DOS - Department of State
DTO - Drug Trafficking Organization
EGY - Egypt
ELF - Earth Liberation Front (*Environmentalist Group*)
ETA - Basque Fatherland and Liberty (*Terror Group*)
EUCOM - European Command
FARC - Revolutionary Armed Forces of Colombia (*Terror Group*)
FID - Foreign Internal Defense
GPF - General Purpose Force
GPS - Global Positioning System
GWOT - Global War on Terror
HADR - Humanitarian Assistance and Disaster Relief
HAM - HAMAS (*Terror Group*)
HQN - Haqqani Network (*Terror Group*)
HUJI - Harakat ul-Jihad-i-Islami (*Terror Group*)
HUJI-B - Harakat ul-Jihad-i-Islami/Bangladesh (*Terror Group*)
HUM - Harakat ul-Mujahidin (*Terror Group*)
HUMINT - Human Intelligence
HVI - High Value Individual
HW - Hybrid Warfare
IA - Interagency IC - Intelligence Community
IDAD - Internal Defense and Development
IDF1 - Israeli Defense Force
IDF2 - Indirect Fire
IED - Improvised Explosive Device
iG - iGuerilla

IG - Gama'a al-Islamiyya (*Terror Group*)
IJU - Islamic Jihad Union (*Terror Group*)
IMINT - Image Intelligence
IMU - Islamic Movement of Uzbekistan (*Terror Group*)
IO - Information Operations
IRA - Irish Republican Army (*Terror Group*)
IRGC - Islamic Revolutionary Guard Corps (*Iran*)
IRN - Iran IS - Islamic State (Terror Group)
ISIL - Islamic State of Iraq and the Levant (*Terror Group*)
ISIL - Islamic State of Iraq and the Levant (*Terror Group*)
ISIS - Islamic State of Iraq and al Sham (Syria) (*Terror Group*)
iT - iTerrorist
IW - Irregular Warfare
IZ - Iraq
JAT - Jemaah Anshorut Tauhid (*Terror Group*)
JCS - Joint Chiefs of Staff
JEM - Jaish-e-Mohammed (*Terror Group*)
JI - Jemaah Islamiya (*Terror Group*)
JOA - Joint Area of Operations
JOC - Joint Operations Center
JSOTF - Joint Special Operations Task Force
JTF - Joint Task Force KH - Kata'ib Hizballah (*Terror Group*)
KSA - Kingdom of Saudi Arabia
LAF - Lebanese Armed Forces
LeT - Lashkar-e Tayyiba (*Terror Group*)
LH - Lebanese Hizballah (*Terror Group*)
LIB - Libya
LIFG - Libyan Islamic Fighting Group (*Terror Group*)
LL / BP - Lessons Learned and Best Practices
LOC - Line of Communications
LOO - Line of Operations
LTTE - Liberation Tigers of Tamil Eelam (*Terror Group*)
MAGTF - Marine Air Ground Task Force
MASINT - Measurement and Signatures Intelligence
MB - Muslim Brotherhood (*Terror Group*)
MEB - Marine Expeditionary Brigade

MEF - Marine Expeditionary Force
MEU - Marine Expeditionary Unit
MJTF - Micro-Joint Task Force
MOIS - Ministry of Intelligence and Security (*Iran*)
MSC - Mujahidin Shura Council in the Environs of Jerusalem
    (*Terror Group*)
NCTC - National Counter Terrorism Center
NEO - Non-combatant Evacuation Operations
NGO - Non-Government Organization
NORTHCOM - Northern Command
NSA - National Security Agency
OCO - Overseas Contingency Operations
ODS - Operation Desert Storm
OEF - Operation Enduring Freedom
OIF - Operation Iraqi Freedom
PA - Palestinian Authority
PACOM - Pacific Command
PFLF - Popular Front for the Liberation of Palestine (*Terror Group*)
PFLP-GC - PFLP-General Command (*Terror Group*)
PIJ - Palestinian Islamic Jihad (*Terror Group*)
PKK - Kurdistan Workers Party (*Terror Group*)
PLF - Palestine Liberation Front (*Terror Group*)
PLO - Palestinian Liberation Organization (*Terror Group*)
POTUS - President of the United States
PRC - Peoples Republic of China
PUP - Pop up Point
PVO - Private Volunteer Organization
RF - Russian Federation
SASO - Stability and Support Operations
SEG - Super Empowered Guerilla
SEI - Super Empowered Individual
SET - Super Empowered Terrorist
SFA - Security Force Assistance
SIGINT - Signals Intelligence
SL - Shining Path (*Terror Group*)
SLOC - Sea Lines of Communication

SOCOM - Special Operations Command

SOF / SF / SPF - Special Operating Forces / Special Forces / Special
    Purpose Forces

SOUTHCOM - Southern Command

SPOD - Sea Port of Debarkation

SPOE - Sea Port of Embarkation

STRATCOM - Strategic Command

SYR - Syria TAL - Taliban (*Terror Group*)

TG - Techno Guerilla

TTP - Tehrik-e Taliban Pakistan (*Terror Group*)

UAV - Unmanned Aerial Vehicle

UK - United Kingdom

UN - United Nations

U.S. - United States

USA - US Army

USAF - US Air Force

USAID - US Aid

USCG - US Coast Guard

USMC - US Marine Corps

USN - US Navy

VBIED - Vehicle Born Improvised Explosive Device

VEO - Violent Extremist Organization

VH - Venezuelan Hizballah

VSO - Village Stability Operations

CHAPTER 1

Trinity
The Divine Shift

State—Nation—Culture

From Red Guards and Red Brigades
to
Revolutionary Guards and Martyrs Brigades

"The first, the supreme, the most far-reaching act of judgment that the statesman and commander have to make is to establish . . . the kind of war on which they are embarking."
—Karl von Clausewitz

The Paradoxical Trinity. The famous Prussian military theorist Karl von Clausewitz defined the dynamics that regulate war as the paradoxical trinity. This trinity represents the three driving forces that animate and drive the decision to engage or disengage in war. According to the master, the tri-polar forces are rationality, chance, and passion. Rationality is represented by the policy making of the state in accordance with its interests; government. Chance represents the probability of success as represented by the military. And passions represents primordial violence, hatred, and enmity; the desires of the masses aka, the people. The trinity can thus be summed up as the government, the military, and the people.[10]

According to Clausewitz, war is held in suspension between the three trinity poles. The interplay between poles defines the terms of conflict if and when it erupts. The triad maps out collective motivation (people) against restraint (policy) and feasibility (military). If the trinity tilts toward policy; conflict tends to be pragmatic. If it favors prob-

---

[10] *On War* by Karl von Clausewitz; Michael Eliot Howard (Translator), Peter Paret (Translator), Princeton University Press, June 1989.

1

ability; conflict tends towards opportunism, adventurism and hyperac-
tivity. When the trinity favors passion it opens Pandora's Box. If the
'mob' goes to war, it does so for emotional reasons, opening up a treas-
ure trove of old but not forgotten hatreds, jealousies, rivalries and
bloodlust that encourage an uncompromising war of annihilation.
Wars of faith and culture are wars of passion.[11]

The trinity describes why we fight which, in turn, defines the
nature of the conflict or how we will fight. Defining the motivation
exposes the motivator and it's not always the state anymore. Loyalty
shifts away from the state for many reasons: declining state legitimacy
given a failure to provide basic services, inability to enforce the rule of
law, appeal of sectarian (above the state) interests, or cultural-ethnic
clashes. These are powerful motivators that can replace the state as the
primary source of loyalty and identification. These competing interests
weaken the state if the state cannot provide compelling reason for dedication to it.[12] Here are some alternative identities for which people
will fight. I propose the priority below from highest to lowest:

- For blood—loyalty to family, clan, or tribe
- For the faith and the culture—loyalty to shared religion and
  shared history
- For the people—loyalty to common nationality
- For the political order—loyalty to the state or to a secular
  ideology
- For the sovereign and his claims—loyalty to the rulers and their
  estates
- For king and country—loyalty to the monarch and his realm

People fought for faith, not the state, during the Thirty Years War
(1618-1648), passion in the trinity model.[13] Each combatant saw him
or herself as the keeper of the true faith whose actions were sanctioned
by God. Although this war was a sectarian based fight, shadowy spon-

---

[12] *The Coming Anarchy; Shattering the Dreams of the Post-Cold War World* by Robert
Kaplan, Random House, August 2000.

[13] *The Harper Encyclopedia of Military History Fourth Edition* by R. Ernest Dupuy and
Trevor N. Dupuy; Harper Collins, 1993.

sors lurked in the shadows backing the Holy Warriors. These puppet-masters fed the bloodlust in pursuit of secular motives. France's Cardinal Richelieu was the prime culprit. He backed Protestants and Catholics in spite of his loyalty to the Pope. Richelieu's goal was to prevent German unification thus perpetuating French continental dominance. He succeeded and in the process, he shifted the state system away from chaotic sectarian based conflict towards rational secular conflict. After a generation of bloodletting to resolve the internecine Christian crises, Europe's leaders built a new system to prevent a repeat. The result was the Peace of Westphalia which radically altered affairs of Europe.[14] The key states in the war were France and Sweden against Spain and the Holy Roman Empire although the fighting was carried out by numerous small groups with a multitude of different loyalties. They decided the sovereignty of each state within the Holy Roman Empire would be recognized. The resulting political reorganization of the German states left France dominant at the expense of the Habsburgs. The provisions regarding ecclesiastical affairs prohibited religious persecution in Germany and, by treaty, the religion of each state would be determined by its prince. Westphalia ended sectarian war of passion in Europe and replaced it with secular wars of rational policy. Wars were to be in the interest of the pragmatic state rather than the passionate congregants. Wars for the state are negotiable while wars for the faith are uncompromising.

The Monarchy replaced the clergy as the arbiter of war until the French Revolution removed their King and replaced him with a Republic nominally in service to public will. Napoleon merged the people (nation) and the state and thus introduced Nation State Warfare. War re-escalated as passion merged as peoples fought for their states, replacing the relatively small dynastic mercenary armies who fought for the sovereign. WWI and WWII saw nation-state war reach its post Westphalian peak. In spite of the bloodshed, we remained nation-state warriors until recently where we see coexistence between nation-state soldiers and resurgent pre Westphalian holy warriors. Let's pause and review some basic definitions.

---

[14] Diplomacy by Henry Kissinger, Simon & Schuster, April 1995

****

"War is not an independent phenomenon, but the continuation of politics by different means."
—Karl Von Clausewitz

When analyzing a conflict we need to assess the sources of identity of the combatant. We should ask where their loyalty and motivation comes from. Is it faith, family, tribe, clan, or nationality—non-state drivers of instability? The answer tells you the likelihood of compromise and the cost to get there. Ever since Westphalia, the prime reason for war was to defend the state or nation-state.

The unification of the people and the state into a single entity with a singular purpose, the nation state, arrived with a vengeance birth of the French Republic.[15] From Robespierre to Napoleon, the people and the state became fused into one. They had to since the revolution had brought France into conflict with all of the Monarchs of Europe. The nation state was a powerful entity and persisted through to the close of the century.

The nation-state dominated warfare throughout the 20th Century and the wars were secular, in service to political goals. The nation state is fading fast in the post-cold war era.[16] In many states, loyalty is shifting away from the state towards non-state entities like Islamism in the Middle East or Drug Traffickers in Latin America. The shift is based on the failure of states to deliver services and disillusionment fueled by Internet global awareness. During the Cold War, one of the Superpowers would step in and ensure stability by delivering services rather than risk losing the state to the opposition. The post-cold war world can't afford to continue the practice thus rising expectations meet declining delivery. The Internet has made people in failing states aware that they are in failing states. Sectarian actors fill the void left by the state by providing a

---

[15] *Holy Madness: Romantics, Patriots, and Revolutionaries, 1776 - 1871* by Adam Zamoyski, Penguin Books, 1999.

[16] *The Coming Anarchy; Shattering the Dreams of the Post-Cold War World* by Robert Kaplan, Random House, August 2000.

unifying identity to the vulnerable population. They also provide basic services at the local level in exchange for loyalty.[17]

Lastly, they provide a form of resistance that promises a future that harkens back to past glory. They provide a way to fight the state, other nationalities, or the world. Their wars lack state structure (uniformed armies) and state rationale (political restraint) but they replace the latter with holy passion. The sectarian non-state actor engages in conflict unable or unwilling to compromise or negotiate. The lack of state driven restraint encourages asymmetric unrestricted warfare given stateless actors' lack of accountability. There is no established global structure that can isolate and hold responsible non-state actors. The trinity is becoming grossly out of balance.

Non-state actors loyal to an extra-state entity employ asymmetric warfare due to their lack of state military resources. Their lack of geographic identity, borderless basing, anonymity, and exploitation of ungoverned space, makes effective retaliation near impossible. There are no capitals to strike or states to invade—does one beat the dog to kill the fleas? The overt state actor facing the covert non-state actor is often reduced to manhunts and whack-a-mole 'hits' as his only option. Conventional kinetic retaliation against the host state endangers innocent geographic cohabitants and may end up swelling the stateless leader's ranks.

So how does this change things? The cold war strategic level was fairly straight forward. Every international act could be traced back to a specific location on the map and a political leader and his capital. Belligerent actors could be singled out and be held accountable. This kept states in check, especially in the shadow of nuclear war. Even insurgents were tied to sponsors. Local cancers like the PLO wandered from state to state only to be ejected when they brought too much heat on their sponsors—see Black September in Jordan.[18]

The operational level of war during the cold war was every bit as complex then as it is now. Our cold war enemy fought us on the land,

---

[17] *The Clash of Civilizations and the Remaking of World Order* by Samuel Huntington; Simon & Schuster Adult Publishing Group, January 1998.

[18] *Blood and Rage: A Cultural History of Terrorism* by Michael Burleigh; HarperCollins Publishers, March 2009.

sea, air, and in space. They countered us globally—politically, economically, technologically, and militarily. The difference was that we could see each other and both sides knew there were limits. Both the US and the USSR were accountable for their actions.

The tactical level of war during the cold war was regulated. Armies fought armies, navies fought navies, and air forces fought air forces; state militaries fought state militaries with a few exceptions. The US and the USSR engaged in posturing rather than direct conflict and occasionally indulged in proxy wars using a client to challenge the other superpower—the U.S. versus North Korea or the Viet Cong and the USSR versus the mujhadeen. Even in these cases the tactical fights were restrained. The superpowers equipped their clients with enough to attrite and exhaust the opponent but not to annihilate it. Major weaponry was under tight state control. Woe to the state whose signature was found in a rogue insurgency's armaments.

Nationality and culture were a largely irrelevant curiosity subordinated to political considerations—see Tito's Yugoslavia. Such issues were not allowed to endanger the 'balance of power'. The US and the USSR could annihilate each other and, knowing this, did not. Our allies, partners, and proxies knew that they would perish if they sparked a superpower exchange and even when they didn't care about the consequences, like Cuba during the missile crises, the superpowers wouldn't allow it. During the Cold War, conflict was forced to acknowledge the political and military logic of mutually assured destruction. Non-political, non-secular, considerations were not tolerated.

****

Westphalia is history for now. Today, we are forced to operate outside of the confines of the secular state regulated system. Our emerging enemy is less conventionally capable, less pervasive, and less powerful but he is also less restrained, less distinct and less visible and his capability is growing. Rogue states can now get away with transferring capability (Iran, Syria, North Korea) and the Internet provides training forums and information exchanges. We now face pockets of fanatics embedded in civilian populations that defy force on force engagement.

Today's strategic level of war is more complex. Bloggers, social media, and cyber-linked hactivists monitor every step taken by highly visible states while the shadowy non-state players only expose what they want exposed. To see this principle in action, one need look no further than Lebanon or Gaza where the Israel was criticized based on doctored Hizballah web photos of Beirut and activist reports in Gaza. The state is the focus while the abuses of Hizballah and Hamas go unreported. The IDF got hammered over collateral damage while Hizballah and Hamas kidnapping and targeting of civilians went ignored. Second guessers plague every state move fostering a zero defect mentality which is impossible to achieve in armed conflict. Non-state actors defy accountability.

Today, we have to deal with nations that span multiple states with varying degrees of complicity. Nationality and culture count now.

If non-state actors get WMD's, they'll be less restrained when it comes to using them. Who would we retaliate against? States can be targeted while nationalities, cultures, and faiths cannot.

> *"Being a revolutionary is about purity and rigidity. But governing is all about compromise and flexibility."*
> **—Mosab Hassan Yousef**[19]

---

[18] *Son of Hamas* by Mosab Hassan Yousef; Saltriver, 2010.

CHAPTER 2

The Edge of Chaos
Wiki World

Wiki-World

"Every era has a currency that buys souls. In some the currency is pride, in others it is hope, in still others it is a holy cause. There are of course times when hard cash will buy souls, and the remarkable thing is that such times are marked by civility, tolerance, and the smooth working of everyday life."
—Eric Hoffer [20]

Global Guerillas and Initial Conditions.   On October 13, 1977, Lufthansa flight LH181 was flying from Palma de Mallorca to Frankfurt with 91 passengers and crew on board. The plane was hijacked enroute by four Palestinian militants wearing Che Guevera T-shirts looking to free eleven Red Army Faction (RAF) terrorists from prison in Stuttgart.

The leader was Zohair Youssif Akache who went by the alias, "Captain Martyr Mahmud." The operation was executed in tandem with a kidnapping of a prominent German businessman named Hanns-Martin Schleyer by elements of the RAF. Mahmud, like the RAF kidnappers, demanded the release of the terrorists along with $15 million U.S. dollars for their trouble. If the terrorists were not freed; the kidnappers would execute Schleyer and the hijackers would blow up flight 181 killing all the hostages on board.

Flight 181 embarked on a circuitous journey, landing in Larnaca, Bahrain, Dubai, then heading on to Oman, where it was denied permission to land. Mahmud changed course for Yemen where he expected a hero's welcome. The captain was not allowed on the main runway and

---

[20]*The True Believer* by E. Hoffer remains the seminal work for discerning the motivation of utopians and fanatics.

was forced to land on a side dirt strip. Following the landing, the captain sought permission to check the condition of the landing gear. He was allowed to leave the plane but did not immediately return even after attempts to recall him and a threat to blow up the plane were issued by Mahmud. When he returned, Mahmud shot him in the head. The Yemeni's allowed them to refuel but would not allow them to stay. Flight 181 took off for the Somali capital of Mogadishu.

On October 17 flight 181 landed at the Mogadishu airport and the captain's body was dumped on the tarmac. Mahmud announced an ultimatum that the RAF terrorists had to be freed by 14:30 that afternoon. As the deadline approached, the terrorists prepared to blow up the plane and kill the hostages. They doused the passengers with the duty free liquor on board, telling them that it would make them burn better. They then emplaced explosives and fuses in full view of the passengers. A German negotiator in the tower convinced the hijackers that the prisoners would be released but that the authorities needed a few more hours. Mahmud extended the deadline to early the next morning.

All along a team of German commandos augmented by British SAS observers had been following the hijacked flight since Larnaca in a commandeered Boeing 737. The team planned an assault of 30 men in six teams of five. They would approach the plane from the rear and, using black aluminum ladders, would assault the aircraft through escape hatches under the fuselage and over the wings. Late on October 18 the Somalis secured the airfield. The team stormed the plane around at 23:00 after the Somalis distracted the hijackers with the airport lights and by setting a fuel tanker on fire in front of the plane. Seven minutes later four of the terrorists were dead, including Mahmud, and one female terrorist was wounded and captured. One commando and a flight attendant were injured and all the remaining crew and hostages were rescued.

Several RAF terrorists awaiting release committed suicide when news of the failed hijacking reached them in prison. Hanns-Martin Schleyer was executed and his body was left in the trunk of a car in France.[21]

---

[21]Michael Burleigh exhaustively reviews modern terrorism from the 1800's to today in his book, *Blood and Rage: A Cultural History of Terrorism.*

What is Wiki War? Is it a gimmick or something? Wiki War is the conflict rooted in the Wiki-pedia model. Everyone has access to Wiki-pedia. Everyone can add to it and everyone can learn from it. It's a living document that is visited and edited daily.

Wiki War where...
Anyone can join, anyone can contribute, and everyone learns.

Progression.   The trajectory of technological development has been phenomenal. From WWI to today we have gone from the Model T to the Lunar Rover, the Biplane to the Space Shuttle, and the Rolodex to the Blackberry. In September 1956 IBM launched the 305 RAMAC, the first computer with a hard disk drive (HDD). The HDD weighed over a ton and stored a whopping 5 megabytes (MB) of data. A common two-inch thumb drive easily holds 64 gigabytes (GB) plus and the capacity is doubling every year. The number of transistors that can be inexpensively placed on an integrated circuit is increasing exponentially, doubling every two years.[22]

Our knowledge, information, and technology are progressing geometrically. They enable us to share what we know and how we do what we discover. What we share is up to us. States have little power to intervene. Todays information is egalitarian and uncontrollable.

Regression.   The counter to the progress above is the resurgence of medieval ethnic and theological motives for war. Wars of blood and faith ended in the west with the Treaty of Westphalia which codified the secular nation-state system. Or so we thought.

Faith based war lingered on a bit longer in the Muslim world only to be terminated with the fall of the Ottoman Empire.[23]   The Ottoman's were the last caretakers of the Caliphate (the Islamic Empire launched by Mohammad around 600AD). The Ottoman Turks expanded the empire to its ultimate limit and then presided over its slow decline as the new powers of Europe ate away at their gains. WWI was the final straw for the Ottomans. Their numerous disastrous

[22] See *Moore's Law* as stated by Intel co-founder Gordon Moore. Moore predicted that the number of transistors on a chip would double every two years. He was right.

[23] *The Harper Encyclopedia of Military History Fourth Edition* by R. Ernest Dupuy and Trevor N. Dupuy; Harper Collins, 1993.

defeats had exposed their anachronistic culture and as a result, Kamal Attaturk led the 'Young Turks' in overturning and secularizing Turkey. In a stroke Attaturk annihilated the Caliphate, an act that is seen by today's Jihadi's as one of the greatest crimes of all time.[24] Attaturk dissolved the Islamic Empire and erased Islamic law (Sharia) and transitioned to secularism.

The Muslim world finally joined the west although many of its people did not. State governance and international affairs stopped pursuing religious (sectarian) interests. They transitioned to non-religious (secular) interests. Faith was, for the time being, a personal issue. Secular fascists and atheist communists replaced Christian Crusaders and Muslim Jihadi's as the new face of radicalism.

Secular causes were passionate but pragmatic. Winning or losing was not a matter of the soul and was not a path to heaven or hell. Secularists could negotiate and compromise and could acknowledge defeat. More importantly, secularists could adjust to life under opposing systems. Secularists choose survival over martyrdom.

The post cold war backslide from negotiable secular movements to antiquated, uncompromising, sectarian movements does not bode well for the future. Given divine sanction, holy warriors are capable of mass murder and unrestrained cruelty.[25] They are propelled by the conviction that their actions are taken in the service of the Almighty Himself. Killing non-believers is pleasing to God. Yesterdays inquisitors are today's Jihadi's—cruel, unyielding, and utterly justified in their pursuit of their implacable goals. They seek the creation of Heavens Kingdom on earth. Any and all actions are valid and beyond human laws, condemnation, or contempt. Sectarians only seek peace in order to regroup for the next attack. They are an insidious and persistent threat to world peace.

Wikifying Warfare. Wiki war is the wedding of progression and regression. It is the merging of modern technology with antiquated motives. Sectarian fanatics, zealots, and fundamentalists can now access a fully modern range of capabilities to pursue their version of Utopia.

---

[24] *The Canons of Jihad* by Jim Lacey; Naval Institute Press, 2008 discusses Qutb's seminal work, Milestones

[25] Robert Kaplan wrote an entire book on this subject: *Warrior Politics: Why Leadership Demands a Pagan Ethos* by Robert D. Kaplan, December 2001, Random House Publishing Group.

The Jim Jones' and Shoko Asahara's of the world can now expand their deadly visions well beyond their myopic and toxic cults.

Social media has become a virtual loaded gun; the Mumbai attackers used satellite phones to maintain contact with their handlers in Pakistan, Egyptian agitators used Facebook to start demonstrations in Tahrir square in Egypt, and Al Qaeda in the Maghreb has adopted Twitter in its campaign win popular support in Mali. Terrorism, insurgency, and insurrection can be planned in the open and on the web. The days of shady characters meeting in smoke filled backrooms to avoid police surveillance are over. The masterminds need not hide and a flashy blog can recruit thousands whereas a corner speech, ala Lenin or Hitler, might reach a few hundred.

The Changing World. The Peace of Westphalia ended the Thirty Years War, a hodgepodge sectarian conflict that devastated central Europe. The result was the birth of secular state sovereignty. War became the province of the state and faith became an internal matter. From Napoleon through the World Wars to Saigon and Baghdad, modern war has been motivated by state interests.[26] Non-state players were not allowed a seat at the table nor were they taken seriously if they tried to horn in. States set the terms, regulate global interaction, and define the interests of the nation.

The state system seemed inviolate until 9-11. Prior to that moment it was inconceivable to imagine anyone, state or non-state, of launching an attack on US soil capable of killing thousands, destroying iconic structures, and generating billions of dollars in damage. Somehow it had become possible. This was the Pearl Harbor of the new millennium but it was more—it was a lethal strike on a world power by non-state actors. The enemy was the precursor to the network of non-state actors motivated by a sectarian (religious) utopian vision. They operated without regard to state borders unconstrained by the fear of retaliation. The end of the Cold War came, and with it came the end of identifiable targets to respond to. There was no government of physically autonomous geographic location that the U.S. could hold accountable.

With the demise of the bi-polarity and its promise of Armageddon,

---

[26]*Diplomacy* by Henry Kissinger, Simon & Shuster; April1995, does an excellent job outlining the evolution or warfare from sectarian to secular.

we faced a multiplication of threats similar to that seen when Rome fell as the global arbiter. Now, there were global terrorists, guerillas, pirates, criminal organizations, and hackers. Aspiring regional hegemons could pursue their goals using these non-state actors as proxies. This is how our newest lethal threats no longer originated from states. Without super power backers, states became so weak that they could not eject the terrorists within their borders. How did the terrorists develop the ability to deliver state like destruction? Do states have a legitimate monopoly on violence and coercion any longer?

It seems trite to say that globalization changed everything—but it did. What is globalization? Let's start with a formal description: *Globalization* is the trend to move from domestic markets to global markets. This increases global interconnectedness and interdependence. Proponents say globalization helps developing nations catch up by providing jobs and access to technology while critics complain that it erodes state sovereignty and encourages wealthy nations to ship jobs overseas to cheaper markets. [27]

Ludwig von Bertalanffy developed General System Theory (GST) to analyze and describe any group of objects that work in concert to produce a result. He identified two types of systems; closed and open. A *closed system* is a one in a state of isolation from the surrounding environment. In reality, no system is completely closed—there are only varying degrees of closure. An *open system* is one that is in continuous interaction with the environment.[28] An engine on a bench, enclosed in Plexiglas, would be a closed system. Put it in a car on the road and it becomes an open system.

Global commercial interaction was relatively closed—limited to very few—before global communications, international corporations, and the World Wide Web. The global security environment was also relatively closed; bounded by the zero sum Cold War world. The end of superpower bipolar restraint opened this up as well.

[27] See the *The Shield of Achilles: War, Peace, and the Course of History* by P. Bobbitt; Knopf Doubleday Publishing Group, September 2003, to read Bobbitt's description of the rise of the 'Market State.'

[28] See the *General System Theory: Foundations, Development* by Ludwig Von Bertalanffy, Braziller, George Inc, March 1969, in the School of Advanced Military Studies-it was illuminating.

Optimal systems operate between order and chaos with the *edge of chaos* being where the rate of evolution is maximized. A totally ordered, closed, system ossifies while a totally chaotic, open, system disintegrates. The goal is be between ossification and disintegration. As the global system expands and adds players, it accelerates and operates in a semi-autonomous manner. This makes it increasingly difficult to monitor.

System dynamics measures complex systems using feedback loops and time delays that affect behavior. These describe how even simple systems display *nonlinearity*. The structure of the system is as important in determining its behavior as the individual components within it are. In some cases the behavior of the whole cannot be explained in terms of the behavior of the parts. In *nonlinear system*, the output is not proportional to the input. The globalized world is nonlinear. Who figured that a Pakistani scientist who studied abroad, would steal and parlay centrifuge technology into an illicit, off the shelf, nuclear weapons black market (AQ Khan)?[29]

We'll borrow a few more concepts from science, then tie it all together. *Complexity Theory* is the study of complex chaotic systems. It looks at how order and structure arise from even though its behavior is non-deterministic and lacks any obvious method for predicting future outcomes.[30] The stock market is a complex system and although trends emerge, actual outcomes are unpredictable. No one saw the crash of October 29, 1929 that kicked off market losses of an estimated $50 billion from 1929 to 1931 en-route to triggering a global depression

Complexity theory introduced *the butterfly effect*: the idea that an insignificant event can cause a disproportionately large effect over time. History is full of examples like the Boston Massacre shot heard 'round the world or Gavrilo Princip's assassination of Archduke Ferdinand. Globalization's butterfly effect was probably the Defense Advanced Research Projects Agency (DARPA) project to develop an interconnected network to facilitate shared research—a network that became the Internet.

---

[29] See Bobbitt's *Terror and Consent: The Wars for the Twenty-First Century*; Random House Inc, April 2008, for a fascinating breakdown of the AQ Khan Network.

[30] *Complexity: The Emerging Science at the Edge of Order and Chaos* by M. Mitchell Waldrop; Simon & Schuster Adult Publishing Group, September 1993.

Chaos in complex environments springs from an excess of complicated information rather an absence of information. Chaos is still somewhat deterministic. With fore knowledge of the initial conditions and the context of action; a reasonable range of likely events can be predicted. A large number of linear interactions generates stable behavior patterns while a small number of non-linear interactions generate chaotic behavior. The vast majority of people who access the Internet will use as intended, in a predictable way. A small numbers of users will exploit it in an unanticipated way. If we are sensitive to initial conditions, we can predict who is likely to abuse it. In retrospect, "Irhabi 007" and his Jihad webpage should have come as no surprise. His posting of Islamist snuff videos to recruit followers from all over the world was inevitable.[31]

Globalization diffuses power, wealth, and knowledge while simultaneously weakening state sovereignty. It's as empowering as it is disruptive. It allows more people to monitor global affairs and spreads discontent by highlighting the imbalance of competitiveness, wealth, and power. Globalization generates jealousies previously nonexistent given the pre-internet info flow. It elevates local conflicts to the world stage—local goes viral and ends up global. Anyone with a credit card and a laptop can get a GPS, night vision goggles, a kit helicopters, or even private sub. Google what you want and see what pops up.

So what does this all add up to? Post Cold War access to global info-systems, knowledge, and technology empowered non-state players and weakened states. Non-state groups used to be an irritant to the state, now they are an existential threat to it. State geographic and political boundaries are dissolving into impotence or irrelevance.

Agents of Change. There are six major trends that have led to the massive transfer of power from the states to the stateless.[32] All are predicated on the proposition that the aggregate power of the state is declining.

---

[31]*Terrorist 007, Exposed*, By Rita Katz and Michael Kern, Sunday, March 26, 2006, *The Washington Post*, www.washingtonpost.com/wp-dyn/content/article/2006/03/25/AR2006032500020.html

[32]Bobbitt's Terror *and Consent: The Wars for the Twenty-First Century* outlines the globalization process.

Globalization Trends that are changing the World:

1. Global Information and Communication
2. Global Weapons Market
3. Global Mobility
4. Global Law
6. Global Trade
7. Global Empowerment

Total Access. Information used to travel at the speed of the Pony express. Next came the telegraph, the radio, and the Internet. With each step, we could send and receive more data, faster, and over greater distances. Today's state has little ability to control the flow of data, information and, most importantly, knowledge. They can't regulate internal information or screen external information although states like China are making deals with information providers to restrict data. Anyone with a computer can proliferate an ideology, no matter how toxic, and recruit followers. The search for like minded miscreants is simplified. Gone are the days of shutting down opposition newspapers and pirate radio stations. Long live the blog! This isn't all bad. The free flow of information has always been a democratic goal but we must be cognizant its second and third order effects—not all knowledge or users are benevolent. The market of ideas has burst wide open and access to all varieties of expertise is readily available to Googlers good and bad. The free flow of information is the key driver of change.

Global communications on the Internet and via global telecoms transcends state control. Information, and the news can go where people want it to go and it can be spun however people want it spun. Throw in social medial like Facebook, Twitter, and YouTube and you have instant comms for organizing a flashmob in NYC, a terror attack in Mumbai, or an uprising in Egypt. Terrorists, criminals, pirates, and smugglers can organize more easily and rapidly than most state intelligence agencies.

The growth of the Internet has been extraordinary. It has penetrated all corners of the globe and is accessible to most peoples in most languages. Search engines allow anyone to seek out high-end scientific and engineering information at the speed of light—you are only limited by your ability to data mine and drill down.

Electronic commerce like eBay and Amazon allows most anyone from most anywhere to buy most anything. Blogs, websites, email, and chat rooms allow esoteric and isolated groups to network across the world. States can't insulate themselves from outside influences nor can they restrict their own disaffected from engaging the outside world in search of support. Local causes effortlessly go global.

A novice surfing the Internet can find and print out advanced research papers and can purchase complex technology given a credit card and a PO box. The cyber marketplace makes technology readily available. The recipe and the ingredients are there for any aspiring cook. Online commerce is near impossible to control.

Expertise can be gained without experimentation given academia's publish or perish culture. The acquisition of knowledge, lethal or benign, no longer requires discipline to attain. The would-be bomber doesn't need a Manhattan Project. All he need do is copy, print, buy, and follow the recipe. For example, a manual for the production of the al-Mubtakkar, a hydrogen cyanide dispersal device, appeared on al-Qaeda websites in 2005. Pulitzer Prize-winning author Ron Suskind, author of the book *The One Percent Doctrine* writes, "In the world of terrorist weaponry this was the equivalent of splitting the atom. Obtain a few widely available chemicals, and you could construct it with a trip to Home Depot – and then kill everyone in the store."[33]

Weapons Weapons Everywhere. In the Byzantine Empire it was a death penalty to share naval technology or techniques with the barbarians. In the old west, arms dealers who traded with the Natives were hung. Today's states have no such ability to regulate arms. Access to weapons of all kinds is on the rise. Non-state groups like Hizballah now have arsenals that once were the sole domain of state armies. Some came from sponsor states while others came from the web. Weapons of mass destruction are becoming accessible and will make state security prohibitively expensive.

For all the ink the catastrophic weapons are getting, the low-end

---

[33] *The One Percent Doctrine: Deep Inside America's Pursuit of Its Enemies Since 9/11* by Ron Suskind, Simon & Schuster, June 2006.

weapons are spilling most of the blood. According to the Control Arms Briefing Note, 26 June 2006, the global value of the weapons trade is estimated at $111 billion. The machete was the worlds biggest killer and the AK-47 is it's favorite firearm.[34]

The Grimmett Report to congress, officially titled as the *Conventional Arms Transfers to Developing Nations, 1999-2006, September 26, 2007, Richard F. Grimmett, Specialist in National Defence, Foreign Affairs, Defence, and Trade Division* makes the following observations.[35] Developing nations are the focus of foreign arms sales by weapons suppliers. Major sales revolve around a select few nations; China and India in Asia, and Saudi Arabia in the Middle East. Petro dollars fund Mid-East arms buys. The Grimmet Report lists weapons on todays market including tanks, artillery, mortars, rocket launchers, armoured personnel carriers, aircraft carriers, destroyers, minesweepers, torpedo boats, patrol craft, motor gunboats, submarines, patrol boats, fighter and bomber aircraft, helicopters, surface-to-air missiles, air defence missiles, Scuds, anti-tank missiles, and anti-ship missiles. These arms used to be state only and it represents only a fraction of what is out there.

U.N. Secretary-General Kofi Annan called small arms proliferation, "weapons of mass destruction in slow motion." According to the UN assault rifles and other small arms including rifles, hand-held rocket launchers, machine guns and pistols, are responsible for 90 percent of all conflict-related deaths in the last decade. This equates to about 3 million people according to the International Red Cross.

If you have a cause and some credit...you can have weapons. Grass roots insurgencies used to require incubation to build up a weapons cache. Today, it's easier to arm a movement given the cyber market, the illicit dealers, and sponsor states like Iran and North Korea and rogue proliferators like AQ Khan of Pakistan.

Full Range of Motion. It used to be traders and explorers who

[34]*Control Arms Briefing Note,* controlarms.org/wordpress/wp-content/uploads/2011/02/The-AK-47-the-worlds-favourite-killing-machine.pdf.

[35]*Conventional Arms Transfers to Developing Nations, 1999-2006,* PDF/Adobe Acrobat, 1999-2006, Sep 2007, Richard Grimmett, Specialist in National Defense, Foreign Affairs, Defense, and Trade Division, fpc.state.gov/documents/organization/93141.pdf.

'saw the world'. Global travel required royal sanction due to the cost. All that you need now is a passport and a plane ticket; the former is easy to forge and there are few restrictions on the latter. The liberalization of movement policies and easy access to travel is dissolving national borders, making them nearly impossible to regulate. States can no longer control immigration or visitation and can't screen cross border travel.

The Airports Council International's World Airport Traffic Report of 2007 reported that air traffic reached an all time high of 4.8 billion passengers, 88.5 million metric tons of cargo, and 76.4 million aircraft movements.[36] The largest market in the world remains the US and the second largest is China, the third was the UK.

The busiest airports in the world were Atlanta, O'Hare, Heathrow (UK), Haneda (Japan), and Los Angeles International. When it comes to international traffic alone, the top five are Heathrow, Charles de Gaulle, Amsterdam, Frankfurt, and Hong Kong. How hard was it for the 9-11 terrorists to move? People are moving at a rate never seen before and its changing the demographic landscape.

Some 11.2 million immigrants arrived in the US between 1990 and 2000. This is in addition to 6.4 million children born to immigrants living in the US and accounts for almost 70% of US population growth in the past decade. Immigrants now represent more than one in every ten US residents, the highest percentage in 70 years. Over the next 50 years, the US Census Bureau projects that immigration will cause the population of the United States to grow to more than 400 million.[37]

Although Mexico provides the largest immigrant population to the US, other groups are showing significant growth. The 3.5 million Arab Americans in the U.S. are becoming a significant minority. The largest concentrations of Arab Americans live in battleground states— Michigan, Florida, Ohio, Pennsylvania and Virginia. Immigrants are

---

[36] *Airports Council International*, 2007 Press Release, Traffic results from the reporting group of over 840 airports will be available, March 2007, www.airports.org/cda/aci.../main/aci_content07_c.jsp.

[37] Immigration Numbers vary; two sources referenced were the *Center for Immigration Studies* at
http://www.cis.org/ and WILLisms.com Trivia at
http://www.willisms.com/archives/2005/09/trivia_tidbit_o_168.html.

welcome, most of us are descendent from immigrants but we must know if they are coming here to assimilate or dominate. Arab American Population in California:

1980 Census—100,972; 2000 Census—220,372; 2008 Zogby Estimate—715,000.[38]

"The basic premise of the Court's argument - that American law should conform to the laws of the rest of the world - ought to be rejected out of hand."
— Justice Scalia (diss) in Roper v Simmons 583 US at 81(2005)

Justice for All. World opinion always mattered, but not much. States did what states did and it took alliances, coalitions and political wrangling to craft treaties to settle disagreements. Today, international law and finance wield deep influence over state internal affairs. The threat exploits western respect for human rights while using international law to suppress state response. These phenomena mount a serious challenge to state independence.

International law is a collection of principles and practices that govern state interaction. It differs from domestic law in that it is not made by legislation nor is there an international legislative body. Most states comply with these rules knowing that violations can evoke significant penalties. The international legal system has no standing enforcement arm. All states are equal and none can claim the right to adjudicate the actions of another. All states are bound by international law but are entitled to interpret that law for themselves—usually a political rather than legal assessment. Refusing to accept international law is the right of each sovereign but defiance is difficult for small states given the negative impact of global opinion and the financial impact of trade restrictions and/or sanctions as 'punishment.'[39]

Some now believe international law trumps state law and they use it to manipulate states. The newly empowered international legal institutions weaken state control of their own internal policy and self-defense. Look at Hizballah. They spun the world press in order to pressure the UN to stop the Second Lebanon War in 2006. They cir-

---

[38] http://en.wikipedia.org/wiki/Arab_American

[39] We again defer again to Philip Bobbitt's *Terror and Consent: The Wars for the Twenty-First Century;* Random House Inc, April 2008.

culated a doctored picture (fauxtography), used rent-a-victims to play dead at multiple sites, emplaced weapons among civilians to draw fire, and regulated media battlefield access thus ensuring biased coverage. These efforts influenced the UN, the global law enforcer, to stop Israeli operations in Lebanon.

Threat exploitation of international law and western values limits state freedom of action.[40]   Again, we reference the masters, Lebanese Hizballah (LH). They regularly violated international law during the Second Lebanon war in '06 but the backlash focused on the IDF when their return fire caused collateral damage. Outrage over civilian casualties was directed at Israel, not Hizballah. LH used Mosques and hospitals as ammo dumps and headquarters and used ambulances to move fighters. Israeli counterstrikes become lightening rods for activists who play into LH hands. When captured, terrorists exploit democratic law to evade punishment, expose sources and collection techniques, and transform public hearings into propaganda platforms.

For Sale.   Global trade will always grow. Wagon trains gave way to the railroad; sail gave way to steam, and cargo gave way to container— today the department store is being gradually displaced by the cyber-store. Virtually unrestricted global trade, currency exchange, the energy market, and the black market, are bypassing and undermine state control of trade.

International trade is regulated by the World Trade Organization and by regional arrangements such as the North American Free Trade Agreement (NAFTA) between the United States, Canada and Mexico. The WTO and the International Monetary Fund (IMF) influence state behavior by restricting trade and state credit unless state internal economic policy is shifted to meet their requirements.

Global trade is exchange of capital, goods, and services across state borders or territories. It expands the available goods and services beyond what is locally produced and is required to get critical supplies such as oil and natural gas. The rising cost of energy forced some states to trade weapons, technology, and expertise for oil. This accelerates the flow of advanced technology into regions that would otherwise not have it.

---

[40]*Learning about LAWFARE,* http://burneylawfirm.com/blog/2010/11/24/learning-about-lawfare/, The Burney Law Firm, LLC, online, 2008.

Weapons components and the systems used to create them are for sale in 'bits and pieces', this is commodification.[41] Commodification eliminates the need to develop weapons since the actor can buy the components and technologies on the market. This alarming trend has fueled the illicit WMD market as exemplified by North Korea's rocket technology sales, AQ Khans nuclear black market, and the great Soviet Union going out of business weapons sale. Commodification will accelerate in the coming years making more capability available to and more actors.

Non state Actors. During the latter days of Rome, non-state groups such as the Visigoth tribes and Hunnish hordes terrorized the empire. States have lost and gained power over the centuries but have held sway since the Treaty of Westphalia.[42] The state reached its zenith in the 20th Century but, with the end of the Cold War, we are headed back to the days of non-state warriors and religious causes. The rise of non-state actors is the most destabilizing characteristic of the modern era. Today's states cannot reign in the passions of the marauders any more than late western Rome could. Non-state entities now exert undue influence over state policy.

The new players include sectarian Islamists, secular socialists, criminal cartels, and legal entities like non-governmental organizations (NGO) and private volunteer organizations (PVO). The former coerce the state while the latter manipulate it.

Transnational threats exploit autonomous zones known as ungoverned spaces. They are ungoverned because the state cannot provide services or guarantee security there. These spaces are not limited to remote geographic areas—in today's world they include ethnic city blocks and cyberspace. Non-state actors step into the void providing order, becoming the de-facto government. They are opportunists who invest in instability.

Non-state actors obviously ignore state borders. They owe their loyalty to tribes, clans, gangs, sects, or ethnic groups—not to states. Lebanon, south of the Litani River; the Pakistani tribal regions, numer-

---

[41] See commodification in *Terror and Consent: The Wars for the Twenty-First Century* by P. Bobbitt; Random House Inc, April 2008.

[42] *Diplomacy* by Henry Kissinger, Simon & Shuster; April 1995

ous Afghan provinces, and the South American tri-border area are examples of ungoverned spaces. The groups exploiting these zones are Hizballah under Hassan Nasrallah, Al Qaeda under Ayman al-Zawahiri, the Taliban under Mullah Omar, and Fuerzas Armadas Revolucionarias de Colombia (FARC) under Alfonso Cano.

Politico-sectarian actors are today's most notorious stateless interlopers but they are not alone. The galaxy of state challengers includes NGO's like Amnesty International and Global Media outlets like Al Jazeera, and diasporas like the Kurds in Turkey or the Palestinians' in Jordan.[43] They exert tremendous pressure on targeted states.

We still haven't exhausted the list of non-state actors in play. Global criminal syndicates like Yakuza of Japan or the Mexican Mafia (La eMe) attack state legitimacy. The Zeta's of Mexico terrorize the population and corrupt state officials.[44] These criminal enterprises are in business to make money and they 'deal' with anyone who'll pay, like global terrorists. They provide access to smuggling 'rat lines' in exchange for money, training, and technology.

Non-state actors can be individuals. The 'Merchant of Death', Victor Bout was a gun runner extraordinaire who inflamed ethnic conflict and fed civil wars throughout Africa to generate demand for his weapons. He built his own airline and ran a number of routes in support of his smuggling operations. Bout's network included a series of airfields, seaports, roads, rails, and ferries that collectively comprised an extensive transport infrastructure for weapons traders who wished to remain anonymous.[45]

Bout's only rival may be Pakistan's AQ Khan—father of the Pakistani Atomic Bomb and godfather of the poor man's nuclear arms

---

[43] *United Nations Office of Drugs and Crime* (UNDOC),
http://www.unodc.org/ngo/list.jsp.

[44] *National Public Radio (NPR)*, The Mexican Drug Cartels,
http://www.npr.org/templates/story/story.php?storyId=126890893.

[45] *Russian arms dealer 'Merchant of Death' convicted by NYC jury of helping Colom-bian terrorists, Viktor Bout guilty on four counts of conspiring to kill Americans,* by Helen Kennedy and Scott Shifrel, New York Daily News, November 2011,
http://www.nydailynews.com/news/world/russian-arms-dealer-merchant-death-convicted-nyc-jury-helping-colombian-terrorists-article-1.971279#ixzz1w0k5ObzY
and *BBC News Europe, Profile Viktor Bout,* 5 April 2012,
http://www.bbc.co.uk/news/world-europe-11036569

market. AQ Khan did for nukes what Bout did for RPG's. He built a fully exportable, state purchaseable, nuclear arms program by trading centrifuge expertise for missile technology etc...he knew the business. Guys like these are the ultimate opportunists who exploit state weakness by building transnational networks that take advantage of corruption, poverty, and shifting spheres of influence. Non-state actors influence political, economic and social arenas. They often support agendas that conflict with the interests of the state they inhabit and can be religious leaders, entertainers, human rights activists, international terrorists, transnational criminals, weapons traders, or international business magnates, to name a few.

Weak, corrupt, impoverished, and badly governed states are a petrie dish that invite non-state actors infection empowered by globalization. They are unencumbered by the obligations and accountabilities of the state. Exploitation of information technologies (IT) enables non-state actors from different regions and sectors to collaborate and build ad hoc coalitions that empower their agendas. They are IT enabled and networked through partnerships, coalitions, and affiliations that can leverage influence through alliances.

States and Nations. We've spilled a lot of ink talking about the declining role and influence of the state but what is a state and does it matter if it's weaker? States used to be the entities that monopolized the application of violence. The notion that any mob could 'invade' his neighbor was suppressed in the hopes that the state, a larger entity with more to lose, would temper the passion and use violence more judiciously. Unfortunately we continually use the terms state and nation interchangeably. They are not one and the same.

A state is a politically organized body of people usually occupying a definite territory. The key here is that the organizing principal is political. Governing ideology binds the group. A state is artificial in the purist sense. On the other hand, a nation is organic. A *nation* is a people having a common origin, tradition, and language. Nations are bound to culture and loosely associated with states. *Culture* is the body of customary beliefs, social forms, and material traits of a racial, religious, or social group shared by people in a place or time. Nations are resilient. They can survive in a single state like the French; in many states like the Jews, or without a state like the Kurds. Nations can break states like Austria-Hungary and Yugoslavia or make states like Kosovo and Israel. It would seem the match made in heaven is the one forged when the nation and the state assume a single identity.[46]

What we describe above is the *nation-state*—a political organization under which a homogeneous people inhabits a sovereign state. It exists now and has existed before and has been a potent historical force. Napoleon was one the most successful leaders in modern history in fusing the nation (French) to the state (revolutionary). The resulting witches brew set Europe afire.

The Nation-Culture Challenge: Accountability. The Westphalian State system dominated state interaction during the Cold War. The operational level was as complex as it is now. The Soviets faced us on the land, sea, and air and challenged us politically, economically, and technologically. The strategic level was simple. Every act was traceable to an accountable state. Even insurgencies had fingerprints. Nationality and culture were not important. Secular ideology dominated world affairs—democratic capitalists versus communist collectivists.

The Westphalian system faded with the end of Cold War and, contrary to Fukayama's assertion, history came back.[47] The ideological glue that forced nationalities together was weakened as evidenced by the suicidal dissolution of Yugoslavia into its nationalistic subcomponents; Croatia, Bosnia, and Serbia. The tribe was back.

The global security framework is more complex. One enemy has been replaced by many. Non-state actors exploit anonymity and if discovered, evade accountability. In the post Cold War world, nationality and culture trump political ideology. We might add that modern Islamist are much more likely to use WMDs if get them than the Soviets were when they had them. If they did...who'd we retaliate against?

---

[46] *The Clash of Civilizations and the Remaking of World Order* by Samuel Huntington; Simon & Schuster Adult Publishing Group, January 1998 discusses the role of culture while *The Soldier and the State: The Theory and Politics of Civil-Military Relations* by Samuel P. Huntington, Harvard University Press, August 2008 discusses the state.

[47] *The End of History and the Last Man* by Francis Fukuyama, Free Press, Feb 2006; Francis Fukuyama optimistically asserted that the collapse of the USSR heralded the global success of the capitalist democratic system-the end of history.

States can be targeted; nationalities cannot. Even given the above, the state remains the world's dominant socio-political organization. It retains a monopoly on the power of coercion although it's grip is slipping. States are most vulnerable in non-competitive regions where there is a little or no national identity; the rule of law is weak; economic performance is poor; and corruption is prevalent. These 'failing states' are ripe for exploitation. All that's needed is an alternative. Stateless challengers emphasize the humiliation of failure, capitalize on envy and highlight government incompetence. When conflict develops, they seek protraction to wear down the state.

The Nation / State Schism. The old ways are back. Tribal and religious identity over-ride state identity. As the state declines and the nation rises; multiple nations within a state compete. Add in the increased mobility that fueled the influx of Muslims to Europe and Latin Americans to the USA and you have a clash of nations—Balkanization. The tribes and sects complain of inequity and uneven progress and dig up age-old grievances. They create perceived relative deprivation (PRD) and fan the flames of envy. The breakdown of services and the rule of law adds insecurity while endemic corruption and kleptocracy mobilize those on the margins. Gone are the days of blind acceptance of Pravda like propaganda and a compliant Soviet nation living in poverty and ignorance.

The post Cold War competition for loyalty has begun. The nations/nationalities are seeking alternative visions and the once suppressed sectarian worldviews are rising to the top of the heap. A new age of religious mass movements and neo-socialism may be upon us. Tomorrow may look more like the holy madness of the Thirty Years War or the secular chaos of the Russian Civil War. A shift in the monopoly of coercion is in progress transforming war from peer competition back to sponsor/proxy war/hybrid conflicts. The iGuerilla and the super-empowered entity are on the rise.

The Wages of Declining State Authority. The state has a few options when the nation pulls away. We are seeing leaders resorting to wholesale repression to enforce cohesion much like Tito did during his time. States can adopt populism in an attempt to provide what the nation demands. This may require a scapegoat minority for the majority to use to vent its frustrations. It also may drive states to bankruptcy. These conditions give birth to Demagogues like Hugo Chavez who exploit insecurity to consolidate power. The state may embrace its ruling oligarchy over the people. In this case, the elites probably resort to kleptocracy in order to maximize their own wealth before they fall. Lastly, the state might simply accept the schism and implode. In this case, the state abdicates large swaths of territory to local rule or anarchy.

A whole series of implications erupt when the state is forced into the final course of action; loss of confidence. The nation or nations within the state lose confidence in security as the rule of law fades and instability grows. As chaos sets in, trade breaks down and barter returns with the black markets. The breakdown approaches catastrophe with the loss of a unifying vision. Eroding state legitimacy spurs an exodus of popular support to those who can provide order. Autonomous zones emerge to provide stability.

State death sees the individuals loyalty revert to primal groups; families, clans, tribes, gangs, militias. This is how Hizballah took Lebanon. Lebanon's Shia felt the coalition government failed them, Arab nationalism failed them, and the Palestinian exodus displaced them. Then came the Iranian Revolution and, on its heels, came the Pasdran sponsored Hizballah (Party of God). They established themselves in the ungoverned space of the Bakka Valley and expanded their influence to the area south of the Litani River. We see the same phenomenon in less mature stages with the rise of neo-Nazis in Moscow, the Mexican Mafia along the US border, and FARC in Columbia. Gangs and militias proliferate whether criminal, ethnic, sectarian, or secular. The strength of personal commitment is based on the establishment of identity and that can inspire the nation's loyalty.[48]

Sources of Identity
- Biological—Family / Tribe / Clan
- Historic—Nation / Heritage / Language
- Land—Region / Territory
- Faith—Sectarian / Secular

---

[48] *Blood and Rage: A Cultural History of Terrorism* by Michael Burleigh; HarperCollins Publishers, March 2009.

- Ideological—Politics / Ethnicity / Eschatology
- Criminal—Cartel / Gang / Smuggler
- Cybernetic—Virtual / Gamers / Bloggers / Social Media

The above patterns are not new, novel, or unique. There are, however new options—the rise of the *Virtual Organization, Nation and State*. These strategies are Internet empowered and are ascendant.

The *Virtual Organization* allows for the preparation and execution of an insurrection while avoiding the historic pitfalls of geographic concentration. The virtual force is dispersed, distributed, and motivated by shared vision and is informed by collective intelligence. The Guerilla overcomes the G-Base which is now a website. The Virtual Organization leads to the Virtual State and Nation.

The Virtual Nation is a social community formed online that seeks to unite, reunite, or create a shared identity or a 'people'. Al Qaeda is trying this on a global scale by recruiting Muslims the world over into the Ummah. Their goal is to create a transnational identity that supersedes the state identity. A Virtual State is a virtual organization that is focused on a targeted state where it attempts to establish a 'shadow government'. Neo-Nazis in Europe use the Internet to build their own covert state within the state. Hizballah built their state within Lebanon without the Internet but they are successfully exploiting it to strengthen and expand their grip. These virtual entities have a whole host of advantages that makes them difficult for the state to combat.

Free from geography. The trade space for the Freikorps in Weimar Germany and the Bolsheviks of Czarist Russia was the city street.[49] They were tied to physical locations and when caught, were jailed, exiled, or deported. Cyber cells need not meet to organize. The virtual entity can be anywhere and everywhere all at once. Their guerilla base is not a city or backwater hideout; it's a blog or webpage and when it's taken down, a new one pops up in hours or days.

Cyber levee enmasse. Napoleon had the revolution as his message, Carnot as his recruiter, and the industrial revolution as his equipper. Today's mass movement has the computer: Cyber doctrine, Cyber

---

[49] *A Brief History of the Birth of the Nazis: How the Freikorps Blazed the Trail for Hitler*, by Nigel H. Jones, Running Press Book Publishers, May 2004.

recruiting, Cyber intelligence, Cyber propaganda, Cyber command and control, Cyber R&D, and even Cyber Arming, training, and equipping.

Gateway to Super Empowerment. The World Wide Web is a natural conduit to super-empowerment. As discussed above, the cyber cell has unlimited access to information that can be parlayed into leverage when combating the state.

Proxy / Sponsor. Cyber groups are good candidates for sponsors seeking regional proxies. When Russia launched cyber attacks against Estonia and Georgia it posted a webpage that gave instructions on how to launch a denial of service attack and provided associated target websites. Faceless masses of hackers and online activists swarmed to the call.

The Virtual Threat is Carnot on the web creating a global *Virtual Mass Movement*. Just as Guderian's radios unleashed the Panzer division the Internet has unleashed the insurgent and the terrorist. It has also unleashed a new type of warfare, resurrected old threats, and expanded vulnerability.

CHAPTER 3

Boxing
Shadows

Enemy States and Stateless Enemies

Back to the Future

*"Yes, we have slain a large dragon. But we live now in a jungle filled with
a bewildering variety of poisonous snakes. And in many ways, the dragon
was easier to keep track of."*
—R. James Woolsey, Former CIA Director, February 1993

The Second Punic War ended in 202 BC on the bloody battlefield of
Zama. Scipio defeated Hannibal and eliminated Rome's only peer
competitor yet, the end of Carthage did not mean the end of war for
Rome. They went on to confront an endless string of 'small wars'
against rogue states and nomadic tribes, clans, and marauders.[50] The
state / non-state struggle hit a high point when Emperor Augustus ven-
tured into an ungoverned space of Germania in 9 BC. His general,
Varus, led three Legions into the Teutoberger Wald where they met
Arminius and his Cherusci tribe. Arminius' army was inferior but they
knew the forrest and they set a trap that forced the Romans to fight as
skirmishers instead of as a unit. The legions were trapped and were
annihilated in the dense woods. Roman expansion in Germania was in
check.[51]

The collapse of the Soviet Union has given the U.S. a brief, or long,
respite from peer competition. No peer threat doesn't equate to no
threat at all. In fact, there's no shortage of enemies determined to strike

[50]*The Grand Strategy of the Roman Empire: From the First Century A. D. to the Third /
Edition 1* by Edward N. Luttwak, Johns Hopkins University Press, February 1979.

[51]*The Harper Encyclopedia of Military History Fourth Edition* by R. Ernest Dupuy and
Trevor N. Dupuy; Harper Collins, 1993.

Americans. We will face our Arminius' just as Rome did. The trick is to not allow Arminius to become Alaric; the Barbarian Goth who sacked Rome and precipitated the fall of the western empire.

America's dance card is changing. America no longer has the luxury of focusing the very visible state dragon. It now face a snake pit filled with a myriad of non-state threats and their shady rogue state sponsors; both exploiting international laws designed to regulate traditional wars between opposing states.

The snakes aren't new but their emerging capabilities are. Not since the Visigoths, Huns and Mongols raped Rome, has the west seen such a swarm of stateless enemies ready and able to strike. The players include; messianic sects, utopians, hacktivists, cyber propagandists, demibloggers, faux tribes (gangs), independent militias, racists, neo-Nazi's, radical environmentalists, and irrational lone wolves are making their presence known all around the world. They can attack the homeland although they aren't an existential threat—yet. They aren't toting nukes or superbugs—yet.

The U.S. has transitioned from the Roman situation to the Byzantine situation with chaos growing on the margins.[52] China, Russia, and most of Europe are also surrounded. States such as Kosovo, Afghanistan, Chechnya, Georgia, Somalia, and Mexico epitomize rising disorder. These struggling states are small, uncompetitive, and are rife with a rogue's gallery of predators skulking in the shadows. These are symptomatic of the declining state losing status as the primary source of identity for the peoples within its borders. As loyalty shifts away from the state, its control erodes and society reforms around new entities. These emergent replacements of the state are elusive, unbounded by borders, are not tied to a capital, and have no head of state thus presenting no identifiable target.

Sometimes the state was never a powerful source of identity. Multi-ethnic Yugoslavia and multi-tribal Somalia are examples of *artificial* states where disparate peoples are glued together by coercion. What happens when the glue weakens? Multi-sectarian Lebanon and cartel plagued Mexico provide some answers.

[52] *Lost to the West: The Forgotten Byzantine Empire That Rescued Western Civilization* by Lars Brownworth, Crown Publishing Group, June 2010.

The end of the Cold War turned the world upside down. The new world took ten years to emerge from 1991 to 2001. The challengers to the west shifted away from secular state, peer competitors to sectarian non-state, non-peer competitors. History came back in an old world / new world point counterpoint.

Bipolar to Multipolar. The Cold War world featured two major players, the U.S. and USSR, as the scorpions in the bottle. Everyone else lined up behind one or the other, like it or not. Europe became NATO versus the Warsaw Pact; in the Far East it was North Korea versus South Korea and North Vietnam versus South Vietnam; in the Middle East it was Egypt against Israel... the lines were drawn and the game was zero sum. Lesser states dared not have unsanctioned wars and non-state groups dared not strike without superpower approval. Any un-managed incident could trigger a superpower confrontation and risk global thermonuclear war.

The U.S. survived; the USSR disintegrated. We emerged with no real peer competitor but we inherited an array lesser threats no longer restrained by a Soviet master. The new enemies tended to be stateless since ambiguity allowed them to evade retaliation. Their newfound freedom has unleashed age old ethnic and religious passions. As the 'Last Man Standing', the US became the target of choice just as Rome had after the defeat of Carthage. If you wanted to make a splash you had to get the attention of Rome or Washington.[53]

COMINTERN to Islamintern. The ultimate goal of the Bolshevik driven state is to unify, or conquer, the world under communist utopian rule. It was the job of the Communist International (COMINTERN) to arrange the political pieces and inspire the proletarian revolution. It took the self-absorbed Stalinism and the A-Bomb to keep the urge in check—although it remained the dream that powered the left even to today.

The goal of global Jihad has a similar goal; to unify the world under a utopian Caliphate governed by Islamic Law—Sharia.[54] Although the

---

[53] *The End of History and the Last Man* by Francis Fukuyama, Free Press, February 2006.

[54] *Voices of Terror: Manifestos, Writings and Manuals of Al Qaeda, Hamas, and other Terrorists from around the World and Throughout the Ages* by Walter Laquer; Reed Press, 2004.

'Islamintern' does not formally exist, it does have an agent, the Organization of Islamic States (OIC). Islamists seek the re-establishment of Sharia in Muslim majority states where intolerance would be confined within their own borders. They also seek the re-conquest of any land ever ruled by Muslims and, eventually, the global Islamist state. For now the Muslim masses, or ummah, remain mostly neutral as if waiting a resolution between appeasement and capitulation in the west. They align with whoever appears to be winning.

Secular to Sectarian. The Soviet state was secular. It was atheist and humanist rather than spiritual or sectarian.[55] Their secular focus made the Soviet Union a rational opponent subject to negotiation within the international nation state paradigm. Mutual survival was preferable to annihilation.

Today's stateless Islamists are wholly concerned with the spiritual world. They are, by definition, sectarian. This makes them uncompromising and intolerant. Negotiation is not an option. War is not only ok, but may be preferable in that it might trigger the Islamic version of the end of times when the world is cleansed and made whole under Allah. The infidel must convert, submit, or die.[56]

From Marx to Qutb. Karl Marx and Friedrich Engles wrote the *Communist Manifesto* to serve as the roadmap to communisms ascendency. They contrasted the decadence of capitalism versus the nobility of communism. They inspired Lenin, Stalin, and Mao and led to de-kulakization, the Great Leap Forward, and the Cultural Revolution and racked up 100 million plus body count.[57]

The Islamists have their own prophets who proscribe death and destruction for non-believers. Sayyd Qutb wrote *Milestones* to serve as Islam's roadmap towards Muslim dominance at home and abroad. His vision is without pity or compromise. Qutb has inspired his own acolytes like Bin Laden and Zawahiri. On the Shia side of Islam, there's Khomeini and his apostles like Nasrallah. The Qutbs and Khomeinis

---

[55] *Russia Under the Bolshevik Regime* by Richard Pipes, Knopf Doubleday Publishing Group, April 1995.

[56] *Terror in the Name of God: Why Religious Militants Kill* by Jessica Stern, HarperCollins Publishers, August 2004.

[57] *Red Holocaust / Edition 1* by Steven Rosefielde, December 2009, Routledge.

have inspired generations of Shahidi (martyrs) who target the defense-less and unsuspecting in pursuit of a world dominated by Islam.

From Che Quevera to Al Zarqawi. Every charismatic movement needs its rock stars. Communism had its fair share of Robin Hood rogues carrying the torch in the countryside. The communist luminar-ies found their way into the headlines and onto t-shirts with Che Quevera being the most famous guerilla to go from predator to Prada. Quevera was Castro's executioner. Like Yagoda and Yezhov, Quevera cleaned house. Having made Cuba safe for communism, Che headed for the mainland to spread the revolution. Unfortunately for him, the people weren't quite ready for revolution as he thought and the gueril-la focused insurgency foundered. He failed to inspire popular support in Bolivia and fell prey to a determined manhunt that ended badly for him—he was caught and killed deep in the jungle.[58]

The Islamists also have commando media darlings. In many ways, Jordanian Abu Musab al-Zarqawi (AMZ) was Al Qaeda's Che. AMZ radical Jihadism loomed over Iraq and was made famous with one of the most vulgar displays of media made mayhem ever to hit the world wide web; the snuff film of him personally beheading Nick Berg. AMZ videotaped the bloody event deep inside rogue Fallujah. It was shock-ing then but is routine now. As the leader of Al Qaeda in Iraq (AQI), AMZ made beheading, maiming, and torture a staple of the 'insur-gency'. His bloody rein even upset his masters in Afghanistan and Pakistan—his sadism was justified by his fundamentalism. Like Che, his fame became his handicap, and he too ended up dead in the sticks.[59]

Soviet Proxies to Iranian Proxies. The U.S. and the USSR had no desire to face off directly so they adopted the time honored and highly successful Byzantine Strategy of war through surrogates and proxies.[60] The Cold War was a proxy war by necessity; it allowed both sides to evade nuclear confrontation. The communists took one side

---

[58] *A History of the Twentieth Century Volume Three: 1952-1999* by Martin Gilbert, Perennial an Imprint of Harper Collins Publishers, 2000

[59] Insurgent Leader Al-Zarqawi Killed in Iraq by Ellen Knickmeyer and Jonathan Finer Washington Post Foreign Service, June 8, 2006

[60] The Grand Strategy of the Byzantine Empire by Edward Luttwak, Harvard University Press, November 2011.

and the U.S. took the other. It might be argued that the last Cold War proxy front was in Afghanistan, the origin and incubator of today's global jihad virus.

The end of a Cold War proxy struggle saw the birth of the Islamist proxy war—this time the goal is not to evade nuclear war but to evade responsibility and retaliation. During the Cold War, the antagonists were peers who faced annihilation should either miss-step. Today's struggle is between a hyper-power and numerous aspiring hegemons. The U.S. doesn't face annihilation but they do; it faces global condemnation. Given the great disparity, America's modern adversaries have chosen proxy war. Iran uses the Hizballah in Lebanon and Hamas in Israel, and Al Houthi in Yemen to name but a few on their client list.[61] Rogue states the world over have adopted terrorists, smugglers, and criminal networks to attack their enemies while providing plausible deniability.

Khruschev and Breznev to Ahmadinejad and Rouhani. The Soviet political icon was the fiery Nikita Khrushchev who famously pounded his shoe on the podium at the UN promising in 1956, "Whether you like it or not, history is on our side. We will bury you." He ascended to power in Stalin's Soviet Union and promptly purged his old master and his cronies but that didn't mean he was ready to give the USA a great big bear hug. He pushed, provoked, and prodded the U.S. up to the point of almost triggering a nuclear war during the Cuban Missile Crises. He was America's nemesis and reminder that it could never be totally safe.

Khrushchev's modern replacement was Mahmoud Ahmadinejad with his proletarian dress, synthetic smile, holocaust denial and 'Little Satan/Great Satan' mantra. He didn't promise to bury us but he did lead crowds of sycophants in chanting 'death to America' from his Politburo like perch in Tehran. The bluster and bravado had been very dramatic but the danger had become real as he created his own nuclear missile crises. Ahmadinejad pumped up the volume by declaring the U.S. is in decline, that Iran is a super power and he pursued nuclear

---

[61] *A High Price: The Triumphs and Failures of Israeli Counterterrorism* by Daniel Byman, Oxford University Press, June 2011.

weaponry for Iran.[62] True to cause too, he claimed the Mahdi is coming, the Caliphate is ahead of us.

And just as Khrushchev's friends, after some rocky political years, showed him the door, a similar door was held wide open for Ahmadinejad by the crowd in Tehran who didn't like his style. Enter Hassan Rouhani with a grandfatherly countenance and hailed as a moderate by the world press but who, with the familiar chants of "Death to America" in the background, embarked on a plan of proxy war and terrorism that has turned the middle east into an inferno as Iran spreads its influence. Cherub-faced Leonid Breznev was hailed as a moderate too but he brazenly invaded Czechoslovakia and pushed the global influence of the Soviet Union. Rouhani may have torn a page from Breznev's book but he didn't need to read it. He seems to be writing his own book.

Communism to Islamunism. Communism emanated from the USSR and thrived in the bipolar world with its nuclear arsenal. The Soviets used Third World poverty to spread their proletarian ideology, fomenting insurgency around the globe. We held them in check with the Mutually Assured Destruction (MAD) policy which promised that if we got vaporized, so would they.[63]

Islamism has stepped into the void as the Cause Célèbre in opposition to the west. It's a sectarian movement bolstered by historical violent Jihad. Islamism lacks a 'home state' yet it still exploits Third World ungoverned spaces where it can grow safe havens and Islamist enclaves. The unique challenge of Islamism is that there is no MAD corollary that can be applied against them. To win this one, we have to win the battle of ideas.

Similar but Different. Communism and Islamism use insurgency and proxy war while maintaining deniability through anonymity. Each pursues its own Domino Theory and each harbors a worldview that is diametrically opposed to the west. Neither can tolerate coexistence with anyone for long. Both require a comprehensive, full government

---

[62] *Fears of a Hezbollah presence in Venezuela: the World The Lebanese militia may be using Chavez's ties with its ally Iran to expand its network, terrorism officials say* by Chris Kraul and Sebastian Rotella, LA Times, August 27, 2008.

[63] *Strategy in the Missile Age* by Bernard Brodie, Princeton University Press, February 1965.

approach to counter; one that includes all the elements of national power—Diplomacy, Information, Military, and Economics (DIME).

Cold War Communism. The shift away from traditional, state based, secular, bi-polar competition began with the fall of the Berlin Wall. The Soviet sphere blew apart and international security lost its Cold War context and the end of the super power imposed restraint. The predictable yet dangerous world of regulated global interaction and accountability came to an end; one we mistook for a Pax Americana.

Instead, we saw the return to Euro-tribalism in the Balkans; the return of faith in the Russian Orthodox Church; the resurrection of repressed nationalism in Eastern Europe and the release of pent up sectarian revanchism in the Muslim world.

Although Cold War interaction was more dangerous, it was less complex. The system was more stable even though perturbations could provoke a global catastrophe. Ironically, the end of the Cold War expanded the list potential enemies; each less dangerous in isolation but the aggregate of which is approaching the level of an existential threat.

Islamist Jihad. Islamist and Islamic aren't analogous. To be Islamic is to adhere to Islam. To be an Islamist is something more. Islamists are fundamentalist or, more accurately, purists. They interpret the Koran literally and are activists. They see their purpose in life as being to spread Islam and Sharia until it dominates the world as per Koranic instructions. They are zealots and, like the *Blues Brothers*, they're on a 'mission from God.'[64]

There's only one superpower—for now. Today, only one state is able and willing to project power globally, suppress regional bullies, police the sea-lanes, provide humanitarian assistance and disaster relief, and place consumer goods in all the worlds markets. Being *that* state means being the symbol of the world order. Being the symbol order means being the prime target for the forces of world disorder. Those who seek a new world order must go through the U.S. to get it.

The new threat is a resurrection of an old one. It's not secular and

---

[64] Y *The Sources of Islamic Revolutionary Conduct* by Major Stephen P. Lambert, U.S. Air Force Research Fellow with the cooperation and support of the Institute for National Security Studies (INSS) USAF Academy, Colorado Springs, Washington DC, April 2005.

it's not a state. It's a sectarian, stateless threat that is becoming a transnational insurgency. They are holy warriors seeking a divine theocracy. The U.S. has gone from the *worker's paradise* to paradise on earth.[65] The Islamist Jihadis filled the power vacuum left behind by communism. They are equally ambitious and are far less constrained. The Soviets would never have attacked New York City. They knew they would never get away with it. Islamists did attack and they continue to attack, relying on Western self-loathing, anti-Americanism, and multiculturalism to give the apologies—it's America's fault and it deserved it... On the one hand, this state of affairs is somewhat unexpected given America's post-Cold War / pre GWOT support to Muslims in Lebanon, Bosnia, Kuwait, Kosovo, Iraq and Afghanistan. On the other hand, its perfectly logical given Islamist Jihad.

Islamists seeks conquest in the name of Allah versus Marx. Marxists required the annihilation of the Bourgeois while the Islamists require the subjugation, conversion, or annihilation of the Infidels. The latter task is bigger to be sure but with Allah on your side, it's not so bad.

The new threat possesses an arsenal of innocuous weapons that are near impossible to defend against. While Soviet attackers and their weapons were easy to find but hard to kill, Islamist attackers and their weapons are hard to find but easy to kill. The Islamist's goal is not mass destruction, which exceeds their current abilities, its mass disruption which does not. They don't need to blow America up—they mean to bankrupt and bleed America, winning by attrition.

The Soviets lived within a defined geographic space dotted with population centers and infrastructure that had to be defended. Islamists occupy ambiguous ungoverned spaces intermingled with the non-combatants, nearly devoid of infrastructure needing defense. Islamists are part of a decentralized network whose sacrament is death. Their lack of presence allows them to hinder retaliation and evade international law.

The U.S. must suppress the Islamists and redirect them towards a peaceful path, if possible, always keeping in mind overextension. Some say Justinian ushered in the Fall of Byzantium by re-conquering west-

---

[65] *Al Qaeda in its Own Words* by Gilles Kepel (Editor), Jean-Pierre Milelli (Editor), Pascale Ghazaleh (Translator); Harvard University Press, April 2008.

ern Rome. On the one hand, if the U.S. focuses solely on its own interests, it will be accused of hypocrisy. If it acts in support of global interests, it is accused of imperialism and becomes overextended.

Wiki-World Definitions. Before moving on, we have to clarify some definitions that provide context. These are based on my notes from the School of Advanced Military Studies (SAMS) that I attended in '99-'00; during our review of the Soldier and the State by Samuel Huntington.[66]

A *state* is an organization of people within and loyal to a sovereign political entity. It is based on shared governing principals. States are legally recognized and defined. The US state is a representative Republic of, by, and for the people; i.e. governed by consent and Rule of Law. It also employs free market capitalism as its economic system. Most other states are Oligarchies where a small body of elites governs by fiat. These states tend to use Command or Centrally Planned economics with limited property rights and close state-business partnerships.

A *nation* is a generally homogenous grouping of people who are bound together by common and shared customs, history, origins, ethnicity, faith, and language. Basques are a nation within the state of Spain. Kurds are a nation within the states of Iraq, Iran, and Turkey. Nations are sprawling and uncontained by state borders which has given rise to much of today's strife; the post war fabrication of state boundaries that disregarded the existing nation boundaries.

A *nation-state* is the politico-cultural union/arrangement where a people (nation) and a political system (state) are aligned and are in general agreement of common goals. Napoleon's France was the consummate nation-state. Much of Europe is nation state tribal as evidenced by the disintegration of Yugoslavia into Serbia, Bosnia, and Croatia and Czechoslovakia which became the Czech Republic and Slovakia.

A *culture* is a shared identity, the totality of socially transmitted behavior patterns, arts, beliefs, institutions, and all other products of human work and thought. Islam is a culture that permeates the world and is defined by the collective term ummah.

The definitions above provide context for international engage-

---

[66] *The Soldier and the State: The Theory and Politics of Civil-Military Relations* by Samuel P. Huntington, Harvard University Press, August 2008.

ment. Each variation inspires loyalty and motivates action. States and nation-states can be held responsible for aggression and can targeted for retaliation. Nations and cultures cannot.

State versus Stateless—Asymmetry, Irregular War, Hybrid War or....

"The resistance withstood the attack and fought back. It did not fight a guerilla war either…it was not a regular army but was not a guerilla in the traditional sense either.
It was something in between. This is the new model."
—Hassan Nasrallah, Hizballah Secretary General,
on Hizballah during the 2nd Lebanon War of '06

On July 12, 2006, a group of Lebanese Hizballah (LH) militants launched a cross border raid from Lebanon into Israel. The attack began with a diversionary rocket strike on a few Israeli border towns followed by an AT ambush on a pair of IDF HMMWV's patrolling the Israeli side of the border. The Hummers carried seven Israeli soldiers. Two were wounded, three were killed, and two were kidnapped.[67]

The incursion was not unusual and came as no surprise. The typical Israeli response would have been to launch a proportional punitive strike. After a series of tit for tat exchanges the two sides would engage in dialogue with LH demanding a prisoner exchange of hundreds of Hizballah for each kidnapped Israeli—often returned dead.

Not this time. Israel's leaders had had enough. They launched a full-scale response. On July 17, 2006, Prime Minister Olmert laid out his strategic goals to the Knesset:

• Return of the hostages
• A complete cease fire
• Deployment of the Lebanese Armed Forces (LAF) into southern Lebanon
• Expulsion of Hezbollah from southern Lebanon
• Fulfillment of United Nations Resolution 1559

[67] *Road to War* by MAJ Sharon Tosi Moore; Lebanon, Joint Center for Operational Analysis Journal, Volume X, Issue 1, December 2007.

The Israeli Air Force (IAF) initiated the conflict by pounding targets throughout Lebanon in order to coerce the Lebanese government to crack down on Hizballah. This demonstrated a fundamental misunderstanding of Hizballah's role as a state within the state. The Lebanese Armed Forces (LAF) had neither the capacity nor the will to coerce LH. In fact, the air campaign convinced many that only Hizballah was able to stand up to Israel thus legitimizing them as the 'true defenders of Lebanon.' This was in direct contradiction to Israeli goals. The air campaign was also designed to hinder LH's supply lines from Syria but LH already had sufficient stockpiles to weather the IDF offensive.[68]

The collateral damage (CD) generated by the IAF played into the hands of the LH media machine who pumped out a steady stream of images of civilian suffering. The fact that LH rocket launchers and command bunkers were deliberately located among civilians was obfuscated. The LH positioning technique was a win-win proposition: avoid the target and the asset survives, hit the target and generate an international media moment.

The air campaign and LH's exploitation of it eroded international support for Israel and alienated potential allies within Lebanon. At the beginning of the conflict most states felt the Israeli reactions were justified; however, as time progressed, LH was able to get their message out triggering the international community to question the proportionality of the Israeli operation. The IDF had no media response. Israel's unattainable objectives and lack of effective communications stood in stark contrast to LH's simple strategy of survival—win by not losing.

The IAF focused on LH's major long range weapons while the short range systems like Qassam and Kaytusha rockets were hitting in northern Israel up to 100 a day; all the way to the cease-fire. The air campaign began to meet with diminishing returns so the ground campaign began. It was kicked off with a series of tentative maneuvers hampered by casualty aversion. Politicians feared high casualties would trigger a loss of public support. This drove ground force leaders to act cautiously.[69] This hesitation limited their ability to pursue basic

68 *2006 Lebanon War: An Operational Analysis* by MAJ Sharon Tosi Moore; Lebanon, Joint Center for Operational Analysis Journal, Volume X, Issue 1, December 2007.

69 *Final Winograd Report: English Summary*, Lebanon, Joint Center for Operational Analysis Journal, Volume X, Issue 1, December 2007

tactical objectives. LH didn't have this problem. For them, casualties were a media opportunity as long they weren't excessive enough to portray defeat. The IDF went in expecting Intifada like mobs throwing stones and the occasional Molotov cocktail. What they got was a coordinated defense fought by well trained and well equipped guerillas. Years of security operations in the West Bank and Gaza left the IDF unprepared for a semi-conventional war / hybrid war.[70]

On the eve of the Korean War, the U.S. Army in Japan found itself dulled by eight years of occupation duty. The result was the Task Force Smith failure.[71] The 2nd Lebanon war of 2006 was an army full of TF Smiths. Infantry, artillery, and armor coordination was poor and tactical skills were atrophied. The IDF ground tactics were fine for Palestinian refugee camps but fell short when facing a prepared defense.

Minutemen / Militia / Military. The Hizballah built a layered defense that called upon locals to act as Minutemen. The volunteers were assigned a fire and forget mission—use an ATGM or pop an IED, then head north for Beirut. The minutemen were backed by traditional guerillas fighting traditional, low tech, engagements until forced to withdrawal. LH hid their long range weapons in sophisticated fighting positions or among civilian buildings—and proved to be more capable then most armies in the region.

LH is an Iranian proxy. They also proved to be able sponsors. In 1992, in the heat of the First Intifada, Israel rounded up the worst hard heads in Hamas and shipped them north to the Lebanese border. Hizballah was waiting there to take the new arrivals under their wing—they weren't worried about the Sunni-Shia differences since they shared a common enemy.[72] They trained them in suicide bombings, rocket attacks, and political agitation; skills they took back to the West Bank and Gaza when they were repatriated. The newly trained Hamas took Gaza and opened up a new and lethal front against Israel which triggered Operation Cast Lead in 2009.

[70] *Terrorist to Techno Guerilla* by Clyde Royston; Lebanon, Joint Center for Operational Analysis Journal, Volume X, Issue 1, December 2007.

[71] *This Kind of War: The Classic Korean War History* by T.R. Fehrenbach, Potomac Books, Inc., January 1995.

[72] *A High Price: The Triumphs and Failures of Israeli Counterterrorism* by Daniel Byman, Oxford University Press, June 2011.

IDF misfires stood in direct opposition to the relative competence of Hizballah. LH skillfully used anti-tank guided missiles (ATGMs) against IDF armor and innovatively used them to collapse occupied buildings. They were disciplined in their use of cover, concealment, and preparation of fortifications. They exploited a witch's brew of IEDs, swarm tactics, and evasion. The 'minutemen' moved to caches, picked up their weapons, moved into position, fired, and then fled. The cadre executed hit and run missions, 'disappearing' into the tunnels when the IDF closed in, only to pop up later forcing the IDF to retake previously taken ground. These weren't back woods guerilla; they were paramilitary soldiers who had war-gamed their enemy's course of action.

LH strategic communications and media exploitation through TV, radio, and print was effective. They executed a robust information campaign. They pushed their message out into the mainstream media.

Second Lebanon emboldened Hassan Nasrallah. His Hizballah as the defender of Lebanon message resonated; "I am carrying my weapons to defend the country which Israel wants to gobble up, and whose waters Israel wants to plunder…" In the end, LH came out of the war with a stronger position. They prepared for the war, fought it, and led the reconstruction; all as the only regional Muslim player to successfully stand up to the IDF—as a non-state actor.

"BEIRUT, Lebanon Aug. 15 — As stunned Lebanese returned Tuesday over broken roads to shattered apartments in the south, it increasingly seemed that the beneficiary of the destruction was most likely to be Hizballah. A major reason — in addition to its hard-won reputation as the only Arab force that fought Israel to a standstill — is that it is already dominating the efforts to rebuild with a torrent of money from oil-rich Iran."
—(*New York Times*, August 16, 2006)

The 2nd Lebanon War wasn't conventional or irregular. It was both. Some call it hybrid war. Whatever it is, it's not new; it's just been dormant since pre WWII. The Thirty Years War, the Russian Civil War, and the recent Georgia-Russia conflict were 'mixed.' [73]

---

[73] *The Harper Encyclopedia of Military History Fourth Edition* by R. Ernest Dupuy and Trevor N. Dupuy; Harper Collins, 1993.

LH *incited* incidents that triggered disproportionate responses that could be *exploited* in the media—a trick for which the IDF is all too willing to fall. These tactics whipped up international condemnation of Israel; transforming Hizballah from aggressor to victim.

- *Media:* LH controlled battlefield circulation of the media by providing transportation and threatening those who might go it alone. The press had to go where LH wanted them to go if they wanted to get to the battlefield.
- *Fauxtography:* LH propagandists *Photoshopped* pictures creating false and exaggerated battlefield images. They duplicated smoke, rubble, fire, and flying rockets to make Israel look ruthless.[74] Hamas, LH's proxy, used the same tricks to 'erase' knives used against IDF weapons during the Gaza flotilla raid in 2010.[75]
- *Human Shields:* LH used apartment complexes and public buildings for rocket emplacements. They stored weapons and ammunition in mosques, schools, and hospitals, counting on western decency and outrage to inhibit further strikes.
- *Lawfare:* They exploited international law by using mosques and hospitals as weapons and ammo caches and as command posts. They used ambulances to deliver arms and ammo before picking up and evacuating casualties. They even built bunkers next to UN positions to shield them from attacks.
- *Rent a Crowd and Mobile Mourners:* LH moved 'victims' from one press covered hotspot to the next, to maximum effect. They were well stocked with professional mourners; some appearing at multiple sites around Beirut.
- *Bait and Blow:* LH lured troops into buildings that were rigged to blow and collapse. They set traps in buildings hoping to take soldiers as hostages.
- *Posters and Broadsides:* Goebbels would be proud of Hizballah's poster and leaflet campaign. They blanketed Beirut with images of Nasrallah in a Stalinesqe personality cult campaign. Hizballah mar-

---

[74] *The Reuters Photo Scandal, A Taxonomy of Fraud,*
http://www.zombietime.com/reuters_photo_fraud/.

[75] *Reuters Admits Cropping Photos of Ship Clash,*
http://www.foxnews.com/world/2010/06/08/reuters-fake-photos-ihh-gaza-blockade-commandos/, Jun 8, 2010.

keting rivals WWII Nazi marketing.[76]

- *Dawa:* Another way of buying good will is to move into an area and build up the infrastructure and provide badly needed services. Good will buys tolerance for LH adventurism.

Hizballah has become the A-Team of terrorism and Iran's most important proxy. The techniques they are developing will proliferate throughout the Middle East and the world. From now on, militaries must be able to operate across the entire spectrum of conflict. The question is, 'can a force fight an irregular war and a conventional war war at the same time? The answer must be yes.

****

Hizballah is the high end version of the new enemy. The stateless franchise terrorists, however lethal, are the low end. Al Qaeda can hijack airliners and use them as manned missiles but they can't field their own 21st Century rocket force like LH. Al Qaeda (AQ) became the Al Qaeda and Associated Networks (AQAN) as it 'franchised' itself. It eventually became one of many in an ever expanding coalition of violent extremist organizations (VEO'S). For now, the terror business is good.

Terror-Crime Coalitions. Most of today's 'big ticket' terrorists are faith based—sectarian. In spite of their righteous roots, they aren't so pure as to avoid profitable alliances with illicit partners; particularly drug trafficking organizations (DTO).[77] Islamists welcome criminals and even recruit them from jail. Criminals provide supplies, access to covert networks, smuggling routes and a drug fueled revenue stream. Both sides thrive on chaos. Smuggling routes become infiltration lanes; the Gaza tunnels now traffic goods and weapons. Somali pirate ransoms pay for AQ camps in return for training and small arms. Terrorists pay to use narco-trafficking routes and counterfeiting services

---

[76] *Hezbollah as a case study of the battle for hearts and minds,* by Dr. Reuven Erlich and Dr. Yoram Kahati, Intelligence and Terrorism Information Center at the Israel Intelligence Heritage & Commemoration Center (IICC), June 2007.

[77] *Seeds of Terror: How Heroin Is Bankrolling the Taliban and Al Qaeda* by Gretchen Peters, St. Martin's Press, May 2009.

to transit from Latin America to the USA.[78] The nexus of terror crime is a mutually beneficial arrangement. Both sides grow in the deal.

The convergence of asymmetric warfare, terrorism and crime is creating a hybrid threat; the Techno-Guerilla enterprise. The TG emerged in Afghanistan when 17th Century Mujhadeen toted Stingers that shot the Soviet HIND attack helicopters.[79] Todays Techno-Guerrilla is an agent of change and not simply a user of technology. The exploitation of technology has delivered greater lethality to small self-organizing and self-tasking groups. The TG uses global communications and the Internet to decentralize planning, preparation, execution and control. Information operations and media manipulation are key tools used to influence peoples and outcomes. The network is replacing the cell and the TG is becoming an iGuerilla using Wiki-War.[80]

Emergent Trends

- *Decentralization:* networks spontaneously spawn cells around the world
- *Compressed levels of war:* tactical events with strategic effects Distributed Vision: Internet transformation of local events into global causes
- *Militarization:* off the shelf technology and online information transformed in weapons
- *Super Empowerment:* individuals and groups able to create mass disruption and death
- *Virtual nations, states, and cells:* cyber communities and distributed radicalization
- *Rise of autonomous regions:* states losing the ability to 'rule' are creating vacuums
- *Utopian terrorism:* anarchistic blood cinema

---

[78] *Terrorist and Organized Crime Groups in the Tri-border area (TBA) of South America,* by Rex Hudson, a report prepared by the Federal Research Division, Library of Congress under an Interagency Agreement with the United States Government, July 2003.

[79] *Charlie Wilson's War: The Extraordinary Story of the Largest Covert Operation in History,* by George Crile, Grove/Atlantic, Inc., March 2003.

[80] *The Internet, and the Homegrown Terrorist Threat,* United States Senate Committee on Homeland Security and Governmental Affairs, Majority & Minority Staff Report Joseph Lieberman, Chairman Susan Collins, Ranking Minority Member, May 8, 2008.

Weaponization. The World Wide Web is enabling innovators to cook up do it yourself (DIY) weapons and techniques at a furious pace. Cyber developers kick out and proliferate prototypes online where anyone can contribute and anyone can learn.[81] Online hackers and dataminers pursue multiple research avenues and share solutions instantly— a much shorter path than traditional acquisition. The Manhattan Project appears antiquated when compared to the self organizing and agile network of swarming cyber Strangeloves and the trend will continue as long as Moore's Law holds.[82] The lag between development and implementation will shrink as online weapons development challenge the linear weapons procurement processes used by state defense acquisition.

The king of successful freelancing is the improvised explosive device the (IED) making it the poor man's ICBM. Continuous improvement in IED tchnology has elevated it from a tactical weapon to an operational one. The IED has seen the addition of shaped charges, remote detonation, cell phone initiation, and much more.[83]

Another weapon on the rise is the do it yourself (DIY) rocket/mortar. Lebanon and Gaza proved effectiveness of rockets and mortars as terror weapons. Homemade rockets are cheap to field but expensive to defend against. They maximize monetary return by bankrupting the defender for pennies on the dollar. DIY rockets are easy to hide, set up and fire. Even given their inaccuracy, they wreak economic havoc in targeted areas.

Asymmetry. The 20th Century was the era of conventional war (CW) between state armies that were similarly manned, trained, and equipped. States fought the wars. They built tanks, bombers, submarines, howitzers, and fielded armies, navies, air armadas, and special forces that looked and fought alike. The 20th Century was a symmetric century. Units and weapons were easy to find and hard to kill.

The Cold war saw more of the same with proxy war as an additive. The U.S. and USSR fielded strategic bombers, nuclear subs, and ICBM's

---

[81] *Terrorist to Techno Guerilla*, by Clyde Royston; Lebanon, Joint Center for Operational Analysis Journal, Volume X, Issue 1, December 2007.

[82] Moore's Law, http://www.intel.com/technology/mooreslaw/.

[83] *Technology of Improvised Explosive Devices*, by Dr. Carlo Kopp, Land Warfare Conference, Defense Today, January 2008.

to counter one another. Both backed insurgents in pursuit of their national interests and as a way to fight without risking Armageddon but everything changed when the Soviet Union collapsed. The U.S. was left alone as the only standing superpower deemed by some to be a hyperpower.

American CW dominance forced wannabe competitors to seek non-traditional ways to take us on. The U. S. military is unmatched on the conventional battelfield. The twin Gulf Wars erased any remaining doubt. America's problems began when conventional war ended.

CW dominance does not mean absolute dominance; the U.S. can be hit and hurt. Troy's walls were invulnerable a pack of Greek 'cheaters' used a hollow horse to get inside. Rome's walls were also impregnable until Alaric bribed insider to open the gates. The American Navy ruled the Pacific until its home port was bombed without warning on December 7th. Of course, the most famous asymmetric attack of all time was David's sling versus Goliath's forehead. Asymmetry has always been a part of war but today, it's the dominant characteristic.

> *"Irregular War is a violent struggle among state and non-state actors for legitimacy and influence over the relevant populations. IW favors indirect and asymmetric approaches, though it may employ the full range of military and other capabilities, in order to erode an adversary's power, influence, and will."*
> —Joint Publication 1-02

Irregular War (IW) is a form of conflict where a significantly weaker player seeks victory through protraction; wearing down the enemy's will versus destroying his military power. The goal is to erode his legitimacy and isolate/alienate the population.[84] The parties to the conflict seek to gain and maintain influence over a targeted population. Irregular war is merely an extant form of asymmetric conflict. Asymmetric means without balance; distorted, irregular, disproportionate, or non-uniform. Asymmetric warfare occurs with the introduction of capabilities or techniques for which there is no ready response. From the Mongol riders to the Spanish Ulcer, asymmetric war has been

---

[84]*Resisting Rebellion,* by Anthony James Joes, University Press of Kentucky, August 2010.

the rule rather than the exception. Even during the heyday of conventional war, there were the Kamikazes.

Media matters: King-maker or breaker... The press has always influenced the conduct of war. During the summer of 1864, Gen Sherman was on his famous march to the sea. He would push Gen Johnston into a corner where he would dig in and await an attack but Sherman wouldn't oblige the invitation to fight. Instead, he would turn Johnston's position forcing him to uproot his defense and withdraw further into the Confederacy in order to keep his army between Sherman and Atlanta. Sherman's strategy was working fine but there was an election brewing up north and the press needed a battle victory headline. The press corps excoriated Sherman for refusing battle and the pressure grew until Kennesaw Mountain. Sherman finally succumbed to media and political pressure and attacked Johnston's defenses and was decisively repulsed. Following the rebuke, Sherman returned to his original strategy and ended up sacking Atlanta and capturing Savannah, effectively cutting the South in half.[85] From *Remember the Alamo to Remember the Maine*; the press has provoked, inspired, or incited. Modern state armies must account for the press given the Internet's ability to send headlines around the world.

"It appears we have appointed our worst generals to command forces, and our most gifted and brilliant to edit newspapers! In fact, I discovered by reading newspapers that these editor/geniuses plainly saw all my strategic defects from the start, yet failed to inform me until it was too late. Accordingly, I'm readily willing to yield my command to these obviously superior intellects, and I will in turn, do my best for the Cause by writing editorials - after the fact."
—Robert E. Lee – 1863

"I published an order that they [reporters] must not come along on pain of being treated as spies. I am now determined to test the question ... I have ordered the arrest of one, shall try him, and if possible execute him as a spy."   —W. T. Sherman, 1864

---

[85] *War for the Union, The Organized War to Victory*, by Allan Nevins, Konecky and Konecky, 1971, by Anthony James Joes, University Press of Kentucky, August 2010.

LH dominated the media arena in 2006. They saw and used the media as a weapon of mass effect. The Israeli's were repeatedly out into "Catch-22" situations where they were damned if they did and damned if they didn't.[86] To strike meant collateral damage; to wait meant rockets falling on Israeli civilians. It was and will remain a lose proposition until state armies learn how to engage with the media and get their stories out. Allowing the enemy to control the narrative is to reduce the chances of success.

Threat media exploitation techniques include:
Fauxtography - Photo-shopping images to exaggerate effects.
- **Trading accuracy for access** - Guerillas granted access.
- **Immediacy** - Satellite links providing images ahead of explana-
- tions.
Death of Context - State actions in secrecy: public response in the
- media.
Rental Victims – Professional mourners.
- **YouTube** - Guerilla videos versus state press releases.
- **Media as Intel** - TV, Blackberry, Twitter, Flickr, and Internet to
- track the state.
Sensationalism - If it bleeds it leads: violence gets headlines.
-

> *"Television's ability to bring graphic images of pain and outrage into our living rooms has heightened the pressure both for immediate engagement in areas of international crisis and immediate disengagement when events do not go according to plan. Because we live in a democratic society, none of us can be oblivious to those pressures."*
> —Madeleine Albright testifying about Somalia
> before the Senate Foreign Relations Committee

The state armies of the west can counter the above by getting their story, based on the truth, out quickly. They can stop suppressing

[86] *The Israeli-Hezbollah War of 2006: The Media As A Weapon in Asymmetrical Conflict,* by Marvin Kalb Senior Fellow, Shorenstein Center, and Carol Saivetz, Harvard University, Joan Shorenstein Center on the Press, Politics and Public Policy Research Harvard University, February 2007.

enemy bad behavior in the name of security and let it out. They can use Facebook. Flickr and Twitter to rapidly rebut false statements and can use their own combat camera to show what their troops are up to. The embedding used during OIF was a start but that's all it was. America must remember that it has to tell the truth while they are under no such obligation. The U.S. needs to get the truth out more rapidly than they get their lies out and it must counter the lies quickly. Today's battlefield is not only a military campaign; it's a political and media campaign.

****

Super-empowerment. Terrorism is on the rise and is the principal component of the Islamist transnational insurgency. Thomas Jefferson's war against the Barbary Pirates was America's first war on terror.[87] The Barbary Pirates were Islamic terrorists who seized ships, took their cargo, ransomed them, and sold their crews into slavery. Terrorism's been around since the Judean Zealots, the Shia Assassins, the Irish Fineans, the Russian anarchists, the Serbian Black Hand that assassinated Ferdinand triggering WWI, to the IRA, and the PLO...[88] The terrorism innovation of the 20th and 21st Centuries is the increased access they have to information and technology. Terrorism has gone from a Finean throwing a stick of dynamite in a London train station to a few terrorists flying a plane into a sky scraper. Moore's Law and Carlson's Curves have, more or less, equalized the playing field between the terrorist and the state. It's increasingly possible for individuals or small groups to threaten states. It used to take a rival state to do that. The Internet powered terrorists may soon deliver state level destruction. How long till a "12 Monkey's" madman unleashes a deadly pandemic?[89]

IMAGINEERING. During an advanced military seminar a question arose There was one particularly vexing question that took some

---

[87] *Jefferson's War: America's First War on Terror 1801 to 1805*, by Joseph Wheelan, Public Affairs, August 2004.

[88] *Blood and Rage: A Cultural History of Terrorism*, by Michael Burleigh; HarperCollins Publishers, March 2009.

[89] *Twelve Monkeys*, written by Chris Marker and David Webb Peoples and directed by Terry Gilliam, Mystery, Sci-Fi, Thriller, January 1996.

time to answer; 'If a super empowered attack is so possible then why hasn't it happened yet?' Obviously, 9-11 had already happened. We were looking to bigger and more catastrophic possibilities.

It's a good question! It makes you think, why not indeed? We finally came to a possible explanation. To answer the question, you have to ask a question, "why didn't 9-11 happen before 9-11?' Why did it take so long? The plan wasn't *that* brilliant. Surly KSM wasn't the first to think of using planes as flying suicide platforms. We know the kamikazes of WWII did just that. They even fit today's homicide bomber profile—fanatics committed to die in the service of their sacred cause. The Empire was the cause and Emperor Hirohito was the divine leader.

How about peacetime airborne terrorism? It turns out that there was terrorism by airliner in 1999. An Egyptian pilot intentionally flew Egypt Air flight 990 out of Massachusetts into the ocean on the 31st of October. His last words came in the form of Muslim prayer in Arabic: "I rely on Allah" which he repeated eleven times before the aircraft began its drop from 33,000 feet to 16,000 feet. Two hundred and seventeen people died in the crash. The incident went unexplained but was catalogued as terrorism.[90]

A trained pilot executed the '99 incident and therein lays the rub. The gulf between the idea (imagination) and actualization (execution) is wide and is bridged by the process of trial and error. The idea of flying planes into buildings was nothing more than a crazy notion until homicidal/suicidal pilots could be recruited, indoctrinated, and trained. That took time. In the 1400's, Leonardo da Vinci imagined the submarine and the tank. The first operational submarine didn't hit the scene until 1864 during the US Civil War and the tanks first credible debut didn't occur until 1918 during WWI. Jules Verne wrote *From the Earth to the Moon* in 1865. Apollo 11 didn't land on the moon until 1969, more than a century later. It takes time for ideas to become reality—or it used to. The world wide web is shortening the distance between idea and action.

In 1995 a Japanese messianic cult dreamt of sparking a global apocalypse by poisoning thousands of Tokyo commuters. The group was

---

[90]*Another look at Egypt Air crash*, by Joseph Farah, WND Commentary, http://www.wnd.com/2001/12/11863/, December 2001.

Aum Shinrikyo and they released Sarin gas on several Tokyo trains.[91] Luckily their delivery method was flawed and the death toll fell well short of expectations.

Four years later in 1999, a pair of teenagers conducted a well rehearsed and multi faceted attack on a Midwest high school in Colorado. They used the Internet to gain the expertise needed to build bombs and timers. They planted a diversionary bomb to divert initial responders, planted more bombs to collapse the cafeteria, and planted two more car bombs to kill the first responders to arrive in the parking lot. They carried hand held bombs and an impressive array of firearms and knives to increase the carnage they hoped to inflict. They almost killed hundreds but for a few mistakes made with their timers and fuses.[92] Columbine '99 looked a lot like Mumbai '09. The Aum Shinryko and Columbine killers were proto-Wiki warriors. They researched and developed novel attack techniques by fully exploiting the public information domain. But for a few technical difficulties these guys might have generated 9-11 or Mumbai like devastation.

The enabling tools of the iGuerilla and iTerrorist used to be out of reach.[93] They were controlled by states or big businesses. The technology was too expensive, too exclusive, too complex, or too hard to get. Today, the technology and knowledge is less expensive, easy to get given Internet access and dual use technology, and is easy to use. In his book *Terror and Consent*, Philip Bobbitt calls this phenomenon *commodification*. We've gone from wonkish MS DOS that requires experts versed in cryptic commands to run to Windows run by graphic user interface (GUI) that is 'user friendly.' Today, if you want it: you can probably get it or find out how to make it. It's probably affordable and it's probably easy to use. *So easy a caveman can do it!*

****

Harbingers.   We've seen forays into *super-empowered* attacks.

[91] *When Religion Becomes Evil*, by Charles Kimball; HarperCollins Publishers, September 2002.

[92] *Columbine by Dave Cullen*, Grand Central Publishing, April 2009.

[93] *iGuerilla: The New Model Techno-Insurgent*, by John R. Sutherland, Armchair General, The Weider History Group, May 2008.

Luckily these early attempts fell short of their ultimate potential but they have served notice.[94]

March 20, 1995: Aum Shinrikyo used Sarin Gas to attack the Tokyo commuter train system; previous attempts included anthrax and cyanide and research included Ebola.

September 11, 2001: Nineteen al-Qaeda terrorists hijacked four commercial airliners and crashed two of them into the World Trade Center, another into the Pentagon, and the fourth crashed near Shanksville Pennsylvania due to passenger resistance.[95]

September 18, 2001: Anthrax laced letters (Amerithrax) infected two post offices and several government buildings enroute to select prominent politicians and reporters. The apparent author of the attack committed suicide seven years later prior to being arrested. He was an American research scientist. This event prompted Gregory M. Poland, M.D. Director, Mayo Clinic Vaccine Research Group and Biodefense, to note, *"Terrorists learned that anthrax can produce infection, panic, and disruption of the entire government and economy."*

May 8, 2002: Jose Padilla was arrested in Chicago for his part in a plot to detonate a dirty bomb in a U.S. city. He was recruited by AQ while in prison.

1976 to 2004: Dr. Abdul Qadeer Khan ran an illicit global nuclear black market becoming the first non-state supplier carrying nearly all components of a nuclear weapons program. AQ Khan used his position as a student and worker in the nuclear tech community to steal technology which he traded for things he didn't have. How long till someone in pharmaceuticals builds a bio-tech black market?

April 27, 2007: Estonia was hit by a three-week cyber attack on its government and financial websites causing Distributed Denial of Service. Estonia lauded itself as one of Europe's most 'wired' states. The cyber-attack almost caused a complete governmental and financial collapse. The removal of a Red Army memorial probably provoked the attack which emanated from Russia.

May 12, 2007: Andrew Speaker unwittingly provided a practical

---

[94] *39 Terrorist Plots Against the U.S. Foiled Since 9/11,* research by Jena Baker McNeill, James Jay Carafano, and Jessica Zuckerman, Heritage Foundation, May 2011.

[95] *The Looming Tower: Al-Qaeda and the Road to 9/11,* by Lawrence Wright; Random House Inc, August 2007.

example of a potential biological attack technique. Speaker flew to Europe for his wedding and honeymoon after having been advised not to take the trip because he had TB. While in Rome, he was contacted by U.S. health officials who told him to stay put because further tests showed he had a dangerous and drug-resistant type of TB. He disregarded the instructions and flew on to Prague and Montreal in an attempt to sneak back into the U.S..

May 30, 2007: Robert Alan Soloway demonstrated individual cyber super-empowerment as the "Spam King." Soloway formed networks of zombie computers into Botnet's that sent millions of spam e-mails. They're called "zombies" because their owners don't know their machines have been hijacked. Soloway was arrested on charges of identity theft, money laundering, and email, mail, wire fraud.

Jihad 2.0: Like everyone else, terrorists are turning to the Internet to improve efficiency and expand their market. Afghan training camps are becoming less available so terrorists are turning to the Internet to create virtual training camps as a cheap and safe replacement. The legendary "Irhabi 007" shared his success stories online, posted snuff videos, and sponsored al-Qaeda led explosives classes.

As the above, incomplete list, demonstrates; super-empowerment comes in many forms. Kinetic super-empowerment focuses on explosions. Nuclear / Radiological super-empowerment looks at portable nukes and 'dirty' bombs. Chemical super-empowerment covers weapons like mustard or sarin gas. Cyber super-empowerment, a fast growing field, includes; hacktivism, malicious code in the form of worms and viruses, identity theft, hacking and crashing, phishing…

Perhaps the scariest of all super-empowerment areas of interest is the biological weapons field. Are The Stand or I Am Legend all that farfetched? Unlike the other forms of super-empowerment, the biological threat can become persistent and mobile.

Bio-weapons. Biological attacks are not unheard of. In 1985 the Rajneesh Cult of Oregon used purchased Salmonella to poison local officials. Between 1985 and 1996 the aforementioned Aum Shinrikyo experimented with Anthrax and Ebola. They even released Anthrax into the Tokyo sky—a failed attempt due to the use of the wrong strain of anthrax, one lethal to animals rather than humans. In 1989, the Minnesota

Patriots Council extracted ricin from castor beans with the intent of poisoning selected government officials. A defection thwarted the plan.[96]

These were tentative first steps by isolated groups into the bio-realm. What would happen if a concerted effort was launched by an international group knowledgeable in data mining and well funded by Saudi Sheiks with bulging wallets seeking pocketbook jihad? AQ has been experimenting with bio-weapons since before 9-11.

Why Bio? Many experts argue that bio weapons are too hard to make, too expensive fund, too difficult to use, and take too much time to make. Some also argue that no one is irrational enough to use a bio weapon. Access to knowledge, training, technology and medical equipment is breaking down the feasibility arguments and the rise in sectarian terrorism is breaking down the rational motivation argument. Carlson is in charge.[97]

The appeal of bio weapons to terrorists is obvious. Bio weapons can be massively lethal. They can be layered or engineered to evade defenses and multiple variations can be implemented sequentially or simultaneously. They are proven asymmetric weapons that evoke terror even when only mildly effective. The knowledge to acquire and make these weapons is dispersed and easy to find given the academic tenet of publish or perish. The materials are accessible and cheap, many can be acquired from dual use, hard to track, and easily hidden sources. Finally, finding attackers can be difficult as Amerithrax demonstrated.

Delivery. The best way to spread most bio agents is through the air and aerosol dissemination technology is common in agriculture. It exists in planes, helicopters, trucks, and even backpacks. A wide variety of systems are available on the Internet such as the Cyclone which sells for $450.00 or so.

The DHS Bioterrorism Risk Assessment of 2006 states that a single attacks using any of long list of bio-weapons could kill more than

[96] *Bracing for Armageddon: The Science and Politics of Bioterrorism in America*, by William Clark; Oxford University Press, May 2008.

[97] *The Pace and Proliferation of Biological Technologies*, by Rob Carlson, http://www.kurzweilai.net/meme/frame.html?main=/articles/art0614.html?

10,000.[98] Bio-weapons can be self-replicating with a "reload" capability. The attacker can make himself immune from his own weapon, a unique characteristic of this type of weapon. Engineering resistance is a common practice. Genetic engineering allows existing biological agents to be turned into designer bugs.

Motivation. Islamist Jihadism, Sunni and Shia, is powered by the faith that Allah sanctifies all actions in the service of Jihad. This sanctification removes typical barriers to mass murder.[99]

- In 1997 Al Qaeda asserted that it was a Muslim's religious duty to kill 4 million Americans, including 1 million children.
- A 2003 Fatwa (Religious ruling) asserts that Muslims are entitled to use biological, chemical, nuclear weapons.
- In 2006 AQ in Iraq called for scientists to join jihad in order to help produce weapons of mass destruction (WMD).

Technology. Systems that use inert ingredients and digital information to create living organisms such as polio, Ebola, and smallpox are within reach.[100] Genetic Synthesizers are available on e-bay and DNA synthesis technology productivity is doubling every 14 months. Synthetic biology is now a major market. All the latest research papers with detailed 'how to' instructions are online—fueled by academia's publish or perish mentality.

Bio-security. Urbanization, overcrowding, poor sanitation, malnutrition, and proximity to animal vectors make modern bio-security problematic. International travel and commerce makes movement of bio agents and actors near impossible to prevent. The industrialization and globalization of the global food supply makes it especially vulnerable to bio tampering. Centralized water sources are equally vulnerable.

---

[98] *Department of Homeland Security Bioterrorism Risk Assessment: A Call for Change*, by the Committee on Methodological Improvements to the Department of Homeland Security's Biological Agent Risk Analysis, National Research Council, DHS 2006.

[99] *Terror in the Name of God: Why Religious Militants Kill*, by Jessica Stern, HarperCollins Publishers, August 2004.

[100] *Living Weapons: Biological Warfare and International Security*, by Gregory D. Koblentz, Cornell University Press, August 2011.

The innocuous nature of bio-weapons coupled with pervasive vulnerability of the targets makes this a worrisome threat.

Epidemics and pandemics are not initially obvious like 9-11—they can spread before their presence is obvious. An attack might take months to materialize and the resulting social and economic disruption could be widespread and sustained. It is doubtful that any state has the medical supplies of vaccines or public health surge capacity to handle another pandemic on the scale of the 1918 Flu.[101]

Terrorists will get WMD's in the future. Recent advances in technology have increased the ability of small groups to damage nation-states and disrupt the global just-in-time economy. Failure to address this emerging threat could be catastrophic. It will require a conceptual change in defense thinking, prioritization, and resource allocation. Assessment of our vulnerabilities and development of containment measures must keep pace with threat adaptation and innovation.

Commercially available electronics, advanced communication technologies, and the exponential growth in basic sciences have made state-like destructive power available to stateless players. The threat is developing ad hoc alliances between rogue states, terrorists, and organized crime networks in order to amplify their potential. Cyberspace is a new battleground where the terrorist is making improvements in all aspects of his operations.

Terror's Rolling Stones / Milestones:
- Dynamite patent - 1867: Fenians launch the London Dynamite Outrage of 1884
- First car bomb: 1905 assassination attempt against Ottoman Sultan Hamid II
- First successful Hijacking of a US airliner: Antuilo Ramierez Ortiz in 1961
- First Extortion Hijacking: Israeli El Al in 1968
- First global media terror event: the Black September takes Israeli Olympic team hostage in 1972
- First suicide bombing: in 1980 a 13-year old blows himself up next to an Iraqi tank in Iran

---

[101] *The Great Influenza: The Epic Story of the Deadliest Plague In History*, by John M. Barry, Viking Penguin, February 2004.

- First large scale terror attack with chemical weapons: in 1995 Aum Shinrikyo uses sarin to attack the Tokyo subway
- First airliner suicide mission: in 1999 an Egyptian Airlines pilot intentionally crashes into the sea off the coast of Massachutsets
- First use of hijacked airliners as weapons: 2001, 9-11 Al Qaeda attack
- First terror/guerilla suicide attack: 2008 Mumbai

"The price of freedom is eternal vigilance"
— Thomas Jefferson

CHAPTER 4

iG

The New Model Insurgent
iGuerilla[102]

Today's Third Wave, high-tech guerilla is motivated by the same force that inspired Oliver Cromwell's 1645 New Model Army – religious fanaticism.

In the winter of 1645, England's Oliver Cromwell instituted a series of critical military reforms, known as the New Model Army, that gave his Puritan Roundheads a battlefield advantage over King Charles' Cavaliers. With religious instilled fervor, his reinvented army conquered Scotland and Ireland and gained control of England by 1649. Over three and a half centuries later, today's insurgents have essentially turned back the clock by embracing one of humankind's oldest motivational forces – religion. The power of religious zeal, coupled with the iPod and iPhone, has resulted in the "iGuerilla," a deadly "New Model Insurgent."

Yesteryear's Insurgents. Until recently, the word "insurgent" conjured images of fearsome Huks in the Philippines and crafty Viet Cong in Vietnam's jungles. In popular culture, the term evoked romantic visions of a revolutionary Che and a young Fidel stalking Cuba, leading ragtag bands armed with hunting rifles and obsolete firearms and aspiring to overthrow corrupt regimes. These insurgents of yesteryear – fighters who were low tech, local and persistent – operated from remote guerilla bases as typically secular and pragmatic forces often motivated by Marxist or Maoist philosophy. They ground through Mao Zedong's three-stage insurgency model until they could transition to a conventional warfare and ultimate victory.

Terrorism has often been the principal tactic of insurgents, with the seemingly random acts of murder and destruction intended either to

[102] *Armchair General Magazine.*

intimidate people to keep them from cooperating with the targeted government or to evoke a massive military retaliation that alienates them from their government. Yet terrorist attacks carried out by 20th –century insurgents killed relatively few, and the shock value was more important than actual body counts. Politics—changing the country's political system—was the motivation, with promises of a better life for the downtrodden held out as the light at the end of the tunnel. Many people tended to view these insurgents as part criminal, part Robin Hood—the "radical chic" among us put their images on T-shirts and designer clothing.

Just as mechanization, radar and the radio revolutionized conventional military operations during the 20th century, so too have technology and globalization revolutionized irregular warfare operations. Che's hunting rifles and the Viet Cong's crossbows and homemade weaponry have been replaced by a wave of technologically sophisticated and highly lethal tools of war. Insurgents still carry the venerable AK-47—the guerillas ubiquitous weapon of choice—but it often serves more as an identification badge than as a primary tool of destruction.

Three successive "waves," however, have swamped the Old Model Guerilla, relegating him to history's dustbin and redefining irregular warfare now led by a New Model Insurgent.

First Wave: The Techno-Guerilla

In a perversion of the power of mass communications to unite far-flung regions of the globe, the First Wave predecessors of today's iGuerillas maximized the effect of improved weaponry by organizing, recruiting members and planning attacks first via telecoms, and then later online.

In retrospect, 1979 seems a watershed year for the techno-guerilla. During that year—which saw the Shah of Iran deposed by Ayatollah Khomeini's fundamentalist followers, Israeli forces moved into Lebanon in response to increased terror attacks, the Somoza regime in Nicaragua fell to the Sandinista rebels, and Irish Republican Army extremists assassinate Lord Mountbatten—the Soviet Union began a Vietnam-like odyssey in the rugged mountains of Afghanistan. The techno-guerilla was born in the Hindu Kush and nurtured by nine years of U.S. and Saudi support—supplies, money, training, equipment and advanced weaponry. The newly lethal rebels bled the Red Army white. The introduction of Stinger anti-aircraft missiles ended Soviet domination of the skies and spurred the Soviets retreat to fortified Afghan cities, transforming 18th century tribesmen into 20th century techno-guerillas who forced a humiliating Soviet withdrawal in 1989.

Afghanistans mujahedeen were a conglomeration of Muslims from all over the world who answered the call to jihad against the "godless" communists. One such group was a Wahabbi sect called al-Qaida ("the base"), led by Abdullah Azzam, who was later assassinated and replaced by Osama Bin Laden. At the time, al-Qaida was just another insurgent group. Yet when civil war broke out among the mujahedeen factions after the Soviets left, al-Qaida and its Taliban allies won. Al-Qaida next redirected its efforts toward a regional Islamist insurgency under the protection of Afghanistan's Taliban rulers.

Another group that benefited from advanced technology and mass communications was the Iranian-supported Hizballah. Its 2006 Lebanon War with the Israeli Defense Forces (IDF) highlighted how deadly techno-guerillas had evolved into iGuerillas. The war which lasted from July 12 to August 14, surprised the Israelis, who expected a low-intensity conflict against unsophisticated guerillas, much like the battles they had fought in Palestinian refugee camps. What they instead encountered was a high tech, well-trained, para-military foe in a high-intensity conflict. Hizballah fired over 4,000 Katyusha rockets (weapons systems common to modern armies but not to insurgent rabbles) and employed advanced Russian-made anti-tank guided missiles (ATGMs). Israel's Merkava main battle tanks took a beating, suffering 50 hit and five destroyed. ATGMs were also used to collapse buildings on top of troops engaged in house-to-house fighting. Hizballah proved to be well trained and highly organized and was equipped with top-shelf weaponry, early detection sensors and cutting edge command and communications equipment. Notably, Hizballah transformed itself into into an asymmetric force with formidable conventional capabilities by capitalizing on the following:

Advanced Command and Control. Hizballah employed networks using protected communications and computers that were slaved to modern sensors. Its members moved through pre-prepared subterranean systems and underground hide positions, repeatedly causing the IDF to retake the same ground.

Direct Fire & Maneuver. They employed advanced intelligence, surveillance and reconnaissance technology and used remote controlled night-vision systems.

Indirect Fire. Hizballah's hid its Kaytusha launchers in apartment buildings thus using human shields to discourage counter fire. When attacked, Hizballah publicly exploited the inevitable collateral damage and portrayed it as Israeli callousness.

Precision Weapons. Hizballah possessed sophisticated anti-armor and anti-ship missiles.

Mass Media. The most effective weapon used by Hizballah was the media. Their digitally manipulated images of destruction inflamed world opinion and fostered the notion that non-defeat equaled victory.

The Hizballah-IDF Lebanon War of 2006 provided a glimpse into the future of

transnational insurgency. iGuerrillas definitely are not yesterday's insurgents – they have closed the gap between traditional insurgent forces and the nation-state's army. Yet the threat posed by the iGuerrilla phenomenon represents much more than localized battles fought with high-tech weapons and mass communications – iGuerrillas have become "super-empowered."

Second Wave: Super-empowerment.

What does one get when nonstate actors mix sophisticated targeting with lethal, hightech, state-like weaponry? The answer is state-like destruction—the potential of iGuerrillas to inflict Hiroshima-like mass casualties. This "superempowerment" gives iGuerrillas the ability to expand their destructiveness exponentially until it has a global reach. The benign-appearing theoretical basis for this is over four decades old. In 1965, Gordon E.Moore, co-founder of Intel, observed that the number of transistors that could be inexpensively placed on an integrated circuit was increasing exponentially, doubling approximately every two years. The trend that he noted, which became known as "Moore's law," influences almost every measure of digital capability, from processing speed to the development of digital cameras, and has improved the usefulness of digital electronics in all segments of the international economy. Moore's law is a driving force of technological advancement (and resulting social change) and is key to the rise of the iGuerrilla. In a corollary to Moore's law—with potentially sinister implications – Rob Carlson, a biologist at the University of Washington, hypothesized in 2003 that the law might also apply to biotechnology. He charted the rates at which various biotechnologies were improving, and then plotted them. The result, known as Carlson's curves, revealed that biotechnology is improving at rates equal to or better than those of Moore's law. If this trend holds, then the technology required to produce lethal biological pathogens will grow increasingly capable, while costs will decline and the knowledge required to execute bio-war will become more accessible. Work that formerly required the specialized skills and knowledge of a PhD can now be done by a trained technician, with much of the information needed to develop dangerous pathogens available online.

The world has already experienced chilling previews of the scope and deadly effects of such superempowerment:

March 20, 1995. An obscure millenarian sect called Aum Shinrikyo unleashed sarin nerve gas in the Tokyo subway system, killing 12 people, injuring 54 and seriously affecting 980.

September 11, 2001. Nineteen al-Qaida terrorists turned Western technology against the West by hijacking four commercial airliners, crashing two of them into the World Trade Center and another into the Pentagon. The death toll was 2,974, with another 24 missing and presumed dead.

September 18, 2001. The first of two waves of anthrax-laced letters was mailed bearing Trenton, New Jersey, postmarks. More than 20 people were infected and five died. Decontamination took 26 months at an estimated cost of over $200 million.

May 8, 2002. Jose Padilla was arrested in Chicago and charged with being part of a plot to detonate a "dirty bomb" (conventional high explosives meant to scatter radioactive material) on U.S. soil.

April 27, 2007. Russia launched a three-week cyber-attack on Estonia, one of Europe's most "wired" societies and a pioneer of "e-government." A webpage explaining how to jam Estonian systems enabled thousands of civilians to augment the attack. Estonia's government and financial websites were flooded, causing massive shutdowns. (See Ralph Peters' "The New Cossacks," *Crisis Watch*, March 2008.)

May 12, 2007. Tuberculosis patient Andrew Speaker boarded a plane to Paris and then traveled on to Athens and Rome, sparking an international scare and providing an unintended example of how an infectious carrier on global transit could spread contagion – and wild-eyed panic.

If Moore's law and Carlson's curves hold steady, the future destructive ability of iGuerrillas provided by the Second Wave, super-empowerment, becomes alarming. A nonstate actor might be able to wage an incredibly deadly war against a nation-state since it may no longer require national resources to build and launch weapons of mass destruction.

The iGuerrillas' motivation for wreaking such destruction, however, is far removed from the latest advances in technology and the state-of-the-art mass communications that give today's insurgents their deadly means. Like Cromwell's New Model Army of 1645, today's New Model Insurgents are motivated by sectarian religious fervor.

Third Wave: Sectarianism

Rebels, radicals, insurgents and iGuerrillas have a new source of inspiration—religious sectarianism. The motivation of 21stcentury insurgents has moved from secular political ideology to fanatic millenarian theology. Insurgents have switched from Marx to Muhammad. As noted strategist Ralph Peters wrote, "Politics may inspire action, but religion inspires sacrifice." The spirit of sectarian sacrifice is now used to motivate suicide bombers—the ultimate "precision-guided missile"—literally to die for the cause with a zeal seldom seen since the Thirty Years War (the religious-based conflict that devastated much of central Europe from 1618 to 1648).

The 19th-century ideologues Friedrich Nietzsche and Karl Marx judged that "God is dead" and declared religion the "opiate of the masses." Their philosophies undermined organized religion in the West and provided the intellectual groundwork to launch the utopian movements of fascism and communism. Their ideas proved spectacular failures in the 20th century, prompting premature claims of the "end of history." But history came roaring back—Nietzsche and Marx are dead, and God has returned with a vengeance. And the new "ism"—sectarianism—is as old as war itself and may prove to be *the* dominant force in history.

In the Middle East, sectarian insurgencies have stepped in where the nationalism of Egypt's Gamal Abdel Nasser and the Baathist socialism of Iraq's Saddam Hussein have failed. Blind faith is being used to mobilize noncompetitive societies whose inadequacies and failures are painfully spotlighted by globalism and the Internet. Faith is touted as the key to identity, making religious-based insurgencies bloodier and more resolute and protracted than secular-based movements.

Sectarian insurgencies have erupted in the past. The Vendee Uprising (1793-95) against revolutionary France, for example, took the lives of 300,000 to 600,000 peasants. But the New Model, Third Wave insurgency of today no longer consists of wandering bands of ill equipped, poorly trained backwater militia-men. The minions of iGuerrillas are semiprofessional armies toting the best weapons, night-observation devices and satellite communications that modern technology has to offer. iGuerrillas carry Armageddon in their knapsacks, and when super-empowerment reaches its full potential, they will be able to wage war with a global reach while protected by non-state anonymity.

The most overlooked aspect of New Model Insurgents is *why* they fight. It may not be politically correct to address, but it is suicidal not to. Today's leader isn't the Bolshevik Trotsky; rather he's a fanatic spouting a perverted interpretation of the prophet Muhammad. The iGuerrillas' cause is not secular ideology, and it isn't about class warfare or "power to the people." It is about power to the prophet and millenarian purification. Insurgents no longer strive to move forward to a utopian future, but fight to move backward to an idealized past. Modern insurgents aren't inspired by politics; they're inflamed by faith. They are in search of theological lebensraum and freedom from globalism and egalitarianism. They seek moral domination and total submission to their sectarian-based worldview. Today's iGuerrillas will not —cannot—compromise; they love war and greet death as a sacrament and a salvation. Such enemies cannot be swayed by logic or argument; they are deterred only through annihilation.

The three "waves" that have created today's iGuerrillas—technology, super-empowerment and sectarianism—have produced a deadly New Model Insurgent. The first two waves raised the potential harm and level of destruction the non-state actor can inflict, while the third wave has added an uncompromising lack of restraint generated by religious fervor. iGuerrillas may soon have access to weapons that can kill tens of thousands. They will be free of state-like accountability and, inflamed with a righteous zeal; have already demonstrated that they will not hesitate to use this newfound capability.

iG Lexicon

Wiki-war. Wikipedia is an online encyclopedia where users read, research, modify and add content. Wikiwar follows the same process. It is open source warfare that anyone can join and to which anyone can contribute. The template is disseminated online and is modified by the users.Wiki-war represents the ability to decentralize beyond the limits of a single group, since the structure expands the number of participants while shrinking the size of the group below normal measures of viability and detection. Virtual cell organization enables new entrants to appear from anywhere at any time, and recruits have already popped up in London, Madrid, Berlin, Canada and New York.
Systems disruption. This sabotage goes beyond simple destruction of infrastructure. It maximizes return on investment through sophisticated targeting that uses network dynamics to undermine interdependent

systems. A $2,000 bomb can blow up a pipeline and end up costing the government $100 *million*. It's not enough to be a nuisance; the goal is to cripple the economy. Creative destruction exploits the interdependent world economic system, and the target set is huge. The number of targets and the unpredictability of attacks make infrastructure defense prohibitive.

Transnational insurgency. The success of iGuerrillas, coupled with the exploitation of global communications, allows militant Islamists to construct a global insurgency. The movement is no longer confined to a single country or region. Ayman al-Zawahiri has made a global appeal to oppose Western influence. Fighters need not be Muslim, as recent domestic terror incidents confirm.

The virtual organization. Exploitation of the World Wide Web produces a new recruiting and training ground. Islamist websites conduct cyber propaganda, recruiting, indoctrination, training, planning and control. Traditional cells are no longer required; networks take their place. Rogues and lone wolves are encouraged and trained for independent, self-tasked operations. Like a franchise, expertise is provided but direct contact is unnecessary. Niche warriors with local grudges are co-opted.

The virtual state. Some organizations become states within states. The virtual state focuses on a specific target, where it establishes a "shadow government." This isn't new, but by exploiting globalization and the black economy, the virtual state has expanded capabilities. It can use global info systems to conduct sophisticated information operations. Manipulation of a susceptible media augments the manufactured legitimacy of this parasitic add-on. Freedom from bureaucracy allows the virtual state to provide services that the legitimate state is unable to in a timely manner. Hizballah and Iraqi Jaish al Mahdi (JAM) have attained virtual state status (although both are supposed to be parties within the state).

The virtual nation. The virtual nation is the transnational insurgency. Its dominant unifying factor is sectarian versus the common 20th-century elements of shared identity – geography, history or linguistics. The emerging virtual nation is building partnerships with disaffected, anti-Western dissident groups as well as global criminal networks. This adds operatives to the network and enhances finance. Such a virtual nation supersedes state identity and is unconstrained by geography. The web-page is the iGuerrillas' base, and the cells need not meet to coordinate. They subscribe to a shared vision offered online and act autonomously or semi-autonomously. The Internet unleashed iGuerillas on the world.

CHAPTER 5

Jihad
Janissaries

Zealots and Assassins
Return

"Absolute faith corrupts as absolutely as absolute power."
—Eric Hoffer

"While Hindus, Sikhs, Christians, Parsees and Jews, along with several million adherents of an animistic religion, all coexisted in relative harmony, one religion that would not accept compromise stood out from the rest: Islam."
—Mahatma Gandhi: *The Power of Pacifism*

Throughout history, people's wars (wars of passion) have been bloody affairs. Passion becomes fanaticism when mixed with faith. The sectarian impulse justifies indiscriminate violence. The Holy Warrior whether crusader, zealot, assassin, or jihadi can't be wrong—his actions are sanctioned by the ultimate moral authority. His victims deserve their fate and innocent bystanders are paradise bound as martyrs. Either way, you can't go wrong.[103]

True Believers need not be 'sold' on the necessity of merciless actions. Often times they agitate for more aggressive options. True Believers are literal. They are purists who shame their moderate co-religionists into tacit support or passive indifference.[104]

The faith warrior's confidence only wanes when they are confronted with a series of exhausting losses over an extended time (the fall of the

---

[103] *Terror in the Name of God : Why Religious Militants Kill*, by Jessica Stern; HarperCollins Publishers, August 2004.

[104]*The True Believer*, by E. Hoffer; HarperCollins Publishers, September 2002.

Ottoman Empire) or with one catastrophic defeat (Omdurman). These events try his faith. Maybe he's lost God's favor; he's not pious enough; he's not worthy... If everything is divinely guided then his losses are the will of God thus his core convictions are shaken—for a while. There's a way out; become more pious he may yet prevail.[105] He never totally goes away and defeat can take generations.

****

Holy War. Rome grappled with religious fanatics for nearly a century. The Jewish radicals emerged under Herod the Great and were known as Zealots.[106] They assassinated gentiles, attacked impious or Hellenized Jews, and agitated for rebellion. To them, Roman rule was heretical; the Kingdom of Heaven could only come from fundamentalist Jewish rule. Their roots ran all the way back to the Maccabeus who had called for Roman help against Seleucid religious oppression and Hellenization.

The Zealots became a major problem during the Judean census of 6AD when Judas of Galilee called for rebellion arguing that the acknowledgement of a pagan emperor denied the authority of God and was tantamount to slavery; themes similar to the complaints of Al Bana, Qtub and modern Islamists.[107]

An even more extreme sect arose called the Sicarii (dagger men). They took up terrorism in pursuit of the Kingdom of Heaven. The Sicarii assassinated Romans in public in a manner designed spread hysteria and fear. Some even dressed as women to get closer to their targets. They terrorized fellow Jews who were friendly to Roman rule, or who didn't rise to their standard of piety, by burning down their homes.[108] Flavius Josephus, the Jewish historian, reports that the Zealots played a major role in inciting the Great Revolt of 66. Kito's

---

[105] *The Canons of Jihad*, by Jim Lacey; Naval Institute Press, 2008.

[106] *Empires of Trust: How Rome Built-and America is Building-A New World*, by Thomas Madden, Penguin Group (USA), July 2008

[107] *The Jews Against Rome: War in Palestine AD 66-73*, by Susan Sorek, Continuum September 2008.

[108] *Terror and Consent: The Wars for the Twenty-First Century*, by P. Bobbitt; Random House Inc, April 2008.

War followed in 115 and the Bar Kokhba revolt of 132 came after that. The sectarian fueled troubles seemed insoluble and unending. The Romans tried though. They gave the Jews political power, religious privilege, and access to trade. They honored the Jewish faith by allowing them to collect tithes for the Temple and allowed them observe Jewish laws. They only asserted control when asked to by Judea's neighbors.[109] None of this brought peace.

Emperor Hadrian decided to end Rome's struggle with the Jews. He realized that the conflict was not political, social, or economic—it was religious. He crushed the revolt, ordered the destruction of Solomon's Temple, and erased Judea from the map. Hadrian's goal was to make it impossible for the Jews to dream of a religious kingdom. The Jewish Diaspora rejected the Messianism that fueled their past rebellions and the local synagogue replaced the central Temple. Jews were force fed toleration.

Religious war is not unique to the Middle East. Faith wars are a global phenomenon. The Crusades were inter-faith wars between Christens and Muslims. The Thirty Years War was a Christian civil war between Catholics and Protestants. Both were sectarian wars that were protracted and traumatic. The Reformation and the Thirty years War cost the Catholics their primacy and restructured Christianity. Islam hasn't faced a similar calamity although they lost the Caliphate to the ossification of its Turkish masters. The Christian west renounced sectarian war but Islam didn't follow suit—it went into hibernation while it was weak.

Understanding the Caliphate is critical. It didn't fall in a firestorm; it was abandoned as a failing anachronism by Kamal Attaturk.[110] This inglorious end gave rise to an Islamist betrayal mythology similar to the German WWI betrayal mythology that fueled the Freikorps and led to the rise of the Nazi's.[111] In many ways, this process is repeating itself.

---

[109] *Empires of Trust: How Rome Built-and America is Building-A New World,* by Thomas Madden, Penguin Group (USA), July 2008.

[110] *Unleashing the Devils; The Ottoman collapse still creates crises today,* by Ralph Peters, ARMCHAIR General Magazine, April / May 2010.

[111] *Knowing the Enemy: Jihadist Ideology and the War on Terro,r* by Mary Habeck; Yale University Press, January 2006.

The Caliphate. The Caliphate was the Muslim Empire. It was the home of the ulemma and the realm of the Caliph; the supreme leader and successor to the Prophet. The Caliphate was a strict theocracy governed by Sharia—Islamic Paradise on Earth. The Caliph's mission was to expand the Caliphate and to convert, kill, or reduce Infidels to dhimmitude. It's vision was Islam and its path was holy war—Jihad.[112] The Caliphate existed in one form or another from the late 600's to the 1920's. Its birth, schism, and fall defines the modern Muslim landscape.

The Schism. The death of the Prophet left his followers, the Salafis, with the inevitable autocratic dilemma; succession. The Sunni majority formulated the rules. The successor should be an Arab from Muhammad's tribe; he should be elected and approved by a council of elders; and he should enforce divine law and spread Islam. They picked Muhammad's father in law, Abu Bakr; an original 'companion'.

The Shia minority believed the successor should be a male blood relative of the Prophet. They backed Muhammad's son-in-law, Ali—thus followers of Ali or Shia. They also asserted that all successors should be descendants of Ali.[113] The resulting schism led to the formation of the two sects and parented today's leading Islamic Theocracies—the Sunni Kingdom of Saudi Arabia and the Shia Islamic Republic of Iran. Sunni Islamism gave rise to non-state terrorism (Al Qaeda) while Shia Islamism gave rise to state backed terrorism (Iranian Revolutionary Guards Command) and proxy terrorism (Hizballah).

Sectarian Warriors. Many westerners see Muslim holy warriors (mujahedeen) through secular eyes. They opine that, "they don't hate us for who we are; they hate us for what we've done." This highlights the western tendency to refuse to acknowledge sectarian, utopian, millenarian, and apocalyptic motivations. This attitude reflects a lack of historical context. The Islamic sectarian impulse has been consistent ever since the consolidation of Mecca and Medina. The brief exception occurred during the Cold War when the superpower struggle

---

[112] *Jihad in the West: Muslim Conquests from the 7th to the 21st Centuries*, by Paul Fregosi; Prometheus Books, October 1998.

[113] *The Middle East: A Brief History of the Last 2,000 Years*, by Bernard Lewis, Scribner, August 1997.

smothered all competing-isms and-ologies. The west cannot secularize the Islamists nor should we paint the false picture that they are an
aberration.[114]

The Manson Family, Aum Shinrikyo, and Jim Jones were sectarian.
As secularists, we write off such groups as the lunatic fringe; a fair
assessment but we ignore their potential mass appeal at our own peril.
No amount of equivocation can get around the fact that these groups
were motivated by demagogic 'faith.'[115] Modern Islamists are no less
sectarian than the groups above. Charles Manson and Jim Jones are
western versions of Bin Laden and Nasrallah. Aum Shinrikyo is a
Japanese Hizballah. The only difference is that the former fabricated
their ideology out of whole cloth while the latter built upon a millennium plus of tradition. The Islamist purists will do anything to serve
Allah. They will exploit any weapons and technology they find, chemical, nuclear, or biological.[116] They don't fight for secular political
causes. They don't compromise or negotiate. They fight for their esoteric, exclusive, prejudicial views of faith. They are intolerant, misogy-
nistic, xenophobic, and uncompromising. They are Manson, Asahara,
and Jones with a turbin.

Some draw equivalence between Al Qaeda, Hizballah, and Hamas
and the Minutemen, Partisans, and Freedom Riders. Absurd! The
World Trade Center is not the Boston Tea Party. It is self defeating to
degrade patriots while elevating intolerant killers. We need to tough-
en up and face the enemy.

Noam Chomsky, Howard Zinn, and George Soros can't project
their worldview on the Islamist Jihadis. These self-loathing socialists
are today's useful idiots; just three infidel heads in a basket. As in
Joesephus' time, the issue is not political, economic, or social—it's religious. The Islamist ideologues are Taymiyyah, Al Banna, and Qutb not
Marx, Nietzsche, or Mao.

114 Y *The Sources of Islamic Revolutionary Conduct*, by Major Stephen P. Lambert, U.S.
Air Force Research Fellow with the cooperation and support of the Institute for
National Security Studies (INSS) USAF Academy, Colorado Springs, Washington DC,
April 2005.

115 *When Religion Becomes Evil*, by Charles Kimball; HarperCollins Publishers,
September 2002.

116 *The Canons of Jihad*, by Jim Lacey; Naval Institute Press, 2008.

Ibn Taymiyyah was a Muslim scholar who saw the caliphate conquered by the Mongols. He rejected the newly converted Mongol rulers as impure for blending their tribal (human) law with Sharia (divine) law. He saw it as the duty of 'true' Muslims to resist. Taymiyyah's contribution to Islamism was the idea of waging Jihad against unauthentic forms of Islam—but who decides what is authentic? [117]

Hassan Al Banna was a schoolteacher in Egypt who saw Abdul Nasser's secular Arab nationalism as un-Islamic. He advocated the overthrow of Nasser's 'apostate' regime in favor of a genuine Islamic state. Al Banna's contribution to Islamism was the covert revolutionary vanguard—the Muslim Brotherhood.[118]

Sayyid Qutb became the Karl Marx of Islamism. An Al Banna's disciple, Qutb introduced the concept of offensive Jihad against the apostate regimes and western influence. He believed in exporting Jihad to the west to weaken their resolve and isolate their Muslim clients. He defined the west as the far enemy and the apostates as the near enemy. Qutb's contribution to Islamism was the his comprehensive doctrine that, like *Mein Kampf*, became the catalyst for modern Islamist non-state terrorism. All added to the Sunni Wahabbi Islamist tradition.[119]

It's dangerous to ignore real Islamist Jihadi voices by supplanting them with contrarian western ones. Western liberal narcissism implies that we are the center of the universe and that we drive all global trends. The notion that no one else is important and non-western action is irrelevant is the ultimate expression of self-centrism. This alienates dispossessed Muslims and provides Islamist Jihadi's with propaganda that highlights our arrogance.

Threat rhetoric matters. Hitler clearly stated his intentions in *Mein Kampf* and Lenin did so in *What is to be Done*. We might have headed off disaster had we taken them at their word? The Jihadi's have written books as well. They present a clear vision of what they want and how

---

[117] *Voices of Terror: Manifestos, Writings and Manuals of Al Qaeda, Hamas, and other Terrorists from around the World and Throughout the Ages,* by Walter Laquer; Reed Press, 2004.

[118] *Blood and Rage: A Cultural History of Terrorism,* by Michael Burleigh; HarperCollins Publishers, March 2009.

[119] *The Al Qaeda Reader,* by Raymond Ibrahim; Bantam Books, August 2007.

they intend to get it. The only thing they have in common with their western counterparts is their lack of compromise.

The Islamist Jihadi's hate Infidels and want sectarian rule. The Jihadi's would just as soon kill a western liberal as a western conservative; a black American as a white American; a white-collar worker as a blue-collar worker; infidels are infidels. Target selection is religious not class or race based. They are not motivated by the fight for multi-cultural egalitarianism. They are utopians who use western policies to excuse societal failure, incite the street, and manipulate the press.

They are xenophobes, bigots, and misogynists in search of resurrecting the Caliphate. We live in the House of War and they live in the House of Islam and the two cannot coexist.[120] Their doctrine is derived from literal interpretations of the Quran, the Hadiths, and the Sura's. Bin Laden summarized the Sunni view in his '96 and '98 declarations while Mahmoud Ahmadinejad presented the Shia view at the UN in 2007.[121] Few westerners read their words and fewer still believe that they mean what they say.

Islamism is not progressive; it's reactionary. It rejects modernity and hates modernity's champion; the west. The war on the west is designed to recapture the lands seized by the Muslim surge following the death of the prophet. Ultimately they desire to conquer and convert the world.

Islamism spawned stateless terror from the Sunni's as embodied by AQ and LeT and state terror from the Shia's as embodied by Iran and its surrogate LH.

We will not offer a Muslim primer here. Islam will only be discussed in terms of its role in providing context for Islamist Jihadi extremism.[122] As with all radical utopian, sectarian, or millenarian sects and cults, a literalist puritanical minority exploits faith to justify extremism. The modern day *assassins* and *zealots* blame Islam's cultural and political decline on apostasy acquiescence to western decadence.

---

[120] *Wars of Blood and Faith: The Conflicts That Will Shape The Twenty-first Century*, by Ralph Peters; Stackpole Books, February 2009.

[121] *The Al Qaeda Reader*, by Raymond Ibrahim; Bantam Books, August 2007.

[122] *When Religion Becomes Evil*, by Charles Kimball; HarperCollins Publishers, September 2002.

They ignore endemic corruption, nepotism, and incompetence in Muslim majority states. They refuse self-criticism in order to transform non-competitiveness into victim-hood whose only redress is holy war. [123]

Today's Islamism builds on layers and layers of Muslim utopianism. It comes in many forms; overt violent Jihad and covert subversive civilizational jihad.

Undeclared, State Supported, 'Soft' Jihad (Conquest from Within). Soft Jihad is a passive, often state backed, infiltration of infidel states. Its leading proponent is the Kingdom of Saudi Arabia's (KSA). The KSA, fueled by western petro-dollars, sponsors the global proliferation of Madrassa's and Mosques that preach their uniquely virulent version of Islam, Wahabbism. They distribute Korans and Islamic textbooks that are harshly critical of the west, Christianity, and Judaism. Prisoners are prime targets given their disaffection. The KSA funds Islamic studies departments in western universities, back Islamic NGO's, and backs Islamic Advocacy and Activist Groups. They promote Wahabism, Sharia, and the establishment of autonomous enclaves that undermine host nation culture.[124]

This approach is reflected in the Islamic poem quoted below:

"The mosques are our barracks, the domes our helmets, the minarets our Bayonets and Muslims our soldiers..."
—Prime Minister of Turkey Recep Tayyip Erdogan

This in your face approach prompted Switzerland to ban further construction of minarets in their country.[125]

Cultural Alienation (Immigration without Assimilation). The idea is to flood a host state with devout immigrants and their families. The new arrivals cash in on all available entitlements while forcing

[123]*Wars of Blood and Faith: The Conflicts That Will Shape The Twenty-first Century,* by Ralph Peters; Stackpole Books, February 2009.

[124]*Hatred's Kingdom: How Saudi Arabia Supports the New Global Terrorism,* by Dore Gold, Regnery Publishing, Inc., An Eagle Publishing Company, February 2003.

[125]*Swiss Ban Building of Minarets on Mosques,* by Nick Cumming-Bruce and Steven Erlanger, New York Times, November 29, 2009, http://www.nytimes.com/2009/11/30/world/europe/30swiss.html.

their culture down their new neighbors throats in the name of multi-culturalism, all the while rejecting host nation culture. The goal is demographic displacement and occupation coupled with democratic disruption. It's called Hijra and it is de-facto Islamist colonialism; an expansionistic strategy designed to suppress and supplant infidel societies. The hope is to transform the locals into submissive dhimmis. The process is Islamization and it is an established part of Muslim history.[126] The Hijra replicates Mohamed's pilgrimage from Mecca to Medina. It symbolizes the Islamist hunt for world domination. It involves millions of Muslims who live outside of Muslim countries who are gradually eroding infidel cultures while striving to install Sharia. The Islamist people bomb is poised to overwhelm many small European countries and is a real threat to the free world.

Cultural Jihad challenges free speech, free religion, women's rights, gay rights and other human rights taken for granted in the Judeo-Christian West. It is justified by a theo-politico-legal doctrine outlined in Islamic texts.

The effect sought is demographic neutralization and insidious cultural destruction and replacement over time. Subtle indoctrination exposes and imposes new expectations and values until a critical mass engineers a takeover. The massive relocation of Muslims west is state sponsored in order to relieve demographic / economic pressure while spreading Islam and building more Londonistans (the largest Europe city in the west). Islamigrants are encouraged to retain and promote fundamentalism by exploiting democratic tolerance, demanding autonomy and recognition of Sharia, and pushing for observation of Islamic cultural practices by non-Muslims. They seek segregation and submission to their religious sensibilities. They become voters and welfare recipients who impact policy while living on the dole and are allied with liberal groups and activists who share their animosity for western culture and capitalism.[127]

The Dutch cartoon incident is an example of Islamist imposed Balkanization. Provocative political cartoons are a tradition of western

[126]*The Myth of Islamic Tolerance: How Islamic Law Treats Non-Muslims,* by Robert Spencer; Prometheus Books, February 2005.

[127]*Unholy Alliance: Radical Islam and the American Left,* by David Horowitz, Regnery Publishing, Inc., an Eagle Publishing Company, March 2006.

press but, for Islamigrants tolerance is a one way street. One dare not satirize Mohammad even though Jesus, Moses, and Buddha are fair game. The incident didn't stop with the Dutch. An academic book published by Yale Press called *The Cartoons that Shook the World* declined to reprint the Mohammad cartoons out of fear of reprisals.[128] A few years later, South Park dropped an episode including Mohammad for the same reason.[129] Islamigrants are redefining western tolerance of intolerance. Elsewhere, Muslim cashiers refused to handle pork products and Muslim cab drivers demanded taxpayer provided foot-baths in airports. Such concessions used to be unnecessary; now they're essential to the cause of multi-culturalism.

****

Sects. All religions fracture as a result of divergent interpretation. What follows are the major Islamic subdivisions by sect. We also need to consider subdivisions by their proclivity to act like; the silent majority, the moderate minority, and the Islamist activists—violent and political. The last group is growing but the real worry is the increasing support and/or indifference of silent majority.

Radical Sunni Islam used to be largely confined to the Bedouin nomads of the Arabian Peninsula and the Egyptian diaspora who were scattered after failing to bring down Nasser's secular nationalism. The Wahabbis partnered with the House of Saud to run KSA while Muslim Brotherhood was smashed and driven underground by Nasser and his successors. They transmitted the Al Banna / Qtub virus throughout the region making it the first genuine Islamist movement since the fall of the caliphate.[130] The virus fermented in exile and in hiding for 40 plus

---

128 *Yale press passes on showing Muhammad cartoons*, The Grand Scheme, http://eileenflynn.wordpress.com/2009/09/10/yale-press-passes-on-showing-muhammad-cartoons/, September 10, 2009.

129 *South Park's Mohammed Episode Censored By Comedy Central*, by Jon Bershad, Mediaite, http://www.mediaite.com/online/south-parks-mohammed-episode-censored-by-comedy-central/, April 22nd, 2010.

130 *Muslim Brothers; Muslim Brotherhood; al-Ikhwan al-Muslimin; Jama'at al-Ikhwan al-Muslimun; Hizb Al-Ikhwan Al-Muslimoon; al-Ikhwan ("The Brothers")* prepared by Prepared by Julie Spears and maintained by Steven Aftergood, Updated January 8, 2002, http://www.fas.org/irp/world/para/mb.htm .

years; organizing, preparing and waiting to hijack the 'Arab Spring' and turn it into the 'Islamist Winter.'

The Saudi extremist variant spread when the most troublesome of the Wahhabi faithful were cast out by KSA in order to answer the call to Jihad in Afghanistan. The resultant flow of Wahhabi's sponsored recruits became a global pool for the coming transnational insurgency.[131]

The modern wave of Islamism was launched by the 1979 Iranian Revolution coupled with the Afghan War against the Soviets. The toppling of the Shah and eventual defeat of the Soviets ignited sectarianism, heralded the end of secularism, and inspired revanchism in Sunni's and Shia's.[132] The Supreme Leader, Ayatollah Khomeini, became the face of resurgent Shia's and the leader of Al Qaeda, Sheikh Osama Bin Laden, became the face of resurgent Sunni's. Both seek restoration of the Caliphate.

The 9-11 premeditated and theatrical mass murder was aimed squarely at the global media. It worked, morphing an obscure and esoteric Mujahedeen cult into a global jihadist insurgency. The media and the Internet made Al Qaeda a 'rock star' start up insurgency. So let's see where the Islamist Jihadis fall out.

Sunnis and Shites. Muhammad's death in 632 triggered an internecine power struggle over his succession. Most of the ummah believed that authority should be passed on to the Prophet's companions. A minority believed that only direct decendents of the Prophet should succeed him.

The majority (Sunnis) won the day when the tribal leaders chose Abu Bakr as caliph (khalifa). Bakr was the father of the prophet's favorite wife, Aisha. A permanent schism between the Sunni majority and the Shia minority has existed ever since.

Succession came up again when the third Caliph was assassinated and Muhammad's cousin and son-in-law, Ali, claimed to be the rightful heir. Ali lost his first bid to Abu Bakr. Ali was met with opposition

131 *Soldiers of God: With Islamic Warriors in Afghanistan and Pakistan*, by Robert D. Kaplan, Knopf Doubleday Publishing Group, November 2001.

132 *Persian Puzzle: The Conflict Between Iran and America*, by Kenneth Pollack, Random House Publishing Group, November 2004.

from many quarters but he defied them all by autonomously establishing a caliphate in Kufa. The ensuing conflict saw Ali defeat his top rival. In spite of his strong position, he agreed to arbitration. He was assassinated during the pause.[133]

Muawiyah, commander of the largest army in the caliphate, claimed the title of caliph and marched on Ali's backers led by his son Hasan. Muawiyah forced Hasan out, he was later assassinated like his father, while Muawiyah founded the Umayyad Dynasty leading to the first Islamic Empire.

The succession argument persisted and the schism solidified into two sects—Sunni and Shia. Most of the world's Muslims are Sunni's who believe in the unity of the Quran, sharia (Islamic law), and the sunna (habits of the Prophet). The Shia or Shiites (followers of Ali) believe in the 12 divinely guided Imams as perfect teachers of the faithful. The Shia ascribe to free will while the Sunni are deterministic.[134]

Sunni's are unstructured and do not have a formal clergy—anyone can become learned and thus become a cleric. The Shia have a formal clerical hierarchy. The Shia are more disciplined given their clerical order whereas anyone can claim religious authority in the Sunni chaotic world. Almost all Shia radicalism can be traced back to its clerical hierarchy in Iran where the Supreme Leader is seen as the equivalent of the Pope to his followers. Sunni radicals pop up anywhere and everywhere given their decentralization that are not necessarily mutually supporting.

A third minor sect exists—it is the mystic tradition of Sufism. Sufis believe they have acquired inner knowledge directly from Allah. The Sufi's are the least militaristic and are the most accommodating of the major Muslim sects and are often persecuted as heretics by Sunni's and Shia's alike.

Let's work our way through the Islamic hierarchy to see how the sects break out.

The Muslim Nation the Ummah. Adherents to Islam; Sunni,

---

[133] *The Middle East: A Brief History of the Last 2,000 Years*, by Bernard Lewis, Scribner, May 1996.

[134] *Islam Unveiled: Disturbing Questions About the World's Fastest-Growing Faith*, by Robert Spencer; Human Events Publishing, Inc. Nov 18, 2002.

Shia, Sufi and smaller sects like the Syrian Allawites; form the Muslim nation aka the ummah. The Muslim nation is sectarian not ethnic or geographic. Most of the ummah are moderates who coexist with each other and with their infidel neighbors. The ummah is not geographically tied to Muslim lands. A Muslim is part of the ummah no matter where they live and many do not warm to outsiders. When in non-Muslim lands, they self-segregate and resist assimilation. The ummah has been hostile to non-Muslims living in or next to Muslim lands.[135]

Infidels who stay in Muslim lands, by choice or not, are designated dhimmis by Sharia Law. While the modern ummah has not been openly hostile to dhimmis since the fall of the Ottoman Caliphate, they used to be and are returning to their old ways in the wake of the *Islamist Winter*. The tradition was to make life so difficult for non-Muslims that they would either leave or convert.[136] Just look at the steady decline of non-Muslim populations in Muslim lands; it's been hemorrhaging for centuries.

Islamists. Islamists are Muslim fundamentalists / literalists. They adhere to the written word of the Quran and believe that religion, politics, and way of life are one. Islamists believe that Sharia should be the law of the land and, eventually, the world. Most believe in a pan-Islamic identity and they seek the elimination of western influences in the Muslim world. They seek a Muslim revival. Islamism is militant but not always violent. Its original focus goal was inward, oriented on the purification of Muslim states through the elimination of 'man made' secular laws. Some decided that the only way to purify the homeland was to expel foreign influence by attacking infidels—thus turning external.[137]

Sunni Salafism. Salafists believe that Islam was perfect and complete during the time of Muhammad and his companions. The Salafi are the 'ancestors.' Salafis believe that Islam has been polluted by

[135] *The Clash of Civilizations and the Remaking of World Order*, by Samuel Huntington; Simon & Schuster Adult Publishing Group, January 1998.

[136] *Jihad in the West: Muslim Conquests from the 7th to the 21st Centuries*, by Paul Fregosi; Prometheus Books, October 1998.

[137] *Y, The Sources of Islamic Revolutionary Conduct*, by Maj Stephen P. Lambert USAF, Joint Military Intelligence College, Center for Strategic Intelligence Research, Institute for National Security Studies (INSS), Washington D.C., April 2005.

impurities, perversions, and deviations based on materialist and un-Islamic cultural influences. Salafism seeks to revive the pure Islam as practiced by Muhammad. Sunni's in general and Salafi's in particular believe ummah should be ruled by the followers of the Prophet.[138]

Salafism can be dubbed as Puritan Islam with Wahhabism as its most virulent sub sect. Wahhabism took root in the Arabian Peninsula when the future king of Saudi Arabia allied himself with the Wahhabis in resistance to the Ottoman Turks. The deal was that the House of Saud would rule the Arabian Peninsula and Wahhabi Islam would be the state religion. The Wahhabis were preceded by the Ikwan who massacred Shia's in what is modern day Iraq in order to purge their heresy.[139] The Wahhabi's inspired the formation of the Egyptian Muslim Brotherhood and its Qutbist offshoot, Al Qaeda, as well as the more traditional Taliban.

Shia Millenarianism. The Shia believe that upon Muhammad's death, true divine leadership was supposed to be passed on through the Prophets bloodline. They focus on the succession of *Twelve Rightly Guided Imams* beginning with Ali (the first) and ending with Muhammad al-Mahdi (the twelfth). Since only descendants of the Prophet should rule, the Sunni Caliphs were illegitimate.

For the Shia, the resurrection of Islamic Glory begins with the return of the *Mahdi*—the Shia Messiah who will purge the world. The Mahdi is one of the twelve Imams mentioned above; which one depends on the sect. The Mahdi didn't die; he disappeared by going into Occultation (divine hiding) in order to escape persecution. This earned him the name of the "Hidden Imam." His return initiates the Day of Judgment that will cleanse the world and bring global Islamic rule. It is important to note that Sunnis also believe in Judgment day but they do not believe the Mahdi will be a Shia or that the day can be predicted or hastened by man.[140]

---

[138] *Terror in the Name of God : Why Religious Militants Kill*, by Jessica Stern; HarperCollins Publishers, August 2004.

[139] *Islamic Imperialism: A History*, by Efraim Karsh; Yale University Press, May 2007.

[140] *Apocalyptic Politics: On the Rationality of Iranian Policy*, by Mehdi Khalaji, Policy Focus #79, Washington Institute for Near East Policy, Published in 2008 in the United States of America by the Washington Institute for Near East Policy.

The Iranian Revolution and the formation of the Islamic republic reinvigorated Shia Millenarianism. Suicide operations in the Iran-Iraq War, Hizballah homocide bombers in Lebanon and Israel, and Ahmadinejad's apocalyptic rhetoric are driven by the resurgence of the cult the Hidden Imam.

Shias disagree as to which Imam is *the* Hidden Imam. The sects follow; the Fifth (Fivers), the seventh (Seveners), or the twelfth (Twelvers). Fiver's and Sevener's are content to wait for the return while Sevener's are activist who believe they can create the conditions (chaos) that will hasten his return.

The Hojjatieh Society. The Hojjatei is the secretive cult of Shia *Twelvers* founded in Iran to combat the Bahá'í faith seen as a heretical to Iranian Islam. The Hojjatieh backed the Islamic revolution but opposed Khomeini's *Velayat-e Faqih* (Guardianship of the Jurist). Khomeini disbanded them in 1983 due to their opposition.

Most Shia await the return of the Hidden Imam. He disappeared in 874 AD. The Sunnis reject the successors of Ali and believe the Mahdi is yet to be born. The Mahdi's identity will be known when he returns. He will rule through a deputy or a deputy will precede him. Ahmadinejad's desire to wipe Israel off the map may reflect his belief that he is the Mahdi's deputy.[141] His warlike rhetoric highlighted the Hojjatieh and in a 2005 speech he openly alluded to the return of the Hidden Imam. This explains his provocative rhetoric and drive for nuclear weapons—to affect chaos and bring his boss back.[142]

Many Twelvers believe the Hidden Imam lives in a Jamkaran town well outside Qom. Followers drop notes down the well to seek his blessing. Ahmadinejad takes the well seriously; he and his cabinet dropped a signed a petition down the well urging the Mahdi's quick return.[143]

Ayatollah Mesbah Yazdi, Ahmadinejad's spiritual advisor and men-

---

[141]*Iranian Video Says Mahdi is 'Near,'* by Erick Stakelbeck, CBN News Terrorism Analyst, http://www.cbn.com/cbnnews/world/2011/March/Iranian-Regime-Video-Says-Mahdi-is-Near-/, April 03, 2011.

[142]*Iran: President Says Light Surrounded Him During UN Speech*, by Golnaz Esfandiari, Radio Free Europe Radio Liberty, http://www.rferl.org/content/article/1063353.html, November 29, 2005.

[143]*Ahmadinejad Promoted Shrine Draws Millions*, by Ali Reza Eshraghi and Raha Tahami, Mianeh, http://mianeh.net/article/ahmadinejad-promoted-shrine-draws-millions, May 4, 2010.

tor, is a high ranking member of the clandestine cult and is the one who introduced him to the group. Yazdi is an ultraconservative cleric sometimes referred to as the "crazed one" or the "crocodile" who may well aspire to ascend to the title of Supreme Leader after Khameini. His acolyte, Ahmadinejad, brought the executive branch and IRGC into the Hojjatieh sphere of influence. It begs the question whether Iran can be considered pragmatic or rational with this group in power.[144]

The Hojjatieh brings messianic and apocalyptic elements to the already volatile theology rooted in martyrdom and violence. While most Shia don't believe that man can prompt the Mahdi's return, the Hojjatieh believe they can generate enough chaos and violence to hasten his return which will usher in the return of global Caliphate while destroying all competing faiths.

The Hojjatieh provide the context to Iranian pronouncements against Israel, holocaust denial, and the destruction of Anglo-Saxon civilization. The desire to create chaos provides a perverse logic to Iran's nuclear program and its partnerships with the Lebanese Hezbollah, Gaza's Hamas, Yemen's Houthi insurgents, and the Taliban of Afghanistan and Pakistan.[145]

Iran has two governments: a Republic run by President Ahmadinejad and a theocracy run by Supreme Leader Ayatollah Ali Khamenei. Mediating the two is the Expediency Council, run by Hashemi Rafsanjani. Power is decentralized among a myriad of patrons and cronies.[146]

A Stateless Army in an Armyless State—Terror's A-Team. Al Qaeda is not the world's top terrorist group; they are only its most notorious. Just as in the criminal world when John Dillenger and Baby Face Nelson were making headlines, the big time bad guys like Carlo

---

[144] *Mesbah-Yazdi: The Regime Ayatullah*, by By Michael Theodoulou, The National [United Arab Emirates], Views from the Occident, http://occident.blogspot.com/2009/09/mesbah-yazdi-regime-ayatullah.html, August 23, 2009.

[145] *Apocalyptic Politics: On the Rationality of Iranian Policy*, by Mehdi Khalaji, Policy Focus #79, Washington Institute for Near East Policy, Published in 2008 in the United States of America by the Washington Institute for Near East Policy.

[146] *Iran's President and the Politics of the Twelfth Imam*, by John von Heyking, Ashbrook, Ashland University, http://ashbrook.org/publications/guest-05-vonheyking-twelfthimam/, November 2005.

Gambino and Vito Genovese represented the real crime wave. Al Qaeda's flash got them in trouble while the low profile Hizballah became the world's top terror franchise. They preceded Al Qaeda by nearly a decade and few outside the Levant knew who they were when they arrived on the scene.

The occupation of Lebanon is over and the traditional power-brokers are out. The Druze Christians and the Lebanese Sunnis lost their internal influence while the Palestinians and Israelis lost their external influence. The Syrians are out of the Bekka Valley and the Americans are out of Beirut. The outsiders have been replaced by an impotent and inert UN Security Force. From the Civil War through the two Lebanon Wars; tiny Lebanon has been a microcosm of the 'troubles' of the Middle East. The Ottoman Millet system failed, Nasser's Arab nationalism failed, Arafat's Palestinian exile failed and Syrian stewardship failed. The 'Party of God' officially rose from the wreckage with their 1985 *Open Letter* Declaration. From the start they were an Iranian creation that would change everything.[147]

The Shia revival blossomed in 1979 in the form of the stern Islamist Ayatollah Khomeini. Khomeini's Islamists united with a number of secular Iranian socialists to overthrow the Shah. The fiery Ayatollah and his coterie of clergy overwhelmed the fractious socialists and formed an Islamic Republic. As with most revolutions, transformation at home wasn't enough; the revolution and its theocratic Utopia had to be exported. The mutinous mullahs looked west to Iraq only to find Iraq's Shia's were more nationalist than sectarian. It took eight years but Iraq stopped the westward push cold.[148]

The failure of conventional war stalled, but did not stop, the revolution. The Ayatollahs looked for other options in other theaters finding the Lebanese hotbed ripe for the picking. The Iranians turned to the time honored Persian tradition of cultivating proxies.[149] The Shia's of Lebanon were their next target and, unlike their Iraqi counterparts, they were a marginalized minority in a failing state. Lebanon had been

---

[147]*Hezbollah: A Short History*, by A. R. Norton; Princeton University Press, March 2007.

[148]*Persian Puzzle: The Conflict Between Iran and America*, by Kenneth Pollack, Random House Publishing Group, November 2004.

invaded by Palestinians, Israeli's, Syrians and Americans. Lebanon was a perpetual host.

Iran's revolutionary leaders seized the opportunity by sending in its revolutionary elite, the Iranian Revolutionary Guards Command (IRGC). They formed, organized, trained, and equipped a local resistance force, the Party (hizb) of God (Allah) or Hizballah.[150] The new Lebanese bad boys used terrorism and guerilla tactics to take on the Israelis. There would be no more conventional force on force fighting. Hizballah introduced suicide bombing such the Mugniyah strike on the U.S. Marine Beirut compound. The new terror war didn't present easily identified targets for response. Opposition faded fast. Hizballah evolved and went viral as Iran's anonymous global road warriors.

Hizballah moved the Shia out of third place and vaulted them into Lebanon's driver's seat while making themselves the worlds real A-Team of terrorism. They have made Lebanon into an Iranian colony. LH has its own army of regulars and militia although their allegiance is not to Lebanon. Lebanon's legitimate army is the Lebanese Armed Forces (LAF) which makes them Armyless. The LAF is poorly trained, equipped, and manned and its leadership is infiltrated by LH. When the IDF invaded Lebanon, it was the LH that fought back, not the LAF. When the IDF pulled out, it was the LH that rebuilt, not the government. They can put weapons caches and rocket launchers inside civilian areas in the name of defending Lebanon.[151]

The LH has built a state within state. They have a leader, Hasan Nasrallah, whose command bunker is in Syria and whose boss is in Iran. They are armed, trained and subsidized by big daddy Iran and their toadie Syria. They can add donations from the Lebanese Diaspora much the same way the IRA did. They have transformed the Lebanese Shia from rock throwing street fighters to first rate terrorists. They may well be the region's most powerful Islamic army. Not a bad trick for a stateless entity.

---

[149]*Persian Fire: The First World Empire and the Battle for the West*, by Tom Holland, Doubleday, May 2006.

[150]*Immortal: A Military History of Iran and Its Armed Forces*, by Steven R. Ward, Georgetown University Press, March 2009.

[151]*A High Price: The Triumphs and Failures of Israeli Counterterrorism*, by Daniel Byman, Oxford University Press, June 2011.

The LH is also a proxy that takes orders from Tehran. The Supreme Leader commands global loyalty like a Medieval Pope. As Iran's agent, LH took the Palestinian Hamas under their arm and helped them take over Gaza. Their new Hamas partner now showers Israel with missiles, rockets and mortars. The Hizballah-Hamas-Syria Axis is Iran's check on US regional influence and puts Israel on the defensive—the latter of which bolsters their claim to be the world's Muslim leader.

The Sunni States disagree. They see the Iran's Shia resurgence as a greater threat than Israel although they won't say so publicly. They fear Shia empowerment in Iraq, a natural outcome of elections in the Shia majority state, and they want Iran's nuclear program stopped. Today, the Saudi's and Turks are presumed to be backing the Syrian opposition in the Syrian Civil War.

Stateless Sunni's, on the other hand, are apt to partner with the Shia in the short run. Hamas is the prime example, having been trained by and become full collaborators with Hizballah.[152]

Hizballah is an Iranian strategic asset used for the 'away game' against Israel and the west. They are being prepositioned for global Jihad should the Islamic Republic ever feel the need or desire to use them. Hizballah released its Second Manifesto on 30 Nov 2009 reassert their strategic vision and world view. The Manifesto confirms that they are an Islamic movement devoted to jihad. They also confirmed what everyone knows; that they are an Iranian movement with Lebanon as their home. They believe the US imperialism must be resisted and that Israel threatens Lebanese order. Interestingly, they state that their opposition to Israel is defensive but that they will not rest until Jerusalem is liberated.[153]

Hizballah seeks to transform Lebanon into a resistance society in a perpetual struggle.[154] This isn't popular since the Israelis withdrew in

---

[152] *Son of Hamas: A Gripping Account of Terror, Betrayal, Political Intrigue, and Unthinkable Choices,* by Mosab Hassan Yousef, SaltRiver, March 2010.

[153] *Hezbollah adopts new manifesto,* United Press International, Nov. 19, 2009 at 12:05 PM http://www.upi.com/Top_News/Special/2009/11/19/Hezbollah-adopts-new-manifesto/UPI-88531258650312/#ixzz22KB3riFN: To read the actual Manifesto go to For a Better Lebanon, http://forabetterlebanon.blogspot.com/2008/02/hizbollahs-manifesto-english-version.html.

2000. Many Lebanese pine for the pre-civil war days when Beirut was the Paris of the Middle East. The remaining fodder for resistance doctrine comes from the Israeli occupation of the Shebaa Farms area.

The LH will not disarm nor will they place their weapons under LAF control. They believe armed resistance will defeat Israel and the final showdown is imminent. The real danger is that they believe they can win. They see themselves as parallel to, but stronger than, the government of Lebanon. This is consistent with the Wiki warrior concept of power without accountability; although stronger than the state they are not the state. As with all genuine Islamist movements, their goal is an Islamic State under Sharia apartheid. They know this doesn't fit Lebanese history. Hasan Nasrallah has demonstrated LH's status as stateless player with state authority by signing a defense treaty with Iran in 2004; a defense treaty with Syria in 2006; and by entering a three-way security pact with both in 2010. Nasrallah would like to establish relations with other states, particularly in Latin America.

LH Capabilities. LH is a hybrid that mixes conventional weapons and techniques with irregular ones. They shift between conventional and unconventional techniques at will and in response to their enemy. They've built a state-like rocket force while maintaining their tried and true suicide bomber capability. They operate in Lebanon; maintain offices in Damascus; support Assad, work for Iran and field operatives all over the world.

Tools. LH has a full bag of tricks, old and new, to use based on the last two Arab-Israeli Wars.[155] [156] (2006 2nd Lebanon and 2009 as Cast Lead vs Hamas).[157]

- *Intelligence Preparation of the Battlefield (IPB):* This is a case if mir-

[154]A High Price: The Triumphs and Failures of Israeli Counterterrorism *by Daniel Byman*, Oxford University Press, June 2011.

[155]*2006 Lebanon War: An Operational Analysis*, by Major Sharon Tosi Moore, Joint Center for Operational Analysis Journal, Volume X; Issue 1, December 2007.

[156]*Winograd Report: English Summary*, Joint Center for Operational Analysis Journal, Volume X; Issue 1, December 2007.

[157]*A High Price: The Triumphs and Failures of Israeli Counterterrorism*, by Daniel Byman, Oxford University Press, June 2011.

roring where the enemy adopts a technique used by their opponent. LH copied western IPB and built an IDF order of battle, studied IDF doctrine, then built a defense to the IDF—no more rock throwing and Molotov cocktails.

- *Militia:* LH made good use of militia. They employed non-combatants to attack the IDF. These Shia volunteers only had to move to a certain house, pick-up an ATGM, and fire it at the first vehicle through a given intersection. Then the volunteer would exit the battlefield like all the other civilians. Other militia would fire from a building to draw IDF patrol in. they would pull out and the building would be dropped by demolitions. Milita-men were rumored to make $10k for their efforts.

- *Fauxtography:* LH knows that a picture is worth a thousand words so they doctored the pictures. They photo-shopped images to maximize their emotional impact. Smoke clouds were cloned to look larger and a single missile caught in flight became several missiles in flight. A smoking house becomes a virtual Hiroshima. A later example of this occurred during the Turkish Flotilla incident where 'aid workers' on the ships had their weapons bearing hands cropped out of widely circulated photos.

- *Human Shielding:* LH placed rocket and missile launchers in apartment complexes; ammo cache's in hospitals and mosques; and headquarters in schoolhouses. The location makes a strike less likely and if a strike does occur it becomes a photo op.

- *Lawfare:* LH exploited international law by using the above off limits sites for combat operations. They used ambulances to push ammunition forward and bring bodies back. They even used vehicles painted to look like UN vehicles to run supplies. LH positioned many of their bunkers adjacent to UNIFIL positions.

- *Information Operations (IO):* LH controlled media battlefield access—go where you're told to go or don't go at all. Ambulances ran media tours to carefully choreographed hotspots manned by on call victims and mobile mourners—the Black Widow was a fan favorite having popped up on film at multiple scenes of carnage. For LH, the Minuteman became the Minute-mourner. They used leaflets, billboards, flyers, to promote themselves as the defenders of Lebanon and own their own TV, radio, and Internet sites. Goebbels would be been proud.

• *Psychological Operations and Recruiting:* LH pays the poor to attend mosque. Once the new recruits are into them for some money they are ordered to attend mosque. They incite the IDF to retaliate in the hopes of a disproportionate response. The deaths of innocent Muslims is an acceptable price of johad.

Jihadism. Jihadi's are Islamists willing to use violence to install Sharia, resurrect the Caliphate, resurrect dhimmitude, and/or trigger the apocalypse. Most post-Qutbist Jihadi's don't limit themselves to terrorizing infidels. They also target 'false' Muslims, (Takfir), whose brand of Islam isn't pure enough. They excuse killing of innocent Muslims since they become martyrs of a holy cause.[158]

Modern examples of Muslim movements include the Nasser Arab Nationalists, Baathist secular socialists, and Fatah's secular Palestinian Nationalists. These groups didn't pursue utopia. They could be negotiated with, deterred, or contained. Jihadists seek Utopia in an 'ends justify the means' campaign that makes them impervious to negotiation and compromise. [159]

There are two paths to the defeat of sectarian fanatics; death or catastrophic defeat. The first option is direct but impractical. It's been called the 'whack-a-mole' approach and is expensive and time consuming. The latter approach is difficult but attainable. When the Zealots stood in the ruins of Jerusalem and Masada, they knew they were defeated.[160] The same was true for the Nazi's and Imperial Japanese in 1945. Neither surrendered until Berlin, Nagasaki, and Hiroshima were in ruins. Fanatics, sectarian or secular, must face utter defeat in order to submit. They won't necessarily reject their utopian ideals but they will recognize that the path they're on is not destined to succeed.

Annihilation only works when lots of people die visibly—not particularly viable in the modern world. Would the modern global media

[158] The Canons of Jihad by Jim Lacey; Naval Institute Press, 2008.

[159] *A Terrorist Call to Global Jihad*, by Jim Lacey; Naval Institute Press, 2008.

[160] *Empires of Trust: How Rome Built-and America is Building-A New World*, by Thomas Madden, Penguin Group (USA), July 2008.

accept another Kitchener led Omdurman massacre? Catastrophic defeat is tough when the threat lacks a state population to demoralize. Perhaps the solution today is a series of local catastrophic defeats coupled with the presentation of a solution such as local democracy.

Jihadism is not a tactic like terrorism, or a temperament like radicalism, or a political pathology like communism—it is sectarian zealotry or holy madness. Jihadism is the refuge of Islamist utopians and nihilists who sanctify atrocities as expressions of faith. Those who die are *Shaheed*, holy martyrs, destined for a bordello Paradise filled where they can pursue the pleasures they are denied in the temporal world.[161] Their families radiate pride for their martyrdom and their communities throw celebrations commemorating their sacrifice. Jihadists are a deadly and persistent threat. They will be defeated but not without considerable bloodletting over an extended period of time.

Shia Jihadis. Ayatollah Ruhollah Khomeini's Iranian Revolution was guided by the philosophy of *Velayat-e Faqih*, or the Guardianship of the Jurist. Khomeini believed that an Islamic theocracy should be established before the return of the Hidden Imam. As *the* Jurist, he became *The Supreme Leader*.[162] When his utopia failed to materialize the Shia apocalyptic vision resurfaced and Iranian leaders turned to the Mahdi (the Hidden Imam).

Khomeini's successor, Ayatollah Ali Hoseyni Khamenei, supports the new line. He belongs to the Islamic School of Mashhad. Mashhad is the center for the study of arcane science such as occultism and antirationalism. Followers of the Mashhad school use bibliomancy (random selection of scripture) and divine prayers to inform decision-making.[163] Khamenei believes in the utopian theocracy and is not adverse to the notion that the return of the Hidden Imam can be accelerated through human action.

Iran's most important proxy is Hizballah. They arose when Arab

[161] *Terror in the Name of God: Why Religious Militants Kill,* by Jessica Stern, HarperCollins Publishers, August 2004.

[162] *The Last Great Revolution: Turmoil and Transformation in Iran,* by Robin Wright, Vintage, February 2001.

[163] *Apocalyptic Politics: On the Rationality of Iranian Policy,* by Mehdi Khalaji, Policy Focus #79, Washington Institute for Near East Policy, Published in 2008 in the United States of America by the Washington Institute for Near East Policy.

Nationalism and socialist secularism failed to head off Israel's 1982 invasion of Lebanon. Hizballah comes in many forms: Lebanese, Iraqi, Venezuelan. Their leader, Hasan Nasrallah, answers to the Iranian Mullahocracy.

Twelvers. Ahmadineajad and Rhouani are Twelvers. He believes in the Hidden Imam whose return will lead to the destruction of unbelief and the establishment of world governed by Islam. Exploiting technology, generating chaos, building ideological armies and weapons of mass destruction will hasten his return. The Twelvers Mahdi was born in 868 AD and became the Shia leader of the Caliphate. He was the political dictator and the spiritual leader. He went into occultation (hiding) to escape persecution and will return when ordained. He will inflict two kinds of death on mankind; the *Red Death* by the sword and the *White Death* by pestilence. Each will kill one third of the world's population leaving the surviving third to rule. The Red Death represents kinetic weapons with the atom bomb as the ultimate tool and the White Death represents biological weapons. Twelver Jihadi's are state backed and can also be held accountable for their actions.[164]

The Question of a Nuclear Iran—Atomic Bomb or Islamic Bomb. It is well known that Iran is seeking its own nuclear weapons. What isn't well known is what their intentions are once they attain it.

The Iranians want an atomic bomb. They seek to use it within the framework of international relations between states. Like North Korea, a would be Iranian Hegemon would use the bomb as its centerpiece in high stakes brinksmanship. They would coerce neighbors and attain concessions from opponents.[165] An atomic state can be appeased (a modern Munich Agreement), contained (policy of Mutually Assured Destruction (MAD)), or engaged (war).

If an Iranian atomic bomb becomes an Islamic bomb designed to trigger the apocalypse, it becomes more dangerous in its sectarian and millenarian use. The only outcome in this case is war. Imagine Hitler and his Nazi true believers armed with a nuclear bomb. The only

---

[164]*Apocalyptic Politics: On the Rationality of Iranian Policy*, by Mehdi Khalaji, Policy Focus #79, Washington Institute for Near East Policy, Published in 2008 in the United States of America by the Washington Institute for Near East Policy.

[165]*Atomic Iran: How the Terrorist Regime Bought the Bomb and American Politicians*, by Jerome R. Corsi, Cumberland House Publishing, April 2005.

options are deterrence (denying acquisition) or pre-emption (striking before war).

Stateless Jihadis. The non-state Jihadi variants that follow are unconstrained by international accountability since they can't be tied to a defined, geographic, political entity. They are mostly stateless and are free to engage in extraordinary violence given their lack of a well-defined target for retaliation. The lack of accountability makes them more toxic even though they lack state level lethality—for now.

Sunni's. In order to unite the tribes of the Arabian Peninsula, Ibn Saud entered into a pact with Muhammad ibn Abl al-Wahab. They would conquer the Arabian Peninsula and the house of Saud would rule and while the Wahabs would be the religious guardians. Each would prop up the other as the Kingdom of Saudi Arabia.[166]

Wahhabism. Wahhab argued that every idea added to Islam after the third century was false. True Muslims must strictly adhere to the original ideas as defined by Muhammad. He opposed praying to saints, pilgrimages, and construction of special mosques, sacrificial offerings, and venerating trees, caves, and stones as sacrilegious. Secularism is more offensive. Wahhabi's reject modernity, democracy (law derived from man) and enlightenment. Wahhabi's preach the unity of God (*tawhid*) and that barbarism and ignorance pre-date Islam (*Jahiliyya*). Muslims who don't observe their version of faith are living in *Jahiliyya*. This allows true Muslims to kill false Muslims. Wahhabi's don't regard itself as a school of thought but as *the* path of Islam.[167]

Qutbism. Sayyid Qutb is the inspiration for the modern Islamism. He built on the teachings of Taymiyyah, al-Wahab, and al-Banna. As a member of the Muslim Brotherhood founded by (Hasan al-Banna), Qutb developed the concept of offensive jihad. He condemned Muslim governments as secular for basing their laws on human authorship rather than the Quran. He was executed in Egypt in 1966 for plotting against the Nasser government.

Qutbism gained notoriety by inspiring extremists like Usama bin Laden who cites him regularly. The main tenet of Qutbism is that the

---

[166] *God's Terrorists; the Wahhabi Cult and the Hidden Roots of Modern Jihad*, by Charles Allen, Da Capo Press, August 2006.

[167] *God's Terrorists; the Wahhabi Cult and the Hidden Roots of Modern Jihad*, by Charles Allen, Da Capo Press, August 2006.

Muslim community has been extinct for centuries after having abandoned true Islam. This led the Muslim nation back to *Jahiliyya*, requiring the Muslim world to be re-conquered for Islam.

Qutb's political views focus on Islam as a total system of morality, justice and governance. He argued for just dictatorship and rejected Arab nationalism and western democracy. The latter placed man in the "servitude to other men" since it obeys man-made which violates Allah's sovereignty (*Hakamiyya*). It takes a revolutionary vanguard similar to Lenin's professional revolutionaries, to destroy the *Jahili*. The vanguard would lead the fight to eliminate everything un-Islamic and establish authentic Muslim Rule.

Qutb's 'Little Red Book' is *Milestones*.[168] Like *Mein Kampf*, it is the vehicle by which the radical outlines his plan of action (Jihad):

- Strict adherence to Sharia
- Rejection of western and non-Islamic ideas including socialism and nationalism
- Vigilance against Western and Jewish conspiracies
- Two-pronged attack consisting of preaching and conversion to eliminate *Jahiliyya*
- Offensive Jihad to remove *Jahiliyya* from Muslim lands and the world

Qutb advocated terrorism against infidels and apostate Muslims (*takfir*) alike—only his followers were true Muslims. This was designed to rally *authentic* Muslims to his call while convicting false Muslims. Qutb's critics feared his declaration of strife (*fitna*) in the Muslim world would be received as legitimate. They were right.

Qutb's inspired multiple bouts of Islamist terror in Egypt and its victims included Anwar Sadat, the parliamentary speaker Rifaat el-Mahgoub, European tourists, and hundreds politicians. Qutb defined the false Muslim governments as the 'near enemy' and he acknowledged that the state was near impossible to defeat given its extensive security network.[169] He proposed that the defeat of the near enemy

[168] *The Canons of Jihad*, by *Jim Lacey*, Naval Institute Press, 2008.

[169] *Knowing the Enemy: Jihadist Ideology and the War on Terror*, by Mary Habeck; Yale University Press, January 2006.

would come about by chasing away their western sponsors thus isolating them. Egypt smashed and dispersed the Muslim Brotherhood and ended up spreading the contagion throughout the region. Qutb's newly distributed followers shifted their sights west.

Qutb's view of the west went beyond the standard template of economic exploitation and Crusader seizure of Muslim lands. Both are expressions of enmity towards Islam that emanated from the Godless and decadent west.

Qutb was sent west in hopes that it would cool his radicalism and keep him out of the Egyptian government's hair.[170]   His destination was the United States and his experiences there troubled his delicate sensibilities. Qutb decided that Americans were decadent, evil, and enemies of Islam. The USA became the 'far enemy' and the key to victory was to bring jihad to the west and force their withdrawal from the Middle East thus exposing the false regimes.

Jews are Qutb's other great enemy. To him, they are conspirators with the west. World Jewry is engaged in numerous plots designed to destroy Islam. They are blamed for diverting the wealth of mankind to Jewish institutions through usury—interest on loans. Anyone who leads the ummah away from Islam or sews division between Muslims is likely a Jew. Qutbists seek the elimination of western influence, annihilation of non-Islamic regimes, and the destruction of Israel.

Convergence. Conventional wisdom states that Sunni's and Shia's don't collaborate—they are enemies who view each other as heretics. Some Sunni's even call Shiism a Jewish plot while many Shia's see the Sunni's as the murderers of Ali. How could these sects unite?

A Muslim saying explains it all; 'The enemy of my enemy is my friend'. Sunni and Shia Islamists can, and do, cooperate in pursuit of common goals; the destruction of Israel, the elimination of western influence, the imposition Sharia, and the resurrection of the Caliphate. The scorpions in the bottle will seek to attain their common goals before they settle their internal differences.

The Iranian Shia Hizballah trained the Sunni Palestinian Hamas, facilitated the takeover of Gaza, and equipped them in order to open up

---

[170] *The Looming Tower: Al-Qaeda and the Road to 9/11*, by Lawrence Wright; Random House Inc, August 2007.

a new front against Israel. Iranian IRGC-Qods Force train Sunni insurgents in Iraq and Afghanistan and elsewhere and are the leading proliferators of Improvised Explosive Devices (IEDs).[171] They taught Sunni's how to use soft power (*Dawa*) through the provision of services that host governments can't or won't provide. Hamas used Dawa to isolate the corrupt and inefficient Fatah in Gaza just as Hizballah used it to isolate the Lebanese governemnt south of the Litani River.[172] Sunni-Shia convergence should have been anticipated.

Throughout history, radicals have shown the flexibility to ally with ideological opposites and morally ambiguous partners. Lenin encouraged such partnerships by reminding his followers that 'useful idiots', criminals, and weak socialists could be dealt with once the Bolsheviks took power.[173] They were. For the Islamists; the final reckoning may be the wedge the west can use if it finds a way to exploit it.

The Hierarchy of Anarchy. So how do the Jihadi masters rank and who are they. The top three are Hizballah, the Muslim Brotherhood, and Al Qaeda. You've probably heard of two out of the three and would be surprised that AQ was last. It's like sports—often the players with the biggest mouths are not the ones with the most impressive records.

Hizballah aka Lebanese Hizballah (LH). The only thing Lebanese about these guys is their home-base—they are a creature of Iran; manned, trained, and equipped. Hizballah literally means the party (hizb) of God (allah) and they are the 'A' Team of terrorism. While Al Qaeda (AQ) blows up buildings and Iraqi Army recruits and Lashkar al Taieba (LeT) sets Mumbai aflame, LH fights wars.

Hizballah is the Jihadist A-Team. They are the Corleone family (The Godfather) of terrorism. Like Vito's family, they are pervasive, powerful, and connected. LH is everywhere (estimated to be in 75% of the worlds countries). They are armed better than most middle-eastern state armies and they are connected—directly to Iran, Syria and

---

[171]*Immortal: A Military History of Iran and Its Armed Forces*, by Steven R. Ward, Georgetown University Press, March 2009.

[172]*Hamas: Politics, Charity, and Terrorism in the Service of Jihad*, by M. Levitt; Yale University Press, May 2006.

[173]*The Russian Revolution*, by Richard Pipes, Vintage, November 1991.

Venezuela and indirectly to Russia and China. They kill where they can and sponsor surrogates where they can't. Hamas is one of their prime clients. They trained them to massacre Fatah and take over Gaza. They are in South America and the USA. When the Iranian Ayatollahs say go, they go.

Muslim Brotherhood. These guys formed in Egypt to oppose the secular Arabs. We reviewed their forefathers (al Banna and Qutb). When they were crushed by Nasser their Diaspora spread the Middle East. The Muslim Brotherhood (MB) is the Grandfather of Islamism. They are like Lucky Luciano (Scarface), the gangster who formed the Commission that organized America's Mafia crime families into a unified criminal enterprise. The Muslim Brotherhood did much the same for Sunni violent extremist organizations (VEO). Recall that Ayman Zawahiri was a MB operative and Sadat assassination conspirator who joined Bin Laden's Al Qaeda thus magnifying their power and influence.[174]

Al Qaeda and Associated Networks (AQAN). As remarkable as it may seem, AQ is the flashiest terrorist organization but is no longer the most relevant. To maintain the gangster analogy, AQ is the Murder Incorporated of Islamism and, like Murder Inc., they garnered much unwanted attention from the 'authorities.' This is not to say that AQ is irrelevant. They are now a franchise whose brand is sought after by local thugs seeking it to bolster their resume.

Before 9-11, AQ added a faction of the Muslim Brotherhood under Ayman Zawahiri and the Taliban under Mullah Omar. They built a network in Iraq under Abu Musab Zarqawi who subsequently alienated the tribal leaders and inspired the Al Anbar Awakening. They are players in the Arab Spring from Libya to Syria, in direct competition with the Muslim Brotherhood and local rebels. They've added Al Shabaab in Somalia, rebels in Yemen, Boko Haram in Africa, the Libyan Islamic Fighting Group in Libya, the Armed Islamic Group in Algeria, Lashkar-e-Tayyiba in Pakistan.[175] They are funneling fighters into Syria around the clock in order to get in on the post war reorganization

---

[174] *The Al Qaeda Reader by Raymond Ibrahim,* Bantam Books, August 200.7

[175] *The rise of al-Qaeda's franchises by Sreeram Chaulia,* Asia Times Online, January 6, 2012, http://www.atimes.com/atimes/Middle_East/NA06Ak03.html.

much as they did in Libya. The list is longer but you get the point.

As terror's leading franchise, they are also its lead educator and mentor through a series of web sites, media centers, and online magazines like: As Sahab, Inspire Magazine Online, and the al-Fajr Media Center. The AQAN are consummate Wiki-Terrorists.[176] AQ continues to inspire terrorists with their bloody 9-11 attack; the ultimate media massacre.

AQ is losing influence in spite of their extraordinary wiki work due to their relative disadvantage with LH. AQ is not a proxy so they do not get the weapons and equipment that LH gets. They are also a franchise instead of a hierarchy which means they have less control over their affiliates. Most of Al Qaeda's toadies are embroiled in local fights rather than AQ's international fight. Few are able or willing to engage far beyond their own regions. They don't want or need the international attention. Al Qaeda in the Arabian Peninsula (AQAP) is one AQ affiliates willing to go the extra mile. They sponsored several failed attacks against the U.S. As a result, their leader was killed.[177] Bin Laden is dead and AQ leadership is dogged by Predator drones that have exposed a key vulnerability—no nation state top cover. It's easier to kill Anwar al-Awlaki than Hasan Nasrallah.

So What? Why this detour into the underbelly of Islamism? We have to understand the enemy if we are to counter them effectively. We ask ourselves 'why do they hate us?' This is the wrong question. We need to know what they want and how we figure in their calculus. This determines how we should respond to them and how we can counter their destructive ideas and misleading perceptions about us.

For example; Bin Laden saw our foray into and back out of Somalia as patent weakness. He also viewed the Clinton retaliatory missile attacks on his camps in Afghanistan as a further weakness. They were proof of impotence. To him, our rapid withdrawal from Somalia following the 'Blackhawk Down' incident was proof that we had no stom-

[176]*Al-Qaeda's Growing Online Offensive*, by Craig Whitlock, Washington Post Foreign Service, June 24, 2008, http://www.washingtonpost.com/wp-dyn/content/article/2008/06/23/AR2008062302135.html?sid=ST2008062302295.

[177]*Al Qaeda's Most Dangerous Franchise*, by Alexander Meleagrou-Hitchens and Peter R. Neumann, The Wall Street Journal, May 10, 2012, http://online.wsj.com/article/SB10001424052702304203604577395611014467928.html.

ach for a fight. Incremental signs of weakness and the Soviet withdrawal from Afghanistan encouraged Bin Laden to pursue his megalomaniacal vision.[178]

They hate America because it ignores their plight, steals their oil, and imposes its values upon them; they are victims; their destitution and autocracy is America's fault. This view is based on the assumption that the world revolves around the west and no one sets their own course-America sets it for them. The U.S. wasn't the lead players during the modern colo- nial period (France and UK); it didn't lead the Arab Nationalist period (Nasser); and wasn't anywhere near the lead in the Arab Spring / Islamist Winter (MB and AQ).[179] This self-centered worldview ignores Muslim motivations and excuses Muslim ambitions. Islamism never needed a western foil. It has always desired global dominance.[180] So how do we address these issues? Do we stop buying Muslim oil, refuse to provide aid to faltering governments, or stop selling them our corrupting goods? The chorus of indignation would be deafening if we 'left them alone,' defacto abandoning the region.

So how do we address these issues? Do we stop buying Muslim oil, refuse to provide aid to faltering governments, or stop selling them our corrupting goods? The chorus of indignation would be deafening if we 'left them alone,' defacto abandoning the region.

Perhaps these are the symptoms rather than the disease. Perhaps what ails the Muslim world is the same thing that transformed the Ottoman Empire into the 'sick man of Europe'. Perhaps it is the convergence of religion and government. Muslim non-competitiveness may be emblematic of its rejection of modernity, repression of women, and embrace of an anachronistic worldview.[181] Perhaps an Islamic

---

[178] *Ghost Wars: The Secret History of the CIA, Afghanistan, and Bin Laden, from the Soviet Invasion to September 10, 2001*, by Steve Coll, Penguin Press HC, February 2004.

[179] *The Islamist ascendancy*, by Charles Krauthammer, The Washington Post, July 12, 2012, http://www.washingtonpost.com/opinions/charles-krauthammer-the-islamist-ascendancy/2012/07/12/gJQArj9PgW_story.html.

[180] *Jihad in the West: Muslim Conquests from the 7th to the 21st Centuries*, by Paul Fregosi; Prometheus Books, October 1998.

[181] *Wars of Blood and Faith: The Conflicts That Will Shape The Twenty-first Century*, by Ralph Peters; Stackpole Books, February 2009.

Reformation is the solution. If so, it has to come from Muslims and no one else.

It may seem pedantic but it's critical to name the enemy. We've been struggling with finding a name for the Muslim Radicals. A top choice has been Islamofascist. It's logical but is also Westphalian. Fascists are secular. Their goal is a centralized socialist state led by an autocrat. Sounds like the Caliphate … kind of.

A better label might be Islamozealots; fanatics in search of a Theocracy, Sunni Caliphate or Shia Imamate. Theocracy was first used by Josephus to describe the Jewish Zealots aspiration to build a Jewish Kingdom subject to the will of God in all things. All the Zealots needed was to be rid of Rome.[182] Theocracy is a government in which God is the supreme ruler; God's laws are interpreted and enforced by ecclesiastical authorities; and civil society is run by clerics under divine commission.

This is utopia; heaven on earth and its warriors were the Zealots. Yesteryear's Jewish Zealots are todays Islamist Jihadi's, anachronistic, and uncompromising. In the west, Bin Ladens Al Qaeda would be cultists akin to Jim Jones' Peoples Temple, Shoko Asahara's Aum Shinrykio, or David Koresh's Branch Davidians—millenarians all.

This struggle is sectarian NOT secular. It's not about western Democracy or Islamic Republicanism. This is the sectarian version of Nasser's Pan Arabism. America's hypersensitivity to religious and cultural Intolerance created a blind spot that prevents it from acknowledging the religious imperative. America can recognize religious extremism with- out being Islamophobes; or can ignore it and pursue inappropriate solutions.

Jihadists, Mary Habeck writes, are not merely angry at U.S. policies. They believe that America is the biggest obstacle to the global rule of an Islamic superstate. Ultimately, in the Jihadist view, "Islam must expand to fill the entire world or else falsehood in its many guises will do so."[183]

---

[182] *Empires of Trust: How Rome Built-and America is Building-A New World*, by Thomas Madden, Penguin Group (USA), July 2008.

[183] *Knowing the Enemy: Jihadist Ideology and the War on Terror*, by Mary Habeck; Yale University Press, January 2006.

CHAPTER 6

Divided Conquerors

The Modern Muslim World
Sunni-Shia-Sufi Schism

*"The fanatic for justice ends by murdering a million helpless people to clear
a space for his law-courts. If we are to survive on this planet,
there must be compromises."*
—Storm Jameson

Back to the Future. The Muslim Middle East of the 21st Century
resembles the Christian Europe of the 17th Century. The former are
in the leading edge of a series of conflicts called the "Arab Spring"
while the latter were mired in a series of conflicts called "The Thirty
Years War." Both are/were internecine sectarian conflicts with overt
political overtones. The Arab Spring is becoming a struggle between
Shia and Sunni represented by Iran and the Kingdom of Saudi Arabia
and their allies. The Thirty Years War was a struggle between
Catholicism and Protestantism represented by The Holy Roman
Empire and Kingdom of France—the Hapsburgs versus the Bourbons.

The analogue to the Catholics is the Shias. The Shia are a monolithic and hierarchical faith led by a religious leader who is God's representative on earth—the Iranian Supreme Leader Ayatollah
Khameini. The Shia are disciplined by their clerical hierarchy and singular leadership.

The analogue to the Protestants is the Sunni. The Sunni's have no
dominant hierarchy or singular leader. There are numerous sects and
variants with many leaders in pursuit of many goals. Their main champion is Saudi Arabia but they are in no way tied to them.

Today's Muslims mainly target other Muslims just as yesteryears
Christians mainly targeted other Christians. The modern Muslim
World is a petri dish loaded with a fermenting myriad of state and state-

less actors who chaotically fall into and out of alliances as the situation develops. Shia align with Sunni and vice versa, when the situation benefits them but the overall mosaic is Shia against Sunni.

The Shia Core. The Shia core revolves around Iran and its Satraps. Iran sees itself as culturally superior to its Arab neighbors given its Persian Dynastic history. They also see themselves as spiritually superior since they are the current home of Shia Islam and the Supreme Leader. They want to be the regional Hegemon and are aggressively in pursuit of that goal. This course of action is even more dangerous given their Twelver leadership with their millenarian belief in that chaos can prompt the Mahdi to return and cleanse the world for Islam.

Iran's two toadie states are Lebanon and Syria. Lebanon is a multi-sectarian state that has been co-opted by the Iranian built Frankenstein known the Hizballah (Hizb or Party of Allah or God). Lebanon gives Iran a northern border with Israel. It also became the first state where the Iranians could export their revolution. The result was war and Syrian occupation. Beirut was once the 'Paris of the Middle East'. Today, it is Sarajevo.

Syria is Iran's arms trafficker and is a key in their plan to create a Shia Levant Crescent. They arm and supply LH while providing safe haven to their leadership by providing offices in Damascus. Syria is a Sunni majority country governed by a Shia minority that is even a minority among Shias—the Alawites. The rulers started out as Arab socialists; the Baathists. The Alawite Baathists never got along with the Sunnis, relying on tension with Israel as a unifier. Assad's father, Hafez, killed 10k to 25k civilians in Hama, the current origin of today's rebellion which is another in the series of Arab Spring revolts. The Syrian Civil War is turning into the modern day version of the Spanish Civil War as Iran and its partners struggle to hold on to its possession while a Sunni coalition struggles to take it away. The result may determine the future of the Middle East and the Levant.

Shia Non-State Actors. The Lebanese Hizballah (LH) are Iran's most important proxy. They are terrorism's A-Team and are an Iranian strategic weapon that can be used with plausible deniability. LH struck the Marines in Beirut and fought the 2006 War against Israel where they earned the reputation as the defenders of Lebanon even though they provoked the war in the first place. They attack without consequences (except concerning Israel) since they are stateless—they pull the strings in Lebanon but they allow a coalition to be the face of the state. LH variants operate in Iraq, Syria, and even Venezuela. Their scouts operate all over Europe, Latin America, and the USA. They do what Iran can't dare do. Their grip on Lebanon may be waning given the unpopularity their directed support for Assad. Syria occupied Lebanon for 40 years and is widely known to be behind the assassination of the popular Prime Minister, Rafik Hariri. Challenges are rising in the Bekka and in the Druze north. Never the less, LH remains a potent global terrorist threat.

Other Shia players include the localized Al Houthi insurgents contesting Yemen; Katab Hizballah contesting Iraq; and the Islamic Jihad Organization (IJO)...the SEALS of Shia terrorism. They are augmented by the Iranian special forces; the Iranian Revolutionary Guard Command—Qods Force (Qods = Jerusalem) and the Ministry of Intelligence and Security (MOIS). This terror team pursues the Iranian Shia Imamate in the Middle East and in the world.

Shia Allies. Iran has collected a nefarious collection of supporters. As Putin rebuilds Russian autocracy, so too he is rebuilding the old spheres of influence with Mediterranean ports in Syria. As such, Russia is Iran's most important backer given their quest to recreate a sphere of influence in the Middle East. Their role is an active one since they see Syria as their ground. They are sending in their navy and troops to bolster Asaad and they are urging him to step up his ruthlessness against the rebellion.

The Peoples Republic of China (PRC) also backs Iran. Their motive is to diminish the U.S. wherever and whenever it can. As we decline, they ascend. As we dissipate our strength in the middle East, we expose ourselves to their chosen sphere of influence in the Pacific. They also see Iran as a cash cow. They sell them weapons and use the proceeds to subsidize their oil purchases. It's a win win for the PRC.

A lesser backer is North Korea. They sell nuclear and missile technology and generally revel in their ability to 'stir the pot.' Agitation is north Korea's main export. The puffed up, wanna be 21st

Century Castro, Hugo Chavez was also an Iranian partner. He did so to burnish his anti-Yankee credentials. Although his influence in the Middle East was negligible; his support was key to Iran's ability to posture terrorists to strike the USA. It was not to be a big deal when Chavez was alive but it may prove to be more than a big deal when, and if, Iran can build a nuclear umbrella like North Korea with Chavez successor Nicholas Maduro, no friend of the U.S..

The Sunni Core.   The Sunni Core is more contested than the Shia Core given Sunnism's lack of a monolithic clerical hierarchy, never the less, the Kingdom of Saudi Arabia (KSA) assumes the lead. They are the Guardians of the Two Holy Places, Mecca and Medina and their Wahabbist theology permeates Arab Sunnism. KSA petro dollars fund Sunnis the world over. Other than their intervention in the Bahrain Iranian Shia backed uprising, the KSA rarely dirties its hands. They fund others and launch their own fanatics who might turn on them.

KSA's coterie of Sunni satellites includes Qatar (home of Al Jazeera), Kuwait (Gateway to Iraq), the UAE (the resort state), and Bahrain (the Shia state ruled by a Sunni monarchy). The allies above provide money, basing rights, and—on occasion—forces. They are our enablers on one hand and terrorisms enablers on the other—a two edged sword.

Sunni Non-State Actors.   The constellation of Sunni stateless players is vast. Al Qaeda and its Associated Network (AQAN) leads the pack. Mullah Omar's Taliban was AQ's first ally. They provided AQ a safe haven and guarded them after 9-11, a decision many of them now regret. AQ has gone from lead killers to lead organizers, trainers, propagandists and recruiters. Their network includes; AQ in Iraq (AQI), AQ in the Maghreb (AQIM), the Haqqani Network in Afghanistan, the Armed Islamic Front in Algeria, Al Jemaah Al Islimayiah in Indonesia, the Libyan Islamic Fighting Group, the Kurdish Ansar Al Islam, Lashkar-e-Tayyiba of Pakistan, Boko Harem of North Africa, Al Shabaab of Somalia, and Jaish-e-Muhammad of Kashmir. It seems like an imposing list but most of these groups are local.

The AQAN is unwieldy and unpredictable. They advance the Sunni cause on a state by state but are not centrally directed. The above Wahabbai line is opposed by an Egyptian strain—the Muslim

Brotherhood (MB). The MB was born and raised in Egypt and it spawned a few charismatic leaders who fueled a global movement that has infected the USA, LATAM, the EU and the Middle East. They were stateless until they took their homeland, Egypt. You won't find an Arab Spring victim untouched by the MB: Tunisia, Morocco, Libya, Egypt, Mali and Syria. Yemen is contested by the KSA and Iran as was Bahrain; the MB couldn't infiltrate these critical KSA allies.

Sunni Allies. The Sunnis are less confrontational than the Shia although they are, in many ways, more dangerous given their insidious nature. It's easier to side with them since their infiltrative threats give America time to rebuke. Thus, the USA backs the KSA, Qatar, Kuwait and Bahrain; the latter three provides the United States with basing in the region. The USA sent troops to defend the KSA and to retake Kuwait in 1990-91. The U.S. is a regional partner. It relies on the Sunni Core for basing in the region and it supports them through the UN and through the application of military might.

The European Union (EU) backs the Sunni Core because the United States does and because the Core provides them with energy. The EU sends troops, as long as the U.S. does, but its most overt support comes at the UN where they support U.S. backed sanctions even without the support of the UN Security Council where Russia and the PRC block the body as a whole.

Sunni Challengers. Turkey and its Islamist Justice and Development Party (AKP) is a new challenger to the KSA as the leader of the Sunni world. The challenge is new since Turkey has been secular since 1922 when Mustafa Kemal Attaturk disbanded the Ottoman Caliphate. All that changed when Recep Tayyip Erdogan ascended to power. He began to Islamisize Turkey by purging the military (Attaturk's guardians of secularism) and the Judiciary (the guardians of secular law). His newly sectarian Turkey refused to allow the US to invade Northern Iraq during Operation Iraqi Freedom; sponsored aid ships to Gaza; and broke away from its alliance with Israel. They moved closer to Iran until Syria offered them the ability to challenge them and take control of the Levant. Today, Turkey is taking an aggressive role in Syria in alliance with the KSA. While the KSA provides money, Turkey provides manpower and equipment—a more tangible contribution.

The Ottoman's were the last, and perhaps most successful, Caliphate. They were the leaders and may well be positioning themselves to usurp Saudi leadership in the future Sunni world.

Egypt is even more ancient than Turkey and Iran and its population and location make it a natural Sunni leader. Egypt led Arab nationalism under Nasser. They led the '67 and '73 wars against Israel. They own the Suez and Mubarak imposed Arab-Israeli Peace upon the Arab world. Egypt's Muslim Brotherhood is global and pervasive. They are not imposing their will as aggressively as they might given the tumult at home as Morsi follows Erdogan's path of purging the military and judiciary in the construction of an Islamic Republic ruled by Sharia. Given the swirling allegiances of the region, they also allowed the Iranians to send warships through the Suez for the first time since the '79 Revolution. 'The enemy of my enemy is my friend'.

Sunni Satellites.   Jordan, Iraq (contested), Yemen (contested), Libya, Sudan, and Mali are Sunni satellites. Most provide safe haven for Sunni non-state actors and little else. Each is more or less fragile, hanging on by a thread. An Iranian/Shia win may be their death knell.

Sunni Wildcards.   Pakistan (a nuclear state) and Afghanistan (Pakistan's toadie) are wildcards. Pakistan can make the KSA a nuclear state over night if Iran becomes one; the Saudi's need only pull out their checkbook. They are unstable and chaotic and an injection of petro dollars couldn't hurt.

Afghanistan has always been sat in a strategic spot between Russian dominated Eurasia, the PRC, and Pakistan-India. The American interest in them emanated from their unique ability to provide a near impregnable safe haven for AQ. America fears that a premature withdrawal will open up a new and improved safe haven. Afghanistan offers the U.S. basing in a difficult region and the US presence there will put India at ease.

The Palestinians under Hamas in Gaza and Fatah in the West Bank are always unpredictable. Hamas, backed by LH, attacked an outpost run by their sympathetic host, Egypt thus incurring their wrath. They possess rockets and mortars that they use to harass Israel. They can provoke a war whenever they want—an event that will always distract the Sunni masses. Fatah rules the Western Bank. They are more conciliatory than Hamas but also have more clout in the international community. Fatah can propose and push ideas like a free Palestine.

Battleground States. The Sunni/Shia War rages in Syria where Russia and China back Iran, LH, and IRGC. Yemen totters on the brink as does Afghanistan. Iraq is under covert attack and may well replace Syria if it falls. These states are under attack by the Shia.

The KSA sends money into Syria and Iraq and troops into Yemen. Iran sends the IRGC-QF, the MOIS, and the LH in as well. AQAN, the Egyptian MB, the Turk military, Kurdish and Libyan volunteers are up to their elbows opposing the Assad regime.

Iran sends the IRGC-QF, the MOIS and LH into Syria to back Assad.

Next Up. Jordan and Bahrain have faced riots. Both staved off defeat. Bahrain needed Saudi intervention in the form of tanks and troops. Jordan needed money. Both hung on for now and both will be top targets after Syria.

What it means. War against infidels; war against Jews; war against takfiri (apostate Muslims); terrorism; instability; and volatile economics due to unstable petrogarchies—Hobbes' Leviathon revisited...

CHAPTER 7

LWFX
Courting Conflict

LAWFARE
STEALTH JIHAD

*"The process of settlement is a "Civilization-Jihadist Process" with
all the word means. The Ikhwan must understand that their work in
America is a kind of grand Jihad in eliminating and destroying the Western
civilization from within and "sabotaging" its miserable
house by their hands and the hands of the believers so that it is
eliminated and God's religion is made victorious over
all other religions."*
—May 1991 Mohamed Akram, Muslim Brotherhood

*"Allah is our objective, the Prophet is our leader, the Koran is our law,
Jihad is our way, and dying in the way of Allah is our highest hope.
Allahu akbar!"*
—Muslim Brotherhood Mission Statement

*"Islam isn't in America to be equal to any other faith, but to become
dominant. The Quran should be the highest authority in America."*
—1998 Omar Ahmad, CAIR's founding chairman

"Assimilation is a crime against humanity"
—2011 Recep Tayyip Erdogan addressing Turks in Germany

Stealth Jihad: Islamist Trojans.   Islamist wiki warriors aren't restricted to traditional weapons used on the traditional battlefield.
They have brought the fight to American shores and America hasn't
acknowledged it. The fight entered the PR realm using websites, spe-

cial interest groups, targeted lawsuits, legal challenges, and more. The bullets of warfare are more dramatic but the blogs of lawfare are more effective.

History shows that it's easier to attack from inside the walls than outside. Just ask the Greeks and the Visigoths: Odysseus got inside Troy and Alaric got inside Rome. The Islamists most effective tool is America's legal system. They exploit expertise gained through a disciplined study of American culture, since they are targeting it. You don't have to be born in the west to understand it and you don't have to be a lawyer to know the law. All you need is a laptop and an ISP. They exploit the values Americans believe while rejecting them all along.

Not all western Muslims are Civilization-Jihadists but enough are to be a concern. The proof is in the polls—western Muslims, particularly Europeans, support Islamist extremism. The struggle among western Muslims is intense but is only a backdrop to the greater jihad.[184] [185]

Dedicated Islamists understand liberal secularism and its trappings like multiculturalism, western self- loathing, moral relativism, political correctness, and hyper-sensitive racism. All these attributes justify their view of the west as the decadent Dar al-Harb in decline.[186] Islamists need tangible differences to validate violence and fuel recruitment. They exploit multiculturalism and reject it. Ditto for political correctness and moral relativity—'Islamophobia' is one of their favorite weapons. America's self absorbed belief that global success and failure revolves around the west makes them vulnerable to any charge of abuse levied against them.

Western Islamists are the Trojan Horse inside our walls.[187] They use all things western to destroy all things western. They use technology that they didn't develop and thus lack restraint in its use. To them,

[184] *Islamic Extremism: Common Concern for Muslim and Western Publics*, by Pew Research Center; Pew Global Attitudes Project, July 14, 2005.

[185] *Muslim Public Opinion on US Policy, Attacks on Civilians and al Qaeda*, Principal Investigator Steven Kull, WORLDPUBLICOPINION.ORG, International Policy Attitudes at the University of Maryland, April 2007.

[186] *Shari'a and Violence in American Mosques*, by Mordechai Kedar and david Yerushalmi, Middle East Quarterly, Summer 2011.

[187] *The Muslim Brotherhood in the United States*, by Steven Merley, Research Monograph on the Muslim world Series No. 2, Paper No 3, Hudson Institute, April 2009.

it's no different than picking up an enemy rifle on the battlefield. Those who use weapons they didn't develop tend not to respect their application and use them carelessly.

The Islamist fifth column exploits western idiosyncrasies to amplify the U.S.'s self destructive tendency to blame itself for the world's ills and to impose racial and sectarian self-censorship against its own people. They don't see self-criticism as enlightenment; its western weakness and proof of Muslim superiority, fuel for the fire.

When the west was confident; Islam was dormant. When Carter faltered; the Shah fell and the Ayatollah ascended. Now, Iran and its surrogates are on the march. Irresolute leadership inspires aggression as surly as Chamberlain's trip to Munich empowered the Nazi's. Aggressors love accommodation / appeasement.

Fitna / Taqiyaa. Fitna is the word that refers troubles between people or the creation of chaotic situations that test faith. Taqiyya is accepted religious dissimulation whereby a believer can deny his faith or commit illegal or blasphemous acts while under threat. The Quran not only permits lying for the faith, it encourages it and true believers take advantage of the privilege.[188] The claim that Sharia compliant enclaves will not encroach on indigenous rights disproves itself when the enclave residents demand non-believers respect Muslim sensitivities such as male only swimming pools, publically funded footbaths, or fully veiled women. The enclaves eventually call for full autonomy as emirates of their own.[189] Islamists claim victimhood via Islamophobia wherever their demands are spurned.

Once Islamists attain *special* status and privilege they move forward to undermine and erode free speech, free worship, women's rights, and overall egalitarianism.[190] The effect is to create de-facto dhimmitude; the conversion of non-believers into second class citizens under the Muslim domination.

---

[188] *Knowing the Enemy: Jihadist Ideology and the War on Terror,* by Mary Habeck; Yale University Press, January 2006.

[189] *British Muslims Urged to Reject Democracy, Embrace Shari'a-Ruled 'Emirates,'* by Patrick Goodenough, CNS News.com, http://cnsnews.com/news/article/british-muslims-urged-reject-democracy-embrace-shari-ruled-emirates, July 15, 2011.

[190] *Radicalization in the West: The Homegrown Threat,* by Mithcell D. Silber and Arvin Bhatt, Senior Intelligence Analysts NYPD Intelligence Division, NYPD, 2007.

Lawfare. Lawfare is an underappreciated realm of conflict. Wiki warriors see law as an asymmetric weapon in their arsenal. They exploit western law and culture to promote their goals and shield their actions.[191] This is the essence of Stealth Jihad aka Civilizational Jihad; to use the democratic processes, institutions and pathologies of the west to undermine and transform the west. Examples include:

- Frivolous and expensive libel lawsuits (often dropped during discovery when evidence must be provided by the plaintiffs)
- Frivolous and expensive defamation lawsuits
- Automatic declarations of 'torture' made by apprehended terrorists
- Using Islamophobia to silence debate
- Exploiting multiculturalism to justify 'Balkanization' over assimilation
- Petitions for *Sharia compliant* courts for cases involving Muslims
- Establishment of *Sharia compliant* enclaves
- Advocating separate and unequal priveledges for Muslims
- Advocating that non-Muslims 'respect' Islam without reciprocation
- Calls for censorship of material offensive to Muslims and Islam
- Criticism of western decadence while condemning any criticism of Islam as racist
- Establishing well endowed 'Muslim studies chairs' in prominent universities
- Screening textbooks and school curricula

Consider full body burqas in Paris, taxpayer funded footbaths in the Kansas City Airport, flying Imams calling their treatment for disruptive activity racist, the Ghalani acquittal of murder of 224 people in the Kenyan Embassy bombing,[192] and the proposed 9-11 civil trial. Think of Mega-Mosques and Islamic Cultural Centers built in provocative

[191] *Learning About Lawfare*, Nathaniel Burney, November 2010, The Burney Law Firm, LLC, http://burneylawfirm.com/blog/tag/lawfare/.

[192] *Ghailani Verdict a Miscarriage of Justice: Al Qaeda terrorist Ahmed Ghailani is certainly guilty of mass murder*, by Thomas Jocelyn, The Weekly Standard, http://www.weekly-standard.com/blogs/ghailani-verdict-miscarriage-justice_518140.html, November 17, 2010. Ghaliani received life in prison for conspiracy, not for murder.

locations adjacent to Olympic Village in London or Ground Zero in NYC. Challenge their choice of location and timing and be condemned as an Islamophobe. Consider of Muslim School textbooks in the USA that call Israel the Zionist Entity or prison Imams who hand out annotated Quran's that condemn western culture while converting and recruiting criminals like the dirty bomber wannabe Jose Padilla.[193] Think of lawsuits that chill legitimate discourse on Islam and incites self-censorship. How about Sharia compliant enclaves in Londonistan and the Eurostans where ads are censored and non-Muslims are harassed.[194] Consider immigrants encouraged transform their new home rather than assimilate. How about ambulances that carry weapons to the front before bringing the wounded to the rear or of photo-shopped images designed to manipulate western media and inflame public opinion. And there's blockade runners covered by NGO's and Muslim Advocacy Groups.

The above are subtle manipulations of the western conscience. They effect given western paranoid sensitivities about race and religion. While the west convert self-examination into self-destruction and self-loathing, criticism of Islam is stifled for fear of prosecution. Western liberals mindlessly default to Chamberlainesque appeasement as retribution for past transgressions that the Islamists are happy to accept.

Who's Who in the Zoo. The lead Islamist subversive group in America is the Muslim Brotherhood (MB).[195] They are the original post Caliphate Islamists. They were founded in Egypt in the '20's by a school teacher named Hasan Al Banna. The MB fathered the Sunni Jihadi premier ideologue, Sayed Qutb, and assassinated Anwar Sadat for making peace with Israel. The MB spawned Ayman Al Zawahirya who allied them with AQ while becoming UBL's top spiritual advisor.[196] The MB is a well organized theocratic/political party that stands

[193] *Islam in the Classroom; What Textbooks Tell Us*, by Gilbert T. Sewall, American Textbook Council, 2008.

[194] *While Europe Slept: How Radical Islam Is Destroying the West from Within*, by Bruce Bawer, Knopf Doubleday Publishing Group, September 2007.

[195] *The Muslim Brotherhood in the United States*, by Steven Merley, Research Monograph on the Muslim world Series No. 2, Paper No 3, Hudson Institute, April 2009.

[196] *The Looming Tower: Al-Qaeda and the Road to 9/11*, by Lawrence Wright; Random House Inc, August 2007.

an excellent chance of co-opting the Tunisian and Egyptian revolutions. Their parties and candidates are poised to win majorities or executive authority outright. The MB has not restricted its activities to the 'Near Enemy' in the Middle East—the Muslim dictators. They have sponsored activist groups throughout the west against the 'far enemy', the west.

The MB backs a multitude of activist organizations in the west. Their mission is to propagate Islamism, exploit the western guilt complex, and prepare the ground for Muslim domination. They are the ISLAMINTERN to the Soviet COMMINTERN. The Muslim Brotherhood's Explanatory memorandum identifies the following groups as 'friends':

- Islamic Society of North America (ISNA)
- Muslim Student Association (MSA)
- Muslim Communities Association (MCA)
- Association of Muslim Social Scientists (AMSS)
- Association of Muslim Scientists and Engineers (AMSE)
- Islamic Medical Association (IMA)
- Islamic Teaching Center (ITC)
- North American Islamic Trust (NAIT)
- Foundation for International Development (FID)
- Islamic Housing Cooperative (IHC)
- Islamic Centers Division (ICD)
- American Trust Publications (ATP)
- Audio-Visual Center (AVC)
- Islamic Book Service (IBS)
- Muslim Businessmen Association (MBA)
- Muslim Youth of North America (MYNA)
- Malasian [sic] Islamic Study Group (MISG)
- Islamic Association for Palestine (IAP)
- United Association for Studies and Research (UASR)
- Occupied Land Fund (OLF)
- Mercy International Association (MIA)
- Islamic Circle of North America (ICNA)
- Baitul Mal Inc (BMI)

- International Institute for Islamic Thought (IIIT)
- Islamic Information Center (IIC)

The MB network is pervasive and inter-connected. They influence Islamic Chairs within western academia that are welcome given the generous inflow of Saudi petro-dollars. This network of community organizers and sectarian activists form a formidable Lawfare phalanx to take on the west from Warsaw to Walla Walla.[197] During the Cold War such organizations were underground and low profile. In today's liberal west, they are 'in your face' advocacy groups.

Stealth Jihadists exploit sympathy for Palestine as the cause célèbre' that justifies all forms of resistance. The Organization of the Islamic Conference (OIC) is one and is the largest voting bloc in the UN and is dedicated to anti Zionism. Only 3 out of the 57 OIC members was rated as "free" by the Freedom in the World Report of 2010.[198] For over a decade, the OIC has worked to criminalize the "defamation of Islam" and to protect Islam from "blasphemy." This is defacto global dhimmitude. The OIC has warned the west that *"freedom of speech to offend Islam and fuel Islamophobia, will alienate 'moderate Muslims' and provide more ammunition for Muslim jihadists."* It's a clever argument...self defense radicalizes normally sedentary Muslims!

Islamophobia is the canard that invalidates valid criticism and justifiable concerns about Islam. It is the shield that immunizes Islamists against all threats. The FBI's hate crime statistics show that Jews are still the top targets of hate crimes receiving 67% of the attention. Muslims rate 12.7% of the attention. Islamophobia?[199]

Islamic Triumphalism. Imam Feisal Abdul Rauf was the leading proponent and fund raiser for the Ground Zero mosque. He claimed the Mosque was designed to bring Muslims and non-believers closer together. If this was the goal, why choose a mass grave caused by

[197]*Blasphemy and Free Speech*, by Paul Marshall, Senior Fellow, Hudson Institute, Imprimus; A Publication of Hillsdale College, February 2012 o Volume 41, Number 2.

[198]*Freedom in the World 2012; The Arab Uprisings and Their Global Repercussions, Selected data from Freedom House's annual survey of political rights and civil liberties*, by Arch Puddington, 2012.

[199]*Hate Crime Statistics, 2010 U.S. Department of Justice*, Federal Bureau of Investigation, November 2011.

Islamist terrorists? Rauf warned that congressional hearings on the *Radicalization of Islam in America* and opposition to the Ground Zero Mosque would promote terrorism and Islamophobia.[200] He wasn't worried about the fact that Muslims killed nearly 3,000 people at ground zero. Was his goal Islamic triumphalism? This is not just a rhetorical issue. The Muslims converted the Arab tribal Kaaba from a pagan temple into one of Islam's most important holy shrines. They built the Dome of the Rock on top of portions of the ancient Jewish Temple after Jersulaem was conquered and the Byzantine Hagia Sofia Christian Cathedral was converted to a mosque and is now a museum. All these sites were taken by Muslims. What about the Twin Towers as a symbol of American global trade?

Strategy and Law. Strategy and law are the twin pillars that guard the state againt internal and external threats. They are complimentary and opposing based on the threats they counter. Strategy is the gatekeeper that looks outward and law is the constable that looks inward. Strategy focuses on war and combatants. Law focuses on crime and criminals.[201]

Wiki warriors straddle the line between war and crime; between strategy and law. Herein lays the dilemma. Strategy uses agencies like the DoD and CIA to find, fix, and finish enemy combatants on the battlefield. Law uses agencies like the FBI and DEA to build cases against criminals to be tried in civil court. The Islamists have blurred the lines. The FBI tracks terrorists in the USA while the CIA tracks them abroad. This is a real problem when the local boys ally themselves with foreign masters for ideology and criminal cartels for ratlines. For a 'rule of law' republic, this attacks the clean lines between strategy and law; between combatants and criminals.

By design, strategic agencies and law enforcement agencies (LEA) don't share information. Defense can't afford to expose capabilities and law can't endanger evidence collection and case construction. Both adhere to different thresholds for action. Strategic agencies can act on

---

[200]*Will the Real Imam Feisal Abdul Rauf Please Stand Up?*, by Eileen F. Toplansky, American Thinker,
http://www.americanthinker.com/2010/08/will_the_real_imam_feisal_abdu.html, August 13, 2010.

[201]*Terror and Consent: The Wars for the Twenty-First Century*, by P. Bobbitt; Random House Inc, April 2008.

less information than LEA's. A threat that blurs the line evades and confounds both. Such threats need unique categorization. They must fit in one bin or the other or be designated their own bin.

Strategy guards against the wolf at the door, enemy soldiers who wage war for foreign states aka combatants. Combatants can be killed or captured but their actions are not criminal, they are legitimate acts of war. Of course there are clearly defined war crimes that are subject to the Geneva Conventions and the Law of Land Warfare etc. We identify combatants by the states they represent and the uniforms they wear. They fight for a political cause on behalf of a state who is a declared belligerent.

Law guards against the fox in the henhouse, individuals (citizen or not) who violate civil rules and regulations for personal gain, aka criminals. From Justinian's Codex to the American Constitution, law defines what individuals can and can't do in civil society. Violators are judged as criminal suspects and are accorded rights under the U.S. Constitution. They are innocent until proven guilty and their illicit actions are not executed in service to a state.

How does the USA handle stateless belligerents who claim to be combatants but act like criminals? How does the USA deal with terrorists; as crimi- nals, as combatants, or as something else?

"Detainees are held at JTF-Guantanamo because they are dangerous and continue to pose a threat to the U.S. and our allies. They have expressed a commitment to kill Americans and our friends if released. These are not common criminals; they are enemy combatants being detained because they have waged war against our nation and they continue to pose a threat."
—General B. Craddock, 2006

Pirate Detainees. The above comment is not completely accurate but it may be the best assessment of America's current reality and the dilemma it creates. The first high profile *Lawfare* issue to arise in the GWOT was the disposition of terrorists captured on the battlefield. The problem came in the midst of Operation Enduring Freedom (OEF) in Afghanistan. The issue was where to send captured Al Qaeda and Taliban and how to handle them. The answer was Guantanamo Bay

(Gitmo) where they'd be called 'detainees' awaiting military tribunal. Gitmo has been used for thorny detention issues before. Bush the elder and Clinton used Gitmo to deal with people who were neither criminal nor combatant such as Haitian boat people and Cuban refugees.[202]

Should terrorists be treated as criminals entitled to a public civil trial? This would expose U.S. collection capabilities, reveal agents, and offer a global propaganda platform from which to proselytize like Trotsky did in 1905 after the failed uprising against the Romanovs.[203] Consider KSM and the Hasan trials as a preview. In both cases, the defendants refused to acknowledge the legality of the court and are making a mockery of the trial.

Perhaps they should be designated as combatants. The problem is that combatants cannot deliberately target civilians or wantonly create collateral damage; the obvious preferred tactics of terrorists. The combatant designation would also elevate terrorists to the honored status held by soldiers, sailors, airmen, and marines.

A *combatant* is a uniformed member of a state's armed services who is engaged in a state directed war. Combatants are *captured* and are subject to the rules of the Geneva Convention as enemy prisoners of war (EPW). They are seen as honorable citizens loyal to their state and are held to prevent their return to battle. They can be *detained indefinitely* until the conflict is settled by treaty or political settlement. Combatants can be interrogated but aren't required to divulge anything beyond name, rank, and service number. EPW's *aren't held accountable* for their actions as long as they have adhered to the Law of Land Warfare.

Combatants can be charged with war crimes like; violating state neutrality, massacring civilians or prisoners or war, maliciously destroying civilian property, or conducting reprisals. When so charged they are subject to a trial by *military tribunal*. Terrorists can't be combatants since their tactics, techniques, and procedures deliberately do what combatants are barred from doing.[204]

[202] *Law and the Long War: The Future of Justice in the Age of Terror*, by B. Wittes; Penguin Group (USA) Incorporated, Pub. Date: June 2008.

[203] *A Concise History of the Russian Revolution*, by Richard Pipes, Knopf Publishers, October 1995.

[204] *Law and the Long War: The Future of Justice in the Age of Terror*, by B. Wittes; Penguin Group (USA) Incorporated, Pub. Date: June 2008.

A *criminal* is an individual who breaks civil laws for self-interest; greed, lust, or desire to harm. They murder, steal, lie, or cheat for passion or profit. They are not honorable men in service to their country; they are villains in search of money, thrills, or notoriety. They break laws they know exist and face acknowledged penalties. That's why they strive to conceal their activities. In America, criminals are *innocent until proven guilty*, they have the right to *habeus corpus* and to *remain silent*, they are allowed to *face their accusers*, have *defense counsel*, and a *speedy trial*. They are *punishable* only if found guilty *beyond a reasonable doubt*. Terrorists don't even recognize the state legitimacy of their victims and their motivation is not self-gain. Their methods are insidious.

The Ghalani trial exposed the vagaries of the 'criminal' approach when he was found innocent of hundreds of murder counts because the information that implicated him was uncovered using coercive interrogation.[205] Does the U.S. want to ban coercive interrogation of terrorists who may know about pending massacres? Does the U.S. want terrorists to confront their accusers and to have *habeus corpus* or pre-trial discovery? Does it want plea bargaining or to face the risk a slick lawyer presenting a 'if it doesn't fit you must acquit OJ argument? Can the U.S. live with terrorist recidivism?

Carbuncles? Terrorists aren't combatants or criminals; they're carbuncles. Citizen terrorists should be deemed insurrectionists but foreign terrorists are something else—but what? They aren't combatants. Terrorists deserve a category of their own, complete with an associated legal regime. This is the business of the Congress not the president or the judiciary.[206]

Today's terrorists are like yesterday's pirates. In their heyday, pirates terrorized the American coastline. They raided ships, killed passengers or sold them into slavery, scuttled ships and formed safe havens in places Tortuga and Port Royal instead of Afghanistan. Vice President Aaron Burr's daughter, Theodosia, was aboard a ship that disappeared off the Carolina coast. It might have been lost in a storm but

---

205 *Not a Suicide Pact: The Constitution in a Time of National Emergency*, by Richard A. Posner, Oxford University Press, USA: September 2006.

206 *Not a Suicide Pact: The Constitution in a Time of National Emergency*, by Richard A. Posner, Oxford University Press, USA: September 2006.

may well have fallen prey to piracy.[207] President Thomas Jefferson launched a war against the Barbary Pirates of Tripoli shortly after his inauguration because he refused to pay ransoms and tributes.[208] The infamy of pirate leaders like Blackbeard and Kidd rivaled todays media monsters like Bin Laden and Zarqawi.

Eventually, the British got fed up with the pirates of the Caribbean. They updated their piracy laws and sent the Royal Navy after them. When a pirate was caught, he was tried by a maritime tribunal. The Captains were hung with their bodies often put on display in Gibbets. Lesser crewmen were sentenced to anywhere from a few years to decades in prison. The pirates weren't treated as enemy sailors or criminals. They were stateless scoundrels and piracy wasn't an act of war or a crime; it was a unique, separate, and distinct act of aggression subject to its own rues and penalties. Perhaps this is the model.

The United States needs an enforcement regime that mirrors the pirate laws of old; sort of a Pirate Protocol. A Pirate Protocol would minimize the need to pursue 'whack-a-mole' tactics in search of famous figureheads. It would target all members of the network to include financiers, support networks, recruiters, propagandists, web trainers, partners, and suppliers. The United States needs open ended detention, military tribunals, and specified penalties. The deliberate and pre-planned mass murder of defenseless and unsuspecting civilians is not a criminal act or an act of war. It is something else altogether. It's a unique outrage that needs to be eliminated the way piracy was eliminated. The first step is a U.S. protocol and the follow up is an international protocol. The United States would not tolerate another Crusade or Inquisition and the United States should not tolerate another Jihad.

The United States must initiate a terrorist legal regime, a **Pirate Protocol**, with the following:
- Trial by military tribunal
- Protection of technology, sources, intelligence, and collection techniques

---

[207] *Duel: Alexander Hamilton, Aaron Burr, and the Future of America*, by Thomas Fleming, Basic Books, September 2000.

[208] *Jefferson's War: America's First War on Terror 1801-1805*, by Joseph Wheelan, Carroll and Graf Publishers, September 2003.

- Open ended detention
- No repatriation
- No habeus corpus
- Capital punishment for key leaders and lesser penalties for the rest
- No right to remain silent
- Legal coercive interrogation
- Warrantless search and seizure
- No Constitutional civil rights for foreign born terrorists
- Access to competent defense council

So what are the new class of beligerants to be called? Terrorists are part criminal since their actions deliberately target defenseless civilians. They are part combatant since their motivation is not personal gain. They are driven by ideology; a nihilist utopian one that endorses any means to their ends. The Romans called their stateless enemies barbarians. Not bad but not PC. Calling them warriors conveys honor. Jihadi is too specific like Viking, Goth, or Hun and it implies prejudicial targeting of Muslims; don't forget Timothy McVeigh or Anders Brevik. When **pirates** were the problem we called the **pirates, pirates**...and tried them as **pirates**. Why not call a **terrorist** a **terrorist** and try them as **terrorists**? Terrorism isn't in the eye of the beholder. A surprise attack resulting in the mass murder of defenseless and unsuspecting civilians is terrorism.

What would the Islamists Want? I think the conventional titles would suit terrorists' fine. Combatant confers legitimacy and elevates the terrorist to the level of soldiers honorably serving their state in war. On the other hand, being a criminal has its advantages such as: access to civil rights, trial by jury, evidence, and witnesses—a great source of intel. Criminals get off on technicalities and can become famous like Charles Manson or the Son of Sam.

Islamist would reject the pirate protocol. It would deny them the public stage and they'd simply disappear. They couldn't claim Geneva or Miranda protection and would be treated as the scoundrels they are, denied recognition, honor and a public forum.

Outsourcing Counterterrorism—Rendition. Should the U.S. hand over terrorists to other countries knowing they'll face harsher treatment there than they would here? This probably wouldn't even be an issue under the Pirate Protocols. This is a good question because we don't have Pirate Protocols. Rendition, initiated under President Clinton, is the practice of U.S. forces handing over captured terrorists to other countries for interrogation and detention. We did this with an Egyptian terrorist sought by us and by Egypt. The latter wanted him for his role in the Sadat assassination.[209]

Rendition would be fine if the terrorist committed crimes against the state he was being sent to but the United States shouldn't use third parties as judicial mercenaries. This damages our reputation. America used treat rendition like extradition is used to transfer a prisoner from one victimized state to another that has more serious penalties for the crime. You see the reverse of this often when a country refuses to extradite a criminal to the U.S. because we have the death penalty. If the gaining state has aggressive interrogation techniques that's their business. It would be beneficial for terror masters to fear falling into the hands of an angry victim police state. There have been indications that some of the offenders would rather be in the U.S. than elsewhere.[210]

What would the Islamists want? They'd probably love to see the United States abandon rendition. It reduces their access to U.S. Civil Law and all the protections it affords them as criminals, their current designation. Furthermore, complaints don't typically come out of Middle Eastern prisons like they do from American and European prisons.

Torture and its Lesser Cousins. Why is it that our most adamant critics are Islamist advocacy groups; the same ones that refuse to condemn terrorism? Why do captured terrorists look for the camera so they can scream torture? Why do detainees toss notes at reporters claiming abuse? Why do AQ training manuals stress the imperative of claiming "that you were mistreated or tortured during your detention"?[211] Might it be exploitation of western navel gazing

[209] *Law and the Long War: The Future of Justice in the Age of Terror*, by B. Wittes; Penguin Group (USA) Incorporated, Pub. Date: June 2008.

[210] *The Cell: Inside The 9/11 Plot, And Why The FBI And CIA Failed To Stop It*, by John J. Miller, Michael Stone, Chris Mitchell, Hyperion, August 2002.

[211] *Al Qaeda Manual Drives Detainee Behavior at Guantanamo Bay*, by Donna Miles, American Forces Press Service, June 29, 2005, http://www.defense.gov/news/newsarticle.aspx?id=16270.

paranoia and our propensity for self-condemnation? As with all things lawfare related, we are vulnerable to self-imposed restrictions designed to end practices that are effective against those who seek its abolition.

The US cannot support torture in any way, shape, matter, or form.[212]

What is torture? Torture is defined as inflicting *excruciating pain* in order to extract information. When we think about torture, we think about Medieval Inquisitors, Nazi's or KGB henchmen so we might add that it is likely to result in the loss of life, limb, sight, sound, or mind. It often leaves the subject permanently damaged, mentally or physically. A torturer is unconcerned about catastrophic damage. His *intent* is confession or divulgence of information. Many torturers know what they want the prisoner to say and will not relent until he says it. They are in search of validation not information.

We must be careful with the definition. Some *activists* claim that bad language or yelling can cause mental damage and are torture. This kind of input would be detrimental to say the least. Generating fear and anxiety, real or imagined, isn't the same as inflicting excruciating pain. We don't need Clarence Darrow or the Simpson legal team on this one. The only winners then would be the terrorists. What we need is common sense and a reasonable definition.

Our most successful form of coercive interrogation is *water-boarding*. It's not torture. Water boarding doesn't leave the prisoner incapacitated and isn't designed to maim, kill or provoke insanity. That doesn't mean that it is risk free. No strenuous activity, particularly one an involuntary one, is without risk but perhaps a terrorist cedes his right to a risk free environment when he attempts or succeeds in mass murder. Water-boarding takes advantage the involuntary fear drowning. An experienced interrogator won't harm the prisoner and most people can't resist an instinctual response. Even when a prisoner knows he won't drown, he panics and most will talk. It works without leaving permanent injury and should not be abandoned. Waterboarding should be restricted to use on terrorists and should be banned for use on criminals or against legal combatants.[213]

[212] *Law and the Long War: The Future of Justice in the Age of Terror*, by B. Wittes; Penguin Group (USA) Incorporated, Pub. Date: June 2008.

[213] *Law and the Long War: The Future of Justice in the Age of Terror*, by B. Wittes; Penguin Group (USA) Incorporated, Pub. Date: June 2008.

What about the ticking bomb scenario? The interrogator who knows there is a ticking bomb and has a conspirator can and should torture him. The torture is not legal but it is moral. Bobbitt counts on the intellect of the jury to recognize the extenuating circumstances and to reward the 'offender' for saving lives or trying to.[214] I would prefer codification of a body of mitigating circumstances that provides a degree of legal protection to the law enforcer who adopts extraordinary means to safeguard citizens under extraordinary circumstances.[215]

What would the Islamists want? They'd love to see us abandon our most effective interrogation techniques while excoriating ourselves in the process—just what we are doing now. Not only does it make life easier, it highlights our lack of resolve. We get squeamish over dunking a terrorist while they videotape beheadings and bombings. It plays well to the clash of the enervated infidel west versus the energized and righteous ummah. What's better is the west's divisive and self-destructive dialogue; evidence of us tearing ourselves apart.

> *"No stronger retrograde force exists in the world. Far from being moribund, Mohammedanism is a militant and proselytizing faith."*
> —Winston Churchill

If it walks like a Duck (Profiling) ... Jewish Sicarri's (dagger men), Shia Hashashins (assassins), Indian Thugees (thugs), Irish Fenians, the Serbian Black Handers, Russian Anarchists, German Baader Meinhoff, and the American KKK are/were terrorists.[216] Terrorism employs all wannabes regardless of race, religion, creed, sex, or political affiliation. It's global and multicultural. Although terrorism has historically been an equal opportunity recruiter; in the 21st Century it has not been an equal opportunity attractor. The modern maxim that *'most Muslims are not terrorists but most terrorists are Muslims'*

[214] *Terror and Consent: The Wars for the Twenty-first Century*, by Philip Bobbitt, Knopf Doubleday Publishing Group, May 2009.

[215] *Not a Suicide Pact: The Constitution in a Time of National Emergency*, by Richard A. Posner, Oxford University Press USA, September 2006.

[216] *Blood and Rage: History of Terrorism*, by Michael Burleigh, HarperCollins Publishers, February 2011.

is accurate, particularly when focusing on attacks against the west. Statistics show that most terrorists, and most of their targets, are Muslim. Muslims span the globe from Alexandria, Virginia to Alexandria, Egypt; from London to Lahore; they are American, European, Asian, and Latino; but most are also Middle Eastern. Accepting this reality is the first step to effective defense.

If most western attackers are Middle Eastern men then why not look for Middle Eastern men when trying to stop those attacks? When a football coach is looking for a lineman, he looks for a kid who is 6'4", 325lbs who runs a 5 second 40 yard dash. If he's searching for a receiver, he looks for a kid who is 6'1", 210lbs, and a 4.4 40 yard dash. Female gymnasts don't do the pommel horse and males don't do the parallel bars. Locals don't interview PhD's to be the dog catcher and universities don't interview high school drop-outs to teach physics. This is sensible profiling based on observed and measurable behavior patterns. The targets are the most likely matches.[217]

America needs to apply the same common sense to the hunt for terrorists. Focus on the most likely offenders rather than randomly hitting everyone in a desperately useless attempt to prove indifference. The U.S. can accept risk regarding the Catholic Nuns, 90 year old grandmas, 9 year old toddlers, the Inuits, and the Japanese tourists and it shouldn't ignore other demographics but it should prioritize the 'usual suspects.' A middle aged Muslim male of Middle Eastern descent travelling from the Middle East should get the first look. If he has nothing to hide then he has nothing to fear. Although its not his fault that most terrorists are Middle Eastern Muslims it is better to inconvenience a suspect minority than to endanger a defenseless majority.

What would the Islamists want? As with most of these issues, the bad guys would love to see the U.S. harass everyone and erode its commitment to common sense and individual freedom. If profiling Muslims males and Jihadi Mosques becomes untenable then the chances of the 'bomber' getting through goes up. The 'flying Imam's' caused a spectacle deliberately to prevent us from reacting to Muslims while British Imam's threaten another 7/7 (Britain's 9-11) in response for counter-

217 *Not a Suicide Pact: The Constitution in a Time of National Emergency*, by Richard A. Posner, Oxford University Press USA, September 2006.

terrorism efforts. If the United States adopts comprehensive and generic profiling that wastes assets and efforts searching the least likely while ignoring the most likely in the name of political correctness, the United States loses.

> *"As great a tragedy as this was, it would be a shame if our diversity became a casualty as well."*
> —Former Army Chief of Staff General George Casey

Islamophobia—Myth and Multiculturalism. The magic phrase that shuts down debate is 'Islamophobia'. To be labeled an Islamophobe is to be labeled a Nazi—one who harbors bigoted and deadly hatred. Acknowledgement of Islamist terrorism is not Islamophobia; its reality.[218] Caution is not paranoia. Vigilance is not prejudice.

America bends over backwards in the name of Islamophobia. Europe has pursued draconian measures to suppress Islamic racism, denying the U.S. access to servers with banking data related to terrorist organizations. Meanwhile back home, we supported the construction of a Mega Mosque at Ground Zero and denied attempts to rebuild a pre-9-11 Christian Orthodox Church and the U.S. Attorney General, Eric Holder, decided to charge the Fort Hood attacker with murder rather than terrorism.[219]

Britain's Channel 4 broadcasted a documentary, Undercover Mosque, that exposed Islamist hate mongers praising Usama bin Laden, justifying the enslavement and murder of kuffar (non-Muslims), and calling for the murder of Jews and homosexuals.[220] The documentary was filmed in *Londonistan*, Europe's largest Muslim city. The police didn't charge the venomous Imams with hate speech but they did file a complaint against the filmmakers for taking things "out of context."

[218] *It's Logical to Be 'Islamophobic,'* by R.C. Marsh, American Thinker, October 18, 2010, http://www.americanthinker.com/archived-articles/../2010/10/its_logical_to_be_islamophobic.html.

[219] *Islamic Supremacism Trumps Christianity at Ground Zero*, by Pamela Geller, American Thinker, July 21, 2011, http://www.americanthinker.com/2011/07/islamic_supremacism_trumps_christianity_at_ground_zero.html#ixzz1zUbw6jVl

[220] *Undercover Mosque*, a Documentary by Hardcash Productions, British public-service television Channel 4, September 2008, www.hardcashproductions.com/recent29.html.

This is multicultural tolerance. The filmmakers were eventually vindicated but the message was clear; shine a light on radical Islam at your own peril.

The Fort Hood attack by the Allahu-Akhbar shouting Army Major Hasan was designated 'workplace violence' for fear of the Islamophobia canard.[221] Rather than worry about Islamists in the military the Army Chief of Staff, General George Casey, was worried about backlash and diversity.[222] Hasan's checkered past was uncovered during the investigation and it was disregarded. Had he been a Christian, he would have made headlines as a dangerous religious fanatic. Don't think the stealth Jihadis don't comprehend the power of Islamophobia as a powerful suppressant. It excuses all kinds of Stealth Jihad measures:

- CAIR telling Muslims not to cooperate with the FBI
- Sharia only zones in the UK
- Cashiers refusing to handle pork products
- Refusing to serve people with 'unclean' seeing eye dogs
- Cabbies demanding airport footbaths at taxpayer expense
- Demands for Sharia in the courts
- Cartoon riots
- Intolerance and hate speech suits against critics ala Mark Steyn[223]

What would the Jihadi's want? They like the status quo—a multicultural, guilt ridden west and a triumphant, sectarian apartheid for Dar al-Islam and their western host nation enclaves. America sensors when a political cartoonist depicts Mohammad with a bomb in his turban or an obscure pastor burns an inanimate object (the Quran). America tolerates, and even validate, the resulting riots, property destruction, killings, and beheadings. On the other hand, when Muslims destroyed the Buddhas of Bamiyan, massacred Christians in Bagdad and Copts in

---

[221] *Lawmakers Blast Administration For Calling Fort Hood Massacre, 'Workplace Violence'* by Catherine Herridge, FoxNews.com, December 07, 2011.

[222] *Army Chief Of Staff Worried About Anti-Muslim Backlash*, by Sam Stein, Huffingtonpost.com, March 18, 2010.

[223] *America Alone: The End of the World as We Know It*, by Mark Steyn, Regnery Publishing, Inc., An Eagle Publishing Company, April 8, 2008.

Alexandria, assassinated Catholic Priests in Istanbul, fire rockets into Israel, hang homosexuals in Iran, or bans infidels from Mecca—the west calls for cultural tolerance. America even helps the 57 states of the OIC codify blasphemy laws.[224] America's inalienable rights become intolerable acts and their intolerable acts become inalienable rights. Thank multiculturalism, moral relativism, and self-indictment. We limit ourselves and unleash our enemies; what more could a Jihadi ask for?

> *"If you tell a lie big enough and keep repeating it, people will eventually come to believe it."*
> —Joseph Goebbles, Nazi Minister of Propaganda

QUICK HITS AND DRIVE-BYE'S

Libel Tourism. The predatory libel lawsuit is a mainstay of Stealth Jihad. Victims of libel tourism include novelists, political cartoonists, and non-fiction critics of Islam, Sharia, and Jihad. Libel tourism is when Stealth Jihadis bring suit in states or countries with liberal libel laws that make it easy to stifle targeted work.[225] The general term for such weak to baseless libel is SLAPP. SLAPP is short for Strategic Lawsuits Against Public Participation. SLAPPs are used to intimidate and silence critics. When a plaintiff brings a SLAPP suit against someone, it is usually disguised as defamation (Islamophobia). These lawsuits are often filed without any expectation of winning but are pursued to bankrupt, demoralize, and silence critics. SLAPPs target First Amendment freedom of speech rights.

The solution is Anti-SLAPP. Anti-SLAPP laws seek to curtail SLAPP lawsuits and defend speech. Where they exist, the defendant being sued enters a motion to strike because the issue as a matter of public concern. The plaintiff then must prove the suit is based on more than allegations and they must show real evidence that could win the case. If the defendant wins, the plaintiff pays. Anti-SLAPP laws guard against frivolous lawsuits.

---

[224] *The 'Istanbul Process': A Success for Muslim Diplomacy* by David Pryce-Jones, National Review Online, March 12, 2012.

[225] *Britain to Seek Curbs to 'Libel Tourism'* by Eric Pfanner, New York Times, May 9, 2012.

No Sharia—No Way.   Muslim Republics are democratic theocracies. Take Iran for example: the government exists in two parts, a western style led by the *President* and the *Majlis* or congress. They are shadowed by a religious government led by the Supreme Leader and his *Council of Experts* that trumps the former. Such states are antithetical to liberal democratic Republics. Islamism is at odds with key democratic tenants of governance such as equal representation, rule of law, equality before the law, blind justice, no cruel and unusual punishment, property rights, and freedom of religion, speech, and association; to name a few.[226] Sharia is divine to Muslims. All other law is manmade and is inferior. The west must show zero tolerance for Sharia within western jurisprudence.

Freedom of religion. Sharia is sectarian and by definition is opposed to freedom of religion.[227] It requires a totalitarianism to implement as any repressive system does. Sharia does not tolerate dissent; proselytizing and religious conversion are capital offenses. It embodies the meaning of Islam—submission of believers and non-believers.

Freedom of speech and press. Sharia considers criticism of Islam or the prophet as heresy punishable by death. One need not look to far; *The Satanic Verses*, the Dutch Mohammed Cartoons of 2005, and the Florida Quran burning generated Muslim outrage and resulted in hundreds of deaths. Theo Van Gough was murdered for producing a film critical of Islam, Ayann Hirsi Ali was forced to flee Europe due to her criticism of Islam and Geert Wilders went on trial for his critique.[228]

Representative Government. Sharia represses the rights of non-Muslims, Dhimmi's, and endorses a special tax upon them for protection called the Jizya. Dhimmi's are restricted in their ability to hold government and judicial offices, form political parties, and participate in government. Sharia does not endorse the separation of mosque and state; they are one.

---

226 *Shariah: The Threat To America, An Exercise In Competitive Analysis Report Of Team B II*, Center for Security Policy, October 2010 Edition.

227 *Hatred's Kingdom: How Saudi Arabia Supports the New Global Terrorism*, by Dore Gold, Regnery Publishing, Inc., An Eagle Publishing Company, February 15, 2003.

228 *Pakistanis Kill Man Accused of Insulting Quran*, by Munir Ahmed, Associated Press, Islamabad July 4, 2012.

Rule of Law. Sharia is not made up of a compilation of codified statutes. There is no analogue to Justinian's CODEX. Sharia is derived from the Quran, the sunna, and the hadith. Under Sharia, a fatwa (extra-legal religious ruling) can be pronounced by any 'holy man' and can become official. Fatwa's have become the stuff of legend ever since the 1989 fatwa issued by Ayatollah Khomeini against Salman Rushdie for his book, *The Satanic Verses.* Sharia trials are presided over by clerics not judges and juries.

Equality before the Law. Men and women are not equal under Sharia. Wife beating is the husband's prerogative. Women are entitled to half the inheritance of men. A female trial witness is worth half that of a male; it takes two women to counter one man. Women are not expected to pursue an advanced education and are not supposed to be outside without male guidance. Non-Muslim women can be captured and used as a combination maid and sex slave—an idea promoted by a Kuwaiti female politician.[229] Lastly, Sharia wholeheartedly endorses slavery. The Kingdom of Saudi Arabia didn't abolish slavery until 1962.

Cruel and unusual punishment. Sharia imposes medieval penalties and enforces medieval crimes. A thief can have his hand chopped off or run over. In Iran, Christian Pastor Youcef Nadarkhani faces death for conversion from Islam although he claims never to have been Muslim. Homosexuals are hung, adulterers are stoned, people are executed for witchcraft, and public lashings are common.[230]

Tolerance for the Intolerant. To tolerate Sharia is to endorse religious apartheid, misogyny, anti-Semitism, and xenophobia. Sharia codifies bigotry, dhimmitude, censorship, and segregation. It allows western Muslims to pursue privileged enclaves rather than assimilating. Western Muslims should not be allowed to elevate their religious law above state law. What does it tell Muslim and non-Muslim alike when the 10 Commandments are banned from public display but a Muslim man can be excused for beating or raping his wife since his behavior is

---

[229] *Female activist: Muslim men need sex slaves to keep from committing adultery,* Acharya Murdock, From the Kuwait Times, 08 June 2011, http://www.freethoughtnation.com/contributing-writers/63-acharya-s/541-female-activist-muslim-men-need-sex-slaves-to-keep-from-committing-adultery.html

[230] *Saudi Arabia execution of 'sorcery' woman condemned,* The UK Telegraph, December 13, 2011.

in accordance with his Quranic Law? This is a key battleground where we must not compromise.

The Jihadi's like it the way it is now; gradual Sharia encroachment into western jurisprudence. They seek self-segregated Muslim communities ruled by Quranic law to supplant western secular law. This creates de-facto dhimmitude by erecting an Islamist wall of separation between the 'chosen' and the infidels.

> *If Sharia says it's legal for a man to beat his wife for disobedience and that is the way they are raised—who are we to judge? If the previous argument is accepted then what happens if an infidel women is raped in a Muslim enclave or a homosexual is beaten of murdered? The culturally sensitive liberal progressive might say the girl provoked the Muslims with her immodest dress and the homosexuals insulted the Muslims sensibilities through their public display of affection. We can't judge them by the standards we hold for ourselves, can we?*

Boiling the Frog. Sharia is the key. It elevates Islam and demotes the rest. It can be implemented gradually. We can be habituated to it. Hobbled by pacifist academics espousing multiculturalism and moral relativity, we submit as an act of intellectual superiority and, in so doing, we sign away our western identity and sign our eventual death warrant. When a civilization loses faith in itself, it loses the will to defend itself.

CHAPTER 8

Detainee
Apples and Bananas
Apples and Oranges
...or Bananas

A Tale of Two Trials. Around midnight on *13 June 1942*, four men departed a German submarine and landed on a beach in Long Island, New York. They carried explosives and incendiaries. Four days later, the rest of their team landed near Jacksonville, Florida. Their mission was to destroy defense manufacturing, supplies and transportation for the Reich while striking fear in America's population.

All eight attackers were born in Germany but had lived in America. One became a naturalized citizen, another gained citizenship when his father was naturalized, and another received an honorable discharge after serving in the Army. Two returned to Germany before WWII broke out and the other six returned after 11 Sept. 1939 but before 7 Dec. 1941.

Ten days after landing, all eight were under arrest after one turned himself in. They were tried by a military commission from 8 Jul to 4 Aug in the DOJ Building. The prosecution was led by the Army Judge Advocate General and the defense included Truman's future Secretary of War and the son of the Chief Justice of the Supreme Court. They were found guilty and sentenced:

- The two who cooperated got life and 30 years. After the war, they were granted clemency and were deported to the American Zone in Germany.
- The other six got the death penalty and were executed on 8 August 1942.

On *1 March 2003*, in Rawalpindi, Pakistan; Khalid Sheikh

Mohammed (KSM) was arrested in a ramshackle apartment looking disheveled and dejected. He ended up in the Guantanamo Bay (Gitmo) Detention camp in Cuba where he confessed to masterminding 9-11, the failed shoe bombing, the Bali bombing, the '93 World Trade Center bombing and the Daniel Pearl beheading. He was charged in 2008.

Gitmo and the detainee designation remain controversial. The debate raged: where to jail terrorists; who would try them; what to charge them with; what rights should apply and so on. The left argued for civil trials in the US with terrorists afforded Constitutional rights. The right favored military tribunals at Gitmo with the terrorists treated as war criminals. Both were right and both were wrong.

Stinging from their failure to close Gitmo as promised, the administration decided to try KSM in a civil trial in NYC. On 13 Nov 2009, the Attorney General announced that he and four co-conspirators would be transferred to New York. By Jan 2010 the military commission dropped its charges "without prejudice" in order to transfer the case to civil authorities. The resulting protest was adamant: NYC couldn't afford it, survivors didn't want KSM in NYC, others opposed granting them constitutional rights, and experts feared the trial would be an intel bonanza for Al Qaeda. In April 2011, the Attorney General sent the trial back to the military at Gitmo.

The trial finally got under way in May 2012. It was immediately disrupted by the defendants who refused to recognize the courts authority, refused listen or respond to queries, broke into prayer during proceedings, and demanded females wear hijab's... Observers say the trial could take years.

70 x (47 / 3405). In 1942, seventy years ago, the time from capture to conviction of eight Nazi saboteurs who didn't manage to blow up anything or kill anyone, was 47 days. In 2012, the capture to conviction of five terrorists who orchestrated the destruction of the World Trade Center, damaged the Pentagon, and killed 2,977 people, stands at 3,405 days and counting. We went from $2^{1/2}$ months to 9 years plus. Why the difference ... clarity perhaps. In June 1942 the US had just won at Midway and in July the Germans were on the outskirts of Stalingrad. We knew who the enemy was and how to deal with them. Today's situation isn't so clear. We're in a Global War on Terror yet we're at peace. Our enemies don't fight for Imperial Japan or Nazi Germany, they fight for global Islamism, whatever that is.

War versus Warlike. The rules are clear in the event of war but what about warlike? The attack on Pearl Harbor claimed 2,402 lives. The 9-11 attack claimed 2,977 lives but it was terrorism not war. The 706 Japanese pilots and copilots were *combatants* operating under the orders of their countries leaders while the 19 Al Qaeda terrorists were *criminals* operating under the orders of a Sunni Cult Leader, at least if you follow western legal precedence.

The Aum Shinrikyo cultists who executed the Tokyo subway attacks were tried as criminals. The Amerithrax attacks, Abdullah al-Muhajir's (formerly known as José Padilla) dirty bomb plot and the Mumbai attack were all investigated and tried as crimes. Meanwhile Hizballah and Hamas attacks are seen as being something more than crime and something less than war. Has a line been crossed when stateless actors can kill and destroy more than state backed military personnel?

The Dilemma. The question arose on the heels of Operation Enduring Freedom in 2002; how do we handle captured terrorists. What laws governed them and were they prisoners of war or criminals? The short term answer was neither. They were designated to be detainees who would be held outside the United States where they were not subject to US legal protections. This extralegal approach allowed the US to evade contentious issues and was consistent with established practice. President's Bush Sr. and Clinton used Gitmo to detain Haitian and Cuban refugees, many with criminal records, until their status could be determined. Bush Jr. continued the trend but his detainees were more sophisticated. A POTUS / SCOTUS ping pong match ensued. The administration said the terrorists weren't entitled to civil protections and the Court said they were. The President went to Congress to get resolution through legislation and the cycle began when the next issue popped up.

The Bush administration favored open ended detention (combatants) and military tribunals (war criminals) while the Obama administration favored closing Gitmo and incarcerating detainees (criminals) and civil trial (criminals). It's clear; the problem is a lack of clear terrorism policy.

Terrorists are either criminals or combatants. Let's walk the dog by laying out each by: definition; relationship to society; the nature of their behavior; motivation; and applicable laws.

Criminal Apples. A criminal is *defined* as a person who commits an act or omission that is prohibited and punishable by law. He engages in unlawful acts. Charles Manson, Bernie Madoff, and Ted Bundy are criminals.

Relationship to Society. Criminals are outlaws. They are called, seen as, and acknowledged as such. Criminals acknowledge the existence of legitimate laws that they are obligated to obey; they simply choose not to. Criminals expect to be punished if they are arrested and convicted.

Nature of their Behavior. Criminals deliberately target helpless, unsuspecting, and defenseless people to be their victims. They don't want to fight for what they seek. They are predators and their actions are covert, designed to evade detection and arrest.

Motivation. Criminal activity is based on the selfish pursuit of personal gain rooted in greed, lust, avarice or the desire to harm others. They plan on benefiting from their actions but do not want credit for them since that would lead to apprehension.

Applicable Laws. Criminals in America are afforded a myriad of civil rights that regulate their arrest and trial. They are innocent until proven guilty and are afforded numerous specific protections under the Constitution:

- The Fourth Amendment prevents unreasonable search and seizure and guarantees warrant based searches based on probable cause.

- The Fifth Amendment denies trial without a grand jury indictment; prevents double jeopardy; grants the right to remain silent and the right to due process. This amendment is the basis of the Miranda Rights.

- The Sixth Amendment guarantees a speedy trial before an impartial jury. It grants the right to confront witnesses and grants discovery—the right to see evidence arrayed against the accused. It guarantees access to defense counsel and the right to be informed of charges beforehand.

- The Eighth Amendment prevents excessive bail and fines and bars cruel and unusual punishment.

- Fourteenth Amendment prevents states from depriving anyone of life, liberty, or property without due process. The state must also provide equal protection under the law and must honor the privileges and immunities provided to U.S. citizens in the Bill of Rights.

Combatant Oranges. A combatant is *defined* as person who serves, or has served, in a states uniformed military. They engage in active fighting with enemy forces at the direction of the state's. Soldiers, airmen, marines, and sailors like Alvin York, Audie Murphy, and David Petraeus are combatants.

Relationship to Society. Combatants are usually viewed as honorable servants of the state. Most are uniformed members of the military and are perceived as society's legal defenders against enemies, foreign and domestic. They are expected to obey the laws of war. They also expect to be detained, but not punished, if captured. They are released when conflict ends.

Nature of their Behavior. Combatants target uniformed enemy combatants and judiciously avoid collateral damage (CD); unnecessary harm to civilians and their property. When combatants disregard or deliberately create CD, it's a war crime. Combatant actions are overt.

Motivation. Combatant service is selfless, rooted in loyalty and duty to the state. They don't seek personal gain from their actions and they cease operations when ordered to. Combatants don't seek credit but they also don't avoid it since their actions are legally sanctioned by their state and recognized by international authorities.

Applicable Laws. The laws governing combatants are largely derived from international institutions. Combatants aren't arrested and tried; they are captured and detained pending conflict termination. Most combatant rights are enumerated in the Geneva Conventions:

- The First Convention covers treatment of the Wounded and Sick in the Field.
- The Second Convention covers treatment of the Wounded, Sick and Shipwrecked at Sea.
- Third Convention covers the Treatment of Prisoners of War.
- The Conventions apply during declared war and armed conflict between signatory nations and between signatory nations and non-signatory nations when the latter "accepts the provisions."

Terrorist Bananas. A terrorist uses violence and threats of violence to coerce targeted populations and governments into changing their behavior, usually for political or theological purposes. Andreas Baader, Shoko Asahara, and Abu Nidal were terrorists. Terrorists clearly don't fit neatly into either of the above categories.

The terrorist relationship to society is that of predator to prey. Terrorists do not acknowledge civil law and routinely ignore laws of war. They deliberately target helpless, unsuspecting, and defenseless civilians, like criminals. Their motivations are selfless, like combatants. They seek maximum collateral damage, unlike criminals or combatants, and they don't seek personal gain although they crave credit for their atrocities. Terrorists are like criminals but are not criminals. They are like combatants but are not combatants...so what are they and how should they be handled by the U.S.? Should they be arrested or captured? Should the U.S. incarcerate them or detain them? Should it send them to a trial by jury or to a military tribunal or should they have the right to remain silent; to confront witnesses; to see evidence; to raise bail...?

Rewind. We've been here before. Past civilizations have been plagued, harassed, and terrorized by stateless nomads, rogues and brigands who had no regard for the law like the Huns, Mongols, and Goths. The most famous and persistent scourge on society has been piracy. Mediterranean pirates snatched a young Julius Caesar and held him hostage. Pirates probably killed Aaron Burr's daughter, Theodosia, in 1813 when the schooner she was on vanished off the Carolina coast.

There have been Mediterranean Pirates, China Sea and Indian Ocean Pirates, Barbary Pirates, Pirates of the Caribbean, and Somali

Pirates. Their leaders were notorious characters like Blackbeard, Captain Kidd and Jack Rackham. They hid out in infamous safe havens like Tripoli, Nassau, Port Royal, and Tortuga. The Romans sent Pompey after them while we sent the SEALS.

The Muslim Barbary Pirates thought it was their divine right to rape, pillage, plunder and enslave infidels. They sold over a million Europeans into slavery throughout North Africa and the Ottoman Empire between the 16th and 19th centuries. They attacked bearing daggers in both hands and one clenched in their teeth to strike terror in their victims.

The Caribbean Pirates were vicious opportunists who preyed on the lucrative shipping lanes between the New World and Europe. They captured, looted, scuttled or stole unescorted ships caught on the open sea. Wealthy passengers were ransomed; deck hands were shang-haied; and extras were sold into slavery, cast adrift, stranded, or thrown overboard. They came out of nowhere and showed no mercy upon arrival.

The Golden Age of Piracy ran from the 1650s to the 1730s and it took a determined effort to end it. It was characterized by three waves of intense piracy. The first wave was known as the buccaneer phase of the mid1600's where Anglo-French sailors preyed on Spanish ships. Next came the expeditionary wave of the late 1600s, where the pirates embarked on long voyages east to target traders in the Indian Ocean and Red Sea. It all culminated with the wave that made the fictional Captain Jack Sparrow famous. The post-Spanish Succession wave made the skull and crossbones a pirate icon. This wave spanned the first three decades of the 1700's and was fueled by newly unemployed privateers from the War of Spanish Succession. This was the Blackbeard crowd.

The Brits, finally unencumbered by war, decided to put an end to piracy in the new world once and for all. They updated their laws by singling out the pirates for specific legal action. Penalties were stiff-ened and the time from capture to conviction was shortened. Then they sent the Royal Navy hunting; armed with the power to kill or cap-ture pirates, try them in Naval Tribunals, and execute sentencing.

The Piracy Act of 1698 got the ball rolling by allowing pirates to be tried where they were caught thus ending the tradition of hauling them back to England. It also specified the death penalty for being an accessory to piracy or engaging in piracy under foreign colors. They stepped up war on piracy in 1718 by ordering the Admiralty to end it. They sent ships to patrol the pirate-infested waters with orders to hunt down the pirates, sack their lairs, execute their Captains, and imprison their crews.

The *Law of Nations* designated pirates as *hostis humani generis* (enemies of humanity). In 1726, the American colonies designated them as common enemies. Justice for captured pirates was swift with hanging as the preferred sentence for the leaders. The executions were reported in detail by the newspapers and as a further deterrence; especially notorious pirates were put on display after death. Their bodies were enclosed in iron cages called gibbets that were hung up at the docks where they rotted in full view of passers- by and would-be pirates. The concerted action of the updated laws and the Royal Navy shut down the safe havens and effectively put an end to the Pirate rampage that had lasted over 80 years.

I call the above rules the *Pirate Protocols* and the United States can learn from them when addressing the modern scourge of terrorism. When a pirate was caught, he was tried by a maritime tribunal and was jailed or hung if found guilty. They weren't treated like enemy sailors or criminals. They were stateless scoundrels. Piracy wasn't an act of war or a crime; it was a unique, separate, and distinct act of aggression subject to its own set of rules and penalties.

Terror Protocols. It's time to classify terrorists. They can't be treated like criminals who are afforded all the civil rights of a citizen and they can't be given the rights afforded honorable and legal combatants. Terrorists have criminal attributes and combatant attributes so are they criminal combatants? Why not treat them like pirates? Let's give them their own designation by calling them what they are—terrorists? If we say terrorists are terrorists and they warrant their own legal regime we can go to Congress and tell them to develop a comprehensive legal regime for them. This set of rules emanate from executive orders as before. It must be legislated.

What might a Terror Protocol look like? We start with definitions. American born terrorists should be treated as criminals unless they renounce their citizenship or actively join a foreign terror cell overseas. When they head to Yemen, Libya, or Palestine to 'join up' or go to training camps in Pakistan, their rights of citizenship should be revoked. As for foreign born terrorists; they should be unambiguously designated as terrorists.

Penalties for terrorists and their supporters should be spelled out based on the notion that mass murder of civilians is not a criminal act of an act of war; its terrorism. Leaders and operatives should face the death penalty while supporters should face decades in jail. Terrorists should be subject to open ended detention and trial by closed military tribunals which should be convened as soon as it has been determined that all intelligence value has been extracted. Terrorists like the 'panty bomber' should not have the right to remain silent which means they should be subject to coercive interrogation. This is not torture but it is waterboarding and intense psychological pressure.

The terrorist regime should entail the following:
- Closed military tribunal that protects sources, agents, acquisition technology and collection techniques
- Open ended detention
- No repatriation or habeus corpus
- Subject to capital punishment
- No right to remain silent
- Subject to coercive interrogation
- No right to a warrant for search and seizure
- Not access to the civil rights of a US citizen

When pirates became intolerable, the U.S. stopped tolerating them and implemented unambiguous laws that targeted the problem rather than shoehorn them into existing but ineffective legal paradigms. Another Crusade or Inquisition would not be tolerated and neither should another Jihad.

CHAPTER 9

Counter-Suit
Cultural Confidence

DEFENSE AGAINST STEALTH JIHAD
No Surrender

"America will never tap into educational innovation and ingenuity without looking at the model that we have in our Madrassas, in our schools where innovation is encouraged, where the foundation is the Koran."
—Rep. Andre Carson (D-Indiana) said at the ICNA-MAS convention, May, 2012[231]

"Evil flourishes when good men do nothing."
—Edmund Burke

Acknowledge Stealth / Civilizational Jihad.   There is no defense against that which is denied. The Islamists have published their goals just like the communists and Nazi's did. The U.S. and the World ignored them and learned with great cost of their reality The Islamists have warned the Free World and the U.S. and those warnings will be ignored at great peril. America can take defensive measures with the following steps require us to restore faith and confidence in our culture, to be proud of Western Civilization without being blind to its faults and allows Americans to acknowledge faults without elevating them as the norm. Americans can only defend their culture if they decide to believe in it.

As Niall Ferguson states in *Civilization: The West and the Rest*; perhaps the most dangerous threat to the post-cold war west is not Islamism but our own ignorance of and growing lack of faith in our own culture.

---

231 *Islamic Circle of North America-Muslim American Society Convention*, May 20012, http://icnaconvention.org/.

> *"Today...the biggest threat to Western civilization is posed not by
> other civilizations, but by our own pusillanimity—
> and by the historical ignorance that feeds it."*
> —Niall Ferguson, *Civilization: The West and the Rest*

- *Free Worship:* Christianity and Judaism should not modify their practices in response to Islamist demands. This holds true for atheists too. The USA is a Judeo-Christian country; check the demographics. While the United States jealously protects the rights of the minority, it is no less a perversion to allow the minority to dictate to the majority.

- *Rediscover Western Civilization*—Americans must rethink the postmodernist trend, augmented by its multi-culturalism stepchild, of bashing the west and lionizing the rest. It's dishonest, inaccurate and ultimately suicidal. Future generations won't defend a culture they aren't knowledgeable of or connected to. In fact, many will contribute to our demise when weaned on a steady diet of west ernophobia—the very definition of a *useful idiot.*

- *Cultural Pride*—American educators used to teach Western Civilization in high school and had Western Civics departments in college. They should resurrect it in primary and higher education. The curricula should highlight western accomplishments without ascribing them to exploitation or theft. Americans should discuss their faults without portraying them as societal norms or uniquely western and should further emphasize the steps taken to correct them. The west should not be painted as the font of all evil, exploitation,greed, and selfishness. It's not true or accurate or helpful. If the truth is told, the story will be grand.

- *Origins*—Americans should celebrate their Judeo-Christian / Greco- Roman roots. The former provided morality and tolerance while the latter provided democracy and the rule of law. It highlights America's national roots and illustrates the American character The Founding Fathers were experts at Greco-Roman studies. They inculcated them in the national development.

- *Original Sins*—Slavery is not a western phenomenon. It's as old as civilization. Egyptians, Assyrians, Chinese, Persians, and Muslims had slaves...among others. Not only is slavery not novel, nearly every race has been on the short end of that stick. Africans and Jews were Egyptian slaves; Brits, Spaniards, and Germans were Roman slaves; and Greeks were each other's slaves; long before anyone was an American slave. Ditto for Imperialism and Colonialism; just take a moment to peruse a book that features history in maps. The U.S. wasn't the first imperfect country and US won't be the last. Our mistakes should not be excused but they also should not be amplified.

- *Foundations*—Americans ought to know whose ideas built it. Today's students know who Nietzsche, Marx (Communist Mannifesto), Mao (*The Little Red Book*), and Che' (The T-Shirts) but are ignorant of John Locke, Edmund Burke, and Alexis de Tocqueville. What student, high school or college, can name the Greek inventor of democracy and the city in which he started it in? Cleisthenes and Athens. Who knows that Rome was a republic for centuries before Julius Caesar converted it into a principate? Who knows who Adam Smith was; what the invisible hand was; and the name of the book he wrote. It would be interesting to see the statistics on who read *The Federalist Papers*, *Common Sense* or *The Wealth of Nations* versus the *Communist Manifesto*, *Mein Kampf* or *Rules for Radicals*. We embrace our critics and ignore our architects—not conducive to long term survival.
- *Free Speech and Open Critique*—Freedom of speech is an American core value that forms the foundation of Democracy and needs to be safeguarded at all costs. It needs to be jealously guarded. America also needs to reduce libel claims designed to intimidate and bankrupt rather than win by setting a higher standard for accepting charges and implementing loser pays rules for defamation harassment. Political cartoons and stories should never be forced to delete from publication and books deemed to be politically unfavorable due to legitimate criticism of Islamism. should never be removed from libraries. If *Mein Kampf* and *TheCommunist Manifesto* can be published and found in libraries, *America Alone: The End Of The World As We Know It* can be published and found on library shelves.
- *Honor History*—Tell the truth. Education should be information not

indoctrination. It should not cater to ideology, moral equivalence, or equivocation. Education should not cave to revisionism. The Red Scare was comparable to a Stalinist purge. America's westward expansion was not like Hitler's eastward expansion. American Slavery was not like the Holocaust. Tell the truth, provide context, and honor scope and scale. Americans are far too generous with specious comparisons that dishonor reality. While we should not slander our own past we should also refrain from whitewashing others past.

- *Sharia*—America cannot tolerate the slightest Sharia creep. America should not allow any form of Islamic finance, sanctioned wife beating, hate spewing Imams, anti-Semitic and anti-Christian textbooks, Sharia courts, gay bashing, infidel raping, fatwa's or Sharia Zones-all zones are Constitution zones. Since the U.S. has so many judges tempted to apply foreign laws and cultural norms, broad voter support of anti-Sharia laws is critical. America doesn't tolerate Mosaic Law and resists posting the Ten Commandments in Courthouses (a legitimate source of western jurisprudence.) There should be no tolerance for the infiltration of the intolerant religious legal code known as Sharia?

- *Dhimmitude*—The notion that Muslims are 'special' and must be catered to flies in the face of western equality. Halal food should not be foisted on non-Muslims; they can get their Halal food the same way Jews get Kosher food. Grocery clerks shouldn't be allowed to refuse to handle pork products. If a job violates Muslim sensitivities then get another job. There shouldn't be any taxpayer funded footbaths. How is it that Christian crosses are being removed from public property while Muslim accoutrements are being installed? NASA should focus on space not Muslim outreach. There should be no special privilege; no 'sanitized' curricula or college chairs; and no madrassas in using their own textbooks. Muslims in America need to go to schools that adhere to the same standards the rest of us follow. There shouldn't be any Islamberg enclaves that practice their 'faith' in defiance of U.S. Law just as there are no legal Mormon communities practicing polygamy. America should not tolerate intolerance or allow fund raising for

Hamas, Hizballah, or the Muslim Brotherhood. American's rights should be rooted in the Constitution not the Quran.

In April 2013 the Associated Press Stylebook eliminated ILLEGAL IMMIGRANT and ISLAMIST from the list of terms used in journalism. This kind of Orwellian 'memory hole' is symbolic of the wave of PC scrubbing of the lamentable truth.

Protect the Critics—America should not allow Islamist organizations like CAIR and the OIC to define hate-speech to isolate and silence legitimate critics. America needs legal definitions of Islamophobia, Judeophobia, and Christiphobia. Blasphemy against any religion is usually unnecessary but shouldn't be illegal. Clear definitions will protect the critics. The U.S. needs to be clear about the difference between informed critique and bigoted hate-speech. America should radically avoid politically correct censorship. Put Islamopohbia in its place: The FBI's 2009 *Hate Crime Statistics* report, released in 2010, reports that the majority of hate crimes target Jews (72%) versus 8.4% against Muslims and 6.4% against Christians.

• *Support Troops and Cops*—America should not modify Law Enforcement Agency (LEA) training or documentation in response to Islamist pressure. The FBI shouldn't be focusing on Muslim outreach while purging 'offense' documents as defined by Islamists. Newspapers shouldn't ignore the religion or nationality of terrorists when reporting on attacks. The US has been transforming the Islamist terrorism into generic terrorism into 'man caused catastrophes' as if attacks are accidental. The DHS should not be warning that war vets and conservative political groups are likely terrorists while the Director of National Intelligence calls the Muslim Borhterhood secular and non-violent. Some celebrities have stated that Christian fundamentalists are as deadly as their Muslim cousins are. Does anyone remember the Christian terrorists who crashed planes into Istanbul killing nearly 3000 Muslims?

• *Trend analysis isn't profiling…or is it…and if it is…so what?*—If 90 of 100 terror attacks were conducted by Middle Eastern Muslim men, it would be illogical and unjust not to look for Muslim men while trying to interdict the next attack. Picking on 5 year old kids and 90 year old grandmas is an absurd and dangerous way to prove you're not prejudiced. The U.S. needs to be vigilant for new modes and means but until there's a drastic change in the demographics of terror—Middle-Eastern Muslim males remain the top prospect.

- *No Islamist Triumphalism*—A mega mosque at Ground Zero is not multicultural outreach, its Triumphalism. Muslims are not to blame for 9-11 any more than Christians are to blame Auschwitz but you don't build a Mosque at Ground Zero or a Cathedral at Auschwitz; it's a matter of respect and courtesy. While it's fair and just to respect other cultures, it's suicidal to venerate them above our own. Islamist misogyny, bigotry, and terrorvangelism are a global phenomenon right now. It's an Islamist Inquisition that seeks global purification and dominance. Now is not the time to venerate them while denigrating everyone else.

- *Back to the Melting Pot*—Islamists seek segregation not assimilation. They want to herd Muslim immigrants into seperatist enclaves where they can be indoctrinated and radicalized. New arrivals are discouraged from interacting with their new host nation and its people. They are told to get all the freebies they can in accordance with their Koranic right—infidels owe Muslims. These habits breed an enemy within. All wanna-be U.S. citizens should be required to assimilate by learning English and going to public school. They should integrate into our communities and obey our laws. If they aren't here to 'join the team' then they need not remain. Immigrant culture should not overwrite our culture. The customs they accept but we condemn, must be left at the door. The United States doesn't allow cannibalism, human sacrifice, suttee, or polygamy. Nor does it accept necrophilia, wife beating, misogyny, pedophilia, stoning, or honor killing. These customs cannot be imported with the immigrants.

- *Over-watch the Activists*—Free speech is allowed but hate speech and incitement are not. American Communists had to renounce the notion of violent overthrow of our government and Mormons drop polygamy. The veritable constellation of MB backed agencies must be watched. Their hidden agenda's cannot be allowed to the surface and their financial operations cannot be allowed to fund terrorism. Religious organizations in America conduct themselves in a prescribed way that the Muslim groups should be forced to emulate. America cannot allow these groups to use liberals, socialists, communists, secular humanists, postmodernists, and multiculturalists to aid in their attacks on free speech via political correctness. The U.S. cannot allow hypersensitivity to racism to shut down criticism. When Islamist activists cross the line, they need to be shut down as quickly as a KKK activist.

- *Detainees and Torture*—America must clarify how it will handle captured terrorists. This requires a new comprehensive legal regime. It also needs to clarify what torture really is and what it is not; as it sees it, not as they see it. If the US makes its position crystal clear, it will disarm a series of major issues exploited by Islamists.

- *U.S. Citizens or World Questions? Answers to questions Americans must consider*—Are we citizens of the world or are we Americans? Do we acknowledge American Exceptionalism or embrace European mediocrity? Do we acquiesce to International Law formed by unelected global elites, many of whom represent autocratic societies, or follow the precepts of the Declaration of Independence and the Constitution ratified by men who threw off the cloak of European mediocrity and fought to bring the dignity and freedom of man to light? If we are part of the Eurocentric cosmopolitan world then we can turn our backs on the efforts of the Forefathers to bring freedom nine generations ago and submit to multiculturalism and moral relativism that elevates the terrorist to the status of freedom fighter. If not, then we can define this as an enemy to freedom and resist him.

The canary in the coal mine. Texas has always been one of America's proudest and most culturally aware states. I spent five years there as an Army brat and my Texas history classes are still vivid in my memory. Texans were proud of Sam Austin, David Bowie, Davy Crocket, and Sam Houston. Texas pride was palpable.

Today many Texas schools teach the Alamo as neutral. The foundational moral event that pitted a small Texas garrison against the full power of Santa Ana to buy time for Sam Houston has been reduced to a morally ambiguous stain—as if the current state of Texas might actually be better off as part of the failed Mexican state. A heroic tale of self-sacrifice is being morphed into a perverted tale of racist bigotry.

A Texas local school system is taking advantage of a U.S. Department of Education grant that provides millions of taxpayers' dollars. To collect the cash, the schools have to teach Arabic as a second language and must present students with Muslim cultural courses. The program describes Arabic as 'the language of the future' thus implying the death of English and its parent western civilization. Are American schools preparing American children for *dhimmitude*?

Cultural Suicide. The west may be temporarily invulnerable to a direct military attack but it is exceedingly vulnerable to ideological infiltration and sabotage via legalistic maneuvering. Westerners don't understand Islamists because its modern secular culture doesn't identify with their medieval sectarian culture. The Islamists, on the otherhand, do understand us. They live among westerners; they go to school here; and have built enclaves among westerners. While the West rejects the essence of who they are—they embrace the essence of who westerners are. Westerners can't reconcile their opposing worldviews so Americans deny the void exists and go on the offensive. There is very little to draw westerners to Saudi Arabia, Iran, Syria, Yemen, or Pakistan but prosperity, representative government, and generous freebies are temptations that draw the Islamists to the U.S., the UK, and Europe.

****

The Danish cartoon controversy began in September 2005. It began when an author announced that he could not find anyone to illustrate a book about Mohammed. They were afraid of Muslim backlash since Islam considers it blasphemy to depict Mohammed. In response, the *Jyllands-Posten* newspaper ran twelve cartoons depicting Mohammed in defense of free speech and to initiate a public debate about the criticism of Islam and the dangers of self-censorship. The Mohammed 'bomb in the turban' cartoon by Kurt Westergaard was the most controversial cartoon. [232]

---

[232]*RIP: Free Speech about Islam*, by Adam Turner, American Thinker, 8 July 2012, http://www.americanthinker.com/articles/../2012/07/rip_free_speech_about_islam.html

It didn't take long for Islamists and politically correct pressure groups to take action. In October, several Muslim ambassadors requested a meeting with the Prime Minister to address their concerns about a perceived Danish smear campaign against Islam. At the same time, three thousand Danish Muslims demonstrated in Copenhagen, demanding an apology, and several Danish Muslim organizations filed suit against the *Jyllands-Posten*. Not to be left out, the Organization of the Islamic Conference (OIC) protested the cartoons as Islamophobic. Since 2005, there have been countless threats, plots, and/or attacks against the Danish:

- In 2005, a Pakistani Islamist party offered a reward to anyone who killed a cartoonist.
- In 2006, the Danish embassies were sacked in Damascus and Beirut.
- In 2008, the Danish Embassy in Islamabad was damaged in a suicide vehicle bombing. The bombing killed six people and wounded 30, mostly Pakistani Muslims.
- In 2009, following the arrest of U.S. citizen David Headley for planning the 2008 Mumbai attacks, American officials learned that Headley had also conducted surveillance in Denmark for an attack against *Jyllands-Posten*, with the codename of "The Mickey Mouse Project."
- In 2010, Danish police shot and wounded an Islamist at the home of Kurt Westergaard. The Islamist broke down the front door with the axe, before being stopped by the door to a panic room. Luckily, neither Westergaard nor his five-year-old granddaughter was harmed. Although sentenced to nine years in prison in 2011, the terrorist appealed the sentence, claiming that he was only trying to scare Westergaard to make him "stop bragging about drawing the cartoon." His sentence was subsequently affirmed.
- In 2011, three Norwegian Muslims were prosecuted for planning to bomb the offices of the *Jyllands-Posten*. On the first day of the trial, the prosecutors said the plot was planned with al-Qaeda in Pakistan, which is where one of the men had been trained.
- On May 28, 2012, Danish domestic intelligence services picked

up two Danish-Somali brothers suspected of plotting a terror attack in Denmark.

In the U.S., the *Washington Post* declined to run a *Non Sequitur* cartoon satirizing the media's fear of offending Islam based on "Where's Waldo" that used Mohammed in place of Waldo. *Comedy Central* censored *South Park* in response to threats over the show's intention to show Mohammed in 2006 and 2010.

****

A Pennsylvania judge dismissed charges against a Muslim man who physically attacked an atheist dressed as "Zombie Muhammad" during the Mechanicsburg, Pa. Halloween parade. A Maryland appellate court enforced a Pakistani sharia court custody judgment in favor of the father, even though the mother argued that she was denied due process; had she gone to Pakistan to contest the case she would have been subject to capital punishment for having a new relationship not sanctioned by sharia.[233] A study by the Center for Security Policy cites 50 appellate court cases from 23 states that involved decisions of lower courts that ruled in cases that appealed to sharia, many of which resulted in judgments in conflict with U.S. law.

The Center for Security Policy today released an in-depth study— *Shariah Law and American State Courts: An Assessment of State Appellate Court Cases.*[234] The study evaluates 50 appellate court cases from 23 states that involve conflicts between Shariah (Islamic law) and American state law. The analysis finds that Shariah has been applied or formally recognized in state court decisions, in conflict with the Constitution and state public policy.

Key Findings:

- At the trial court level, 22 decisions were found that refused to apply Shariah; 15 were found to have utilized or recognized

---

[233] *Shariaphobia*, by Richard Butrick, American Thinker, 25 June 2012, www.american-thinker.com/articles/../2012/06/shariaphobia.html.

[234] *Shariah Law and American Courts: An Assessment of State Appellate Court Cases*, Center For Security Policy; The Center For Security Policy Occasional Paper Series, 20 May 2011.

- Shariah; 9 were indeterminate; and in 4 cases Shariah was not applicable to the decision at this level, but was applicable at the appellate level.
- At the appellate Court level: 23 decisions were found that refused to apply Shariah; 12 were found to have utilized or recognized Shariah; 8 were indeterminate; and in 7 cases Shariah was not applicable to the decision, but had been applicable at the trial court level.
- The 50 cases were classified into seven distinct "Categories" of dispute: 21 cases dealt with "Shariah Marriage Law," 17 cases involved "Child Custody," 5 dealt with "Shariah Contract Law," 3 dealt with general "Shariah Doctrine," 2 were concerned with "Shariah Property Law," 1 dealt with "Due Process/Equal Protection" and 1 dealt with the combined "Shariah Marriage Law/Child Custody."
- The 50 cases were based in 23 different states: 6 cases were found in New Jersey; 5 in California; 4 each in Florida, Massachusetts and Washington; 3 each in Maryland, Texas and Virginia; 2 each in Louisiana and Nebraska; and 1 each in Arizona, Arkansas, Delaware, Illinois, Indiana, Iowa, Maine, Michigan, Minnesota, Missouri, New Hampshire, Ohio and South Carolina.

"I fear all we have done is wake up a sleeping giant and filled him with a terrible resolve."
—Admiral Yamamoto upon hearing of the successful attack on Pearl Harbor

COMMENTS AND OBSERVATIONS

- A bill was introduced in the House of Lords entitled "One Law for All" that would restore the supremacy of British law and deny the jurisdiction of the more than 75 sharia tribunals that have asserted authority over Muslim marriages, family law, and contract negotiations in the UK.
- When last we heard, the 9/11 hijackers did not chant "Shma Yisrael," "Hare Krishna," or "Jesus Saves," although "Allah akbar!" figured prominently in what was last heard from the doomed aircraft.
- The late Erbakan was the keynote speaker at a European "Brotherhood and Solidarity Day" in Arnheim, the Netherlands, during June 2002, he proclaimed triumphantly—if ominously—to his mainly Turkish audience of 23,000: "The whole of Europe will become Islamic. Like the army of the sultan we will conquer Rome."
- The CIA's *Book of World Facts* (and trends) doesn't even mention religion as a significant factor in politics
- A Civilizational jihad technique is **takiya**—deception. It is legal to lie to an infidel.
- During a 1974 Organization of the Islamic Conference meeting in Lahore, Pakistan, OIC general secretary Mohammed Hasan Mohammed al-Tohami highlighted two key related goals:

  (1) Urgent [convening] of a meeting of specialists in the propagation of Islam on a world level, and the establishment of a Jihad Fund...this fund is open with no restrictions ... in all fields of Jihad.

  (2) Caring for the affairs of cultural centers in Europe, and the establishment of [additional] cultural centers in the continent.

- Dutch filmmaker Theo Van Gogh was brutally assassinated on November 2, 2004 by a Dutch Muslim of Moroccan descent named Muhammad Bouyeri.

- Danish Muhammad turban bomb cartoonist Kurt Westergaard was chased around his home by an axe-wielding Islamic fanatic.
- Winston Churchill proclaimed Hitler's *Mein Kampf* to be *"the new Koran of faith and war: turgid, verbose, shapeless, but pregnant with its message."*
- Today, most Christians will tell you that the Inquisition was unacceptable but not many Muslims will dare to say that sharia is unacceptable.
- "We will be able to make a logical case for Auschwitz. As a lawyer, I know that any action can be defended." —SS Nazi Erik Dorf.

THE FOUNDERS AND ISLAMISM

In 1786, Thomas Jefferson, ambassador to France, and John Adams, ambassador to England, met with the emissary of the Islamic potentates of Tripoli to Britain, Sidi Haji Abdul Rahman Adja, regarding the demands for tribute being made at the time by the so-called Barbary Pirates.

Afterwards, Jefferson and Adams sent a four-page report to the Congress describing this meeting. The relevant portion of their report reads:

> We took the liberty to make some inquiries concerning the Grounds of their pretentions to make war upon Nations who had done them no Injury, and observed that we considered all mankind as our friends who had done us no wrong, nor had given us any provocation.
>
> The Ambassador answered us that it was founded on the Laws of their prophet, that it was written in their Qur'an, that all nations who should not have acknowledged their authority were sinners, that it was their right and duty to make war upon them wherever they could be found, and to make slaves of all they could take as Prisoners, and that every Musselman who should be slain in battle was sure to go to Paradise.

After this, Jefferson read the Quran in order to know his enemy. That knowledge of his adversary led to his doctrine of "Millions for defense, but not one cent for tribute." John Adams' son, John Quincy Adams, whose formative years coincided with the founding of the republic, offers further insights into the early presidents' views on this subject. Like many Americans, he took an oath to uphold and defend the U.S. Constitution from all enemies, foreign and domestic. And, when faced with an Islamic enemy, he understood his obligation to be educated on the factual aspects of the principles, doctrines, objectives, jurisprudence and theology of shariah that comprised his enemy's threat doctrine.

John Quincy Adams' 136-page series of essays on Islam displayed a clear understanding of the threat facing America then—and now, especially from the permanent Islamic institutions of jihad and dhimmitude. Regarding these two topics, Adams states:

- …[Mohammed] declared undistinguishing and exterminating war, as a part of his religion, against all the rest of mankind….The precept of the Quran is, perpetual war against all who deny, that [Mohammed] is the prophet of God.
- The vanquished [dhimmi] may purchase their lives, by the payment of tribute."
- As the essential principle of [Mohammed's] faith is the subjugation of others by the sword; it is only by force, that his false doctrines can be dispelled, and his power annihilated.
- The commands of the prophet may be performed alike, by fraud, or by force.
- This appeal to the natural hatred of the Mussulmen towards the infidels is in just accordance with the precepts of the Quran.
- The document [the Quran] does not attempt to disguise it, nor even pretend that the enmity of those whom it styles the infidels, is any other than the necessary consequence of the hatred borne by the Mussulmen to them—the paragraph itself, is a forcible example of the contrasted character of the two religions.
- The fundamental doctrine of the Christian religion is the extirpation of hatred from the human heart. It forbids the exercise of it,

even towards enemies. There is no denomination of Christians, which denies or misunderstands this doctrine. All understand it alike – all acknowledge its obligations; and however imperfectly, in the purposes of Divine Providence, its efficacy has been shown in the practice of Christians, it has not been wholly inoperative upon them. Its effect has been upon the manners of nations. It has mitigated the horrors of war—it has softened the features of slavery—it has humanized the intercourse of social life.

The unqualified acknowledgement of a duty does not, indeed, suffice to insure its performance. Hatred is yet a passion, but too powerful upon the hearts of Christians. Yet they cannot indulge it, except by the sacrifice of their principles, and the conscious violation of their duties. No state paper from a Christian hand, could, without trampling the precepts of its Lord and Master, have commenced by an open proclamation of hatred to any portion of the human race. The Ottoman lays it down as the foundation of his discourse.

CHAPTER 10

iForce
Swarm-Troops

A Force for all Seasons
iForce Swarm Troopers

"Tell me what brand of whiskey that Grant drinks. I would like to send a barrel of it to my other generals."
—Abraham Lincoln

"You may not be interested in war, but war is interested in you."
—Leon Trotsky

Lincoln was lamenting the lack of adaptation in the Union Army during the Civil War while Trotsky was cynically reminding people that no matter how much people want to forget about it, war won't be forgotten.[235] When we're at peace, we'd better remember that the next war is just around the corner—like it or not.

Lincoln was wrestling with a reoccurring military frailty; the dogged determination to do things the way they're always done, even if they're not working. Trotsky was cynically addressing a broader societal issue; the refusal to acknowledge war until it becomes inescapable. Both problems wish away real problems; how to fight the fight you've got versus the one you want and how to prepare for the next fight.

The New Equation. The democratization of information access *plus* the proliferation of easily acquired and exploitable technology *times* the expanding ability to 'share' dreams and nightmares through social media *equals* a relatively dramatic change in warfare mixing conventional linear symmetric with hybrid non-linear asymmetric.

---

[235] *History in Quotations*, by M.J. Cohen and John Major; Cassell, 2004.

156

*info access + exploitable and accessible tech x social media = **hybrid war***

> * Note: Hybrid war includes; elements of conventional war like uniformed armies and terrain oriented battlefield clashes; elements of irregular war like guerillas and terrorism; and includes rogue elements like criminal cartels, militias, and stateless 'international' entities. The nature and threat composition of hybrid conflict is fluid. US forces on a hybrid battlefield must be ready and able to rapidly transition from conventional battles to COIN and counter terrorism to counter drug and weapons smuggling and counter corruption and back again.

Wiki-War accelerates and flattens threat adaptation and innovation to levels that cautions Americans not to repeat old habits of ending the fight, coming home, declaring victory, drawing down, and cashing in the 'Peace Dividend.' Adaptation, the adjustment to the environment and innovation, the introduction of something new is not unique to the west or the U.S. who were the best at it given the cultural tendency to critically analyze efforts. However, success breeds imitation and now the enemy is in the imitation mode using the proven success tools. The environment may not be more complex but it is more dynamic. Wiki warriors, state and/or stateless, can change their stripes, reemerge, and reinitiate conflict more quickly than America's Warsaw Pact opponents did. The U.S. can't stop preparing for war during relative peace when our enemies are wiki-warriors. The U.S. must use lulls, and that's all they are, to learn from past successes and failures. The U.S. has to keep a close eye on the enemy to see what they are up to and be ready to work around the clock just to stay even. The best way to keep the peace is to maintain and demonstrate our ability to *defend it*.

> *"There is no avoiding war; it can only be postponed*
> *to the advantage of others."*
> —Niccolò Machiavelli

We have to remember that adaptation and innovation goes both ways. It's not unique to the west or the U.S. although we used to be the best at it given our cultural tendency to critically analyze our efforts. Success breeds imitation and now the enemy does what we do, using the tools that we made. Before we go on we need to define what we mean by adaptation and innovation.

> **Adaptation**—adjustment to the environment
> **Innovation**—the introduction of something new

Given U.S. experience in Afghanistan, Iraq, Libya, Egypt, and around the world; it has collected a load of lessons, best practices, and lingering challenges. When Baghdad fell the conventional war ended and a hybrid war began; the U.S. didn't see it. The new fight included a media war, an info war, a guerilla war, a cyber-war, and a tribal war fought by insurgents, militias, foreign fighters, state proxies and terrorists. The fight in Iraq included nation building, security and stability, counter-terrorism and counterinsurgency.[236]   The threat went from tanks to improvised explosive devices (IED's). The battlefield became nonlinear, decentralized and distributed. This was a new paradigm, or more accurately a return to an old one. After 56 years of Cold War, the U.S. military was used to well-defined battlefields occupied by uniformed state armies even given the 10 year anomaly called Vietnam. The institutional military wasn't ready doctrinally or materially for the shift.

The military fought in the traditional way until it became untenable; then it adapted from the bottom up. This is natural since the tactical units are the ones fighting for survival. They are the ones most intimately engaged with the enemy. They see what's happening first hand rather hearing about it second hand through reports and dispatches. They adjust or perish. That's why the best solutions to emerge were developed and implemented by small units in the field.

Lessons learned are merely lessons observed until they are integrated into training, adopted by doctrine, and are translated into new equipment. Although the U.S. must change to accommodate the future; we cannot forget the past. Our military must adjust to meet the

---

[236] *A Revolution in Military Adaptation: The US Army in the Iraq War,* by Chad C. Serena, Georgetown University Press, September 2011.

new challenges but must not forget the old ones. Conventional war may be less likely for now but it remains the most dangerous threat. It's the low probability side of the problem; failure here would be catastrophic. In the short to mid-tem; the most likely threat is the stateless irregular or hybrid war. We currently can win the 'big' war we *want* but we need to win the messy 'little' war we'll likely *get*.

When facing a battlefield that defies traditional tactics, techniques and procedures (TTP), soldiers and Marines pursue trial and error experiments with non-standard solutions. When they are up to their necks in alligators and needed to find a way out. Solutions that didn't work were discarded and ones that did were shared. Emergent solutions developed by small units made their way up the chain of command where they were embraced by operational leaders. Ad hoc solutions became theater TTP.

From Learning Lessons to Implementing Them

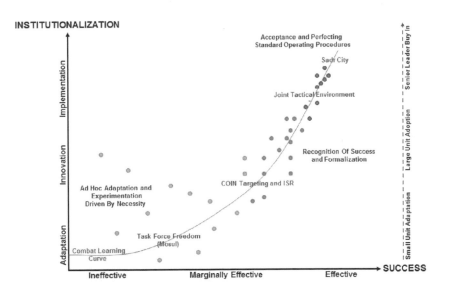

It's time to analyze and institutionalize workable solutions that have broad application. Solutions that appear to be episodic should be captured as case studies for implementation if and when similar circumstances arise again in the future. History repeats itself so archiving esoteric adaptation is useful.

Now, more than ever, armies that excel are ones that adapt and innovate. The reason I say *now more than ever* is due to the pace of adaptation among wiki-warriors. Islamist Jihadis have graduated from hijacking planes in the 70's to hijacking revolutions in the 10's. When defeated on the battlefield, Islamists attack from within by using trusted insiders to gun down their western partners. When lacking technologically guided precision munitions, they employ; suicide/homicide bombers. When lacking air defenses they pile 'human shields' on top of targets. All these challenges defy standard TTP's developed to counter the Soviet Army. They require new and creative approaches.

A famous western strength is introspection and critical analysis. We indulge in self-criticism and reflective analysis almost compulsively. This western idiosyncrasy has served us well.[237] Many, if not most, cultures avoid self-criticism. They deny self-induced failure. Saddam Hussein denied his failures after his disastrous defeat in Operation Desert Storm and Hamas did next to nothing to adjust to the thumping they too in Operation Cast Lead. If shortcomings are ignored the set-up is for disaster as described by Cohen and Gooch.[238] The U.S. acknowledged its shortfalls in Iraq, albeit grudgingly. It chose a new commander (General Petraeus) and executed a new strategy (theSurge) in 2007-08. In Afghanistan the U.S. plugged in Provincial Reconstruction Teams (PRT's) and executed Village Stability Operations (VSO) in addition to pursuit of traditional counterinsurgency (COIN). The new, deeper, approach improved the situation. The improvement drove the development of a new threat approach; insider shootings.

The U.S. collects lessons but is often slow to codify them and is reluctant to acknowledge that change might be more than episodic. To deny their potential permanence is to defer meaningful change. The conventional model is comfortable. It's been the basis for our force design, equipment purchases and war fighting doctrine for decades. It led to battle-field victory and helped win the Cold War. It's been the basis for R&D and acquisition of sexy, big ticket, hardware. The U.S.

---

[237] *Carnage and Culture: Landmark Battles in the Rise of Western Power*, by Victor Hanson, Doubleday, August 2001.

[238] *Military Misfortunes: The Anatomy of Failure in War*, by Eliot A. Cohen and John Gooch, Free Press NY, 1990.

likes our very visible Cold War tanks, fighter jets and combat divisions. We have been less enamored with our less lethal Special Forces, infantrymen, drones and brigade combat teams (BCTs). The problem is that, for now, our enemies can't and won't face those conventional tanks and fighters.

****

The most relevant since 2002 came from the tactical level in places like Mosul, Fallujah, Al Anbar in Iraq and Sangin in Afghanistan. The changes migrated from the *bottom up* and happened in spite of head-quarters rather than because of them. Fortunately, the upper echelon commanders endorsed and proliferated the innovations throughout the theater. It's time to codify the lessons for development and refinement. Here's a snapshot of some big ideas...

> *Our strategic focus needs to change.* The U.S. strategic focus needs to change. The Cold War emphasis on conventional war (CW) and nuclear war (NW) is outdated. These types of war are far from obsolete but in today's world, they are the exception rather than the rule. They are the most dangerous types of war. The U.S. must retain the ability to win them but should not exclude preparation for irregular war (IW) or hybrid war (HW) yet to be fully defined. It must prepare for the most likely and most dangerous.
>
> *Foster Joint Adaptation and Innovation.* The Army, Navy, Air Force, Marines and Special Forces learned a lot about working together in ways that didn't fit the doctrinal mold. The U.S. must capture and refine the collaborative tools and teaming techniques that were designed on the battlefield. It needs to preserve small unit leader's ability to employ operational and strategic assets that previously were only used by Colonels and Generals athigher echelons. It takes a network.
>
> *It takes a network.* Conventional war organization is vertical and hierarchical. We need flat, self-tasking, networked and distributed organizations to pursue IW/HW. The new model needs to make strategic and operational assets available to tactical units. It is nec-

essary to reverse the flow of plans, intelligence and combat supportflow from top down by request to bottom up on demand, directly to tactical leaders that have ground truth. Small unit leaders know what's happening on the distributed battlefield versus a dispersed enemy who leaves little or no signature. Efforts to find, track, and engage them must be led from the front rather than the rear.

Hives. Collaborative and purposive combat units enabled by knowledge fusion, and intelligence, planning, and target sharing retain the flexibility and responsiveness to strike fleeting targets. They are empowered to act without seeking permission. They gather, exploit, share and act on the intel they gather on their own. The units are dispersed and semi-autonomous and are propelled by a shared vision that frames their actions and allows missions to be 'handed off' from one unit to another.

Swarms. The hive-mind facilitates tactical 'swarms' to form against emerging and elusive targets. Collaboration and sharing allows tactical units to converge where they are needed when they are needed. If unit A's high value individual (HVI) appears in unit B's sector, a quick exchange of digital chat messages allows A to strike it or track it for B. neither must 'go up the chain' for permission.

Super-Empowered Tactical Units (iForce). A key to successful swarming is tactical access to strategic and operational assets once reserved for brigade, division and corps commanders. Squads, platoons and companies need immediate access to and direct control of operational ISR, close air support, and precision strike munitions. BCT's should be *Micro-Joint Task Force's* (MJTF).

The 'New Model Insurgent' or Techno-Guerilla or, in its most advanced form, iGuerilla is the latest iteration of the stateless enemy. The terrorist / guerilla evolved from the nomadic bands of wild eyed, AK toting, bush stalking hit-men to tech savvy, lethal, networked paramilitary groups carrying top shelf equipment. They are relatively well trained and, in most cases, are sectarian. The Katyusha multiple rocket launcher replaced the AK47; the network replaced the cell; and the

Holy Book replaced the Little Red Book. The threat has attained state-like destructive capacity and martial discipline while retaining non-state and proxy invisibility. The U.S. has solved the motorized rifle regiment (MRR) but has yet to solve the Islamist VEO.

Are U.S. forces Adapting?   The short answer is yes. The real question is whether it will retain and implement what is learned. The bulk of meaningful adaptation emerged in Iraq between 2006 and 2010; in Afghanistan it occurred between 2007 and 2011.

> **OPERATION CYCLONE.**   The U.S. supported the Afghan resistance against the Soviet invasion in a manner that introduced the Techno-Guerilla.[239]
>
> **OPERATION JAWBREAKER.**   Special Forces, conventional forces, and other government agencies (OGA), integrated to unseat the Taliban.[240]
>
> **OPERATION AL FAJR / PHANTOM FURY.**   The second major combat operation in Fallujah in 2004 was joint (Marines, Army, Air Force, Navy), combined (Iraqis), and used innovative information operations that protected civilians and isolated terrorist / insurgents.
>
> **MOSUL.**   Task Force Freedom inherited a disintegrating situation in Mosul and adapted by adopting shared and collaborative operations. They tied strategic and operational assets directly to tactical units. Units under different headquarters and in different sectors shared targeting and execution; a destabilizing practice during conventional linear war but a multiplier in irregular non-linear war.[241]
>
> **TEL AFAR.**   The clear, hold, build counterinsurgency strategy that was adopted and executed in Tal Afar reflected a deeper

---

[239] *Charlie Wilson's War: The Extraordinary Story of the Largest Covert Operation in History,* by George Crile, Atlantic Monthly Press, April 2003.

[240] *Jawbreaker: The Attack on Bin Laden and Al-Qaeda: A Personal Account by the CIA's Key Field Commander,* by Gary Berntsen and Ralph Pezzullo, Crown, December 2005.

[241] *Decade of War, Volume I; Enduring Lessons from the Past Decade of Operations,* Joint and Coalition Operational Analysis, June 15, 2015.

understanding of *'people's war'* and the adoption of a proven approach.[242]

ANBAR AWAKENING. U.S. forces in the hostile province of Al Anbar used Al Qaeda's brutality to turn the local tribes against the terrorists thus converting from adamant enemies to determined partners.

THE SURGE. MNF-I forces finally match tasks as it spreads counterinsurgency tactics, techniques, and procedures developed by tactical units throughout the theater.[243]

Adaptation and innovation has been excellent but episodic and reactive given U.S. failure to foresee the insurgency in Iraq, the Taliban resurgence in Afghanistan, the rise of AQAP in the Arabian Peninsulaand AQIM in North Africa and the resurrection of Al Qaeda as demon strated in Benghazi, Libya. [244] These (re)emergent threats weren't anticipated therefore the adaptation that occurred was forced upon the forces in contact. This kind of massive adaptation and innovation was symptomatic of the underestimation of the threat. These (re)emergent threats weren't anticipated therefore the adaptation that occurred was forced upon the forces in contact. This kind of massive adaptation and innovation was symptomatic of the underestimation of the threat.[245]

Adaptation and innovation are key attributes for a military to cultivate. It is necessary to analyze how they emerge and to preserve the mechanisms that enabled them. By institutionalizing the adaptation process then the next time when facing a hybrid threat adjustments will be systematic and proactive rather than reactive. [246] America owes it to

---

[242] *On War*, by Karl von Clausewitz, Howard Michael and Peter Paret editors and translators; Princeton University Press, 1984.

[243] *Resisting Rebellion: The History and Politics of Counterinsurgency*, by Anthony James Joes, University Press of Kentucky, September 2004.

[244] *Why Benghazi is a Crucial Strategic Moment*, by James Lewis, American Thinker, americanthinker.com/2012/10/why_benghazi_is_a_crucial_strategic_moment.html#ixzz29laGVK8Z, October 2012.

[245] *A Revolution in Military Adaptation: The US Army in the Iraq War*, by Chad C. Serena, Georgetown University Press, September 2011.

[246] *Decade of War, Volume I; Enduring Lessons from the Past Decade of Operations*, Joint and Coalition Operational Analysis, June 15, 2015.

its military to prepare them to adapt to succeed rather than forcing them to adapt to survive.

****

The U.S. should formally recognize four *levels of war* versus the traditional three levels. Each level defines motivation, scope, and scale while framing aims, ends, means, and ways.

National Strategic Level—This level is where the state determines its aims and identifies the type of forces required to achieve them. Switzerland's aim is to protect its borders. A small defensive forceis all that is required to guard the narrow passes into the homeland. Hitler's Germany wanted 'lebensraum' which required a massive offensive capability; the *Wehrmacht*. When the U.S. focused on the USSR and war in Europe it needed a large conventional force. Now that it faces a myriad of hybrid forces and non-linear battlefields, it needs a more diverse and joint capable mix of conventional and Special Forces. National strategy is the purview of the President and Secretary of Defense.

Theater Strategic Level—This level is where the Combatant Commander reconciles national strategic, global, aims with geographic, regional, aims. During WWII the U.S. had two major theaters: Europe and the Pacific. One required land formations under a land commander and the other required amphibious and naval forces under a naval commander. Today the U.S. has several theaters, each assigned to a Geographic Combatant Command (GCC). (GCC). Each Combatant Command (CCMD) must design a strategy for its region that supports the National Military Strategy (NMS), is synchronized with the other Combatant Commands and addresses the specific challenges of its geographic region of responsibility. The relative peace in European Command (EUCOM) means they can get by with fewer resources while the constant tumult in Central Command (CENTCOM) demands lots of resources. The National Security Council (NSC) must harmonize the CCMD's theater strategy.

Operational Level—This is where Joint Task Force Commanders (Flag officers who command forces that include units from all services; Army, Navy, Air Force, Marines) link theater strategy to tactical actions by planning major operations and campaigns. These plans link a series of tactical objectives over time, space and purpose to achieve operational objectives that contribute to strategic objectives. Campaigns avoid tactical battles that are irrelevant to the desired outcome or end state. Operational commands like MNF-I in Iraq and ISAF in Afghanistan design operations in support of Combatant Commander's theater strategy.

Tactical Level—The tactical level is the most celebrated and familiar level of war. This is where battles and engagements are fought. Cumulative tactical successes drive towards the attainment of an operational objective that, in turn, drives towards the attainment of a strategic objective. Tactics include engagements and battles. An engagement is a single armed clash while a battle is a series of related engagements. Tactics is the purview of front line units in direct contact with the enemy.

For Example… To illustrate how the levels of war inter-relate we'll take an anecdote out of the American Civil War. President Lincoln's national strategy was to prevent the Confederacy from seceding from the union. He saw control of the Mississippi River as "key" and stated he needed that key in his pocket—National Strategy. The Western Department, ultimately commanded by US Grant, pursued a two pronged approach that integrated Naval, Riverine, and Army forces targeting New Orleans and Baton Rouge in the South while eliminating Confederate forts along the river from the North—Theater Strategy. Grant commanded the main effort whose objective was the seizure of Vicksburg, the fort that commanded the river more than any other—Operational Campaign. Over a period of eight months, Grant methodically prosecuted a number of engagements and battles from Chickasaw Heights to Champion Hill en-route to the Siege of Vicksburg, an operational objective. The seizure of Vicksburg achieved control of the Mississippi River, both a theater and national objective.[247]

In the immediate future, we can expect the four levels of war to engage in fewer conventional contests and more irregular contests. We face an increase in insurgency and a need for counterinsurgency expertise. The move away from conventional, linear, state on state warfare and the move towards irregular/hybrid, non-linear, state on stateless warfare will increase the overlapping of the levels of war. In fact, the levels of war may well become nested. A Mi Lai or Abu Ghraib, although unacceptable, would have no impact on WWII while they can absolutely derail U.S. national interests in Iraq or Afghanistan. The 'strategic corporal' and the 'three block war' are manifestations of the small wars of insurgency and counterinsurgency.[248] The threat to the nation in these wars is insidious rather than overt therefore, the public's tolerance for bad news is lower. Tactical actions can have strategic implications.

Insurgency—An insurgency is a political or sectarian militaristic struggle carried out by a covert organization(s) seeking to subvert or overthrow a sitting government. Insurgents seek to dominate state resources and influence the population. Insurgent methods include guerilla warfare, terrorism, political mobilization, propaganda, and media exploitation. The insurgent seeks to emplace an alternative government. The insurgency is the contest between the insurgent and the state for the popular support.[249]

Counterinsurgency (COIN)—COIN is the combination of actions taken to defeat an insurgency including; political, security, economic, and information operations. COIN seeks to reinforce government legitimacy while reducing insurgent influence. The military plays a supporting role to political action. Protection of the population and reduction of violence

---

[247] *Grant Wins the War: Decision at Vicksburg*, by James R. Arnold, Wiley, October 1997.

[248] *The Strategic Corporal: Leadership in the Three Block War*, by Gen. Charles C. Krulak, Marines Magazine, January 199.9

[249] *Insurgency & Terrorism: Inside Modern Revolutionary Warfare*, by Bard E. O'Neill, Brassey's (UK) Ltd, November 1990.

is critical. Reinforcing government institutions while address-ing legitimate grievances allows the state to isolate and margin-alize the insurgents politically, socially, and militarily.[250]

ARMIES ADAPT IN RESPONSE TO DILEMMAS. From 1914 to 1917 the armies of Europe faced a deadly *dilemma*—the trench-es, presaged by the American siege of Petersburg. Massive armies faced off on fronts without flanks. Europe's armies were reduced to bloody frontal assaults that resulted in staggering body counts and gains meas-ured in yards. Morale plummeted and leaders struggled for solu-tions.[251] Both sides trotted out a parade of silver bullets that mostly failed. The initial solutions were techno-wonders like chemical weapons, flamethrowers, airplanes, and the tank. Other innovations included shoulder fired automatic weapons and light mortars. Other approaches included the intentional bloodletting of Verdun and the attempted starvation of the U-boat offensive and the allied blockade. The allies tried to go around the trenches by opening new fronts at Gallipoli, Salonika, and Italy but the carnage continued.

The real adaptation came from the German side of the Eastern Front and the innovators were Erich von Ludendorf, Max von Hoffman, and Georg Bruchmuller.[252] They didn't have the luxury of

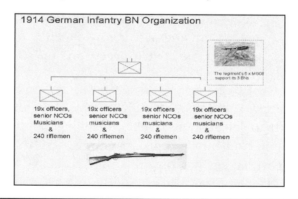

[250]*Resisting Rebellion: The History and Politics of Counterinsurgency*, by Anthony James Joes, University Press of Kentucky, September 2004.

[251]*The First World War*, by John Keegan, Vintage, May 16, 2000.

[252]*Steel Wind: Colonel Georg Bruchmuller and the Birth of Modern Artillery*, by David T. Zabecki, Praeger, December 1994.

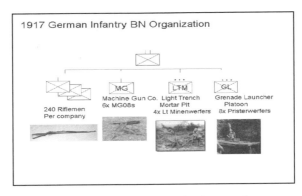

1917 German Infantry BN Organization

240 Riflemen Per company

Machine Gun Co. 6x MG08s

Light Trench Mortar Plt 4x Lt Minenwerfers

Grenade Launcher Platoon 8x Pristerwerfers

pursuing technological solutions. They had to seek non-material solutions. They built new organizations and designed new training. They re-distributed equipment and developed new tactical and operational concepts. The infantry battalion was redesigned and high echelon weapons were pushed down to squads led by sergeants trained to lead autonomous units.

Generals no longer led troops crashing through the lines; they followed them through as gaps were found. Fronts narrowed and artillery went from the traditional and monotonous weeklong barrage to an intense hour-long prep. Ops were decentralized down to the rifle squad which became a combined arms formation. The new formations were equipped with machine guns, grenadiers, and flamethrowers. The new Stosstruppen or Stormtroop did not lead charges across no man's land; they slipped through enemy lines and pulled the main body behind.

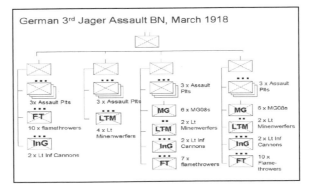

German 3rd Jager Assault BN, March 1918

3x Assault Plts

FT 10 x flamethrowers

InG 2 x Lt Inf Cannons

3 x Assault Plts

LTM 4 x Lt Minenwerfers

3 x Assault Plts

MG 6 x MG08s

LTM 2 x Lt Minenwerfers

InG 2 x Lt Inf Cannons

FT 7 x flamethrowers

3 x Assault Plts

MG 6 x MG08s

LTM 2 x Lt Minenwerfers

InG 2 x Lt Inf Cannons

FT 10 x Flame-throwers

The new approach succeeded but the Germans couldn't exploit it—they lacked reserves. The shift from command push (Befelstaktik) to recon pull (Auftragstaktik) was too little too late but became the foundation for Blitzkrieg, linking the tanks of Cambrai with the infiltration of 1918.[253]

In the 1790's the French Republic was surrounded by hostile monarchies determined to smother the new Republic. The *dilemma* was how to meet so many threats from so many directions and the innovation was the *levee enmasse* that enabled the creation of the nation at arms.[254] Likewise, in the 70's and 80's the U.S. faced a Soviet military that had technological and numerical superiority in Europe. The Fulda dilemma led to Airland battle, which linked the tactics to the operations.[255] Adaptation and innovation are standard fare when war doesn't go the way we planned.

Korea brought the helicopter for MEDEVAC and Vietnam expanded it to troop carrier giving birth to vertical envelopment.[256] We adapt.

CAN A STATE FIGHT CONVENTIONAL WAR (CW) *AND* IRREGULAR WAR (IW)? Some argue that a conventional army trained for CW can obviously fight and win IW. This view is problematic; see Arminius versus Varus', Alaric versus Stilicho or the Hoche versus the Vendee.[257] [258] [259] Today the U.S. military struggles

---

[253] *The Dynamics of Doctrine: The Changes in German Tactical Doctrine during the First World War,* by Timothy Lupfer, Combat Studies Institute US Army Command and General Staff College, July 1981.

[254] *The Harper Encyclopedia of Military History Fourth Edition,* by R. Ernest Dupuy and Trevor N. Dupuy; Harper Collins, 1993.

[255] *In Pursuit of Military Excellence: The Evolution of Operational Theory,* by Shimon Naveh, Routledge, March 1997.

[256] *Pleiku: The Dawn of Helicopter Warfare in Vietnam,* by J. D. Coleman, St Martins Mass Market Paper, February 1989.

[257] *The Lessons of Terror: A History of Warfare Against Civilians,* by Caleb Carr, Random House Publishing Group, January 2002.

[258] *The Grand Strategy of the Roman Empire: From the First Century A. D. to the Third,* by Edward Luttwak, Johns Hopkins University Press, February 1979.

[259] *Resisting Rebellion: The History and Politics of Counterinsurgency,* by Anthony James Joes, University Press of Kentucky, September 2004.

to fight IW while maintaining CW capabilities. The Israelis also struggled to apply an IW skill during the 2nd Lebanon War in 2006 as well. It seems a CW military struggles in an IW environment and an IW military struggles in a CW environment. We had time to do adapt while the IDF didn't.

The issue today isn't an either or proposition. Not only do modern state militaries have to maintain proficiency in both environments; they must be prepared to do them sequentially at best or simultaneously at worst. You can either build specialty units that do one or the other or train general purpose to do both. The first choice is a manpower issue and the second choice is a training issue and both require multiple sets of equipment.

Can a generic military dominate conflict in both environments? Probably not. Overt *conventional war* typically is a series of armed clashes between state militaries on the behalf of their state leadership. *Irregular warfare* is a cover to semi-covert clash between state militaries and non-state entities and/or extra-state proxies employing asymmetric modes of conflict. Non state *soldiers* didn't wear 'regular' uniforms and were thus called irregulars. Irregulars are weaker than their state counterparts so they avoid direct firepower based confrontation and large scale combat. Their relative weakness forces them to pursue small scale, hit and run, indirect combat and protracted warfare.[260] Their tactics are a blend of guerilla hit and run and terrorist subversion and coercion. Insurgents don't 'choose' to fight this way—they have to fight this way.

Mao's three phases of insurgency are as relevant today as the day he put them to paper.

> **Phase 1** focuses on building the *political organization* needed to establish a base that can win popular support or coerce general indifference.
>
> **Phase 2** is the *transition to guerrilla warfare* where the insurgents use irregular tactics and terrorism to challenge the state. The goal is to harass, disrupt, and propagandize in order to weaken

---

[260] *Invisible Armies: An Epic History of Guerrilla Warfare from Ancient Times to the Present*, by Max Boot, Liveright Publishing, January 2013.

resolve and consolidate power. Territorial conquest is irrelevant during this phase.

Phase 3 begins once the insurgency gains enough momentum and support the *transition to conventional warfare*; the conventional war of movement involving large-scale battles and territorial seizure.

The wiki-war innovation to the above is the acceleration between phases. Wiki warriors empowered lethality and enhanced capability allows the insurgent to 'spike' sooner and more often. This creates a dilemma for the state since the commitment to conventional war is a major and often irrevocable decision. Too rapid a shift implies loss of control and the escalation of violence can be used to reinforce the insurgents.

The conventional and unconventional battlefields are worlds apart and transition is hard for state armies unprepared for it. The guerilla usually gets to set the tone so they are ready. Here's a compare and contrast to illustrate the challenge…

The CW battlefield is linear. Friendly and enemy territory is distinct and opposing armies are separate and identifiable. The IW battlefield is non-linear and non-contiguous. State and threat forces are interwoven in a mosaic that includes the non-combatant population. The guerilla force is dispersed and innocuous while the state army is concentrated and in uniform given its requirement to provide security for the non-combatants.

CW is fought on the strategic, operational and tactical levels with slight overlap. The military struggle overrides politics and is synchronized and mutually reinforcing. IW blurs the levels of war and subordinates the fight to political considerations. Tactical actions can have strategic implications and strategic actions can be irrelevant. An irrelevant but well publicized guerilla raid can strike a disproportionate blow to the state while a statewide tightening of security can provide a propaganda bonanza to the insurgents.

CW operations are centralized and executed in sequence by linking tactical objectives together over time and space to cumulatively achieve operational and strategic objectives. IW, on the other hand, is decentralized. Action is simultaneous and focused on small, tactical, units. Plans and intel flow from the bottom and are collaborative rather than directive.

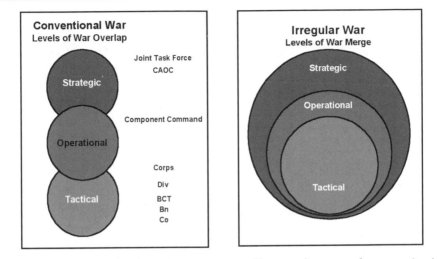

CW employs high tech recon to collect and target threat units in depth such as reserves and artillery groups. Divisions, Corps and higher control deep strike assets to hit high value targets to the enemy rear. There are no 'deep threats' in IW. The threat is everywhere and high value targets are guerilla leaders not rocket battalions. High tech recon has to support squad leaders in the fight who know where the enemy is. The targets are people and places. The rule of thumb for joint/operational/strategic recon and fires is: CW—easy to find, hard to kill. IW—hard to find, easy to kill.

In CW, captured soldiers are enemy prisoners of war (EPW) who are sent to the rear for interrogation. In IW, captured fighters are criminals or detainees who are interrogated forward since information is time sensitive making rapid exploitation critical. Linguists and interrogators go with small units rather than hanging out at HQ waiting for prisoners to arrive; they do their job forward and under fire.

In CW, air assets are centralized and directed from above. Attack sorties are massed to maximize the operational effect. There is no massing in IW. Air is tasked piecemeal in support of tactical units in the fight.

CW intel collection plans are made and prioritized at the top and execution is centralized to maintain optimal control. Intel collected at the top and pushed down; intel drives operations. In IW, the opposing forces are in close contact and the guerilla is an indistinct and fleeting target. Intel is collected at the bottom by troops in contact and is pushed up. Operations generate intel which triggers more operations in rapid succession. HQ can't even keep up when in a tight cycle. The fusion of operations and intelligence enables this accelerated execution cycle. The intel and ops functions must co-locate and collaborate and decision making authority must be pushed down.

THE UNITED STATES CAN ORGANIZE, TRAIN, AND EQUIP FOR CW AND IW. The *'Auftragstaktik'* of WWI was an example of decentralization and power down operations. Special weapons, and decision making occurred at the tactical level-the formula for modern IW. The U.S. Air- Land Battle bridged the gap between tactics and strategy by defining operations and introducing the shaping deep attack, adapting when the established solutions no longer worked.

The U.S. needs new approaches for hybrid war and has examined many. The U.S. has collected a decade of adaptation and innovation lessons in Iraq and Afghanistan and they must be the basis for new methods of war fighting.

The vacillating (CW-IW-HW) battlefield demands flexibility and agility that comes from units able to transition from conventional centralized command to irregular decentralized command. Units must be able to execute power- down decision making as autonomous units on a distributed battlefield.

The U.S. <u>must</u> also retain 'big war' conventional dominance. The future military must be agile enough to shift back and forth between conventional, irregular, and hybrid environments. International criminal cartels, iGuerilla's and their rogue state sponsors who will shift the nature of war to their advantage. The U.S. must respond with greater than or equal speed and competence. Lebanon 2006, Estonia 2007, Georgia-Russia 2008, Gaza 2009 and the Arab Spring 2010 from Tunisia to Syria are the 'new normal'.Aum Shinrikyo 1995, Los Zetas 1999, and Al Qaeda 2001 have added their services to the 'traditional' band of stateless outlaws Hizballah and the Muslim Brotherhood. Super empowered individuals like Viktor Bout 'the Merchant of Death' and AQ Khan 'the nuclear arms salesman' and super empowered groups like Anonymous, and Wiki-Leaks will proliferate and threaten society and stability around the globe.

The answer to this complex challenge emerged in Iraq from 2006 and 2009 when tactical units adapted by refining the ability to fight in multiple environments nearly simultaneously. The U.S. learned; how to decentralize command and control; how to rely on bottom-up intelligence collection and analysis; operate as a distributed force on a non-linear, non-contiguous, mosaic battlefield; how to employ air support at the tactical level; special and conventional force teaming; interagency integration; ops-intel fusion; and how to provide national strategic and joint operational support to tactical units. We did it in places like Mosul, Sadr City, and many others throughout Iraq and Afghanistan.

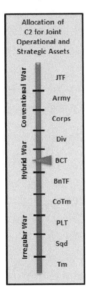

The U.S had developed autonomous, joint capable, tactical units. Leaders at battalion, company, platoon and even squad level became able to perform the tasks that were once carried out by Colonels and Generals at much higher levels of command. As the tactical units became proficient in the application of these expanded capabilities, the high commanders developed a rheostat mentality that allowed them to decide when and where and for what missions these tools should be pushed down-not all tactical units need joint capability all the time. We must preserve these gains even as our political and legal systems lag behind.

The Army accelerated prototyping and fielding of new COIN specific equipment that enhanced survivability and success. Following withdrawal from Iraq, there was a movement to dismantle and mothball the new gear, a mistake that would be criminally shortsighted and irreversible. Such a move would doom American forces to the drearily predictable process of 'relearning' lessons from the past at the onset of a new conflict. The proactive thing to do is to store the new equipment, like the MRAP, in contingency stockpiles that augment are conventional war stockpiles. The IW/HW contingency stocks could then be drawn upon occasionally for IW/HW training and exercises.

MOSUL 2004. Mosul was an island of stability in 2003, experiencing a relatively low number of insurgent attacks each week. The 101st Airborne Division (Air Assault) provided security at a ratio 1 sol-

dier for every 105 citizens. Early in 2004 the 101st headed home and was replaced by the much smaller force; TF Olympia. TF Olympia was a brigade sized unit about one third the size of its predecessor; the 101st. The move made sense since Mosul was relatively calm.

Things in Mosul began to change in fall 2004 with the coalition assault on the terrorist stronghold of Fallujah. Many of the terror leaders fled north to Mosul to escape the heat on Fallujah. Insurgent attacks increased four fold. TF Olympia was suddenly too small although it managed to keep the pot from boiling over.

Task Force Freedom (TFF) replaced TF Olympia at the end of 2004. TFF was comprised of a Stryker Brigade capable of achieving a ratio of 1 soldier for every 420 civilians. TFF faced a rapidly disintegrating situation with attacks escalating to as many as 150 per week. The local police were overwhelmed. They lost 27 police stations to insurgent attacks as TFF moved in. Task Force Freedom faced a stark situation and had to do something new to survive.

Synchronize - to cause to go on, move, operate, work, etc., at the same rate and exactly together.

Collaborate - work together on a common enterprise or project.

They partnered with the local special forces and internal security forces by sharing targets, intelligence, plans, and collaborating on missions. TFF improved their use of their tactical HUMINT teams (THT) and the special forces added to their flexibility by teaming with the infantry. Unprecedented levels of decentralization enabled bottom up execution of this new team effort. [261]

What was new was the unprecedented degree of sharing and collaboration. TFF and local SOF organized and coordinated horizontally rather than vertically. The new partnership was ground breaking. Information flow was flowed horizontally as opposed to the traditional manner where it goes up the chain to be analyzed by staff then handed back down. Breaking the hierarchical vertical information flow accelerated operations—key in a COIN environment where the enemy is elusive and fleeting. Adoption of Internet Chat allowed small unit leaders to directly communicate and collaborate across units, echelons, and

[261] *Decade of War, Volume I; Enduring Lessons from the Past Decade of Operations,* Joint and Coalition Operational Analysis, June 15, 2012.

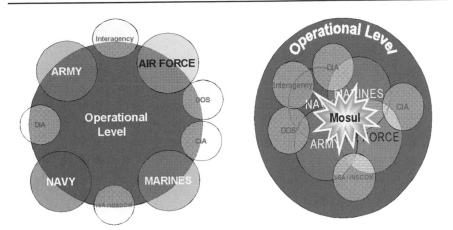

specialties. Sharing and collaboration lowered the threshold 'actionable intelligence'. Tips and successful missions triggered further action and exploitation. The immediate collection and dissemination of intel created a cascading mission effect since units could act on what they found without waiting on the go ahead from higher—cutting out the middle man. The role of HQ was to monitor the battlefield and provide timely support.

The integration of tactical, operational, and strategic capabilities created shared awareness that enabled small unit collaboration and accelerated operating tempo. The streamlining of procedures coupled with shared plans allowed TFF to regain control of Mosul. Their actions spawned theater wide development of operations and intelligence fusion centers that facilitate replication of the techniques that made TFF successful.

THE JOINT TASK FORCE. When Americans go to war we bring the Army, Navy, Air Force, and Marines. Each service brings unique capabilities that are applied against the enemy. They are grouped in service or multi-service formations but are usually somewhat separate and distinct from one another. The Army and Marines fight in pure units in assigned zones or sectors with the Air Force, Naval Air, and Marine Air providing limited support. Airpower focuses on enemy air and ADA then infrastructure and the Navy focuses on enemy naval power, controlling on the sea lines of communications (SLOC), and dominating the coast line and littorals.

A task force (TF) is a temporary formation derived from a single service that is established to accomplish a defined task. An Army mechanized or armored task force is made up of a mixture of US Army armor and infantry units. A Marine Air Ground Task Force (MAGTF) is made of Marine armor, infantry, and air. Tactical warfare is usually fought by service task forces supported by specifically allocated amounts of airpower.

A joint task force (JTF) is a formation designated by high level authorities such as the Secretary of Defense or a combatant commander. The twist is that a JTF includes subunits from two or more of the services under a single command. Operational warfare is fought by joint task forces typically commanded by a flag officer.

THE HIVE MIND AND THE SWARM. The modern threat is a transnational terrorist *network*. It is adaptive, distributed, purposive and self-tasking. Our threat model has shifted or, more accurately, has grown. Land, air and sea dominance are critical but now we need *network dominance, information dominance, and media dominance*. We need a military network to defeat the terrorist network.

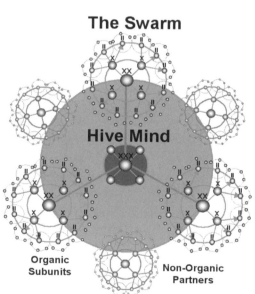

The military network must be collaborative, aware, proactive and distributed. The network needs to be illuminated by shared awareness and animated by a shared vision **(the hive mind)** that drives an initiative oriented, joint empowered, self-tasking tactical and operational force **(the swarm)**. [262] This is the iForce to oppose the iGuerilla.

[262] *Out of Control: The New Biology of Machines, Social Systems, & the Economic World*, by Kevin Kelly, asic Books, April 1995.

The iForce could be a *Micro Joint Task Force (M-JTF)*; a small tactical unit organized like a Joint Task Force with the access and skill to employ direct support from strategic and operational intelligence and targeting assets.

The Micro JTF should be interoperable and tailor-able; shaped to fit the characteristics of the area of operations. It would share command, control, and surveillance systems to generate a genuine common operating picture (COP). The Hive Mind uses *ops-intel fusion cells, joint interagency task forces (JIATF),* * *company intel centers (CIC), autonomous air operations centers, and joint targeting boards.* *A JIATF is a temporary grouping of inter-agency organizations in support of the assigned mission, which may include: DoJ, Border Control, USCG, DoS, LEA's...

The M-JTF would habitually maximize conventional-SOF partnering. Analysis, assessment, and exploitation is horizontally shared rather than vertically. Data flow will be as close to real time as possible. The legacy process used versus the motorized rifle regiment would not be tossed in the trash, just subordinated to the more immediate process needed to fight an elusive opponent on a non-linear battlefield.

Planning, targeting, and execution is decentralized and pushed down to small units empowered to self-task and respond to threats as

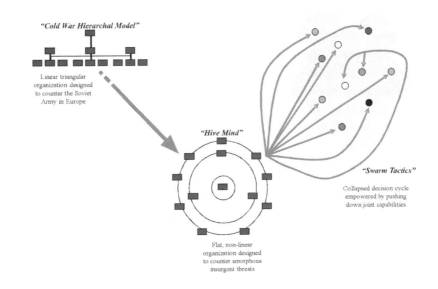

"Cold War Hierarchal Model"

Linear triangular
organization designed
to counter the Soviet
Army in Europe

"Hive Mind"

"Swarm Tactics"

Collapsed decision cycle
empowered by pushing
down joint capabilities

Flat, non-linear
organization designed
to counter amorphous
insurgent threats

they are identified (Swarm). Collaborative tools are pushed down and information is transportable across units and echelons. Trust, teamwork, and cross training will make the M-JTF a viable, versus ad hoc, organization.

The Hive and Swarm thrives on shared purpose, vision, and awareness. Each MJTF sub-units 'sees' what its partners 'see'. A common information system fuses joint capabilities to tactical forces while the hive mind provides motivation and direction and purpose without issuing specific operations orders as in CW.

A day in the life of the MJTF begins like a patrol day for the boys in blue on *Hill Street Blues*. Small unit leaders, or their representatives, assemble in person or virtually for 'the' daily brief where they get the lowdown on what's up in the AO. They find out who's wanted, what the local patterns are, and what to focus on for the day. Once they're 'spun up' they hit the street. When someone runs into a high value individual (HVI) or uncovers an IED factory during the course of their patrols; they fire up the comms and rally whoever is in the area and is uncommitted.

Operations and intelligence fusion is critical. The two feed off, and reinforce, one another. Intelligence triggers operations while operations uncover more intelligence. When they are effectively fused, tempo is increased and cascading operations executed by collaborative autonomous units is possible allowing the iForce to outpace the iG. Swarm leaders must be patient and trust of partner units and subordinates is essential. The leaders on the line must be ready and willing to act without permission. They must be purpose driven and initiative oriented.

So what's stopping us from building Hive HQ's and Swarm-Troops? The answer is; not much. We've been there and done that. We saw the prototype MJTF smother an insurgent network in Mosul eight years ago. It was a necessity driven innovation / adaptation brought on by the need to sink or swim. The TTP's were proliferated and were perfected over the following few years but have not been codified in doctrine or training yet; a required step to build the personal relationships, trust, and teamwork needed in the future. As we institutionalize the Mosul model we must keep in mind that these techniques

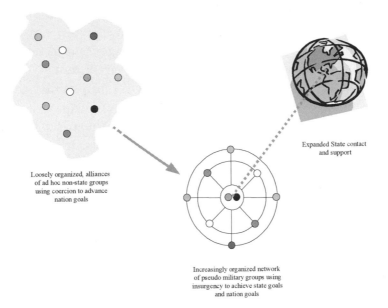

Loosely organized, alliances
of ad hoc non-state groups
using coercion to advance
nation goals

Expanded State contact
and support

Increasingly organized network
of pseudo military groups using
insurgency to achieve state goals
and nation goals

augment existing doctrine rather than as a replacement. Conventional war is not gone; it's just in waiting.

The hindrances to innovation are lack of cooperation and barriers to the flow of information between services. Incompatible systems coupled with institutional resistance can stymie the Hive and the Swarm. A single example can be found in the Air Force's desire to retain central control of airpower in order to mass it in accordance with the Master Air Attack Plan (MAAP)—the cold war TTP for air power. Many resist the decentralization and dispersal of airpower as seen in IW. We continue to allow ourselves to be victimized by our cold war paradigm. As stated; the IW/HW TTP's mentioned above are not to replace CW war fighting skills. They should augment them.

The MJTF cannot work under traditional hierarchical central command. It must be decentralized and networked across services and echelons. Commanders must be comfortable with relinquishing control to their tactical subordinates: its 1918 all over. Today's Stormtroops are Swarmtroops and we have excellent candidates for the MJTF in the Army's Stryker Brigades and Marine's Expeditionary Brigades. These units are already versatile and used to decentralized operations.

It's difficult to fight a distributed network with a centralized hierarchy. It's like using a sledge hammer to drive home a ten-penny nail. It's imprecise, messy, and causes the collateral damage we can't accept in a hyper-aware media driven world. Our cold war system is great for defeating nation-state's but, when the enemy is an iGuerilla network, the conventional system is too ponderous and must adapt.

We've gone from the Soviet leviathan trolling the world for proxies to sponsor to insurgent proxies looking for sponsors. It's a bottom up threat that requires a bottom up response. A series of geographically aligned standing MJTFs might be the answer. Each might have astanding fusion cell, air operations center, targeting board, and joint interagency team. The MJTF would build teamwork and expertise through career progression assignments and shared training. Human terrain teams and academia might provide regional databases that generate cultural awareness. The M-JTF would be multi-functional including non-combat missions like disaster relief, humanitarian assistance and support to domestic civil authorities. Forces could be aligned but not assigned; ie a Stryker brigade combat team may be on the list but not employed until a mission activates them. It's time to capture the adaptations and breakup the stovepipes to enable a new way of war fighting.

CHAPTER 11

Super-Empowerment
In-Defensible?

Embracing the Unthinkable
Counter SeG/SeT and Civil Defense (CD)

"We must try to find ways to starve the terrorist and the hijacker of the oxygen of publicity on which they depend."
—Margaret Thatcher

It's time to think the unthinkable and admit that the American homeland is vulnerable. Not since the height of the Cold War have the United States faced an enemy who is both able and willing to hit America. During WWII the enemy couldn't range the continental United States (CONUS). They struck on U.S. soil versus the Pacific Fleet in Hawaii. Once! During the Cold War a strike CONUS was tantamount to suicide given the doctrine of Mutually Assured Destruction (MAD). To hit the American homeland was to contemplate nuclear devastation.[263]

Today's Jihadi's outrange Nazi Germany and Imperial Japan exploiting global transportation thru open borders and, unlike the Soviet Russia, can strike the homeland cloaked in stateless anonymity. They are approaching the state like destructive ability through cyber war, dirty bombs (radiological dispersion device—RDD), chemical weapons, and biological weapons.[264] While they mutate and advance they can continue along the traditional line of bombings, massacres, and hostage taking. They can also surprise us in the short run with evolutionary bursts of 'progressive' attacks like Mumbai. Training can occur in Venezuelan Hezbollah training camps. They can stage in

---

[263] *Strategy in the Missile Age by Bernard Brodie*, Princeton University Press, February 1965.

[264] *Super Terrorism; Biological, Chemical, and Nuclear*, by Yonah Alexander and Milton Hoenig, Transnational Publishers, 2001.

Mexico under the cover of any of a number of drug cartels. They can find in-country safe houses through paid criminal gang surrogates such as M18 or MS13. They can launch shallow attacks against any of a number of vulnerable border communities or go deep into the heartland. Of course there are non Latin American (LATAM) routes such as the Canadian route used by the millennium bomber, the aerial route used by the shoe bomber, or the urban cell like the blind sheik, the Lakawana seven or the Fort Dix six not to mention the seaborne routes used by dope smugglers.[265]

The United States faces a full range of homeland defense scenarios.[266] Our response is in question given our politically correct, multicultural, denial of the religious imperative and the reality that there are people dedicated to our destruction. Will America rise to the challenge?

Back to the Future. During the 50's we acknowledged a possible Armageddon. America's willingness to think the unthinkable enabled it to take the steps required to defend ourselves. The United States dealt with the threat rather than not denying it.

Cold War tensions dominated the headlines. The movies were nuclear nightmares about radiated giant ants, spiders, and people. *Doctor Strangelove or How I learned to Love the Bomb* exposed our nuclear-alter ego. Kids got under school desks for nuclear duck and cover drills. Everyone knew what the black and yellow triangles meant and everyone watched the emergency broadcast Super-Chief TV tests. America didn't seek nuclear war but knew the enemy had a vote. Everyone took homeland defense seriously.[267] It is now time to dust off self-defense practices; catastrophic attacks against the homeland are possible again.

It took Bin Laden three years to pull off an attack on U.S. soil after his 1998 declaration of war against the Zionists and Crusaders. When it came, he hit America's first city and the capital killing nearly three thousand while generating images that captivated the world. Luckily, 9-

[265] *39 Terrorist Plots Against the U.S. Foiled Since 9/11*, research by Jena Baker McNeill, James Jay Carafano, and Jessica Zuckerman, Heritage Foundation, May 2011.

[266] *7 Deadly Scenarios: A Military Futurist Explores the Changing Face of War in the 21st Century*, by Andrew Krepinevich; Bantam Books, January 2009.

[267] *Makers of Modern Strategy from Machiavelli to the Nuclear Age*, by Peter Paret, Princeton University Press, March 1986.

11 set the bar too high. After a few years America suffers from amnesia and cynicism. Americans seemed to think it will never happen again or will be insignificant if it does. Both assumptions are dangerous.

The enemy—the Jihadi, Qutbist, Islamic fundamentalists—are scheming, researching, and testing ways to meet or beat 9-11.[268] The flurry of less than spectacular attacks America experienced since then, have not been significant but they demonstrate will. They are simply waiting for aspirations to align with means. Given the globalization of knowledge, commodities, and expertise—it seems to only be a matter of time.

The United States should guard against improvised explosive devices (IED's), homicide bombings, assassination, sniping, cyber terrorism and hacking, chemical attacks (sarin or ricin), nuclear attack (RDD's), and the big daddy, biological attack (anthrax or small pox). The US can detect some of these threats, deter others, and mitigate most. The first step is to acknowledge that a threat exists. Once the United States admits it and describes then it will be on the road to understanding, which reduces fear and enables the building of defenses.

Definition of Hybrids in the Homeland. The modern threat shifts back and forth between conventional and irregular techniques and can employ both simultaneously. The US has seen this play out on the battlefield but how does it play out at home? Today's Jihadis are not classic guerillas, terrorists, or criminals. They resemble a mixture of modern day commandos and latter day zealots. The Mumbai attackers used GPS and Blackberries to carry out a raid designed to inflict precise and maximum death and destruction.[269] They dropped bombs to mislead first responders, watched TV to track the reaction and torched hotels to glean media attention. The Mumbai terrorists took hostages and executed Infidels. They awaited their deaths, all the while being bolstered by their handlers in Pakistan via sat-phone. The handlers encouraged them when they were wavering, reminded them of their imminent trip to paradise. They kept them focused. They watched TV and waited for the hotels to burst into flames and when they didn't, they called the Mumbai operatives and urged them to get busy. Mumbai is

---

[268] *A Terrorist Call to Global Jihad*, by Jim Lacey; Naval Institute Press, 2008.

[269] *i Guerrilla Version 2.0 - The Terrorist and the Guerrilla Converge at Mumbai*, by John Sutherland, December 2008.

more likely to happen here than another 9-11 is. It's a headline hungry way to kill lots of people. Terror is a free market enterprise that flourishes given attention and media feedback. The iTerror techniques seen in Mumbai provide the Jihadi's with a way to bide their time until they can deliver a mass killing like 9-11.

Terror-Criminal Nexus. To maximize their capabilities, global terror networks are forming coalitions with regional and global criminal enterprises all around the world.[270] Drug cartels offer clandestine smuggling networks from South America to the U.S.. They offer access to gangs, counterfeiters, money launderers and funding. South American Coyotes who traffic illegal aliens can also traffic terrorists.[271] The criminals can provide underground services such as providing false ID's, weapons, safe houses and more. The criminals get cash and expertise for their support. Both benefit from chaos, they thrive in an environment of weakened governance. Both ignore boundaries and exploit state sovereignty to gain safe haven. The nexus of crime and terror enhances the attributes of both.

Although the American focus is on the Transnational Islamic Insurgency outside of its borders The US must remember that its involvement began with an attack within its borders. It must prepare for thenext strike. It is impractical to think that another 9-11 is impossible. The reality is that the world is full of terrorists seeking to kill infidels in large numbers and in spectacular ways and Americans aretheir favorite targets. Americans must decide how to respond.

The Problem. In 2004, Israel was successfully fighting rock throwing refugees in Ramallah and its main problem was concerned with best to isolate and eliminate key Palestinian militant leaders. By 2006 Israel faced a formidable paramilitary guerilla force the Hizballah, and by 2009, it faced a modernized Hamas in Gaza that learned in 18 months what Hizballah learned in 18 years. [272] This short tour through

---

[270] *Seeds of Terror: How Heroin Is Bankrolling the Taliban and Al Qaeda*, by Gretchen Peters, St. Martin's Press, May 2009.

[271] *Terrorist and Organized Crime Groups in the Tri-border area (TBA) of South America*, by Rex Hudson, a report prepared by the Federal Research Division, Library of Congress under an Interagency Agreement with the United States Government, July 2003.

[272] *Winograd Report: English Summary*, Joint Center for Operational Analysis Journal, Volume X; Issue 1, December 2007.

the Levant illustrates the problem—the evolution of terror and insurgency from local movements to tech savvy paramilitary super empowered guerillas and terrorists. The problem is the Darwinian Jihad which is the proliferation of biological, chemical, nuclear, and cyber knowledge, equipment, and personnel, coupled with a declining costs and a reduction in barriers to access. This combines to make mass (disruption or destruction) likely in the near future.

Counter SeT—A Way Ahead. It's time for the U.S. to resurrect its erstwhile Civil Defense and to update it. The Jihadi's are more likely to attack America than the Soviets were since they don't have need to fear nuclear annihilation. The United States needs its our own hybrid—a mixture of Cold War Civil Defense, super-SWAT, INTERPOL, and Elliot Ness' Untouchables. Lets break it down...

Areas of Operation and Concern. Although the campaign is local, the effort is global.[273] Each area is a concern and requires its own strategy, one that is nested into the overall strategy.

- The homeland: Civil Defense begins here, in the US and inherently must also cover the Canadian and Mexican borders.
- Latin America (LATAM) is the terrorists chief conduit into North America with its plethora of Cartels, ungoverned spaces (Tri-Border Area: TBA), criminal enablers and a growing coalition of hostile and willing sponsor states like Venezuela.[274]
- Europe: It is necessary to monitor Europe, it is a prime source of information, technology and 'white' Islamist recruits. This portion of the campaign requires close cooperation between domestic law and intelligence services and European ones to include INTERPOL.
- Africa: The problem in Africa is the proliferation of ungoverned spaces, poverty inflamed recruitment, blood diamond funding, and exploitable tribalism.
- The Middle and Far East: These areas are the hub of Islamism

---

273 *A Terrorist Call to Global Jihad*, by Jim Lacey; Naval Institute Press, 2008.

274 *Fears of a Hezbollah presence in Venezuela: the World The Lebanese militia may be using Chavez's ties with its ally Iran to expand its network, terrorism officials say,* by Chris Kraul and Sebastian Rotella, LA Times, August 27, 2008.

with the greatest density of Muslims being found in Indonesia. The Muslims of the Middle East harbor the most virulent sects while the Muslims of the Far East remain largely moderate—a trend we need to nurture.

- Russia, North Korea, Iran, Syria, Venezuela, China (Axis of Instability): These states are the world proliferators, enablers, and terror sponsors who see any diminution of the west as advantageous to their regional and global aims.

The above listing illustrates that for Civil Defense to work, it must be a component of an American global strategy much as Cold War Civil Defense was. The U.S. 'contained' communism abroad and in South America, actively opposed it domestically when sponsored by the Soviets, applied political and economic pressure where necessary, and prepared detailed steps to deter Soviet strikes against American allies and the homeland. It took a nested approach for all these strategies to be complementary and effective.

Potential Strategic Phases. Prevention is far more effective than reaction. Planning prevention or response are two factors that are always critical in war time. It should be assumed that they will occur. An inherent part of the process is the implicit effort the U.S. must make to define the threat, inform the public, and acknowledge the potential for catastrophic events. This mirrors the public information effort that accompanied the U.S. preparation for possible nuclear war.

I. Pre-Attack (Prevention): This phase includes all the actions taken before an attack occurs. Detect the threat, deter the attack, and prepare for internal defense. This requires monitoring the infrastructure, transportation, communications, Internet, and academia. It may also require keeping an eye on key industries and expert personnel. During this phase, hopefully the one we stay in the longest, DHS works to build public awareness of threat groups and techniques via public information programs and selected news releases. A simple color-coded alert system is insufficient to build awareness and is likely to become so ubiquitous as to be ignored. The goal here is to isolate and preempt attacks while educating the public and normalizing the threat. Although nuclear war was incomprehensible, we never prepared for it and comprehended the real danger it posed.

II. Attack (Internal Response): In the event of attack, the U.S. must cycle through and apply local first responders, state and regional second responders, and if required, federal third and special purpose responders. This process needs to be pre-planned with the authorities in place and the lines of communication open. Failure to synchronize local, state, and federal response will lead to disjointed effort such seen during HurricaneKatrina. Cities and towns must have some form of reliable and compatible immediate response communications and must make provisions for social distancing (cordon), mitigation (inoculation & decontamination), containment (isolation), and eradication. All effort must be followed up with rapid restoration of critical functions. Throughout the response, law enforcement (LEA's) continue-tracking sources of attack. The purpose is to mitigate the initial-effects of an attack, reduce casualties, prevent expansion, and reduce panic, in response. In parallel, LEA's begin to identify threat weapons, techniques, perpetrators, and sponsors. Communications is key; both in the immediate target area and nation-wide. Public communications should tap into TV, am/fm,radio, cell phone text messaging, Facebook, Twitter (any virtualsocial network), and the Internet—forming a 21st Century Emergency Broadcast System.

III. Post Attack (Recovery): Full recovery and prevention of re-emergence or re-attack are key in this phase. Essential services are restored and any attackers or support personnel still in the US must be apprehended. The goal is to return to the status quo, re-stock critical mitigation supplies, and prepare for the external response to attack.

IV. Post Attack (External Response): Once the attackers and their sanctuary are identified they, their sponsors, their financiers, their accomplices and their information networks must be attacked relentlessly and ruthlessly.

Critical Players. The U.S. will need a team of teams to execute a comprehensive and logically sequenced strategy. Below is an incomplete list of players that will expand as law and strategy merge-a network work tooppose a network.

The Guardians: provide purpose, direction and motivation:
- DHS, DEA, DOJ, Federal Marshals, FBI, USCG, State and Local LEA—the homeland enforcers who uncover the plots and hunt down the bad guys.
- The Department of Defense (DoD), Department of State (DoS)—the overseas synchronizers who build the whole of government approach (Patraeus / Crocker team).
- Geographic and Functional Combatant Commands (COCOM's)—the overseas hammer and regional partner to allies.
- Border Service and INS—key allies to the IC and homeland enforcers.

Intelligence: find and track emerging threats and perform predictive analysis:
- Director of National Intelligence (DNI) and the Intelligence Community (IC); NSA, CIA, NCTC, DIA, the Secret Service and LEA intelligence (especially NYPD and LAPD)—the folks responsible for early warning and predictive analysis.
- The NSA—leader of CNA/CND effort that includes all of America's cyber warriors.

Bio Detection, Response, and Containment: monitor biological threats:
- WHO—Pandemic trackers who should resurrect smallpox and polio protocols.
- USAMRIID—America's epidemic/pandemic research, rapid detection, diagnosis, and vaccination.
- CDC—global pandemic partner to the above.
- DHHS—monitoring the home front.

Response Team: disaster relief:
- DART—America's rapid consequence management and response team.

- FEMA—America's federal aid coordinator and emergency management team.
- USAID—America's foreign aid coordinators.
- NEST—America's nuke hunters.
- NORTHCOM and the NGB—the federal first responders who coordinate with local and state first responders.

Coalition Partners: allies who add breadth, expertise and experience to the effort:

- FFRDC and Think Tanks—brain trusts who ensure we avoid repeating the mistake of lack of imagination as highlighted by the 9-11 Commission.
- EU, NATO, ASEAN and International LEA's—global partners that make Joint-Interagency-Multinational (JIM) possible / partners in an International rule of law enterprise.
- Commercial / Private Industry—the key to resilience and reserve capacity.

The Civil Defense (CD) Enterprise must be collaborative, maximizing fusion through vertical and horizontal communications and free flowing information sharing. It must be networked and include interagency participation. It should be seamless and transparent among members. It must be interactive between the national, state and local levels and yet remain decentralized and self-tasking in nature. The end state will be an enterprise in pursuit of a shared purpose and common aim; shared vision and common understanding; shared knowledge through common nets; and shared execution with common objectives. Given bureaucratic inclination to 'guard their own equities' and resist sharing power and responsibility difficulties this enterprise demands a George C. Marshall, the man who melded America's military and the allies into a coherent force in opposition to the axis. This contemporary man should live apart from Washington and be free of the political paralysis that exists there.[275]

The History of Civil Defense. Civil defense includes the largely non-military efforts taken to prepare American citizens for military

---

[275] *The American Way of War: A History of United States Military Strategy and Policy,* by Russell F. Weigley, Indiana University Press, January 1960.

attack.[276] The name and practice of CD have fallen out of the mainstream having been replaced by emergency management (FEMA) and homeland security (DHS)—neither of which does what Civil Defense did. Nows the time to resurrect the dead!

CD used to be defined by the city walls and castle moats, overwatched by the omnipresent lookout and chronicled by the crier; "10-oclock and alls is well." The later is the precursor to the nuke attack sirens of the Cold War and the tornado sirens they inspired. An approaching army with accompanying siege engines was easy to spot. In many ways, this mentality guided the United States into and beyond WWI.

The U.S. lacked any substantial civil defenses given its unique position between two great oceans. America was never exposed to a viable homeland threat before or during WWI so when the war erupted, we organized anti-saboteur vigilance and ran army recruiting campaigns in the name of CD. WWI CD facilitated the draft, participated in Liberty Bond drives, and helped to maintain soldier morale. We were free from the new warfare, aerial bombardment, so it focused on a broader scale.

WWII saw the emergence of real CD, called Civilian Defense and Comprehensive Emergency Management.[277] Japan's surprise attack on the US led to a more robust version of CD. Responsibility was bumped up from the local level to include the state and federal levels with leadership residing in the federal Office of Civilian Defense (OCD) within the Office of Emergency Planning (OEP) under the President. The OCD was charged with promoting protective measures and elevating morale. Its first leader was the famous NTC Mayor LaGuardia. Many disparate government organizations worked together to mobilize the civilian population. The Civil Air Patrol (CAP) was created to commission civilian pilots to patrol the coast and borders and provide in search and rescue. The Civil Defense Corps was organized to recruit and train millions of volunteers to fight fires, conduct post chem attack decontamination, provide first aid, and perform a myriad of other emergency

---

[276] *Consequence Management, Joint Center for Operational Analysis Journal,* Volume XI, Issue 1, Winter 2008-2009.

[277] *A History of the Twentieth Century Volume Three: 1952-1999,* by Martin Gilbert, Perennial an Imprint of Harper Collins Publishers, 2000.

tasks. Most of this evaporated folling the war.

WWII saw rationing and recycling added to the list—WWI had mobilized the nation while WWII mobilized the nation and the state. As the war progressed, the threat of air raids and invasions receded and CD shifted its focus back to simplistic air raid drills and border patrols.

The WWII activities became the baseline for the civil defense that re-emerged in response to the Cold War. Cold War CD was more comprehensive—it fulfilled the following functions: *education, evacuation, continuity of government, fallout shelter production*, and *early warning*.[278]

Education. A new Cold War component of CD was the education program. It was comprehensive—from the kid friendly *Duck and Cover* to the adult focused *Survival Under Atomic Attack*. The former inspired school nuke attack drills and the latter taught atom bomb survival. Booklets and pamphlets were common such as Fallout Protection and *Nuclear War Survival Skills*. This was a start but it didn't go far enough. It was time to expand the message to include modern technology, the radio. Radio Public Service Accouncements joined printed material and even included children's songs designed to discuss nuclear war.

Evacuation. At the dawn of the nuclear age, the federal government argued that citizens should remain in the cities in the event of a nuclear attack to repair the infrastructure and man recovering industries. Never the less, evacuation plans were drawn up. Drills were conducted that included the evacuation of city centers and hospitals. In 1957, CBS aired A Day Called 'X,' a dramatization of how a city should respond to nuclear attack. X was produced by CBS in co-operation with the Federal Civil Defense Administration. It was narrated by Glenn Ford. Evac plans were plausible when the nuke threat was confined to strategic bombers but the entry of the Intercontinental Ballistic Missiles (ICBM's) changed everything—early warning was no longer guarenteed. The lead time on detection went from hours to minutes. The world changed and America was insecure!

Civil Defense evac plans lasted into the modern era. In 1983,

---

[278] *Conflict after the Cold War: Arguments on the Causes of War and Peace*, by Richard Betts, Longman Publishers, Columbia University, 2001.

President Ronald Reagan introduced the Crisis Relocation Plan. His five-year $10 billion plan was intended to evacuate victims from targeted urban areas to rural areas. The goal was to save 80% of the post war population. The plan assumed a three day warning period given that a nuclear war would be preceded by an extended period of rising tensions between the U.S. and USSR.

Continuity of Government. Cold War governments wanted to survive a nuclear war whether they were NATO or Warsaw Pact. In the U.S., CD took the lead in the planning effort. National and State Capitals plus key cities built atom bomb Emergency Operation Centers (EOC). Key leaders would disperse and constitutional government would persist.

Fallout Shelters. JFK launched a nation-wide effort to build fallout shelters throughout the nation. The shelters would not protect against a nuclear blast or the thermonuclear heat but protect against radiation. CD officials encouraged civilians to build bomb shelters to incorporate nuclear defense into local building plans.

Early Warning. CD would be strictly reactionary and untrustworthy if it could not provide warning of imminent danger. To address this fundamental requirement the US created systems at the local, state, and national levels to communicate emergencies. In 1951, President Truman established CONELRAD (Control of Electromagnetic Radiation). The system consisted of a few stations that would be alerted in the event of an emergency. They would, in turn, broadcast the warning around the country. All broadcast stations would listen to and pass on the warnings. After the broadcast, all radio communications would be shut down save two designated AM frequencies. This was done to prevent Soviet bombers from using the signals for direction finding and navigation.

The arrival of the ICBM with their internal guidance made bomber monitoring academic. In 1963 the FCC created the Emergency Broadcast System (EBS). The EBS became the primary alert system and was used throughout the remainder of the Cold War and on into the 90's.

Post-Cold War. The end of the Cold War saw interest in and commitment to CD decline. The nuclear war focus shifted to an all-hazards approach of Comprehensive Emergency Management. Natural disasters and terrorism pulled attention away from traditional civil defense. In 2006, the triangle logo was retired and replaced with a new logo featuring EM (for emergency management). The new logo was announced by the National Emergency Management Association.

From 1979 on, CD was handled by the Federal Emergency Management Agency (FEMA). In 2001, President George W. Bush created the Department of Homeland Security (DHS) in response to 9-11. FEMA was subordinated to DHS in 2003.

New CD Functions. Modern terrorism CD needs to address homegrown fanatics, foreign teams, sleepers, bombers as well as cyber, chemical, biological and nuclear attack. It should include these basic functions: *public education, early warning, consequence management, quarantine, continuity of government, decontamination, mass casualty care, and restoration of services and commerce.*

Public Education (The Fungus Among Us). The education program needs to be a three tiered: the threat, threat attack methods and civil response. The program needs to use TV, newpapers and magazines, movies, the Internet, flyers and pamphlets, school documentaries, social networking sites, billboards and any other public messaging vehicles and venues available. The messages need to be consistent, honest, and should avoid caricatures. The point is not to demonize or dehumanize the enemy but to understand them and the threat they pose in a sober and accurate way.

Part one is the description of the threat. This portion needs to honestly and frankly discuss the threats; who are they, what do they want, why do they want it, how do they think they are going to get it... Citizens need an unfiltered, non-politically correct, description of threat ideology and goals. The discussion should not be designed to legitimize their grievances but to describe them. The average citizen has little to do with manufactured victimology and can do little to rectify percieved injustices. Threat writings and doctrine should be published and shared—they tell the truth about who they are and what they will do. Whenever possible, selective actual footage of terrorists (prisoners or propaganda videos) talking should be used. This has to be handled carefully since we definitely don't want to do is become an extension of the threat propaganda.

Part two or our public education programs focuses on what the threat will do in pursuit of their goals: cyber, kinetic, chem-bio-nuclear, as well as tactics like hijacking, hostage taking, massacres, assassinations. This is the crux of the education program—what to expect. We need to expose how the threat uses the Internet to recruit and propagandize and how to recognize cyber intrusions. The program should also cover threat finance but the ultimate topic is threat attack tactics, techniques, and procedures. All potential methods of attack need to be discussed and prior terror attacks need to be publically autopsied in order to make people more aware of what to expect.

Parts one and two are designed to convince the public that the threat is real and that concern for it is not pointless. An awareness must be cultivated rather than an excitement that might stimulate panic. Once they acknowledge the presence of a threat their vigilance will be added to the detection system. The response plans show that although the threat is real and dangerous, the U.S. is ready for them.

Part three is where CD makes its money by building confidence. In part three, we outline our response plans to show that, although the threat is real and is dangerous, we're ready for them. Part three covers the actions the individual takes in the event of an attack. it then relates those actions to local, state, and national responders. It tells citizens what to do, where to go, how to get information, and how to avoid becoming a casualty. Virtual (Internet) and actual rehearsals should be employed to inculcate plans into daily life.

We also have to find an updated version of the 'duck and cover' drill.

Early Warning (One if by Land, Two if by Sea). The new 21st Century CD will need a new 21st Century early broadcast system. The new early warning system (EWS) should incorporate TV, the Internet, social networks, cell phone texting.

Consequence Management (Brushfire not Prarie Fire). This program seeks to weave together the first responders and build in triggers, with associated authorities, to activate state and national second and third responders. This programs takes its cues from lessons learned from Hurricane Katrina. State and Federal governments must function smoothly in contrast to the lack of cooperation demonstrated in Louisiana.[279]

Roles and regulations needing clarification: Posse Comitatus, National Guard,

Quarantine (Slow Go or No Go). If the attack is by contaigon then there may be a requirement to isolate the infected to prevent further spread of hazard. If quarantine is required it will be very tricky in terms of what's legally possible and how it can be done. Once again, the authorities would have to be prepositioned for this to work.

Continuity of Government (Decapitation). This was a viable Cold War objective for the Soviets but for terrorists, it would be a way to generate panic and fear not topple the USG. Issues include: *Decon, Mass Casualty, and Restoration.*

Civil Defense (CD). It is imperative that the US review the procedures from the 1950's to determine the effective procedures used then replicate the network and rebuild the mentality that drove it under the auspices of the DHS.

- **Public Affairs:** educate the public about CBRNE
- **Emergency Broadcast System (EBS):** radio, TV, Internet, cell phone text
- **Build Reserves:** stockpile critical supplies, manufacture likely vaccines, build production capacity
- **Build Redundancy**: create back-up systems for critical functions and infrastructure—back-up power
- **Resurrect CD:** man and resources: possibly dual-hat of FEMA, Reserves, NG, EMP hardening
- **Reinforce Domestic DART:** CBRNE capable in coordinate with US Mil capabilities
- **Integrate Response Plans:** National, Regional, State, Local (public and private)
- **CD Website:** Situational awareness and collaboration
  Stand up CD boards, centers, cells

---

[279] *Consequence Management*, Joint Center for Operational Analysis Journal, Volume XI, Issue 1, Winter 2008-2009.

The Thuraya satellite phone is emerging as the key tool in the iG and iT tool bag. The Thuraya of 2008 and 2009 is revolutionizing irregular warfare and terrorism much like the radio of 1939 and 1940 revolutionized armored warfare. This trend is most visible in the 'third world.' It made its urban terror debut in Mumbai 2008 and is currently making a splash in Darfur 2009.

Telephone service used to be almost non-existent in Africa. What service there was was limited to elite sections of urban areas. Folks in the countryside had to rely on anachronistic two-way radios. Important communications had to be delivered face to face or by messenger. The cheap and accessible cell phone changed this in the cities and slums but the rural folks were still left out in the cold and thus were incapable of challenging the urban hubs for political dominance.

Then, along came the rugged Thuraya and its full service satellite network. Now folks in the deepest backwaters can communicate with the same ease as a commuter on an inner-city bus line. When communications change; conflict follows suit. As exemplified in modern times by Lawrence of Arabia in WWI and Rommel in WWI, desert warfare is all about mobility and surprise. This is as true in Darfur as it was in the Arabian Peninsula and North Africa. Lawrence's camels and the Desert Foxes Panzers have been replaced by the ubiquitous "technical" aka the 4WD Land Cruiser and the key to C2 is the Thuraya equipped commander—no more Somali burning tires!

Pre-Thuraya desert guerrilla ops required detailed planning and disciplined execution. The wristwatch time hack was the last chance for voice communications until the mission was over. The lack of in-stride comms meant that desert warriors relied on surprise, violence, tightly choreographed execution and momentum to prevail. Now, add in the Thuraya and the commander is transformed from being a remote observer watching his plan unfold, able to make minor adjustments using visual signals to an active participant able to impose his will and vision upon his troops on the line. He can now mass distributed forces and concentrate them against targets of opportunity in short order.

A Thuraya empowered commander and his subordinate 'technicals' have been transformed from a chaotic semi-autonomous mob to a tactically capable small unit. Rival factions with a shared overall goal can form ad-hoc coalitions in order to coordinate and execute joint operation against a common enemy. Airtime can be transmitted from one Thuraya to another, funds can also be transferred, and instant communications can be backed up by instant resources. Before the Thuraya, political negotiations had to be face to face and once a bargain was struck between a tribal leader and a provincial governor, it was difficult to renegotiate. Now, the bargaining process is dynamic. The rebel can conduct several negotiations at once and can rapidly renegotiate more advantageous deals. Thuraya enabled war is another globalization and information technology innovation that effectively deregulates violence. It has progressed much more quickly than regional security forces have and presents an emerging challenge to the global mechanisms for resolving conflict.

The terrorists who attacked the city of Mumbai on 26/11/2008 used Thuraya satellite phones for conversation with their handlers in Pakistan. Thuraya phones were preferred by anti-India terror groups because they are not licensed to be sold in the country and, therefore, their logs cannot be readily accessed by its agencies.

Thuraya, the Arabic name of the Pleiades, is a regional satellite phone provider. Its coverage area is most of Europe, the Middle East, North, Central and East Africa, Asia and Australia. The company is based in the United Arab Emirates and distributes its products and service through authorized service providers. Most Thuraya handsets (except for the Thuraya SO-2510 and XT) have a dual-mode feature that allows them to operate in the Thuraya satellite network and GSM terrestrial mobile networks. Thuraya has concluded roaming agreements with over 200 wireless (cellular) operators around the world, providing its customers the ability of using their Thuraya phones outside the satellite coverage. The dual-mode feature of the handset is similar to the Telit (GSM/Satellite) and Qualcomm (CDMA/Satellite) handsets on the Globalstar system. Roaming for outgoing calls is only available for subscribers. For pre-pay (scratchcard) users of Thuraya roaming is only available for receiving incoming calls. Third Generation - In 2009 a new rugged model came on the market the Thuraya XT. This handset is dust, shock and splash-water proof and offers GSM-like options like phone-calls, SMS / text services and internet access.

Services

- Voice communications with hand held or fixed terminals
- Short message service
- 9.6 kbit/s of data & fax service
- 60 kbit/s downlink and 15 kbit/s uplink "GMPRS" mobile data service on SO and SG handsets
- 144 kbit/s high-speed data transfer via a notebook-sized terminal
- GPS is supported by all handsets
- Value-added services: news, call back, call waiting, missed calls, voicemail, WAP.*
- Prayer service: after sending the GPS position to a special number a reply is sent back containing exact prayer times and heading towards Mecca. The service accounts for the prayer time difference between Sunni and Shia.
- A one-way 'high power alert' capability that notifies users of an incoming call, when the signal path to the satellite is obstructed (e.g. inside a building)
- Marine Services: a combination of a special (fixed) base station and subscription offering voice, fax, data and always on internet-access. Also an emergency service which, when activated, sends multiple SMS messages containing alarm-status and actual position to pre-defined destinations

* Wireless Application Protocol (commonly referred to as WAP) is an open international standard for application-layer network communications in a wireless-communication environment. Most use of WAP involves accessing the mobile web from a mobile phone or from a PDA.

** Virtual country codes - Satellite phones are usually issued with numbers in a special country calling code—Thuraya does not. Thuraya's country calling code is +882 and is not part of the ITU-T International Networks numbering group. Thuraya is also not associated with the country calling code numbering group in the Global Mobile Satellite System. Thuraya is a regional rather than a global system and as such is allocated numbers in the +882 code designated for "international networks" not used exclusively for satellite phone networks.

THURAYA 🌐

The Problem: *Proliferation* of biological, chemical, nuclear, and cyber; *knowledge, equipment*, and *capable personnel*, coupled with a *declining costs* and *reduction in barriers* to access making mass (disruption or destruction) attacks more likely in the near future.

Threats (by type of WMD): Proliferation makes knowledge, technology, and equipment accessible to informed individuals who can exploit it to create WMD's. The threats are listed in order from most dangerous to least based on; potential effect & impact, ease of development & production, deliverability, ambiguity of source, and expense (cheaper is better).

1. **Bio:** Viral—Influenza, Smallpox, Ebola, Hanta...
   Bacterial—Salmonella, Anthrax...
   Agricultural—Hoof in Mouth, Mad Cow...
2. **Nuke:** Dirty Bomb / Radiological Device, suitcase nuke, conventional nuke
3. **Chem:** Sarin, Ricin, Cynaide, Mustard...
4. **Cyber:** Hacking, Denial of Service Attacks, Viruses, Botnets...

Threats (by type of group): Threats groups are listed in order from most likely to least likely based on; ideological motivation, deniability / responsibility, and capability.

1. **Non State / Virtual State**—Al Qaeda
2. **Non State / State Sponsored**—Lebanese Hizballah
3. **Nation State**—Iran, North Korea, Venezuela
4. **Domestic crime / terror**—Earth Liberation Front, MS13
5. **International crime / terror**—Mexican Mafia, FARC
6. **Rogues**—(eg. Jim Jones, Ted Kazynski, Rajneesh)

Areas of Operation and Concern: The campaign is global; each area is a concern for different reasons and requires its own sub-strategy.

- The homeland: US, Canada, and Mexico
- LATAM (ungoverned spaces and enablers)

- Europe (source of information, tech, and 'white' AQ recruits)
- Africa (ungoverned spaces, source of recruits)
- Middle and Far East (hub of Islamist movement)
- CIS, NK, IN, SY, VEN, (PRC) (proliferators and enablers)

"It appears we have appointed our worst generals to command forces, and our most gifted and brilliant to edit newspapers! In fact, I discovered by reading newspapers that these editor/geniuses plainly saw all my strategic defects from the start, yet failed to inform me until it was too late. Accordingly , I'm readily willing to yield my command to these obviously superior intellects, and I will in turn, do my best for the Cause by writing editorials—after the fact."
—Robert E. Lee, 1863

"I published an order that they [reporters] must not come along on pain of being treated as spies. I am now determined to test the question ... I have ordered the arrest of one, shall try him, and if possible execute him as a spy."
—W. T. Sherman, 1864

Chapter 12

The Islamic State

It was early; the sun was barely up in the sky, when the Army of the Faithful descended on the City. While the attack wasn't completely unexpected; its ferocity was. The cities defenders were overwhelmed in a matter of days. They might have held out longer had they known what the attackers had in store. The next two weeks saw the city hurled into a merciless orgy of rape, maiming, pillage, and the wholesale execution of infidels.

The assault on the population was accompanied by an assault on their most cherished beliefs by destroying their Churches and Shrines. The city's people wept as they were forced to watch the demolition of an ancient Saint's Tomb. When everything of value was taken and all symbols of faith were smashed, the Muslim victors razed the ruins. Once the deed was done and burned into the minds of the survivors and the surrounding communities; the army withdrew. They were followed by a small army of chained prisoners of war now serving as slave porters hauling the loot back to the Caliph's capital.

Upon the army's return the women were sold as sex slaves, mostly to the soldiers. Some of the men were put to work as slave laborers tasked with renovating the Grand Mosque by integrating items plundered from their own Churches and Shrines. It was always good to see infidel slaves working on a Mosque. The rest of the men were marched down to the river where they were lined up and publically beheaded one by one. The severed heads were paraded through the capital and the market in celebration of the victory over the Christians. When the victory lap was done, the heads were put on display at the ceremonial gates of the city.

The army's leader was none other than the Caliph himself. He had recently laid claim to the title, usurping it from the previous leader of

203

the faithful whom he deemed insufficiently pious. In fact, the Caliph held most of his contemporaries in contempt for lacking piety and commitment; he had to be fearsome to justify his claim to the mantle. This is where the severed heads came in handy. They served two purposes; to cement his right to lead in the eyes of the faithful and to strike fear in the hearts of the apostates and infidels.

"I will instill terror into the hearts of the Unbelievers: smite ye above their necks."
—Quran 8.12

Mohammad, himself, had been presented a head in the wake of his first great victory and so the new Caliph presented heads to commemorate his victory and to show his fitness as leader of the faithful. The new leader had experienced some internal dissent when he expanded his army by recruiting foreigners, many from North Africa. He needed to demonstrate mastery of his multi-ethnic followers while luring more into the fold. His was an old fashioned unapologetic jihad; heresy, idolatry, un-Islamic writings and un-Islamic behaviors were to be eliminated.

The new Caliph adopted the age old ultimatum policy when dealing with anyone with the unfaithful; convert, or submit (to Sharia and pay *jizyra* as a *dhimmi*), or die. Submission was only offered to 'Peoples of the Book' meaning Christians and Jews. They could retain their faith in the Caliphate if they accepted their second class stauts as dhimmis without legal or property rights while paying *jizyra*; the protection tax better described as tribute.

The new Caliph was not going to be seen as a *Taifa* or faction king. He was to be recognized as the genuine leader of the faithful and the Caliphate and it was his right to command the loyalty and obedience of all Muslims.

The time was August 10th, 1997. The self-declared Caliph was Abd al-Rahman. The city was Santiago, Spain. The warriors were Saracens who hailed from the capital in Cordoba, the foreign fighters were Berbers from North Africa and the desecrated Shrine was that of Saint James. The Saracens ranked alongside the Vikings for predation in the eyes of the medieval world and all trembled when they were on the march. The behavior of ISIS is not unprecedented.

When Abu Bakr al-Baghdadi and the Islamic State of Iraq and Al Sham (ISIS) conquered Mosul in June of 2014, it did so using traditional purist Jihad. The conquerors announced the reestablishment of the Caliphate with Baghdadi named as Caliph. In deference to the resurrected Caliphate decrees were issued and tribute was demanded. Apostate Shiite Iraqi soldiers were lined up and shot or beheaded; Christians were beheaded, hung, maimed and crucified and Shia Yazidi women were sold into sexual slavery. In honor of tradition, Shia mosques and Christian Churches were demolished or converted into torture chambers and historic cemeteries were destroyed. Even the ancient Tomb of Jonah was destroyed for being idolatrous.

A visitor from 10th Century Santiago would have not been surprised in the least by the atrocities in Mosul. Purist Jihad has always been bloody, pitiless and intolerant business whether it's Mohammad's followers massacring the Jews of Medina in the 600s, the Saracens of Al Andalus massacring the Christians of Santiago in the 900s, the Ikhwan of Arabia massacring the Shia of An Nijaf in the 1700s or the Islamic State of Iraq massacring the Kurds of Mosul in the 2000's.

The Islamic State is the essence of regression back to medieval Islamist tradition.

STATELESS TO STATELET

"What we've got to appreciate is that Islamic State... is not just a terrorist group, it's a terrorist army and they're seeking not just a terrorist enclave but effectively a terrorist state..."
—Australian PM Tony Abbott

The Islamic State (IS) is the latest iteration of the Frankenstein's monster that is Al Qaeda. As is often the case in virology, the newest variant of the pathogen is more virulent than its progenitor. The son set out to upstage the father and he did.

The Islamic State was founded in 2003 by a Jordanian jihad junkie named Abu Musab al-Zarqawi or AMZ as his pursuers called him. He had been toying with terrorism since the late 90's and the end of the Iraq War was his chance to get into the game for real. His 2003 terror start-up was called the *Organization of Monotheism and Jihad* (JTJ) and its goal was to get on the terrorist map. Zarqawi had no intention of languishing in the bush leagues; he intended to get called up to the majors. To get the attention required for Al Qaeda Center to notice, the JTJ launched into a frenetic 9 months of bloody attacks against the coalition and Iraqi Security Forces. It worked and AMZ caught Al Qaeda's eye. As hoped, the JTJ was given the AQ Iraqi franchise after AMZ swore allegianceto Al Qaeda and Usama Bin Laden, the boss of bosses. The mayhem merger triggered name change as the JTJ became the *Organization of Jihad's Base in the Country of the Two Rivers. Awkward: most just called them Al-Qaeda in Iraq*(AQI).

Zarqawi was not a suave businessman like Bin Laden or a learned theologian like Zawahiri. He was a street thug; the Frank Nitti to their Al Capone. As a 'made' terrorist, he was all over Iraq like a Mesopotamian John Dillinger. Video clips of him firing captured weapons popped up as he roamed western Iraq in search of targets to blow up and convoys to ambush. He was a certified AQ gangster.

AMZ may have been addicted to Jihad but he also wanted to be taken seriously, a dedicated Islamist. He made and communicated a simple four phase plan for conquering Iraq that he sent to Ayman al-Zawahiri, Bin Laden's deputy and spiritual advisor.

1 – Kick the U.S. led coalition out of Iraq
2 – Establish Islamic law and an Iraqi Caliphate.
3 – Take the revolution to Iraq's neighbors
4 – Take the war to Israel

In May 2004, Zarqawi and AQI got the headlines they craved when the beheading video of American Nicholas Berg went viral on the web. The vicious tactic wasn't new; Khalid Sheik Mohammad slaughtered Daniel Pearl the same way two years earlier. The difference was that KSMs vile act was captured on videotape and its copies were distributed while AMZs terror clip was released on the web making it readily viewable around the world. During 2004, AQI's torture chambers in the outlaw city of Fallujah were targeted twice by coalition attacks. The second attack was decisive. While AQI's 'soldiers' fought, its leaders slipped away headed for Mosul.

Zarqawi couldn't contain himself in 2005 and cracks began in his Al Qaeda alliance. AMZ was determined to enforce his uniquely draconian version of Islamic Law in the areas he controlled while accelerating his harassment of the Iraqi Security Forces and the coalition. AQI attacked Abu Ghraib, blew up Iraqi voters at the polls in protest of evil democracy, then kidnapped and killed the Egyptian Ambassador for being an ally to Jews and Christians. What really opened up a rift with the suits in AQ Central was his anti-Shia campaign consisting of attacks, bombings and massacres of Iraqi Shias and their Mosques. The year ended with Zawahiri openly criticizing the attacks on Iraq's Shia.

In 2006, AMZ went to work alienating everybody in Iraq; especially his Sunni supporters. In September, 30 Anbar tribes formed a local alliance dubbed the Anbar Salvation Council, to counter al-Qaeda in their province by brazenly aligning with the Iraqi government and the U.S.

AMZ continued moving to the top of the coalition target list and in June 2006, he was killed. Few lamented his loss. He probably made a better martyr than warlord.

The new boss was Abu Abdullah al-Rashid al-Baghdadi and he was just as dedicated to the Zarqawi plan as Zarqawi was. He kept the heat on and by October 2006 had declared AQI to be Islamic State of Iraq (ISI). The newly minted ISI claimed dominance over six provinces including; Baghdad, Anbar, Diyala, Kirkuk, Salah al-Din, and Ninawa. Naturally, Baghdadi declared himself the state Emir. AQI's conversion to ISI wasn't taken too seriously since few believed they controlled the area they claimed.

Under the Emir ISI, continued its abuse of the Sunni tribes and alienating their Chieftains. Their heavy hand was stalled in Iraq by the combination of the Surge and the Anbar Awakening.

The 2007 loss of the Diyala province and continuing abuse of Sunni locals aggravated a growing rift between ISI and the locals who began to shift their support to the U.S. With the Surge in full swing, the new alliance generated results; dozens of ISI leaders were killed or captured.

The 'blowback' against ISI became known as "the Anbar Awakening" and its troops called the "Sons of Iraq" who were paid by the U.S. and motivated by their tribal chiefs.A series of 2008 offensives drove ISI out their hideouts, notably Fallujah, and into a Little Big Horn last stand in Mosul. ISI looked cooked and the U.S. began to pull out in 2009 prompting fears of a resurgence. While they managed an impressive bombing campaign, their foreign fighters fled and the slide deepened. Baghdadi was killed in Tikrit in April 2010; thirty-four of forty-two top dogs were killed or captured; and attack and casualty stats dropped to their lowest point in seven years.

Another Baghdadi, Abu Bakr al-Baghdadi, was next in the chute as boss. He made his way up running the ISI's sharia committees and serving on the senior council. The new Baghdadi went to work rebuilding ISI leadership by recruiting former Ba'athist buddies from his Hussein days. Most were military or Intel officers who had done time in post-Saddam prisons. The new core was professional, trained, and angry at the exclusionary pro-Shia Maliki regime in Baghdad.

In the summer of 2011 with ISI's fortunes in Iraq on the rocks, Baghdadi turned west for new opportunities. He decided to jump the jihad caravan headed for Syria where the door on the Arab Spring was being slammed shut by Assad's guns. The anti-Assad resistance was a grab bag of Sunni groups; a few small secular and a host of Islamists. Like Iraq 2003, Syria 2011 was in chaos and was ripe for a terrorist start-up.

Not one to neglect the home front, in 2012 Baghdadi kicked off Operation Breaking the Walls to free former members from Iraqi jails. The highlight came with simultaneous raids on Taji and Abu Ghraib that freed 500 prisoners, many being former insurgents.

ISI's advanced party in Syria was furiously recruiting fighters and building cells in Syria capitalizing on the military expertise their former Baathists brought. They formed the Jabhat al-Nusra li Ahl as-Sham and the al-Nusra Front with the latter eventually integrating the former into a single group called the Islamic State of Iraq and al-Sham. They were also referred to as the Islamic State of Iraq and the Levant (ISIL).

Throughout their history, the name and venue changes weren't random; they were all about recruiting and open source warfare. The move west saved ISI from extinction by jumping the anti-Assad bandwagon tying them to the Arab Spring. Instead of oppressing Anbar Sunnis they were now liberating Aleppo Sunnis…great PR.

ISIS's motives were obscure until summer 2014 when the game changing announcement came. On June 10th, 2014, ISIS seized Mosul and Tikrit. The Syrian campaign had turned back East on the Iraqi homeland where Maliki's ham-handed abuse of the Sunni's had re-inflamed the resistance. The resulting acquisition of a contiguous stretch of desert running from Aleppo in Syria to Mosul was just the beginning. It was ISIL's coming out:

- **12 June:** ISISdemanded that their new subjects "offer their unmarried women so that they can fulfill their duty of jihad by sex to their brotherly mujahideen. Failure to comply with this mandate will result in enforcing the laws of Sharia upon them."
- **29 June:** ISIS declares the reestablishment of the Caliphate and re-branding itself as the Islamic State (IS). Baghdadi became leader of the faithful as Caliph Ibrahim. The self-proclaimed caliphate is composed of 16 vilayets or provinces stretching from the Iranian border through Mosul, Iraq to Aleppo, Syria with its capital in Raqqa, Syria. With this land IS has probably become the world's richest terrorist organization based on theft of state wealth and access to oil petro-dollars.
- **2 July:** Caliph Ibrahim announces that IS will march on Rome, conquer Spain (Al-Andalus) and expand the Caliphate from the Middle East to Europe, India, the Balkans, and North Africa. IS passes AQ as the world's top Islamists by actually seizing ground.
- **15 July:** IS decrees that no public gathering other than those organized by ISIS will be allowed and no guns will be allowed outside its ranks.
- **18 July:** IS issues the Nineveh Decree or, dhimmi contract triggering a Christian exodus that endangers their two millennia presence in Mosul.

"We offer them three choices: Islam; the dhimma contract —involving payment of jizya; if they refuse this they will have nothing but the sword"
—IS Decree

In just $2^{1/2}$ weeks the Islamic State turned the clock back to the 7th Century by resurrecting the Medieval Caliphate that had been euthanized 90 years ago by the Young Turks who booted out the Ottomans. They resurrected the barbarity of Baybar's sack of Antioch and Tamerlane's pyramid of skulls in Bagdad. The cold bloodbath IS unleashed is unrivalled in the post-World War II era with their videos reminiscent of Katyn Forrest, Nanking, and BabiYar. Will a Levantine Auschwitz follow; one for Jews, Christians, and Shiites?

They also brought back dhimmitude whose demise preceded the Caliphate's demise after being nixed by the Ottomans, under pressure, in the early 1900's. IS isn't fighting for the liberation of the oppressed from sock puppet dictators; they're fighting for revenge and religious apartheid. They seek an earlier age when the Saracens roamed the world with scimitar in hand and slaves in tow. This is sectarian clash of blood and faith versus a secular clash of politics and economics. IS is uncompromising, anachronistic, sectarian, and chauvinist. This is an existential war over the definition of civilization—rule by consent or submission to terror.

Although the above history is interesting, it doesn't say much about what makes the Islamic State an emerging leader of the iGuerilla herd. Why? Their goal is to terrorize their enemies and in reestablishing their theocracy they aren't unique. The fact that they've taken, and are holding ground, is unique but might be a reflection of the lack of western resolve than the awesome might of the Islamic State.

What makes the Islamic State the latest 'upgrade' to the iGuerilla network is their comprehensive exploitation of the full spectrum of global communications to recruit, train, fund, and equip an army rather than build a cell. The Islamic State is the current poster child for 21st Century Wiki War.

> *"This is a new battle, a great battle, similar to the great battles of Islam, like the conquest of Jerusalem."*
> —Usama Bin Laden, October 2001

The Islamic State is an outgrowth of Al Qaeda; founded by opportunist and terror entrepreneur Abdul Azzam. He lured Bin Laden to

Afghanistan to fund the operation. Bin Laden inherited the business after Azzam spontaneously combusted in a car bomb after a disagreement over Al Qaeda's future; Azzam wanted to focus on the region while Bin Laden wanted to go west. AQ didn't create the Islamic State but they did legitimize it by subletting their Iraqi operations to it. AQ and IS had a falling out in Iraq and Syria but AQ was forced to accommodate the upstart—it seems the pupil and prodigal is taking over the business.

Al Qaeda's early success as the command central of the Transnational Islamist Insurgency was based on progressive public relations; seize center stage with a big event, advertise-advertise-advertise, diversify, adapt and innovate to the changing environment.

The Big Event. As with any start up; this is the tough part...how to gain attention. The gold standard is probably Black September's attack on the1972 Olympics. They delivered a slow-mo terror show that was broadcast around the world.It took AQ twenty-nine years to deliver a sufficiently novel and bloody event to rival '72. Zarqawi's big event was the viral video beheading of Nicholas Berg and the Islamic State's big event was the resurrection of the Caliphate. Each event fired up 'the base' upon which all the rest is constructed. In their spirit of their leader, IS released a series of online videos showing the beheading of numerous western journalists. They added gruesome footage of Iraqi and Syrian soldiers being executed, Shia Mosques being blown up, sex slave markets and more. IS cornered the gore and atrocity market not only to sew fear but to excite potential followers to the adventure of killing in Iraq and Syria.

PR. AQ regularly distributed messages from its CEO, UBL, via video tapes. Al Qaeda didn't intend to be lost in the news cycle or forgotten as a drive by. In 2010 Al Qaeda added the online magazine, *Inspire*, to their propaganda portfolio. *Inspire* is a *Better Homes and Bombings* for aspiring Islamist killers searching for permission and targets such as the brothers Tsarnaev or the brothers Kouachi. The former found their pressure cooker bomb plans in *Inspire* and the latter found their target *Charlie Hebdo* there. *Inspire* was designed to do just that; inspire self-organizing and self-tasking lone wolf Shaheedi's.

AQI broke into the PR realm by peddling terror- vision snuff clips. Once they became the ISIS, pretty much evicted from Iraq, they went in search of enlarging and diversifying their army through global out-reach. They shocked the civilized world by releasing videos and images of their battlefield successes that resemble the grainy black and white films shot by Nazi SS voyeurs documenting the Einsatzgruppen. They added Jihad rap videos and Islamist versions of Call of Duty and Grand Theft Auto to the warnography, ending up with a comprehensive PR campaign to attract bored, adventure hungry, glory seeking, and shallow millennial janissaries.

Perhaps IS's most sophisticated propaganda and recruiting tool is *Dabiq* magazine which went on line in 2014.It is deliberate, calculated and refined, even the name speaks volumes. *Inspire's* name is illustrative but not deep or imaginative. *Dabiq's* name is both. It appeals to the seasoned terrorist with its nod to history and to the aspirant with its allusion to adventure. Dabiq is a town on the Syrian-Turkish border where, in 1516, the Ottomans defeated the last Arab Caliph. This led to the fall of Cairo and the ascension of the Turks to the leadership of the Caliphate. Dabiq is an Islamist version of *Meggido*, the site of the last battle of Armageddon. Its name evokes the unification of the ummahunder an empowered Caliph. Dabiq is where the Prophet said a clash between Muslims and "Rome" (the West) would occur. Issue 2 "The Flood" parallels IS with Noah's Ark with IS as the Ark; come on board or drown.

Dabiq uses Islamic literature to legitimize the caliphate and the Caliph. It argues that their rule is based on religious principles. The seizure of territory and establishment of Sharia compliant government is the basis of their authority and Baghdadi is the rightful leader given his battlefield successes. *Dabiq* differentiates the Islamic State from Al Qaeda and will surely be a propaganda platform if the cold war goes hot.

Diversify. Once on the board, AQ expanded from their Afghan base to new terror markets:

- Yemen: home to Al Qaeda in the Arabian Peninsula (AQAP)...AQ's bomb makers
- Iraq and Syria: JTJ, AQI, ISI, ISIL, ISIS, IS...AQ's possible usurper

- North Africa: Al Qaeda in the Maghreb (AQIM)...AQ's African franchise
- Nigeria: Boko Haram...A particularly vicious spinoff trying to destroy Nigeria
- Somalia: Al Shabaab...an early AQ training ground and financier via piracy
- Indonesia, the Philippines, Spain and more.
- Pakistan and Afghanistan: Taliban are partners not subordinates

Like a Conquistador seeking the Seven Cities of Gold or a neo Nazi looking for the Fourth Reich; any Sunni Salafist fantasizing about the resurrection of the Caliphate knew where to go. Make up a name; kill enough infidels or take fire to get some press; earn a blessing from the Jihad father and gain access to funding and recruitment then sit back and enjoy the ride. Black flags for everyone.

Adapt. The Arab Spring, which evolved into the Islamist Winter, changed the market. The far enemy (the West) had always been the focus given the strength of the international security forces of the near enemy (the apostate dictators). Just as Lenin didn't see the Petrograd uprising coming; Bin Laden didn't see the Arab Spring coming. The people under the dictators took events into their own hands in Tunisia...on their own. The Islamists came in late and usurped the movement just as the Bolsheviks did in 1917. Morsi and the Muslim Brotherhood took Egypt, the Mullahs held on in Iran where the internal security forces were more fearsome than before, Libya fell into Islamist chaos and Syria's Assad held on given his external support from Iran and Russia. IS seems to have seen itself as the Sunni version of the Shia Khomeini's theocratic overthrow of Iran. Bin Laden and the terror masters would duel with Jefferson and the Patriots for the hearts and minds of the Arab street.

Al Qaeda's prodigy may be stealing the limelight for now but it seems likely that their high profile and geographic identity will ultimately doom them. In the interim, expect a low grade civil war between the Al Qaeda establishment and the upstart Islamic State. Like scorpions in a bottle, their reach for terror headlines was illustrated by their competing claims for the recent attacks in France. AQ will probably outlast IS by profiting from its anonymity and ubiquity—its uncanny ability to be everywhere and nowhere. As long as IS sticks to its geographic state it remains vulnerable since, like all states, they can be held accountable. They have no safe haven.

iGuerillas and Wiki War

In his book *Leaderless Jihad*, Marc Sageman offers one of the best descriptions of the impact of the Internet information and communication revolution on transnational Islamism. Sageman contends that up to 2004 terror recruiting and plotting was accomplished by face to face interactions between recruiters and recruits. From 2004 on the majority of terrorists arrested were recruited online.

Sageman notes that the World Wide Web is divided into two domains; one passive and one active. The passive side is the information transmission and dissemination side populated by web pages, articles and news. It's where we go to read about what's going on and it plays an important, yet subordinate, role to the rise of the iGuerilla. True, this is where the aspiring terrorist goes to read propaganda and find articles on the tactics, techniques and procedures and it is where terrorists want to see their atrocities reported but it's not where hearts and minds are won.

Enticing, recruiting and radicalizing wannbe jihadis takes place on the active domain of the web. This is where true interaction and two way communications occur. This is the realm of email, social media like Face Book, online forums, blogs and micro-blogs, chat rooms and Twitter. It includes texting, smart phones, and blackberries. These unmonitored virtual spaces replace the physical spaces that have been under surveillance all over the world since 9-11. Their anonymity facilitates unfiltered interactions freed from the typical inhibitions and restraint common to face to face dialogue. The safe virtual space of a chat room also creates a sense of intimacy allowing virtual partners to bond. Some studies indicate that virtual partners can become even closer than physical partners. Hatred and passion flow freely in such spaces where the recruit takes on the group identity as a 'member' of the stateless terrorist group. He is anonymous and unaccountable.

Dynamic and direct interaction with the prophets of Jihad is far more powerful than the reading revolutionary tracts, leaflets and pamphlets of the pre-Internet era. How much more powerful would it be to speak to Thomas Paine rather than read his pamphlet *Common Sense*?

Sageman's research also show that the recruits are getting younger with the average age of recruits dropping from 26 to 20. This makes perfect sense since it is the young who are most apt to effectively use the Internet. Likewise, the role of women has also increased since they are now able to listen in on the online forums. They are no longer excluded as they had been under traditional male dominated jihadism of the past.

As stated above, before 2004 most recruits were a result of face to face interaction when a trained operative would 'raise' his own team much as Mohammad Atta did for 9-11. Post 9-11, such spaces were watched. The need for unmonitored space was filled by virtual space that is almost impossible to monitor. The problem was access. While 90% Europe has Internet access, only 6% of the Middle East did although that figure is constantly growing. The solution has been to use the ubiquitous Internet Cafes that replaced coffee shops and to distribute communal laptop computers. Getting into the terror recruiting corridors has never been easier and it's the young who know the way; the very people most likely to foment rebellion.

The Cowering Inferno

Of course the goal of all this Internet outreach is two pronged; instill terror in the targeted population and intimidate their governments and project strength and power to potential recruits. They also show IS fighters building schools and pursuing domestic activities like swimming with their children in an effort to show the Islamist Utopian State as a place where the faithful can flourish. To those ends, a cottage industry has emerged that offers a wide array of products and services to meet the goals of the terror masters.

Products and Services. IS makes and peddles its own propaganda through its own Al-Hayat Media Center and are said to own more than a half dozen TV stations. Their products include:

Mujatweet: with its distinct black bird logo, used for micro-blogging and dissemination of multiple links to online videos so that, as they are taken down, there are still options for viewing. As of 2013 there were 20,000 followers using:

YouTube: for training videos and propaganda with 450,000 views in 2013

CDs, DVDs, posters, pamphlets, T-shirts, and Websites

The *Lend Me Your Ears* news reports by British war correspondent and IS captive since 2012, John Cantlie, are short, western style, news reports that highlight IS progress and counter western narratives – Cantlie wrote an article in *Dabiq* issue #6 titled *Meltdown*.

*shortly thereafter he was beheaded as a video propangda subject.

The above only scratches the surface. The Internet also facilitates data mining, finance, networking, mobilization, supplying doctrinal materials and manuals, downloadable books and can be used for hosting planning and coordination of operations. The range of possibilities requires a book of its own but suffice it to say that the rise of transnational Islamist terrorism mirrors the rise of the Internet unleashed by globalism.

Their global pick-up army is attracted by IS blessed barbarity that allows miscreants to indulge their darkest fantasies. Their recruits scour the battlefield scarfing up goodies left behind by the incompetent armies of Assad and Maliki—taking rather than building.

The Islamic State's sophisticated and multi layered message, recruiting, and operations machine is working. An estimated 3,000 westerners have joined the Islamic State's Jihad in Syria and Iraq, to include roughly 100 Americans; a number not seen since the Spanish Civil War of 1936. One young western recruit called it, *"not unlike a student holiday without the booze."* Comments like these highlight the twisted allure of beheadings, firing squads, slave markets and unrestrained pillaging. It's medieval. It's a new Dark Ages for the victims.

Perhaps the most frightening observation came from an American recruit:

"If you guys only knew how much fun we have over here.
This is the real Disneyland."

Wiki World
Essays

Cold War II

A Strategy for a New Cold War

Cold War I. Cold War I was the global struggle between the U.S. and USSR that took place from 1947 to 1991. It was called 'Cold' because the contestants did not engage in open conventional war. Both were nuclear superpowers making open warfare too risky. The U.S. began its effort by defining the enemy; who they were, what they stood for, and why they opposed us.

George F. Kennan's famous article defined the Cold War for American generations to come. *The Sources of Soviet Conduct*, appeared in the July 1947 issue of *Foreign Affairs* magazine under the pseudonym X.[280] In the article, Kennan asserted that Stalin's policy was shaped by a combination of Marxist–Leninist ideology and its dictum to defeat global capitalism. He claimed that Stalin's dedication to "capitalist encirclement" was a a cover designed to legitimize his consolidation of power. Kennan believed that Stalin could not moderate the Soviet determination to overthrow the Western democracies; therefore:

> "the main element of any United States policy toward the Soviet Union must be a long-term, patient but firm and vigilant **containment** (emphasis added) of Russian expansive tendencies.... Soviet pressure against the free institutions of the Western world is something that can be contained ..."

Taking Kennan's highly accurate and non-politically correct definition of the enemy and using it to design a workable strategy of **containment**.

---

[280] *The Sources of Soviet Conduct*, by George F. Kennan (aka - X), *Foreign Affairs*, July 1947.

Cold War II. The U.S. may well be on the road to another Cold War. The reasons for avoiding direct engagement aren't based on mutual annihilation as before but are based on the historic volatility of sectarian war similar to the Thirty Years War,. Before designing Cold War II strategy It is necessary to define the enemy.

The Threat? The U.S. joined the current struggle following 9-11 attacks. The enemy had been at war with the US long before but had been ignored. Al Qaeda and its Saudi billionaire leader got America's attention and it declared a Global War on Terrorism (GWOT). The identification of terrorism as the object of the war was problematic from the outset. Terrorism is a tactic. It's not an ideology, movement, party or worldview. It is the use of violence, usually against 'soft' defenseless and unsuspecting targets, to attain political objectives. It is typically employed by those too weak to engage in conventional war, like Al Qaeda, or by those who are too powerful to be stopped, like the Nazis.

How do you fight a tactic? It is necessary to address the motivation. If the terrorists are secular then pragmatic political solutions may be offered or legitimate discussions initiated but if the motivation is sectarian or utopian, another approach will be necessary since pragmatism is useless.

If the U.S. is going to target motivations then it needs to know what they are. Since the threat isn't terrorism per se, what is it? Inventorying the forces arrayed against the U.S. is a must and then the search for commonalities.

First on the list is the Saudi-Egyptian, Sunni-Wahabbi violent extremist organization (VEO) known as Al Qaeda; the 9-11 attackers. They were actually preceded by the Iranian-Lebanese, Shia VEO, Hizballah; the '83 Beirut Marine Barracks attackers. We can add the Palestinian PLO and their successor, Hamas; Yemen's Al Houthi; Somalia's Al Shabaab; the Philippine's Abu Sayaf, the Pakistani Pashtun Lashkar e-Taieba; and on and on…all are stateless Muslim VEO's. They include Sunni's and Shia's; Arab's and Persians; Asians and Africans; and more. The U.S. might devise a blanket definition for this plethora of bad guys if this was all there were but it isn't. This list leaves out hostile Muslim states pursuing similar goals to include the Shia Islamic Republic of Iran; the former Sunni Taliban Islamic republic of Afghanistan, and numerous VEO enabling states like; Lebanon (safe haven), Syria (safe haven), Sudan(safe haven), Qatar and Saudi Arabia (finance).

The threat is expansive. It includes states and the stateless; Sunni's, Shia's and Sufis; it spans the globe from the Middle East to Asia to Africa to the Balkans and the former Soviet Republics. The one commonality, the dedication to a strict, literal, and purist version of Islam as the basis for law and governance. Each seeks an Islamic Utopia based on an idealized and romanticized past-the 14th Century Caliphate. The Islamic world is divided between those that wish to conquer the world through different means: war or peace. The ultimate Islamist goal pursued by all sides of the issue is to restore the historic caliphate and expand it globally by eliminating 'unjust manmade law' and the democratic consent of the governed, with submission by all of the faithful to the Islamic theocracy.   Islamism's beliefs are summed up in the credo of the Muslim Brotherhood:

Allah is our objective; the Quran is our law, the Prophet is our leader; Jihad is our way; and death for the sake of Allah is our highest aspiration.

Cold War II Islamism is similar to Cold War I Communism. It doesn't seek coexistence or compromise. It seeks the creation of a 'Kingdom of Heaven' on earth governed by Islam.

Past as Prologue.   Muslims know their history. Islamists remember it, and use it to develop their world view. As an immigrant nation discovered by Europeans in the 1400's, and colonized in the 1600's, America has heterogeneous roots and a short history. The American mindset doesn't get the old world's almost tribal dedication to ancient grievances and dead empires. A Canadian General who led troops in Bosnia during the disintegration of Yugoslavia said that our advantage was our ignorance of the history that all sides had so emotionally tied themselves to. That was then. Today, we need to be aware of the history in order to understand how it drives the threat.

Islam was invented in the 610's, spread to Mecca in the 630's, began its imperial expansion in the 650's, and was abolished in 1924's-a period of 1300 years. The fits and starts of the Caliphate defined the nation of Islam, the ummah, and it animates the revanchist Islamism.

Rapid Expansion. Mohammad began the conquest and consolidation of the Arab tribes under Islam after he unified Medina and Mecca. He died before the job was done prompting Islam's first crises—the succession. The ummah divided into two camps; the Sunni's and Shia. The majority Sunni believed the next leader (caliph) should come from among Mohammad's closest companions. The followers of Ali, Shia, believed the successor had to be a male blood relative. The Sunni's won, Ali was assassinated and the *Sunni Shia schism* was born, grew and persists to this day. The schism explains, in part, the bitter rivalry between the Sunni Saudi Kingdom and the Shia Islamic Republic.

As important as the schism is, it was a footnote in the early years of the Caliphate. The united Arabian tribes embarked on a Jihad that conquered peoples and lands from Spain to India; and it all took less than 130 years to complete. It was probably the fastest imperial growth since the conquests of Alexander the Great and it seemed to validate the Quranic claim of Islamic superiority and divine mission to rule. This *Muslim Manifest Destiny* is a key concept to modern Islamism.

The newly conquered subjects of the Caliphate were forced to convert to Islam until the empire realized it could enrich itself by extorting protection money in the form of a tax (jizyah) on the people in error (dhimmi's). The new subjects could retain their faith as long as they submitted to second class status under Islamic rule. Dhimitude reflects Islamist belief in the *Domination of the Master Faith*.

Decline. The Caliphate experienced internal strife and divisions as do all large empires that engulf a diverse array of peoples, faiths, and languages. The leadership of the Caliphate and its subordinate Sultanates reflected the divisions. The Caliphate traded hands between Sunni Arab Abbasids and Umayyids, the Shia Arab Fatimids, and finally, the Sunni Turkish Ottomans. Meanwhile, the Persian Sufi and Shia Safavids broke off and established their own Islamic Dynasty that clashed with the Ottomans. The *factionalism* persists today.

An interruption to Arab rule occurred with the Mongol conquest and rule in the 1200 and 1300's. Although the Mongols converted to Islam, they ruled using a mix of Sharia and tribal tradition. The Islamic scholar Ahmad ibn Taymiyyah (1263–1328) saw these innovations un-Islamic, unjust and the cause of decline. He sought to eradicate beliefs and customs foreign to Islam as the way to rejuvenate Islamic thought. He saw the first three generations of Islam (the Salaf) as the infallible guide authentic Islam and any deviation should be forbidden. He opposed borrowing from Christianity or any infidel faith. Taymiyyah created *Islamism* as rejection to Mongol rule.

The few challenges and setbacks the Caliphate faced came at the hands of the emergent Christian West. Charles 'the Hammer' Martel, grandfather of Charlemagne, stopped Muslim expansion into Western Europe at the Battle of Tours in 732. From the 1100's to the 1300's the west launched a series of Crusades to regain the Holy Lands. Don John led the Holy League in defeat of the Ottoman Navy at Lepanto in 1571 and the Polish King Sobieski's mounted Lancers broke the Ottoman Janissaries at the gates of Vienna. Spanning all was the 600 year long Spanish Reconquista that ended with Spanish freedom from the Caliphate in 1492. The impact of Western rivalry grew as the European Empires nibbled away at the fringes of the Caliphate. Imperial Russia encroached in the east; Britain snatched Egypt and India, and France took North Africa. By the 1800's the Ottoman Caliphate was derided as the 'sick man of Europe.' The *Christian West the hated 'Other'* was well established in the Islamist mind.

Fall. Islam was humbled from the 1700's on but catastrophe finally struck in the wake of WWI. The Ottoman Caliphate predictably sided with the autocratic Central Powers and fell with them with the help of a Saudi Arab Revolt. A secular nationalist movement arose in Turkey under the leadership of Mustafa Kemal Ataturk and the Young Turks that resulted in the abolishment of the Caliphate.

The abolition of the Caliphate coupled with British colonial domination of Egypt inspired the birth of the Muslim Brotherhood under its leader, Hasan al-Banna and its doctrinaire, Sayyid Qtub. The latter called the end of the caliphate a 'catastrophe.' Qtub saw post Caliphate Muslim rulers as despots backed by the west. Their manmade law made them un-Islamic and justified their deaths. As the 'near enemy' they were too powerful to defeat so he proposed Jihad against the far enemy—the west. Qtub was sent to America to study in the hopes he would lose is revolutionary fervor. Instead, he ended up deciding that western culture was the ultimate expression of un-Islamic decadence. Thus the 1920's saw *Islamism reborn* in a more radical form.

Humilitation.   The post WWII world saw the Muslim world gradually granted independence from their colonial masters. The victory was hollow to the Islamists when, in 1947, the state of Israel was created by the United Nations. The combined armies of the Arab Middle East experienced a string of humiliating defeats by tiny Israel in '48, '56, and '67. The war to exterminate the Christian imposed Jewish state of Israel and replace it with a new Palestine became the New Crusade; *the cause célèbre of the Muslim World*. The Arabs tried to win as Soviet client states and failed. They tried secular socialism and Nasser's Arab Nationalism and failed. The Arabs were as inept as the Israelis, with their American support, were invulnerable.

Revanchism. Muslim fortunes began to change in the 70's. In 1972, the Palestinian Liberation Organization (PLO) transformed their cause from a regional one to a global one. The following year, the Egyptians and Syrians managed to launch a surprise attack on Israel that almost worked. Although it ended in defeat, it proved that the IDF was not invincible. When the U.S. resupplied Israel, the Petro-States comprising OPEC shocked the western world and provoked a recession by enacting an oil embargo. The Muslim world discovered that oil *was a weapon*.

Real change came in the late 70's and early 80's. *The Iranian Revolution of 1979* was as momentous to the Muslim World as the Russian Revolution of 1917 was to the Western World. The Iranians overthrew the Shah's pro-western, secular, monarchy and replaced it with an Islamic Republic. The revolution's spiritual leader was an exiled Ayatollah who returned and usurped the uprising. Islamists could actually overthrow their secular masters. The Islamic Republic rapidly went to war with their secular neighbor just as the Soviets had against the Poles; and just like the Russians they lost. They weren't deterred and they exported their revolutionary Islam with the first target being Israeli occupied Lebanon.

The Iranian Pasdaran went to Lebanon and organized the Shia minority into an Islamist militant group called the Party of God or Hizballah. They were trained in the tactics of suicide attacks that harkened back to the Shia Hashishin sect (assassins) of the late 1200's.

Hizballah bombed Israeli targets and the U.S. Marine Barracks in Beirut in 1983. American and Israeli forces withdrew although Israel didn't fully withdraw until 2000. Hizballah stood up to the Israelis and won, something no Muslim state had succeeded in doing.

The Soviet invasion of Afghanistan also began in the watershed year of 1979. The call to Jihad prompted a flood of Islamist fighters to the war, turning Afghanistan into a Soviet Vietnam. The Soviets withdrew in 1989, leaving a civil war behind. By 1996, an Islamist insurgency (the Taliban) under Mullah Omar had taken control. Another Islamist State was born in the span of 17 years and it came with a safe haven for Al Qaeda. The successes of Hizballah and the Taliban led to faith in the *indirect means of waging war* against the west.

On September 11, 2011, a VEO hiding out in the Islamic State of Afghanistan attacked the US. It was an unprecedented action that saw a non-state Muslim group actually attack the US Homeland. Islamists all over the world celebrated. In their eyes, they had prompted the fall if the Soviet Union, one of the two super powers and they had opened up a new front against the second super power, the USA.

The 2000's saw the birth of two more Islamist states. The formerly outlawed Islamic Justice Party (AKP) won the 2003 elections in Turkey. The result was the placement of Islamist Recep Erdogan as Prime Minister. As an Islamist, he went right to work by; denying US use of Turkish territory to move troops into Northern Iraq during Operation Iraqi Freedom removing military and judicial proponents of Turkish secularism and cooling off relations with Israel. Turkey is no longer a secular Muslim partner with the west.

In 2012, Egypt jumped on the Arab Spring bandwagon. The west supported the protestors of Tahrir Square and forced Mubarak from power. The military, the traditional guardians against Islamism in Egypt as they had been in Turkey, tried to delay elections. They know that only the once illegal and underground Muslim Brotherhood (MB) would be organized and ready for an election. The west mistook the Arab Spring as a democratic movement so we pushed for elections. The MB won and Mohammad Morsi became Mubarak's replacement. Now the Iranians are welcome in the Suez for the first time since '79, the Sinai crossings are open to Hamas, Israel's pipeline is cut, the U.S.

Embassy has been attacked and Morsi has demanded that we curtail free speech in our own country in order to prevent insulting Islam. Islamists are usurping the Arab Spring to *create an Islamist Winter*.

The Tenets of Islamism—Triumphalism and Grievance.

- *Sunni Shia Schism.* The succession debate grew into a bona fide religious schism pitting the majority Sunni against the minority Shia. The Shia champion has become Iran while the Sunni's have many potential champions to include the Turks, the Arab Saudis and the Arab Egyptians. Sunni's do not want to see leadership in the hands of Shia and vice versa.
- *Muslim Manifest Destiny.* The rapid expansion of the Caliphate validated their belief that they are destined to 'rule the world.' The decline and fall erased this idea but the events from 1979 to today are resurrecting it. The perceived western economic decline adds to the sense of Islam ascendant. Islamism is increasingly revanchist. Calls to reclaim all the ground that made up the Caliphate at its height will increase.
- *Factionalism.* Islamists hate the west but they hate insufficiently Islamic Muslims almost as much, if not, more. The sects consider each other apostates and all Muslim ethnic groups can make arguable claims to the mantle of leadership / caliph. There will be infighting and disunity.
- *Islamism v 1.0.* The Salafi way or the highway. Taymiyyah condemned Mongol rule as unauthentic. The model for Muslim governance was the one used during the time of Mohammad and his companions. True Muslims must emulate their rule and lifestyle. No interpretation, deviation or innovation should be tolerated. Pure and literal Islam is the way.
- *The Christian West the hated 'Other.'* The Christian West became the 'other' by resisting, halting and then rolling back the Caliphate. Today, the western bogeymen are the Big Satan (the USA) and the Little Satan (Israel). The west takes the blame for the decline and fall of the Caliphate and western culture is blamed for the corruption of the faithful. Western freedom of speech,

individual liberty, religious tolerance, and rule of law are antithetical to Islamism. The west will remain in the forefront as scapegoat for Muslim inability to compete in the modern world.

- Islamism v 2.0. The post Caliphate Islamism upgrade used version 1 to explain the death of the Caliphate but they faced new challenges. The post Caliphate world was run by petty dictators with police states. Islamism 2.0 legitimized killing un-Islamic Muslims and admitted that the faux Muslim states (the near enemy) were too tough to topple. Leaders were corrupted by western decadent culture and were propped up by western support (blame it on the west). The solution was to attack the west (the far enemy) and demonize its culture. Perpetual Jihad would go abroad and the west would be Ummah Public Enemy Number 1.

Muslim Brotherhood Declares 'Mastership of World' as Ultimate Goal through 'Resurrection of a caliphate.'

- Cause Célèbre Palestine. Islamists claim that no one has a legitimate claim to the Holy Land other than them. This seems absurd given western rational historicism. After all; the Jews built their Kingdoms more than a millennium before Mohammad was born, Jesus rode into Jerusalem more than six centuries before Mohammad was born and Constantine declared Rome a Christian state three centuries before Mohammad was born. Mohammad never set foot in the Holy Land, accept in his imagination. Before he died, Mohammad told a tale of being whisked away on a winged horse to Jerusalem where he met Musa (Moses) and Isa (Jesus) after which he was returned. Even with the Magical Mystery Tour the Muslims were last in so how do they do it? Islamists call the time before Islam Jahiliyah, the time of ignorance. It doesn't exist. Mohammad's excellent adventure served two purposes for his followers; it reinforced the superiority claim of Islam/Mohammad as the replacement to Judaism/Moses and Christianity/Jesus and it gave the aspiring empire a divine target for expansion. Islamists use Palestine the same way; to highlight their inherent superiority, exploit victimhood, and create a

Muslim rally point. The oppression of Palestinians and eradication of Israel justifies any Islamist atrocity and reclaims a historic piece of the Caliphate.

- *Oil as a Weapon.* The OPEC embargo card has not been played since '73 largely because of division among oil producing Muslim states. If the Shia Iranians cut production, the Sunni Saudi's increase it. The modern way to attack oil is to blow up pipelines, like the one that used to pump oil to Israel, or disrupt LOC's. For Iran, that means the Straits and for Egypt, that means the Suez.
- *Iranian Revolution.* The Arab Spring that began in 2010 was presaged by the Persian Spring of 1979. Islamists, Sunni and Shia, are continually inspired by the Iranian Islamic Republic and its tough stance with the USA, Israel and the West. Schism or not, Iran continues to inspire the Islamists and will ally with them in the short run or until a sectarian civil war breaks out—now a distinct possibility given the Syrian uprising pitting a Sunni majority rebelling against a Shia minority in power.
- *Indirect War.* Muslim armies have been a dismal failure in the Arab Israeli Wars, the Iraq Iran War, and the two Gulf Wars but Islamist insurgents have been successful. Lebanon 2006 saw Hizballah win simply by surviving. The Iraqi insurgents were broken but the gains evaporated due to a premature withdrawal but the Taliban is imitating Hizballah. State and stateless Islamists will use terrorism wherever possible—only a terrorist could attack an embassy and kill the ambassador and get away with it. They will use 'civilizational jihad' as defined by the Muslim Brotherhood to subvert the west from within by exploiting victimhood to erode western values such as free speech.
- *Islamist Winter.* Islamists are repeating the Bolshevik strategy of piggy backing on the moderate revolt followed by usurping power during the void created when the old regime collapses. They are converting the Arab Spring from within. In Egypt the Muslim Brotherhood rushed the elections before the moderates could organize. They benefitted from their covert organization that had operated underground for 70 years. Yemen, Bahrain, and Jordan are all battling Islamists disguised as Arab Spring freedom

fighters. Tunisia and Libya are battling the Islamist surge and it remains to be seen who will prevail. Look for Islamists behind every Arab Spring movement.

Towards a Cold War II Strategy. As previously noted George F. Kennan wrote the X Article, titled The Sources of Soviet Conduct, which was published in Foreign Affairs magazine in 1947. Kennan was the Deputy Chief of Mission to the USSR from 1944 to 1946 under Ambassador W. Averell Harriman. In the article, Kennan described confronting Soviet Communism as "undoubtedly greatest task our diplomacy has ever faced and probably greatest it will ever have to face". His proposed concepts became the basis of U.S. Cold War policy:

- The USSR saw itself at perpetual war with capitalism
- The USSR saw left-wing non-communists as worse enemies than capitalists
- The USSR would use controllable Marxists in the capitalist world as allies
- Soviet aggression was not aligned with the views of the Russian people or with economic reality, but was rooted in historic Russian nationalism and neurosis
- Soviet government structure prohibited objective analysis of internal and external reality

Kennan stated that the Soviet Union did not believe in peaceful coexistence with the capitalist world. Their persistent aim was to advance the cause of communism. Capitalism was a menace to their ideals and could not be allowed to influence the Soviet people. Conventional war was not desirable but they would remain ready to exploit opportunities wherever they might arise. Kennan closed by defining Soviet weaknesses and proposing US strategy. He believed we could solve the problem without resorting to "general military conflict," arguing that the USSR was vulnerable to internal instability. He wanted the U.S. to define communism while championing America and the superiority of the Western Civilization over the Soviet collectivist model.

Kennan's view of communism parallels what we see in Islamism. If we substitute Islamism for USSR and Soviets we see a stunning similarity. This should come as no surprise. Communism can be accurately described as a secular religion whose doctrine and WWII success implied to its adherents its destiny to rule the world. They would avoid open warfare but would exploit social unrest wherever it appeared while using western leftists to subvert the West from within.

The cornerstone of U.S. Cold War I strategy was containment of communist expansion. Wherever the communists were, the US was. It challenged them around the world and within their own borders by making the human rights of their dissidents a global issue. It worked but it required patience.

Our Cold War II strategy against Islamism should resemble our Cold War I strategy against Communism. It should contain four pillars; Contain Expansion, Exploit Factionalism, Defend Israel, and Champion the West.

Contain Expansion. America's top priority is to prevent the jump from VEO to CEO. In Egypt, it saw the Muslim Brotherhood move from underground terrorists to the head of state. The consequences of this transition are just beginning to become evident with the sack of the U.S. Embassy. It is easier to deal with Islamism in the form of terrorist violent extremist organizations than to check an Islamist state. As a state, the Islamist gains Westphalian legitimacy, the backing of international institutions and laws, access to the resources of the state to include its treasury, manpower, brainpower and military. The U.S. can target Al Qaeda's Wahhabis but we have to negotiate with Iran's Twelvers.

Exploit Factionalism. The U.S. should highlight and make use of historic Muslim rivalries based on, sects, ethnicity, ideology and nationalism. The U.S. should cite their divisive history often. Refer to the Iranians as Safavids or remind Iranians that the Wahhabi Ikhwan massacred the Shai in Iraq. The divide and conquer strategy exploits the natural divisions and competition within the Muslim world:

- *Sectarian:* Sunni, Shia, and Sufi as major sectarian competitors and
- Wahhabis, Twelvers and Alawites as minor sectarian competitors
- *Ethnic:* Arab versus Persian versus Turk
- *Ideology:* Muslim Brother Qtubism versus Hizballah fealty to the Supreme Leader

- *Nationalist:* Egyptian versus Saudi for Sunni Leadership and Iranian versus Turkey for overall leadership

Defend Israel. The battle for Palestine is the lightning rod that unites the ummah in the 21st Century just as the Crusades united them in the 12th-14th Centuries. If Jerusalem becomes al Quds it would be seen as the greatest Islamic victory over the west since the conquest of Constantinople. Muslims all around the world would rally around the victor; for a while. Israel's demise would be a bloody holocaust that would trigger a global wave of Islamist Triumphalism. Western Muslims would erupt in a burst of 'in your face' violence that would make the Danish Cartoon riots look mild. The destruction of the only western democracy in the Middle East would be justly defined as a sign of western decadence, fear and weakness and be seen as a harbinger of the Caliphate's return.

Champion the West. The west cannot win while apologizing for itself. The United States amplifies its vulnerability by elevating its transgressions to norms while denigrating its triumphs as exploitive. A civilization lacking pride and self-confidence is destined to decline. Reforming the failure doesn't mean rejecting the principals. The U.S. should vigorously defend freedom of speech, expression, and religion while championing consent and rule of law. Domestically The U.S. needs to reinvigorate Western Civilization studies from public school through post graduate school. Internationally, the U.S. needs to promote the western values of the Enlightenment, the American Revolution, and the values of the founding fathers while contrasting American Greco-Roman governing tradition and Judeo-Christian moral tradition against the dreary, stoic and stultified Islamist tradition where individual liberty is sacrificed to submission. And it is absolutely necessary to resist civilizational jihad within our borders and support dissidents within the Islamic states supporting jihad.

Operational Imperatives. The above strategy can be boiled down to a handful of Islamist objectives we must deny.

- No safe have and no rest for non-state Islamists
- No support or legitimacy conferred upon Islamist heads of state

- No Islamist regional hegemony in the Middle East or North Africa
- No monolithic Islamist leaders; state or non-state
- No Islamist victory over Israel
- No compromising western values to appease Islamist sensibilities
- No allowance for Islamism to dominate the narrative
- No Islamist Super State / Caliphate

Summary. It is apparent that Western Democratic Capitalism will not be allowed to coexist with Eastern Theocratic Islamism—the latter cannot tolerate the former. America's existence and economic success highlights their internal flaws, contradictions, and failures. A united Islamist world would not engage in a conventional war with the west; they are too weak economically and militarily. Instead, they will pursue 'death by a thousand cuts' from without while subverting western values with 'civilizational jihad' from within. The U.S. can wear them out in the same way we wore the Soviets with a coherent, patient, persistent, and dedicated strategy. The U.S. keeps the Islamists in their stateless cells and out of their state capitals; inflame their natural and historical rivalries; guarantee Israel; and 'sell' western civilization at home and abroad, we will win over time.

The Arab Bureau of Britain's Foreign Office conceived a campaign of internal insurgency against the Ottoman Empire in the Middle East. The Arab Bureau had long felt it likely that a campaign instigated and financed by outside powers, supporting the breakaway-minded tribes and regional challengers to the Turkish government's centralized rule of their empire, would pay great dividends in the diversion of effort that would be needed to meet such a challenge. The Arab Bureau had recognized the strategic value of what is today called the *"asymmetry"* of such conflict. The Ottoman authorities would have to devote from a hundred to a thousand times the resources to contain the threat of such an internal rebellion compared to the Allies' cost of sponsoring it.

Sacred Causes

Strategies to Defeat Sacred Causes

By John Sutherland | War College | Published: June 22, 2011 at 10:49 am

77 British soldiers clash with the Mahdi Army during the Battle of Omdurman.

"The savior who wants to turn men into angels is as much a hater of human nature as the totalitarian despot who wants to turn them into puppets."
—Eric Hoffer

During the summer of 1881 Muhammad Ahmad bin Abd Allah declared himself Mahdi—the Muslim Messiah who would purge the world for Islam. The announcement came as anger against Sudan's Egyptian rulers and their British masters was growing. Ahmad's sacred cause was to cleanse Sudan of impure influences and form an Islamic state. Sound familiar? The call to arms inspired the masses and an army sprang up over night. From June 1881 to January 1885 the Mahdi Army racked up a series of impressive victories including the seizure of Khartoum. Not even the death of the divine Mahdi himself (typhus) dampened their enthusiasm; his deputy, Abdallahi ibn Muhammad, carried on as Khalifa of the Mahdiyah (Mahdi state).

In 1898 the Brits finally decided to assert their client-state, Egypt's, claim to Sudan. General Horatio Herbert Kitchener received the task. Mahdist brutality and expansionism stirred public support for the enterprise. The newly formed Anglo-Egyptian Army was armed with the best equipment available to include the new Maxim machine-gun. Kitchener needed whatever advantages he could get given the 60,000+ size of the Mahdi Army.

Kitchener began the operation by wiping out a Mahdi fortress, foreshadowing things to come. Next he moved on to the capital, Omdurman. In response, the Mahdi horde attacked into Kitchener's Maxim guns with predictable results; 10,000 dead, 13,000 wounded, and 5,000 prisoners. Kitchener's force suffered only 47 dead and 382 wounded. The Khalifa fled, only to be eventually cornered and killed – the Mahdi uprising died with him. The Anglo-Egyptian administration under British control lasted for 58 years until Sudan was granted independence.

Sacred Causes

The Mahdi's sacred cause took an extraordinary defeat to end. A sacred cause is uncompromising. Negotiation, accommodation, or toleration is not acceptable. If pursued, it's merely to buy time. Sacred warriors seek utopian perfection through absolute victory and nothing short of the loss of their mandate will stop them.

Sacred causes come in two flavors; sectarian and secular. The sectarian brand tends to be more persistent and more difficult to dissuade. A sectarian sacred cause is led by a prophet who has fashioned a theocratic worldview based on an esoteric interpretation of a given faith. Sectarian sacred warriors believe they are divinely entitled or compelled to impose their worldview on 'unbelievers' and/or 'sinners'. These sacred warriors will relent only when they believe the almighty has withdrawn his blessing usually due to a lack of purity and fidelity.

The secular brand may be less persistent but is no less violent. The secular sacred cause is led by an ideologue who has fashioned a cultural worldview out of an esoteric interpretation of socio-political economic theories. Secular sacred warriors believe they are the intellectual vanguard leading the revolutionary reconstruction of society based on their utopian vision. For the secular sacred, the ends justify the means. They will only submit when they believe the world is unprepared for their progressive leap forward or if their followers are deemed unworthy.

The Kingdom of God

The Jewish-Roman wars were a series of revolts by the Jewish Zealots of Judea against Rome. They include the Great Jewish Revolt (66–73), Kitos War (115–117), and the Bar Kokhba revolt (132–135). The Romans tried economic integration, political empowerment, and religious toleration to satisfy the Zealots but their efforts failed to suppress the desire to create a Heavenly Kingdom on Earth

The final uprising was the final straw. It began when Simon Bar Kokhba identified himself as the 'Messiah'. His name means "son of a star" and is derived from Numbers 24:17: "There shall come a star out of Jacob." The revolt quickly spread across the Judean Province. The Romans were caught napping and the Jerusalem garrison was isolated. Simon Bar Kokhba had restored the State of Israel announcing the "Era of the redemption of Israel."

Emperor Hadrian assigned Sextus Julius Severus to quell the unrest; it took 2$^{1}/_2$ years. Modern historians claim a half million Jews were killed and over a thousand villages were razed. Hadrian was tired of the repetitive uprisings so he decided to eliminate the source; Judaism. He banned Torah law, the Hebrew calendar, and executed Judaic scholars. He built statues of Jupiter on the Temple sanctuary and renamed Judea as Palaestina; after the Jews old enemy the Philistines. He banned to Jews from Jerusalem, allowing them yearly entry to mourn their defeat at the Western Wall. As a result, Judaism became mobile, focused on local synagogues instead of the national Temple. The Diaspora was born, Messianism was discredited, and Bar-Kokhba was denounced. Like the Sudanese Mahdi, the Judean Messiah led a multi-year revolt against the most powerful empire at the time. Both established sectarian states and required catastrophic defeat to end.

The French Empire. The French Revolution (1789–1799) turned Europe on its head. In the wake of the American Revolution, the French challenged King Louis XVI's divine right to rule and took on the class system that placed the clergy and nobility above the law and exempt from taxes. The *New Republic* declared the Rights of Man and embarked upon a sacred cause to remake France. The revolution inspired Europe to form a series of coalitions to smother the movement in its infancy and preserve the monarchical system—they failed.

Internecine arguments became self destructive bloodbaths requiring a changing of the guard from purists to pragmatics—thus Napoleon ascended to leadership in 1804, establishing the French Empire (1804–1815). Napoleon was a dictator and a true believer so he took the Revolution on the road.

Napoleon gives orders during the Battle of Austerlitz

The Napoleonic Wars imposed French influence over most of Western Europe and into Poland. By 1812 the Empire ruled over 44 million subjects and maintained a military presence in Germany, Italy, Spain, and the Duchy of Warsaw, counting Prussia and Austria as allies. Napoleon's victories exported the revolution's ideology throughout Europe. Aristocratic privilege was all but eliminated and the Napoleonic Code codified legal equality, the jury system and legal divorce. Napoleons family occupied Europe's thrones. After his victory over the Austrian Empire, Napoleon launched the invasion of Russia in 1812. It was an ill advised disaster. Shortly thereafter the Sixth Coalition kicked the French out of Germany in 1813. The pressure built and the Empire fell when Napoleon abdicated at Fontainebleau on 11 April 1814. But that wasn't the end. After a brief exile on Elba, Napoleon returned to resurrect the Empire in the Hundred Days.

He was defeated yet again by the Seventh Coalition at Waterloo. The British captured him and re-exiled him, this time to Saint Helena, a remote island in the South Atlantic. He lived there until his death in 1821. he removal of Napoleon saw the end of the revolution and its gains. The Bourbon monarchy was restored and France lost the territories it had won between 1795–1810. It took Napoleon's removal (leadership decapitation) to decisively end the hyper-secular French Revolution.

The Caliphate. The caliphate is literally the "dominion of a caliph" (successor). It's the rule of Islam over the Muslim Nation (ummah). The first Caliphate was led by Mohammad's closest followers and was known as the 'Rashidun caliphate'. Sunnis believed the caliph should be selected by a Shura (council) while Shia's believed the caliph should be a descendent of the Prophet—the source of a future Islamic Schism. The caliphates went from anointed leaders to familial dynasties; the Umayyad followed by the Abbasid, the Fatimid, and the Ottoman.

Mohammad expanded his rule from the city of Medina to the entire Arabian Peninsula driven by his sacred mandate to conquer the world for Islam. The Caliphate was a continuation of his sacred cause and so it embarked upon a 600 year Jihad (Holy War). The Rashiduns conquered Persia and most of Byzantium; the Umayyads took North Africa, Spain and expanded east to the Indian border; while the Abbasids added portions of southern Italy and pressed into modern day Azerbaijan and Georgia. The Ottomans capped it off by adding Anatolia, Greece and the Balkans. The Caliphate met resistance at the Battle of Tours (732), the Siege of Vienna (1529), the naval Battle of Lepanto (1571). Finally, the sacred cause stalled and began to recede in the late 1600's as conquest became defeat and dynamism became stagnation. Sectarian apartheid, poor education, economic failure, and technological inferiority eroded Ottoman influence. The Caliphate began losing so often it earned the moniker of "the Sick Man of Europe". They sealed their fate by siding with the Central Powers during World War I—a choice that led to their partition and eventual dissolution.

The Ottoman Caliphate collapsed with the occupation of Istanbul in November, 1918. They signed the Treaty of Sèvres but the final disposition of the empire was delayed by the Turkish War of Independence. The final agreement with the Grand National Assembly of Turkey came in 1923. The resulting imperial partition created the modern Middle East and the Republic of Turkey. France received mandates over Syria and Lebanon while Britain got Mesopotamia and Palestine. A year later (March 3, 1924) the President of the Turkish Republic, Mustafa Kemal

Atatürk abolished the institution of the Caliphate and transferred its powers to the Grand National Assembly. With a few brief exceptions, the title has been dead ever since. The sacred cause of the Caliphate with its divine mission to spread Islamic rule died of exhaustion brought about by poor comparative performance.

Triumphant return of a Caliph from the battlefield.

Strategies to Defeat Sacred Causes

War, cold or hot, is a clash of wills. Resolution comes when one side finally acquiesces to the other. The question is, 'how difficult is it going to be to get that acquiescence?' The answer is based on commitment. A sacred cause inspires more commitment than a mundane one.

Committed leaders and followers. This represents the most toxic of sacred causes and is most often associated with an expeditionary cause such as Nazism and Islamism. Nazism was neo-Darwinist racism and Islamism is sectarian imperialism. These are viral sacred causes whose leaders are infected with 'Holy Madness' and whose adherents are fanatic disciples. These causes are not content with dominating their homelands; they are aggressive in their 'mission' to export their vision in search of regional and/or global domination.

Causes like these require catastrophic defeat to be quelled. Only an unambiguous and total defeat discredits the messenger and the message. The egregious abuses of Nazism, a racist form of Fascism, were so profound that total defeat was the only option. Today, racist fascism is so discredited that it is virtually extinct. The same can be said for Japanese militarism; another racial superiority based fascism.

Committed leaders with reluctant / lukewarm followers. Some sacred causes are almost wholly dependent upon a charismatic leader to carry them through. In these cases, the leader is the inspiration to the masses and is often the only influence able to control subordinate rivalries. These causes are dominated by the cult of personality. They can be deadly but are vulnerable.

Decapitation can bring a cultist cause to a rapid end if the leader can be removed before dedication and unity emerge among the vanguard and/or the masses. Frederick Barbarossa led the largest and most dangerous contingent of the Third Crusade. His army turned back when Frederick fell from his horse and drowned during a river crossing. Some believe Barbarossa's local scouts led them to the river on purpose. Attila's Huns disintegrated after he died on his wedding night. Some believe he was poisoned. Arminius' assassination ended German unity against Rome and the capture and exile of Napoleon ended the French Empire.

Entrenched leaders with indifferent followers. Causes like these are usually mature. They achieved their initial goals and settled into lassitude and/or ossification. While the leaders and their followers may still believe in their system, they no longer feel compelled to 'fight' or 'sacrifice' for it.

The communists conquered Russia, successfully defended themselves in a three way civil war, and then failed in their attempt to spread the contagion into Poland. Under Stalin they became content to pursue 'Socialism in one Country,' repudiating the 'Permanent Revolution' philosophy of founding father Leon Trotsky. The communist war with capitalism became a Cold War until final *exhaustion* caused the Soviet economy to collapse and precipitated its disintegration. The USSR voluntarily faded away just as the Ottoman Caliphate had in the face of a western world that outpaced it.

Islamist/Jihadism – Islamic Revanchism

So what path do we take to roll back the medieval jihadist impulse emanating from the Muslim world – state and stateless? Jihadi motivation is clear; to recapture the ancient Caliphate which includes conquering Spain (Al Andulus), North Africa, parts of Italy numerous Mediterranean Islands, much of India. They want to restore their perceived medieval dominance and return the infidels to dhimmitude. The most overtly aggressive Islamist state is Iran. The most covertly aggressive state is Saudi Arabia. The pantheon of non-state Islamist/Jihadists is too numerous to account for here.

With Iran seeking an Islamic bomb, Turkey resurrecting the Ottoman Empire and Saudi Arabia subverting the west with a petro-dollar tidal wave—all backed by steady drumbeat of stateless Jihadi terrorism – what is our approach?

Decapitation? Probably not—there are too many chiefs. There is no single charismatic leader. There are many: Ahmadenejad, Khameini, Erdogan, Nasrallah, Qardawi, Abbas, Meshaal, Asaad, Gaddafi. Some lead Sunnis, some lead Shia, some are nationalist and some are theocrats. All extol Islamic triumphalism. It's a hydra so whose head do you choose?

Exhaustion? Again, probably not – there's not enough time. Iran could have a bomb any day; Saudi Arabia builds a new Mosque or Madrassa every day; Erdogan's party was re-elected June 12; Palestine is going to declare statehood any day; and Gaddafi seems to be holding on versus NATO's fearsome offensive. It's hard to exhaust an opponent who is convinced he has the wind to his back.

Catastrophic Defeat? The above leads us to the conclusion that catastrophic defeat is the only path available today. The problem is will – does the west have what it takes to follow this path? Given the west's current self destructive trend of self loathing bolstered by the twin pillars of political correctness/Islamophobia and multiculturalism/moral relativism, it seems unlikely. The west will not challenge Islamism until it regains its confidence or it is so grievously provoked that the masses are moved to action.

Until then, the west must tolerate the intolerable: religious apartheid, medieval morality, misogyny, cultural bigotry, and virtual dhimmitude—all in the name of western enlightenment. It seems odd to embrace eastern regressive ideology in order to reinforce western progressive ideology.[281]

---

[281] John Sutherland is the author of several acclaimed articles published in *Armchair General* magazine, including "iGuerrilla: The New Model Techno-Insurgent" (May 2008) and "Persian Arrows: America's Winning Iran Strategy" (March 2011).

Techno-Terrorism
Mumbai

iGuerrilla Version 2.0 – The Terrorist and the Guerrilla Converge at Mumbai

John Sutherland's article "iGuerrilla: The New Model Techno-Insurgent" appeared in the May, 2008 issue of *Armchair General* magazine.

An Indian soldier aims his weapon toward The Taj Majal Hotel in Mumbai, Nov. 29, 2008. Indian commandos killed the last Islamic militants holed up inside the hotel, ending the more than two-day terror assault on India's financial capital. *Pedro Ugarte/AFP/Getty Image.*

News reports claim that the attackers carried handheld GPS navigators, the tool that probably guided the speedboats to their insertion points and then would get the teams very quickly to their targets. [283]

The designation iGuerrilla first appeared in the May '08 issue of *Armchair General* as the New Model Techno-Insurgent, a high-tech guerrilla motivated by religious fanaticism. The article stated that the terrorist Hizballah paramilitary force that fought the '06 Lebanon War was the modern-day embodiment of the new wave warrior / iGuerrilla. Hizballah had made the leap from boonie-hopping bands of AK-toting, would-be revolutionaries pulling off the occasional raid or ambush to a

The recent attacks in Mumbai, India, may have opened a chilling new chapter in terrorism and guerrilla warfare.

well-trained force consisting of semi-professional troops executing a well-conceived elastic defense while armed with anti-tank missiles, computers, night vision, and long range rockets. These guys ran Lebanon from the shadows, built bunkers, established an extensive network of caches, took on the Israeli Defense Forces (IDF) and, all the while, managed to retain their non-state actor status. The fighters of the 2006 Lebanon War were highly trained, well equipped, and even better armed with modern weapons and technology than any non-state guerrilla force we've ever seen … but they were still guerrillas.

As if the rise of the iGuerrilla wasn't enough, the threat has morphed yet again. Like a virus, the iG has reorganized its DNA in order to form a new and more lethal variant. The latest version of the iG has taken on a more terrorist-like flavor while preserving its original guerrilla foundations. It can now strike at a new host. iG v 2.0 has exploited technology just as the original did in order to facilitate its attack. The new virus doesn't fight with state armies; rather, it prefers to commit a sort of prolonged and theatrical suicide that maximizes media exposure, generates massive societal disruption, and inflicts maximum mayhem, violence, and destruction. The iG 2.0 employs guerrilla tactics, techniques, and procedures while in pursuit of terrorist effects and objectives. For this to make sense, we'll have to initiate the discussion by paraphrasing a few sources that address some basic definitions and descriptions.

What is a Guerrilla? According to *The American Heritage Dictionary*, a guerrilla is a member of an irregular, usually indigenous, military or paramilitary unit operating in small bands in occupied territory to harass and undermine the enemy, as by surprise raids. Guerrilla is the diminutive form of the Spanish word for war (Guerra). One can envision in the mind's eye a group of plotting, armed, Robin Hoods who seek the overthrow of the Sheriff of Nottingham and his replacement by their own exalted leader.

What is Guerrilla Warfare? For this description, we'll rely on the definition from the International Relations Program at University of California, Davis. Guerrilla war is unconventional warfare (not army against army) and combat with which a small group of combatants use mobile tactics such as ambushes and raids to fight a larger and less mobile formal state army. Guerrilla war includes certain kinds of civil wars and is warfare without front lines or boundaries. The irregular forces that fight guerrilla wars operate among the civilian population and are often hidden or protected by them. The purpose of guerrilla war is not to engage the state army directly but rather to conduct continuing operations to harass and punish it so as to gradually limit its operation, liberate territory from its control, and erode its support.

In guerrilla war without lines there is territory that neither side controls; both sides exert military leverage over the same place at the same time. This makes guerrilla wars extremely painful for civilians because conventional armies fighting guerrillas often cannot distinguish them from civilians and so punish both. This aspect allows non-state actors to exploit international law—a concept known as *Lawfare*. Guerrillas operate from bases established in remote and inaccessible terrain, such as forests, mountains, and jungles. They depend on the support from the local inhabitants in the form of recruits, food, shelter, and information. Striking swiftly and unexpectedly, guerrillas raid supply depots and installations, ambush patrols and convoys, and sever lines of communication with the goal being the disruption of the state's activities and the capture of equipment and supplies for their own use.

What is a Terrorist? This is a bit tougher to pin down since there are literally hundreds of definitions for terrorists out there. We'll go with Princeton University's WordNet on this one. A terrorist is a radical who employs terror as a political weapon, usually organizes with other terrorists in small cells, and often uses religion as a cover for terrorist activities. For this one we envision a Guy Fawkes–type of character packing the sewers under the Parliament with gunpowder with the plan of blowing up the place while in session, or maybe we see the skulking PLO gunman, complete with full face ski mask, patrolling the roof of the Olympic Village in Munich.

What is Terrorism? We'll stick with Princeton University's WordNet. Terrorism is the calculated use of violence (or the threat of violence) against civilians in order to attain goals that are political, religious, or ideological in nature; this is done through intimidation or coercion or instilling fear. Terrorism requires violence that provokes psychological impact and fear that is perpetrated for a political goal.

Terrorism deliberately targets non-combatants, is executed (at least in part) incognito, and is viewed as unlawful by the population at large.

All in all, terrorists and guerrillas are quite a bit alike ... and yet are somewhat different. Both represent weak forces taking on much stronger opponents and because of that, the guerrilla and terrorist are forced to resort to asymmetric warfare techniques. Historically, guerrillas tend to focus locally. They attack state sources of power in pursuit of a pragmatic goal while trying to win over the populace. Terrorists, on the other hand, tend to be more sporadic and are willing to strike anywhere if it promotes their cause. They seek the de-legitimization of the state through coercion of the public. Much like a protection racket, they'll protect you from their own attacks if you turn on the police who are supposed to protect you. Guerrillas resort to terrorism as a tactic from time to time when they are weak, while terrorists typically cannot resort to guerrilla tactics and thus rely almost exclusively on public displays of violence. Let's do a hasty comparative analysis to see if we can sort out one from the other.

The common perception of a guerrilla is personified by Lawrence of Arabia, Mao, and Ernesto "Che" Guevara. Common perceptions of guerrilla wars are the Vendee Uprising in the early days of the French Republic, the Boer War, the Malayan Emergency, the Battle for Algeria and the mujahedeen of Afghanistan. All of these scenarios are familiar. They remind us of partisans, freedom fighters, and communist insurgents. Some gain popular approval, others disapproval, but they all seem conventional and somewhat respectable-at least they are understood. Guerrillas are hard but rational. They negotiate, and even the sectarian guerrillas will strike a deal if concessions are made that address their perceived grievances.

When terrorists come to mind, the Irish Republican Army (IRA), the Palestinian Liberation Organization (PLO), Baader-Meinhof, the Red Brigades, Shining Path, and Al Qaeda show up. Unsavory characters like Abu Nidal, Usama Bin Laden, Timothy McVeigh, and Ilich Ramirez Sanchez (Carlos the Jackal) appear. They are relentless zealots, nihilists, and utopians. They will kill, kidnap, and bomb their way through anyone to get what they want. They don't cut deals; either you're with them or you're dead. Terrorism prompts the mind to remember events like airline hijackings, bombings, and assassinations of famous leaders like Lord Louis Mountbatten and President Anwar Sadat. Mental images of Munich, the *Achille Lauro*, and 9-11 appear. Terrorist events seem more criminal than warlike, and often shock the terrorists' supporters. They come across as unjust-why toss Leon Klinghoffer, in his wheelchair, overboard on the *Achille Lauro*? How does this simple act of personal cruelty help to liberate Palestine? Unlike guerrillas, terrorists come across as irrational. The guerrilla resembles Robin Hood, while the terrorist resembles Jack the Ripper.

The writings of Chinese leader Mao Zedong helped shape modern guerrilla warfare.

Convergence. Mao Zedong shaped modern-day guerrilla warfare and, in a way, made room for the terrorist and guerrilla to coexist. The Maoist theory of People's War divides warfare into three phases. In phase one the guerrilla earns the population's support by distributing propaganda and attacking the organs of government. In phase two, he escalates his attacks against the state's military forces and institutions— there is room for some terrorism here, but it must be measured so as not to undo phase one. Phase three sees the conflict shift to conventional warfare in which guerrilla armies seize key terrain and cities, overthrow the government, and take control of the country. The initial phases of insurgency see a blurring of the lines between terrorism and guerrilla warfare, making a clear-cut designation problematic at times.

Similarities and differences. Guerrillas seem larger than life and even somewhat romantic—see Che Guevara T-shirts—while terrorists come across as wild-eyed maniacs. Guerrillas attack what they see as their inherently guilty and corrupt enemy, while terrorists attack the inno-cent in order to indirectly coerce their enemy. Both use asymmetric techniques but guerrillas seem to take a more or less legitimate, if aggravating, path that holds out the promise of political resolution. Terrorists follow a bloody and uncompromising path.

What is iG v 2.0? As I watched the Mumbai attack unfold over sev-eral days in late November I got the feeling that this was something dif-ferent. It wasn't a high-tech, one-shot deal like 9-11, nor was it anoth-er garden-variety, chaotic bombing like the one that struck the Marriot in Karachi. This was more like a military raid that had no planned with-drawal. It seemed to have been launched with the surgical precision of a special operation. It was quick and slick. It seemed like the iGuerrilla had left the battlefield arena and entered the realm of the terrorist.

iG v 2 is a hybrid that includes genes from the guerrilla, the terror-ist, and techno genes from the iGuerrilla. I suspected that Mumbai had the latter and news reports on that came in on December 3 and 4 bore out my suspicion. The attack itself wasn't all that original but the tools that made it so precise were. Mumbai was an outbreak of the iG v 2 virus—a Hizballah-like iGuerrilla entity augmented with an Al Qaeda–like flare for public suicidal violence. The Mumbai attack was very guerrilla but the end state was very terrorist and the innovation was very iGuerrilla.

The Mumbai attack represents the merger of the terrorist and the iG. For five days, from Nov 30 to Dec 1, somewhere between 10 and 40 operatives captured and held the world's attention by pulling off at least seven attacks in the high visibility heart of Mumbai, India.

The Guerrilla Element. The Mumbai attackers employed old-fash-ioned guerrilla tactics. They used speedboats for rapid insertion. They were broken down into several small assault teams. They hit soft targets and they used small arms, grenades, and explosives in their attacks.

The Terrorist Element. The attack was very visible; there was no attempt at stealth. They took hundreds of hostages, some of whom they tortured and killed. The casualty figures were around 170 with anoth-er 300 or more maimed (none of these figures are final at the time of this writing). The targets were not political or military; as usual, the victims were non-combatants. The sites they attacked were not government buildings, they were innocuous civilian hangouts like the Leopold Café, the Chhatrapati Shivaji train terminal, the Oberoi Hotel, the Trident Hotel, the Taj Mahal Hotel, and the Chabad House Jewish Center (the only nonpartisan objective). The attackers were members of the Deccan Mujaheddin, an AQ affiliate that apparently operates out of the tribal regions of Pakistan. They were not executing a guerrilla hit-and-run, their goal was clearly to wreak as much death and destruction as possible.

The iG Element. News reports claim that the attackers carried handheld GPS navigators, the tool that probably guided the speedboats to their insertion points and then would get the teams very quickly to their targets. No more landing at the wrong pier or running to the wrong building. No more taking the wrong turn down the dead end alley, now you can get where you have to be when you have to be there. (Fox News Report, "Technology Gave Mumbai Terrorists Tactical Edge," Wednesday, December 03, 2008)

They also carried satellite phones and BlackBerrys ("Gunmen Used Technology as a Tactical Tool, Mumbai Attackers Had GPS Units, Satellite Maps," Emily Wax, *Washington Post* Foreign Service, Wednesday, December 3, 2008). These would obviously enhance command and control and mission coordination. The Mumbai mob used satellite phones and Voice over Internet Protocol (VOIP) in Pakistan, thus making their calls hard to trace. Once the attacks were underway the terrorists took victims' cell phones and swapped the SIM cards to further confuse anyone hoping to intercept their communications. The teams could have easily reported all the way back to Pakistan given these tools—no more waiting breathlessly in a cave with the shortwave on and a cup of chai in your hand! These devices would eliminate the time-honored tradition of synchronizing watches or waiting for the initial casualty-producing burst that kicks off the entire operation. My guess— just a hunch—is that there were probably multiple observation posts manned by spotters who could vector assault teams to their targets and away from Indian security forces. Once on the ground, the attackers monitored the Indian response by watching TV. They also may have monitored Internet reports, blogs, *YouTube* and other sources of streaming and constant situation updates.

Reports state that the Mumbai mob used the Internet to dig up information on their planned objectives. Apparently they downloaded what they needed, then burned mission CDs containing detailed maps and *Google Earth* images of their targets. The only terrorist captured has told police that he was shown video and satellite images of the targets before the attack! No more paying off desk clerks and cab drivers to snap drive-by photos or pace off intersections—simply go on line and do a cyber recon. Welcome to point-and-click mission preparation and rehearsal.

An internal security expert at the Center for Policy Research in New Delhi, India, told the *Washington Post* that, "they were not sailors, but they were able to use sophisticated GPS navigation tools and detailed maps to sail from Karachi to Mumbai."

"Most of their rehearsals to familiarize themselves with Mumbai were done on high-resolution satellite maps, so they would have a good feel for the city's streets and buildings where they were going," terrorism expert Praveen Swami told the *Post*.

The precision of the movement rendered clandestine infiltration unnecessary. This wasn't like Munich where the attackers had to dress like athletes, then had to bluff their way into the complex, and then had to figure where things were after arriving on site. The Mumbai teams knew exactly where they were and where they were headed. This is iG v 2.0. Mumbai was a terrorist attack that exploited modern information technology. Like the Hizballah fighters in 2006, the Mumbai attackers of 2008 used all the modern technology within their reach to conduct their operation.

This type of attack isn't new or even novel. Terrorists have carried out these types of attacks before and have hit these kinds of targets before. They've even been able to "make it last" like Mumbai did. Below are two very similar examples:

November 17, 1997; Tourist Attack in Luxor, Egypt: Al-Gama'at al-Islamiyya gunmen killed 58 tourists and 4 Egyptians and wounded 26 others at the Hatshepsut Temple in the Valley of the Kings near Luxor. Thirty-four Swiss, eight Japanese, five Germans, four Britons, one French, one Colombian, a dual Bulgarian/British citizen, and four unidentified persons were among the dead. Twelve Swiss, two Japanese, two Germans, one French, and nine Egyptians were among the wounded.

And more recently . . .

September 1–3, 2004; Beslan, Russia: Islamist gunmen take over 1,000 hostages, mostly children, at a school in North Ossetia. After a three-day siege, many of the hostages are killed in an explosion in the school gym, after which Russian troops storm the building. The final death toll is over 330, many of them children. Eight hundred more are injured.

This attack profile isn't new. The targets aren't new and neither are the victims. Only the extent of the infusion and exploitation of technology is new. Just like Hizballah's defense south of the Litani River wasn't really new, the unexpected appearance of a full array of sophisticated technology and weapons augmented by an aggressive information operations campaign were new. The unanticipated combination forced the Israeli Defense Force to leave the field appearing, at least nominally, to have been beaten, thus bursting their all-important invincibility persona. The Israeli military expected to meet *intifada*-like refugee mobs throwing rocks and firing potshots, but they got paramilitary commandos fighting from a coherent and well-prepared defense system.

The Mumbai attacks will have a similar chilling effect once the whole story is known. The lessons learned might point to the introduction of a new type of special ops terrorism whose capabilities will extend their reach while enabling them to execute surgical strikes that will surely be transformed into grand theater for the "if it bleeds it leads" media. The virgin-seeking suicide bomber may give way to sectarian suicide "A-Teams" whose final moments resemble a Blackhawk Down movie clip versus a series of grainy surveillance stills of a car driving up, parking, and detonating. With terrorists armed with Information Age technology, there will be more Taj Hotels, more Luxors, and more Beslans on the horizon. It's not difficult to train someone how to use a GPS and to pull up the Internet on a Blackberry.

The U.S. must now brace itself for iG v2 terrorist-guerrillas who will launch pseudo-guerrilla operations in the west with the ultimate goal of pulling one off within the continental United States. They won't require a long incubation period and an extensive sleeper network and, with the U.S.'s porous borders, they will have little problem getting into the country. Their attacks won't be hit-and-run; they will be stick-and-kill. Cyber recon and distributed cyber command and control and cyber navigation will enable terror guerrillas to execute precise, Special Forces-like operations. Low-cost, readily available, easy-to-use modern information technology has accelerated all aspects of modern society. It would be folly to think that the bad will not accelerate alongside the good. The newest killer virus is among us. The iG v 2 is the West's newest and potentially most lethal non-state threat

War and Peace
2013

WAR AND PEACE: 2013 AND BEYOND

What you *must know* about the global strategic situation.

THE QUEST FOR POWER

International relations, at the most fundamental level, is the quest for power: some nations have it, and want to keep or expand it; other nations (and, increasingly, stateless groups that are not "traditional nations") want it. Yet, the calculus of power is ever-shifting as nations struggle with the inevitable ebb and flow of their military strength, wealth and influence. This competition to gain, hold or expand power has several profound implications for today's global strategic situation.

Ambiguity: Traditionally, diplomats have sought to create a "balance of power" among nations, a condition essentially of ambiguity in which no nation feels threatened. Yet, if nations do not feel threatened, they are not *deterred* from engaging in military, political or economic adventures to expand their own nations' power at the expense of others. Ambiguity or uncertainty created by the balance of power promises at least some expectation of "victory." One tragic historical example is World War I—although the interlocking web of treaties "balanced" power among European nations, each side marched off to war in 1914 because each side expected victory.

Clarity: When power is extremely "unbalanced," with one nation or bloc of nations clearly and unambiguously dominant, the result of such clarity typically is general stability and relative peace. With no expectation of victory, there is no incentive for less powerful nations to

Editor's Note: The author is a senior operations and intelligence analyst whose influential articles include the widely-acclaimed "iGuerrilla: The New Model Techno-Insurgent" (May, 2008 ACG) and "War on Terror: A Global Update" (May, 2010 ACG). This insightful strategic update presents readers the author's assessment of today's most critical global security challenges.

challenge the status quo. Although such clarity of power does not mean the absence of all conflict, it makes the outbreak of any *cataclysmic* war impossible or extremely unlikely. Historical examples include the "Pax Romana" of the Roman Empire, "Pax Britannica" during the heyday of the British Empire and, some might argue, "Pax Americana" while the United States is the world's sole remaining Superpower.

Will: Power is relative, not absolute. Regardless of a nation's *apparent* military, political and economic power, such power is irrelevant if a nation's leaders lack the will to use it. In the late 1930s, for example, the combined power of France and Britain greatly outweighed Adolf Hitler's rising Nazi Germany; yet, French and British leaders were unwilling to use it until it was too late, preferring "appeasement," despite Hitler's oft-demonstrated appetite for new conquests. Lacking the will to exercise France's and Britain's national power, French and British leaders' goal of "Peace in our time" became "war on Hitler's schedule."

Rationality: Historically, the successful conduct of international relations has depended upon the expectation that national leaders will act rationally in a given situation—although, admittedly, what might seem "rational" to one nation has at times and under particular circumstances appeared distinctly "irrational" to another. Yet, "rationality" is not always a hallmark of sectarian-led nations (or stateless groups) in which religious tenets and beliefs trump any seemingly "rational" secular concerns. The increasing proliferation of sectarian states and groups in the Middle East presents diplomats representing the world's secular states with perhaps their greatest challenge in many decades.

An assessment of today's global strategic situation clearly reveals that the quest for power among nations has not diminished – nor is it likely to.

STRATEGIC ASSESSMENT: EUROPE

Europe was the hub of power and influence for centuries. There were so many great and powerful nations that none knew which was *most* powerful -- hence two cataclysmic World Wars and a Cold War dominated 20th century Europe, changing everything.

Welfare State Debt: The Cold War (1946-91) during which the United States assumed the main burden of defending Western

European allowed those nations to redirect their defense dollars to their economies. Given essentially a "blank check," Euro-socialists built a cradle-to-grave nanny state. Free markets gave way to utopian equality, bloated bureaucracies, lush entitlements and imminent bankruptcy. Today, Spain has 24-percent unemployment and empty banks, Greece is broke, and Germany is being strong-armed to ruin its own stable fiscal situation by subsidizing everyone else. Europe has fulfilled Margaret Thatcher's prediction: "The problem with socialism is that you eventually run out of other people's money." This problem is worse given the creation of the European Union (EU), Europe's attempt to counterbalance U.S. power and influence. EU nations have a shared currency (the Euro), resulting in the problems of the few becoming everyone's problems. Portugal, Italy, Greece and Spain lead the debt derby with Ireland and France close behind. The EU is an unnatural political creation that seems now in danger of fragmenting. Yet, the dissolution of the EU would birth a plethora of impoverished states seeking to reclaim ancient rights to land, resources and possible re-aggregation that reverses post-Cold War fragmentation. That could well bring revolution and dictatorships reclaiming center stage as old solutions re-emerge.

Debt Coping: Europe has few ways of coping with this self-inflicted implosion. They can cut budgets and thereby strand legions of dependent citizens, tax wealthy citizens and redistribute their wealth, or extort the solvent states to bail out the failing ones. Greece and Spain are experiencing the pain of austerity as a dependent citizenry erupts in violent rioting upon the announcement of each new austerity measure. France has decided to exploit class warfare by taxing the rich at a 75-percent rate, causing the flight of wealth to more taxpayer-friendly nations.

Welfare State Demographics: Growing entitlements and eroding values have generated a society more interested in entitlements than families. European populations are declining: no kids=no tax base=no future. Europeans aren't even replacing the current generation. No generation after next means no workforce to fund entitlements.

Demographic Coping: Europe's demographic death spiral has only one solution—immigration, legal or not. Europe essentially eliminated national borders and has rolled out the multicultural red carpet to predominately Muslim immigrants. The newcomers, however, are not all fans of democracy beyond the generous entitlements democracies provide. Thus, firebrands like Khomieni (France) and Qardawi (Britain) are coddled in the West while fomenting militant Islamism abroad. And since European nations do not demand assimilation from the new immigrants, imported religious intolerance threatens the very continuance of liberal Western democracy.

Welfare State Defense: No money for defense and eroding confidence in European culture have created endemic weaknesses and declining influence. The continent that once fielded massive armies and built global empires can no longer field a complete combat division. The EU looks to NATO and the U.S. for salvation. EU nations deploy bits and pieces as a conglomerate force that is so hobbled by national caveats that its aggregate effect is to burden their allies more than their enemies.

Defense Coping: The way to cope with being defenseless is pseudo-isolationism and nuclear proliferation. Much of Europe self-righteously rejects any external engagement beyond writing indignant letters or issuing official condemnations. The ghost of "appeasement" is back. Europe has traded the threat of military intervention for ineffectual economic sanctions - unless facing a low risk environment like Libya - and the results are predictable: Iran builds nukes; Syria slaughters dissenters; Russia mugs Georgia and Ukraine; and Israel is blamed for Hamas and Hizballah rockets. National pacifism yields homeland defense without an army, navy or air force. The answer is nukes: aggressive nations will leave you alone if they know you possess nuclear weapons. If Iran "nukes up," expect Europe to follow suit.

STRATEGIC ASSESSMENT: THE MIDDLE EAST

The Middle East became the main battleground following the Cold War. The expiration of old spheres of influence and their secular imperative reinvigorated the ancient sectarian impulses. The time came for the Muslim world to replace its earthly dictators with divine theocrats.

Arab Spring – Sectarianism: The West mistook opposition to dictatorship as support for democracy. This isn't new; France swapped a

King for an Emperor, Russia traded a Czar for a Bolshevik dictator, and Iran booted a Shah for a Supreme Leader. In each case, the cure was usually worse than the disease and the pattern was consistent—liberals may start a revolution but radicals finish it. The "Arab Spring" has become an "Islamist Winter:" Hamas took Gaza; Hizballah got Lebanon, Al Shabaab runs much of Somalia; the Al Houthi are taking Yemen; Al Qaeda hid in the shadows of New Libya and is headed to Syria; and the Muslim Brotherhood bagged Egypt. Iran and Bahrain were misfires, while Tunisia, Mali and Libya have more in common with the Iranian Spirit of 1979 than the America Spirit of 1776. Secular dictators have been replaced with sectarian theocrats, and the rule of law has become the rule of Sharia with the goal of resurrecting the Caliphate.

Sectarian Coping: To date, the West's way of coping has been to pretend the Arab Spring is democratic, while the region's new sectarian rulers give public lip service to secularism but condone, abet or actively encourage increasingly violent waves of religious-based persecution. The West pressures old allies to step down and foolishly backs sworn enemies in the vain hope that the region's new rulers will appreciate such magnanimity when they take power. So far no good — witness Al Qaeda's flag flying in Benghazi and murdered U.S. diplomats.

Arab Spring – Triumphalism: Muslim triumphalism leads to political over-extension, unrestrained avarice, and strategic overreach. The response is pursuit of the Caliphate and cultural/sectarian war, meaning Jihad. Targeted for "return" to the Dar al Islam would be Spain, India, North Africa and the Balkans. The recent warming of Egyptian-Iranian relations is ominous at best. Iran has long-range missiles, Egyptians destroyed the Israeli oil pipeline and stormed the U. S. Embassy. Libya followed suit, killing the U.S. ambassador on the anniversary of 9-11. Europe would be threatened in the traditional border areas of Southern France, Italy and Austria. Israel would be doomed.

Arab Spring – Civil War: A Shia-Sunni civil war may come sooner rather than later. It would be a natural repeat of the wars of succession to Mohammad between Ali and the companions. Iraq's Shia President indicted his Sunni Vice President who fled to Sunni Turkey, and a series of bombings killing a hundred Shias followed. The Turks are backing the Syrian Sunni rebels, with Saudi financial support, and Iran and Hizballah are backing the Shia Alawites. The Syrian Civil War is looking a lot like the Spanish Civil War. Iran will lead the Shias while a number of candidates might lead the Sunni block. If Iran develops nukes, so will Saudi Arabia and possibly others. The result will be global disruption of Middle Eastern oil, a rise in terrorism and a region unsafe for non-Muslims. In the end, one side will win or, more likely, both sides will return to obscurity and the serial failure that followed World War I.

Coping: The West will need to keep trade routes open, defend Israel and promote secularism as an alternative to sectarian bloodshed. If a Shia-Sunni civil war erupts, it will be Ireland of the 1970's on a much more massive scale.

STRATEGIC ASSESSMENT: THE BIG THREE

The world's Big Three States – America, Russia and China – have held and continue to hold the global center stage. The first is the reluctant "top dog" increasingly looking to relinquish the lead in exchange for a simpler life; the second single-mindedly pursues the path of recapturing old glories; and one is a manpower giant seeking regional hegemony and increased global influence.

America: The United States seems to be repeating its flawed war-ending game plan from the Vietnam War: declare victory; recall the troops; slash defense funding; and spend the "peace dividend" like a drunken sailor. U.S. forces turned out the lights in Iraq and have provided the Taliban with an end date in Afghanistan. Iraq is now Iran's puppet – as just two examples, consider that Iraq abstained on an Arab League vote to sanction Syria and the country now has an Iranian Transportation Minister. The U.S. appears to be leaving the future of Afghanistan to the Taliban and Pakistan—who will be only too happy to fill the void left in the wake of America's withdrawal. After several years of U.S. foreign policy fiascos—if not having a coherent foreign policy can be described as a "policy"—America appears weak, distracted and irresolute. Even the murder of a U.S. ambassador provoked only a "strongly-worded note" in response. Add to this America's fiscal troubles and it becomes clear that the world's only remaining Superpower lacks the will to act like one. America is dangerously exposed.

Russia: The veneer of democracy in Russia is wearing thin. The parade of anti-Putin demonstrations leading up to his impending 2012 election as "President for Life" was met with old fashioned, "Soviet-style" repression. Nationalism, virtually a state religion in Russia and a useful tool to dictators, is fanned by re-starting the Cold War—bombers have reappeared over American airspace, Russian subs roam the Gulf of Mexico, and Russian knee-jerk opposition to the U.S. has returned to block UN actions on Syria and Iran. Russians are weary of Putin's oligarchy, his toady Medvedev, and his millionaire cronies, but any effective opposition to Russia's corruption and heavy-handed governance is kept in check by robust "organs of state security." Russia is a lead victim of the Euro-demographic death spiral. The country's population dropped by 2.5 million from 2000 to 2012 and the number of retirees joining the pension rolls is skyrocketing. Putin made population decline a campaign issue by offering cash to families who have 3+ children with the goal of getting Russia's population up from 142 million to 154 million by 2050. Meanwhile, expect Putin to continue to use "foreign threats" to distract from domestic abuses.

China: Today, socialists the world over point to the Peoples Republic of China as the model for the new world order, just as they pointed to the Soviet Union back in the 1930's. They were wrong then and they're wrong now. China may have one of the world's largest economies, but "big" doesn't mean "rich." The size of China's economy is based on its massive population, but actual "wealth" lags. China's current Gross Domestic Product (GDP) is only $4,000 per person, one-tenth that of the U.S. ($40,000). At the most optimistic rate, China *could* reach a GDP of $20,000 by 2030; half that of the U.S. today. Add to that the challenge to China of spillover from the EU crisis – there is already an economic slowdown in China's response. The problem is that the expectations of China's population have risen rapidly, making any fiscal downturn a shock that could shake the very foundation of the Beijing government. China perpetually faces a difficult balancing act between the industrial coast region (40-percent of the population) and the vast rural interior (60-percent). China's wealth is focused in the manufacturing and export coast and the inland folks periodically grow restless—prompting wealth redistribution to calm the masses. Finally, China's male-to-female imbalance ranges between 119 to 130 men for every 100 women. The longstanding one child policy fuels a high abortion rate and may leave 24 million men without wives by 2020.

UNITED STATES' COPING STRATEGY FOR 2013 AND BEYOND

The United States faces serious but not insurmountable challenges in 2015 and beyond. Yet, meeting these challenges requires a thoughtful and deliberate coping strategy.

Maintain Power: The surest path to security is to remain the most powerful nation in the world. The U.S. should not allow sequestration to gut its military forces. Now, more than ever since the 1991 Soviet collapse, the U. S. should appear strong, be strong and act strong. America's strength includes dominance in conventional, special operational and nuclear forces (the triad of missiles, bombers and subs). To allow any other nation or bloc of nations to achieve parity is to invite war.

Design a Strategy for Maintaining Power: The U.S. needs to create, communicate and execute a viable and coherent global strategy that guards its vital national interests. The strategy should be clear and uncompromising in laying out America's global goals and objectives. The U.S. needs a 21st century version of the Monroe Doctrine that sends an unambiguous message to friends and enemies alike that weds the nation's intent to its power.

Independence: An independent nation maintains freedom of action through self-reliance. Dependence upon foreign energy, finance and manufacturing puts America at the mercy of other world nations whose own goals may be inimical to those of the U.S. Energy is increasingly the key component of power and America has plenty of reserves in oil and natural gas and could—if it chose to—lead the world in nuclear energy. There is no reason to allow energy blackmail via politically-motivated embargoes and production reduction by foreign producers. Financially, America cannot allow itself to be trapped by foreign debt. For example, U.S. debt payment to China, America's largest creditor, skyrockets and subsidizes the explosive growth of the Chinese military buildup. Financial independence requires cutting the U.S. deficit and dramatically reducing foreign debt payments—it is clearly a vital national security issue that demands prompt action. America should also bring its industrial manufacturing base back home from China, India and Mexico, thereby creating jobs, independence and a surge capacity.

No "Islamist Winter:" While America should support popular uprisings against dictators, it should do so with an eye on U.S. national interests—and should never back Islamists, regardless of the meaningless rhetoric thrown up to camouflage what is, in effect, an oppressive sectarian coup d'état. When a dictator is benign like Egypt's Mubarak or Iran's Shah, America should follow policies and actions that temper the process in order to buy time for liberal secular parties to organize and take root. Likewise, when the target of a Middle East revolution is an unambiguous enemy like Iran's Ahmadinejad or Syria's Assad, the U.S. should back the movement aggressively. Turkey must be drawn back into the secular world as a counterbalance to Iran's undisguised quest for Middle East hegemony. The U.S. must remain Israel's staunchest ally—for Israel's sake and America's.

WHICH PATH FOR AMERICA?

Increasing global debt implies that many nations today cannot afford a powerful conventional military. Thus, when lacking overt force, nations will pursue asymmetric warfare through terrorism, insurgency and cyber-attacks (weapon of mass disruption). Ominously, the lure of the acquisition of nuclear weapons promises a tempting "wall of immunity" to external coercion that those nations capable of acquiring nuclear weapons will seek. Declining wealth may also trigger desperation as it did in 1930's. The result then was the rise of the dictators, the imposition of "command" economies and aggressive, revanchist war.

In the short run, a nation vs. nation challenge to the U. S. is unlikely. As of now, no single nation can match American power. In Europe, no money equals no resilience and no surge capacity. Should conflict arise, it likely would be abrupt and decisive—any protracted conflict would have to be asymmetric and prosecuted by proxies. Yet, the assessment of relative power among nations is becoming less obvious. And, as uncertainty grows, so does the likelihood of war. Today resembles 1933 more than 1914. In 1914, each of the European nations saw themselves as powerful enough to win. None had a decisive edge and a stalemated bloodbath followed. In 1933, the aggressors perceived a shift in power and, particularly, in will. This produced a comprehensive test of relative power and a global bloodbath that ultimately rearranged the world security environment.

To the casual observer the West appears in decline; Putin and Ahmadinejad have openly said as much. Britain, France, and Germany are no longer military powers; they're bankers, diplomats and historical curators. The West refuses to defend its values and its borders, inviting aggression by showing weakness, indecision and foolish accommodation with those who seek to destroy it. The U.S. may be forced to join those nations proceeding along this lamentable path as it sinks into its own debt hole. America in 2013 remains the world's only Superpower; but it stands at a historic crossroads. The country's ultimate fate rests firmly in the hands of the nation's political leadership.

High Angle Hell
Truly Indirect War
PERSIAN ARROWS

"The wave of Islamic Revolution will soon reach the entire world."
—Mahmoud Ahmadinejad

Hegemony Then. In 490 BC, Persia was one of the world's greatest empires. No one dared challenge them regionally and few stood up to them beyond. When Cyrus the Great took power he quickly dispatched the existing regional powers, co-opted their aristocracies, and liberated their captives. When he conquered Babylon, he freed the Jews and financed the rebuilding of Jerusalem in a move that was less altruism than opportunism. Cyrus coveted the other great empire of the time, Egypt, and he knew that a Judean ally would come in handy down the line. Persia was growing in power.

Now. In the mid 2000's, Iran sees itself as the dominant regional power; a global power broker equal to anyone. Hegemony fell into their laps when their worst enemy, Iraq, was crushed by the 'Coalition of the Willing' in 2003. Afghanistan, a perpetual basket case since before Alexander the Great, sits on her eastern border. To the west are the petro-dollar addicted Saudi's and the Emirates all of whom prefer buying security over earning it. To the north is newly minted Islamist Turkey, dreaming of resurrecting its regional leadership. Also to the north are the Caucuses and Central Asia—the "Great Game" playground. On the edges of Iran's empire are decrepit Egypt, bankrupt Jordan, puppet Lebanon, and lapdog Syria. It's a lamentable collection considering that the most powerful army among them belongs to stateless Hizballah. Iran is growing in power.

259

"The fighting in Palestine is a war between the whole
Islamic Nation and the world of arrogance…"
—Mahmoud Ahmadinejad

Legitimacy Then.   Darius the Great ascended to the throne through regicide. When Cyrus was killed during another attempt to expand the empire, his sons ascended to the throne… for a while. Cambyses took the lead. His first major feat was to bag the biggest prize of them all, Egypt, in 525 BC. When rumors reached him that his brother, Bardiya, was leading an uprising at home, Cambyses rushed back home to set things right. In his haste, he jumped onto his horse and was accidently stabbed and killed by his own sword. Conveniently, his lance-bearer Darius was by his side. Darius assembled a group of associates and rode off to settle with Bardiya, now the legitimate successor to the throne. They ended up killing Bardiya leaving Persia leaderless. Fortunately Darius was willing to assume the role although he faced legitimacy problems since he had been close at hand during the deaths of both of Cyrus' sons.

To justify his actions, Darius reasserted the Cambyses accidental death and advanced a supernatural excuse for Bardiya's death. Darius claimed that the man he had had killed was an evil usurper who magically made himself look like Bardiya who was actually already dead. Darius had avenged both sons in the name of the Zoroastrian God Ahura Mazda. He was a servant of God in the eternal struggle between the 'truth' and the 'lie' and his followers were entitled to direct passage into Paradise. Darius was legitimate by divine writ.

Now.   Mahmoud Ahmadinejad won re-election through fraud. His first term as President of the Islamic Republic was less than successful and he was less than popular. He left Iran financially weakened and isolated. Ahmadinejad was on the decline and the reformers were poised to make a comeback. His conservative supporters disqualified most of his competitors and predetermined the elections outcome as evidenced by the near instant release of the results just hours after the polls closed—impressive given the millions of paper ballots that to be counted by hand. Ahmadinejad not only won—he won big! He even took a majority in regions where he was unpopular. The resulting riots were crushed before the world's eyes via online cell phone videos. The western silence was deafening and it encouraged an intensification of the crackdown on the Green Movement reformers.

To justify the election, President Ahmadinejad and the Supreme Leader Ayatollah Khameini, called the results divine. Ahmadinejad stepped up his apocalyptic rhetoric, intensified Iran's pursuit of nuclear weapons, and made it known that he personally communicates with the Hidden Imam, the Shia Messiah. He portrays himself as an agent of God at war against the Great Satan and the Little Satan. He is engaged in the divine pursuit of Gods will on earth and his followers are martyrs guaranteed a spot in Paradise. Ahmadinejad is legitimate by divine writ.

The Road Bump Then. Persia's expansion seemed unstoppable until troubles arose on the empires west flank. The Ionian Greeks along the east coast of the Aegean had heard rumors of a revolution in Athens. The uprising had replaced the tyrants with a government elected by the people called democracy. Some newly freed Athenians helped the Ionians overthrew their Persian Satraps in order to establish their own democracies. Darius had to be put down this challenge to his rule. His new enemies, the Greek City States, were notorious for internal quarrels and disunity and now they were offering a system of governance that challenged the natural order of things. Democracy was a 'lie' that had to be ripped out.

Now. Iran has assembled an extensive list of allies from Anatolia to Asia to South America. Some are states and others are stateless entities embedded in reluctant hosts. Iranian proxies infect every state in the region and have even become the de-facto rulers of Lebanon. They have gained the Syrian subservience, Lebanese acquiescence, the partnership of the Sunni Hamas, and have intimidated the rest of the region to sit quietly on the sidelines. Iran has infiltrated the resistance movements in Iraq and Afghanistan and is postured to wait out the promised US withdrawal. They face no serious external challenge other than a defiant little state of six million people renowned for divisive politics and political isolation whose biggest backer has grown recalcitrant.

Direct Combat Then. Darius sent an expeditionary force to police the rebellious Ionians. The western Greeks shuttered at having awakened the Persian giant but readied themselves to face the attack.

The Persian effort to punish the Greeks was a minor one for such a large empire. The Ionian invasion was a rousing success but the Athenian invasion was another matter altogether. Darius sent 20,000 troops and 600 ships to take on Athens – a seemingly large enough force for the task at hand. The troops landed south of Athens at Marathon while the ships threatened the Athenian harbor. Even given a two to one advantage in ground troops, the Persians were decisively beaten. The Greeks lost 192 men to 6,400 lost by the Persian invaders. Spartan observers visited the battlefield and were underwhelmed by Persian wicker shields and lack of armor. Greeks had worn bronze for years.

Although Darius had failed, he had not forgotten. After suppressing another minor rebellion in Egypt, he died during the return trip before he could return to Greece. He was replaced by his son Xerxes who was even more determined than his father to make an example of the upstart Greeks. Xerxes amassed the largest army ever assembled and marched on West with the goal of adding a new province to the burgeoning Empire. Like his father, he met the first determined Greek defenders in a narrow pass and held an enormous numerical advantage. Like his father, Xerxes could not defeat the Greeks, Spartans this time, at Thermopylae Pass.

Now. Iran has made Israel its most important enemy. They are the infidel infiltrators in Muslim lands however Ahmadinejad already knows that direct combat is not a winning proposition. In 1967 the Arab Muslim World united behind Nasser of Egypt with the goal of pushing the Zionists into the sea. Not only were they spectacularly defeated but they lost the Sinai, Jerusalem, and almost lost Damascus. A second attempt in 1973 saw Syria lose the Golan Heights and the IDF cross the Suez into Egypt. It seemed the little Israel was too much to handle.

Iran sought proxies to meet the Israelis in their stead and came up with the Lebanese Hizballah, a terrorist / guerilla organization they trained and equipped. Hizballah fought the IDF in the First Lebanon War of 1982 and the Second Lebanon War of 2006. They lost both but gained prestige. Next, through Hizballah, they propelled Hamas to power in Gaza mirroring Cyrus' strategy of acquiring new allies for future wars. Their new partners took on the Israelis again in Gaza

2008—another loss. The 2006 and 2008 struggles taught Iran and their proxies some new lessons.

Persian Arrows. Xerxes was frustrated by his inability to defeat the Greek coalition in Thermopylae (the Hot Gates). Even his elite shock troops, the Immortals, couldn't crack the Spartan Phalanx. He resorted to a Persian specialty, the cultivation of spies and traitors. He found a Greek who knew of a secret pass that would enable his army to bypass the Hot Gates and encircle the defending Greeks. When word of the betrayal made it to the Spartans, they released their allies and remained with a token force of 300 to die in the pass, buying time for the others to spread the word to the rest of Greece.

Xerxes' army moved into place but did not close on the embattled Greeks. They demanded surrender and when it was denied they still did not attack. Instead, the Persian archers unleashed a rain of arrows that killed or wounded almost all of the defenders. Once crippled, the army then closed in for the kill. In the end, it was all for naught. Xerxes advance had been slowed enough for the rest of Greece to organize a defense and his army was finally vanquished at Plataea where his archers could not overwhelm the defenders.

"The first step would be that all areas in Israel are in reach of our missiles; I mean, there is not a single place in Israel outside the range of our missiles. Even some European countries are within the range of our missiles."
—Hossein Shariatmadari, editor-in-chief of
Kayhan, Iran's major state-run newspaper

Iranian Arrows. Iran has aggressively sought to acquire as many missiles as possible of every size, shape and description. What they lack in quality, they are making up in quantity. Their mad dash to produce, procure, and proliferate missiles may be more than just the musings of megalomaniac Mullahs with a bottomless bank account. It just might be a deliberate strategy to capitalize on lessons from the '06 Second Lebanon War. That lesson was that having lots of missiles limits enemy's options, threatens enemy population centers, avoids force on force contact, demonstrates resolve, and influences the media. A missile fleet becomes a poor man's air force—a strategic weapon.

The strategy might be to whip up anti-Israeli sentiment with inflammatory rhetoric while drawing international attention to the 'peaceful' nuclear program; all the while surrounding Israel with missiles, mortars, rockets, and artillery. The 'archers' are the plethora of Iranian proxies and surrogates. The combination of provocative language and a suspect nuclear program might provoke a preemptive strike against Iran. Preemption is Israeli policy as evidenced by strikes against Osirak, Iraq, in 1981 and a suspected site in Syria in 2007. If such a strike were to befall Iran, they would claim to be the aggrieved party and would be justified in striking back. The result would be steel rain on Israel. Being confined to a small geographic, the onslaught might bring them to their knees. The Iranians would count on universal Muslim animus to rally support thus propelling them to the status of regional hegemon. This is a risky proposition and is only a theory.

Iran has surrounded Israel with its proxies. Hizballah occupies southern Lebanon, Hamas owns Gaza, and Syria stands opposite the Golan. All have been armed to the teeth with missiles, mortars, rockets, and artillery. Iran could add their own long range missiles to the mix. There are many potential advantages to such a policy:

- Sold as a response to aggression versus initiation of aggression
- Swarm tactics that should overwhelm local anti-missile defenses
- High volume of fire to overwhelm the IDF
- Missile mix (small + cheap + numerous) + (large + expensive + scarce)
- Asymmetric low tech volume to overcome high tech precision and skill
- Avoids air war against the vastly superior IAF and ground war versus IDF
- Exposes Israeli civil population
- Employs a multitude of systems launched from a multitude of locations
- Exploits all proxies—all of whom stand to gain by a weakened Israel
- Avoids Iranian weaknesses—ground combat
- Does not require nuclear weapons

- Uses deception and misdirection—focus on nukes versus the real threat of mundane conventional missiles
- No nuclear or chemical battlefield

Like the Spartans of Thermopylae, the Israelis are surrounded by Persian archers ready to unleash steel rain. The way to overcome direct combat inferiority was to pursue indirect combat superiority through the employment of numerically overwhelming standoff weapons. Persia / Iran pursued killing without closing.

"We are clearly dealing with a country that has made no secret of its desire to develop a robust, plentiful, increasingly capable missile arsenal."
—Geoff Morrell, Pentagon Press Secretary

Iran Today. There is a real struggle going on within the corridors of power in Iran and the players are not who we think they are. We've assumed the battle is between the Hard-line Conservatives and the Green Party Reformers—it's not, completely. The 2009 stolen election and subsequent Green Movement crackdown that elicited little more than a disinterested yawn from the west, settled that score. The Reformers lost and they did so decisively. Sure, the main honchos are still out there but they are Chiefs without Braves or Indians; most of their lieutenants are dead or in jail and their followers, although willing, are powerless. Make no mistake; the Greens aren't friends of the west. Khatami oversaw the initiation of the nuclear program and he has made anti-Israeli statements nearly as scary as those made by Ahmadinejad. In modern day Iran the choices are ugly with a spectrum ranging from bad to worse. The players go from willing to wait for Armageddon to willing to trigger Armageddon.

The real struggle is between the semi-pragmatic Hard-line Conservatives and the fanatic True Believers. As with the Reformers mentioned above; neither of the main contenders is kindly disposed towards the west. It's a matter of degree; the hard-liners are dangerous but the true believers are potentially deadly.

The Hard-line Conservatives are dedicated Islamists but chief among their goals is preservation of the Islamic Republic. They favor

confrontation and provocation but would most likely oppose any conflict that would threaten the survival of the regime. If they had nuclear
weapons, they would likely use them like the North Koreans do. They
would use them to empower brinksmanship and to coerce their neighbors but their most important use would be to deter any and all forms
of foreign intervention. The newfound freedom to maneuver would be
exploited to gain and maintain regional hegemony and acceptance as an
equal to the world's top powers.

The True Believers are Shia millenarians who belong to a shadowy
sectarian group true called the Hojjatieh Society. The Hojjatieh
Society believes that the Shia Messiah, known as the Hidden Imam or
the Mahdi, is the twelfth Imam of the Caliphate. They are often identified as 'Twelvers.' According to Shia eschatology, the Hidden Imam
/ Mahdi will reemerge from hiding to lead the faithful in the Great War
to purify the earth for Islam. Both Shia's and Sunni's are millenarians
but the Twelver's are unique in that their philosophy that if they generate enough chaos they can hasten the Mahdi's return. Twelvers with the
nuclear bomb (Islamic Bomb) would be sorely tempted to use it offen-
sively since they need not fear the consequences—the Mahdi will be at
their side. In fact, use of the bomb might well be construed as a religious imperative.

Regional Strategy: First, we must acknowledge the limited impact
of UN Sanctions even though we have to continue to pursue them.
Iran is using the ancient Byzantine strategy of paying off adversaries
and allies, knowing that the money would come back through their
markets. Similarly, Iran is showering Russia and China with contracts
knowing that much of the money will come back via energy payments.
Russia and China have no incentive to back sanctions that would kill
their cash cow.

Iran appears to have at least three major factions: the
Conservatives, the Twelvers, and the Greens. Each can be played
against the other but none will be friends to the west. All you can hope
for is a less confrontational approach.

The Conservatives are Khomeini's revolutionary hard-liners.
Their leader is the Supreme Leader, Ayatollah Seyed Ali Khamenei, the
ultimate authority in Iran. This group is confrontational but it is also

preservationist and dynastic. They want the regime to survive and they want it to stay in their hands—this they don't want to risk regime collapse and they want Khamenei's son to inherit the mantle of Supreme Leader. The way to shake this group is to openly discuss the looming difficulties of dealing with Khamenei's replacement (his health is waning), the Ayatollah Mesbah Yazdi. Yazdi is an opponent. Secondly, the west should make it clear that a regional war will be brutal for Iran thus threatening collapse of the regime.

The Twelvers are the next faction and they are on the rise. Their overt leader is President Mahmoud Ahmadenijad although he is under the influence of Ayatollah Mesbah Yazdi. This group is aggressive, ascendant, and millenarian. They seek the return of the Mahdi / Hidden Imam and the Apocalypse. There are two ways to get after the Twlevers: ask to negotiate with the Supreme Leader rather than the President; and target IRGC businesses. Asking to talk to the Supreme Leader may inflame rivalries between the two groups whether he agrees to talk or not. The Twelvers rose up given a healthy dose of nepotism from Ahmadenijad who doled out leadership and business interests to his IRGC cronies.

The weakest faction is the one with the greatest latent power—the Greens. The leaders of the Green Movement are Mir-Hossein Mousavi, Mehdi Karroubi, and Aatollah Seyed Mohammad Khatami. The Greens are reformers, though no friends of the west, and they seek to liberalize the Islamic Republic. The west needs to support them very carefully. We can't afford a Mossadeq moment where the Greens become perceived as western puppets, a death sentence. The best way to support them is through sustained criticism of the 2009 elections and through covert and clandestine support. What any nascent movement needs most is communications and that's what we ought to give them. They will persist as long as they can talk.

The west should target IRGC and MOIS operatives working in Iraq and Afghanistan.

Syria is Iran's most important regional ally. They are the weapons conduit to Hizballah and, by extension, Hamas. The west should make it clear that regional weapons proliferation is an act of war that Syria will be held accountable for. We should be above board and vocal about what we know about weapons transfers and should be clear that we will not oppose Israeli efforts to suppress them.

Hizballah operatives working outside Lebanon should be targets with the same zeal as are AQAN operatives. The West should also increase support to the LAF. Hamas funding and support should be routed through Fatah on the West Bank – not a single penny or product should go directly from the west into a Hamas members hands.

Turkey has been drifting east ever since Erdogan and his Islamist AKP took power in 2002. A way to dampen their zeal might be to aid their anti-terror campaign directed against the Kurdish PKK. We also might begin to question their place in NATO and threaten to drop EU discussions.

Israel is the region's top power. The west could help them most by providing pro-democratic dialogue. The west could also help out by enhancing Israeli targeting to improve acquisition and accuracy.

The Iranian Republic has been schizophrenic from its inception. On one side we have the powerless Political Establishment with its elected officials and toothless bureaucracies. On the other side we have all powerful Clerical Theocracy with its Mullahs and overseeing bureaucracies. The former exudes the façade of democracy while the latter reflects the reality of theocracy. There are factions upon factions within both and agendas upon agendas. Some are pragmatic and others are fanatic and most are somewhere in between. Today's Iran mimics yesterdays Soviet Union:

> *"Soviet Union foreign policy is a puzzle inside a riddle wrapped in an enigma, and the key is Russian nationalism."*
> —Winston Churchill

Similarly, Iranian foreign policy is a puzzle inside a riddle wrapped in an enigma, and the key is Shia nationalism—not Iranian or Persian nationalism.

Mali Matters

WHY MALI MATTERS

An Islamist takeover offers terrorists a safe haven – and launching pad for future attacks – in northwest Africa.

"A QUARREL IN A FAR AWAY COUNTRY"

On September 30, 1938, Britain's Prime Minister Neville Chamberlain signed the infamous Munich Agreement that sacrificed Czech-oslovakia in what ultimately proved to be a vain attempt to appease Nazi dictator Adolf Hitler's rapacious aggression. During a radio broadcast to the British public three days earlier, Chamberlain had explained why: "How horrible, fantastic, incredible it is that we should be digging trenches and trying on gas masks here [in England] because of a quarrel in a far away country between people of whom we know nothing." To the leader of one of the world's great powers, tiny Czechoslovakia was merely "a far away country" that simply didn't matter. Yet, encouraged by Britain's (and France's) cowardly behavior at Munich, Hitler continued his aggression, invading Poland in September 1939 and starting World War II that unleashed Nazi terror against all of Europe. In hindsight, it is clear that Chamberlain was tragically wrong – "far away" Czechoslovakia mattered very much indeed.

Fast-forward 75 years. To most Americans today, the Republic of Mali, a former French colony in West Africa, is "a far away country" beset by a quarrel "between people of whom [they] know nothing." Yet, like Czechoslovakia in 1938, "far away" Mali matters. Here's why.

TERRORISTS, SAFE HAVENS AND THE CALIPHATE

Terrorist organizations around the globe today – whether they be drug lords, smugglers and pirates seeking ill-gotten wealth or, more dangerous, Islamists waging jihad – cannot thrive without safe havens.

The groups need secure, remote locations where they can plan, organize, recruit, train and build weapons arsenals, and from which they can launch attacks to strike distant targets. For Hezbollah, it is eastern Lebanon's Beqaa (Bekka) Valley; for the Taliban it is the Tora Bora cave complex in eastern Afghanistan; for Al Qaeda in Afghanistan it is the mountainous Pakistani tribal regions; and for Al Shabaab the desolate Somalia hinterlands. Mali's vast northern region, composed of the Sahel (south Sahara Desert) and the rugged Adrar des Ifoghas Mountains, is a devil's playground that can support the manning, training and equipping of a veritable legion of terrorists that could strike forth from Mali to all points of the compass.

Of all the terrorist groups that might covet Northern Mali as a perfect safe haven, none poses more of a threat to Western security and values—and U.S. national interests – than Islamist jihadis. The principal strategic goal of the jihadis is to re-conquer the Late Great Caliphate. According to their pan-Islamic vision, any land conquered by Muslims must remain Muslim or be returned to Muslim rule. At its peak a millennium ago, the Caliphate ranged from Morocco and Spain in the West to India in the East, and from the Balkans in the North to Yemen in the South. The extent of the Caliphate rivaled that of the Roman Empire at its height, and Muslim armies very nearly overran Europe more than once were it not for timely defeats inflicted by Charles the Hammer at Tours (732), Don John of Austria at the naval battle of Lepanto (1571) and the Holy League at Vienna (1683).

By 670AD, the Caliphate encompassed all of North Africa (beginning in the Middle Ages, represented by Ottoman Empire rule); but in the 19th century Muslim control was lost to European colonizers (France, Britain, Spain and Italy). Today, Islamist jihadis want it back. Remote, ungoverned Northern Mali offers the safe haven needed to host jihadists' efforts to destabilize North Africa—and, not incidentally, bring them ever closer to Europe.

MALI: "FROM HERE TO TIMBUKTU"

Americans today likely know only one thing about Mali – the country's most famous city is the exotic, almost mythical Timbuktu. As the epitome of any far distant or outlandishly remote place at "the end of the Earth," it has become immortalized in the commonly-used phrase "from here to Timbuktu." Located on the southwest edge of Northern Mali, Timbuktu (population 55,000) is the capital of Mali's Tombouctou administrative region containing the entire western *half* of the potential terrorist safe haven in Northern Mali. Timbuktu is, indeed, physically remote from the U.S. and the West; yet, if Northern Mali becomes an Islamist jihadi safe haven and launching pad for terror attacks, Timbuktu is going to feel a lot closer to home. But, for their own good Americans need to know much more about Mali than merely Timbuktu.

Land: Mali is landlocked and is bounded by Algeria on the North, Guinea, Ivory Coast and Burkina Faso on the South, Mauritania and Senegal in the West, and Niger in the East. It is the world's 24th-largest country — double the size of Texas, Afghanistan or France. About 65-percent of Mali (northern and eastern portions) is dry and arid desert or semi-desert, while the country's much smaller wet, tropical region is in the southwest along the Niger River. Less than four-percent of Mali is arable land suitable for growing crops. Although a poor country, Mali has substantial deposits of salt, uranium (at least 17,400 tons are known) and gold (it is Africa's third-largest producer of gold).

Northern Mali is ideal guerrilla country comprised of the Sahel (southern Sahara desert ecological transitional zone) and the rugged, 3,000-feet high Adrar des Ifoghas Mountains. It is figuratively "Lawrence of Arabia meets Bin Laden of Tora Bora."

People: Mali's population is 14.5 million, most living in rural areas with a sizable nomadic minority in the north. More than 90-percent of Malians live in the lush south in and around the capital, Bamako. Bambara or "black" Malians are Mali's largest ethnic group (37-percent). Their language is Mali's "lingua franca" (80-percent of all Malians speak Bambara) although French remains Mali's official language. Nomadic Tuareg (10-percent of the population) are Arab Berbers seen as "white" Malians. Recent persistent droughts forced the Taureg to temporarily abandon their nomadic life as many of them fled to Algeria and Libya. Other ethnic groups include Fula, Voltaic and Songhai (totaling 35-percent of Mali's population).

Longstanding ethnic tensions pit "white" Tuareg of the north against "black" Africans of the south. The animosity dates back to the Caliphate-era slave trade—Arab Berbers kept and sold black slaves until stopped by early-20th century French colonizers (although there are claims that some black Malians are still enslaved in the north). Given this history coupled with the backlash against the Tuareg after Malian independence, both groups complain of racial discrimination.

Religion: Islam came to West Africa in the 11th century and remains dominant today with 90-percent of Malians being Sunni or Sufi Muslim. Five-percent of Malians are Christian (Roman Catholic and Protestant) and the remaining 5-percent animist. The Malian constitution provides for a secular state and freedom of religion. Yet, that is under fire by Islamists seeking Wahhabi-style Sharia.

History – From First to Worst: One must travel back seven centuries to Timbuktu to find history's wealthiest man -- Mansa Musa I. He ruled the Malian Empire 1280-1337 and grew fantastically rich on the salt and gold trades. Things have changed. Mali today is one of the world's poorest countries with an average annual per capita income of only $1,500. In 1892 Mali became a French colony and for the next 68 years supplied France's labor needs along the West African coast. Mali gained its independence in 1960 and quickly emplaced a one-party socialist state. Mali withdrew from the French Community and built a close relationship with the USSR-dominated Communist Eastern bloc.

Politics – From Coups to Insurgencies: Economic woes caused Mali to rejoin the Franc Zone in 1967 and to initiate economic reforms. Mali's first military coup came in 1968. Its leaders attempted economic reform but failed in the face of internal struggles and devastating drought. They intended to install civilian rule but the military stayed in power. Mali stabilized in the 1980s and economic reforms were resurrected under an austerity agreement with the International Monetary Fund (IMF). The populace resented the austerity measures believing the ruling elites didn't share their sacrifices.

Calls for a multiparty democracy intensified in 1990 and opposition to one-party rule emerged; yet, so did ethnic violence in the north. Large numbers of Tuareg, who had fled the droughts, returned from Algeria and Libya sparking unrest in the north. Fearing Tuareg secession, the Mali government imposed a state of emergency to put them down. Rioting in 1991 triggered yet another military coup. This time a majority civilian body was established to appoint a civilian-led government. In 1992 a free election led to the inauguration of Alpha Oumar Konaré as Mali's president. Konaré stepped down after his mandated two term limit and the 2002 election became a first when Mali transitioned from one democratically-elected leader to another.

In January 2012, the National Movement for the Liberation of Azawad (MNLA) rebelled (Azawad is the Tuareg name for Northern Mali). Although expected, the Tuareg insurgency came as a double surprise—the timing and alliance with Islamists were unforeseen. The Malian Armed Forces (MAF) were soundly beaten in the initial engagements. Given the years of training and support it had received from the West in preparation for this very event, MAF losses were also unexpected. The MAF's poor performance cast doubt on the government's effectiveness.

In March 2012, amidst the panic and confusion of a mutiny at Kati military camp six miles from the Bamako presidential palace, MAF officer Captain Amadou Sanogo joined the mutineers and led another coup. Rebel MAF soldiers appeared on state-run television announcing the overthrow of the government due to its mishandling of the conflict in the north. In response to the coup, the Economic Community of West African States (ECOWAS) froze Malian assets and imposed an embargo. The new government promised but found no answer for combating the insurgency as the rebels seized Timbuktu and took Northern Mali without serious resistance. Apprehension turned to panic when news arrived that Islamists were marching on Bamako.

RE-ENTER THE FRENCH

In December 2012, a day after Konna (360 miles north of Bamako) fell to the Islamists, French forces intervened with their launch of Operation Serval. A French colony for nearly 70 years, Mali's connection with France runs deep (French is Mali's official language and French nationals still live there). Operation Serval's multiple aims were: to block the Islamist advance on Bamako; regain control of Northern Mali; secure the lines of communication all the way to the Algerian border; and then hand off stabilization operations to the African force fighting alongside French troops. To accomplish these ambitious aims, France fielded a versatile 4,000-man force that included mobile infantry, paratroopers and Special Forces, backed by Mirage fighters in close air support and U.S. surveillance drones.

Realizing the importance of putting an "African face" on the effort, the French quickly went to work recruiting African partners from their former colonies with Chad leading the way by pledging 2,000 troops to the mission (other countries contributing include ECOWAS members Nigeria, Ghana, Ivory Coast, Burkina Faso and Niger). Ultimately, the French would leave and Africans would fulfill a UN peacekeeping role. This was a smart move: when Westerners keep the peace in Africa it feels like imperialism; when Africans keep the peace in Africa it feels like teamwork.

French forces proceeded systematically by securing the chokepoint in the Sahel connecting Northern and Southern Mali, thereby blocking the invasion route to Bamako. Next, they recaptured two key northern cities, Timbuktu and Gao. They then worked their way north, securing the lines of communication between Bamako and the Algerian border while re-taking Kidal and Tissalit along the way. Finally, the French gradually put the African ECOWAS forces in the lead. All the while, the French nurtured a new partnership between the MAF and ECOWAS.

The French exploited their overwhelming tactical firepower and superior mobility by employing the *Véhicule Blindé de Combat d'Infanterie* (VBCI—armored vehicle for infantry combat similar to the U.S. Stryker) supported by AMX 56 Leclerc tanks and 155mm CAESAR self-propelled howitzers to dominate the road networks. They also capitalized on superior operational mobility through the use of paratroopers and air-inserted Special Forces to rapidly seize remote locations in the north. French forces achieved their objectives quickly and with ease – perhaps too much ease.

It is entirely possible that Mali's insurgents were repeating the tactics Lawrence had taught Arab insurgents fighting the Ottomans nearly a century earlier: fade into the desert when the enemy is strong and attack when he is weak. When fighting an insurgency in its infancy, it is common for counterinsurgency forces to gain the upper hand. But, the difficult part is maintaining the upper hand after the guerrillas fade away and before they are defeated—they come back. Insurgents seek protracted conflict to wear down the government's will and exhaust the people's patience. Suicide bombings are already taking place in the newly re-captured northern cities. If this continues it will widen the gulf of mistrust between Mali's urban population and the desert and mountain nomads.

MALI MATTERS

If one or more of Mali's Islamist insurgent groups manage to regain and maintain control of Northern Mali they will have captured their largest safe haven ever. The Adrar des Ifoghas Mountains are the perfect guerrilla stronghold and hideout, essentially Mali's Tortuga, Fallujah or Tora Bora. The mountains are the region's historic "bandit badlands" (the home of drug smugglers, gun runners and bandits for decades), made even worse by having a porous Algerian border nearby that facilitates the flow of weapons and supplies to the insurgents. These mountains are riddled with caves formerly used as shelter from sand storms. Now they provide shelter from counterinsurgency drones and helicopter gunships.

Al Qaeda in the Islamic Maghreb (AQIM) and their Islamist allies know the area well. AQIM set up shop there in 2003, using the mountains and the Sahara desert to hide hostages and to train recruits such as Niger's Boko Haram jihadist organization. The largest town in the area, Kidal (population 25,000), has been the epicenter of every Tuareg rebellion since 1962—tellingly, it is also home to a 90-year old French Foreign Legion fort, a lasting symbol to the longstanding danger of this remote center of resistance. Larger than other terrorist safe havens such as Lebanon's Beqaa Valley, Afghanistan's Tora Bora, and Pakistani tribal regions, the area is rife with potential Islamist terror clients. In addition to Mali's "home grown" insurgents, these include Boko Haram from Niger and Burkina Faso, Islamists from Algeria and Libya, the Muslim Brotherhood from Egypt, and Al Shabaab from Somali.

There are plenty of weapons to be had as well from Libya's abundant stocks captured in the wake of Dictator Muammar Gaddafi's fall. Insurgents based in Northern Mali can also count on political top cover from sympathetic North African regimes in Islamist Tunisia, Libya and Egypt. Already, Egypt has condemned France's military intervention in Mali, while a wary Algeria will most likely keep quiet in the hopes that its own Islamist tormentors will stay "south of the border" in Northern Mali.

That's why Mali matters—and why it compels U.S. policymakers to develop and implement a strategy to do something about it.

U.S. STRATEGY

If Northern Mali continues to live up to its historic reputation as a safe haven for bandits and guerrillas it will remain a magnet for North Africa's Islamists, particularly AQIM. After having lost their 10-year insurgency against Algeria as the Armed Islamic Group (GIA) and the Salafist Group for Preaching and Combat (GSPC), the newly branded AQIM is seeking a home. Northern Mali more than fits the bill. Moreover, AQIM has ready clients with deep pockets like Boko Haram, masters like Al Qaeda with decades of experience planning and executing deadly strikes, and a clear, if nonetheless apocalyptic, vision— restoration of the North African Caliphate. AQIM has an "arms room" called Libya and enjoys the support of the sympathetic regional states Tunisia, Libya and Egypt. If the Northern Mali safe haven is permitted to exist, North Africa—and the West, including the United States—will be at great risk. U.S. strategy, therefore, must address the key players and most compelling issues.

The Tuareg are the key to the security of Northern Mali. If the Tuareg reject the Islamists, the Islamists will be gone. If they embrace Islamists, the Islamists will stay. The Malian Tuareg are much like the Afghan tribes in the wake of 9/11. When the Afghani tribes turned on the Taliban and Al Qaeda in 2002, the terrorists were defeated. The rejection of the tribals in Al Anbar in 2006 had the same effect on Al Qaeda in Iraq.

One of the most profound observations of Carl von Clausewitz (1780-1831), the famed philosopher of war, was: "Everything in war is simple; but the simplest thing is difficult." This dictum applies to the problem confronting U.S. policymakers in Mali. The solution to the problem presented by Northern Mali is simple to define yet difficult to execute. The tension between the former slave-owning white Arab Berbers and their former slaves the black southern Malians is long-standing. The sedentary northerners and the nomadic Tuareg also distrust one another. Add the Sunni/Sufi Muslim sectarianism antagonisms exemplified by the insurgents' destruction of the Timbuktu Sufi Temples and rampant banditry and one ends up with a complex problem set. The U.S. must build up and professionalize the MAF while weakening the Islamists and, simultaneously, begin bridging the political gap between the Tuareg and the rest of the Malian population.

The U.S. objective must be to rid Northern Mali of Islamists while forging long-term solutions to the region's political, social and economic problems, arrested economic development, poverty, institutional chaos, government power vacuum and ethnic tensions. Specific actions to achieve these goals should include:

- Semi-autonomy for the Tuareg in the North—perhaps a provincial governorship.
- Tuareg political representation in Bamako.
- Upgrade and maintain the North's deteriorating infrastructure.
- Provision of basic government services in the North.
- Political mediation between sedentary and nomadic northerners.
- Discredit Wahhabism—most Malians already oppose Sharia.
- Crackdown on drug running, kidnapping and smuggling in the north while providing viable economic alternatives.
- Improve MAF professional education to decrease the likelihood of future coups.
- Restore the Mali population's democratic spirit that flourished 1992-2002.

On October 22, 2012, during the U.S. presidential election's third candidate debate, Republican nominee Mitt Romney stated: "Mali has been taken over, the northern part of Mali, by Al Qaeda type individuals." Yet, since then Mali has largely dropped off of the American public's radar. Mali matters and it needs to reappear on the U.S. radar screen—soon.

TERRORIST SAFE HAVENS

- **Khowst, Tora Bora and Hindu Kush (Afghanistan); Northwest Frontier Province and Baluchistan (Pakistan)**—Harbors Afghan Taliban and Pakistani Taliban, Al Qaeda, Al-Jihad, Black Guard, 055 Brigade (Arab Legion of Al Qaeda), Libyan Islamic Jihad, Tehreek-e-Taliban Pakistan (TTP), Tehrik-e-Nafaz-e-Shariat-e-Mohammadi (TNSM), Lashkar-e-Taiba, Lashkar-e-Janghvi, Hizb-i-Gullbudin, Hizb-i-Khalis, Islamic Party of Uzbekistan, Islamic Jihad Union, Jaish-e-Mohammed, Haqqani Network, and Iranian Revolutionary Guards/Quds brigades.
- **Beqaa (Bekka) Valley (Lebanon)**—Home to Lebanese Hezbollah and its allies; used for training other Islamists, e.g. Hamas and Islamic Jihad Organization (IJO).
- **North Caucasus between Black Sea and Caspian Sea (Chechnya)**—Home to the Islamic International Peacekeeping Brigade (IIPB), Special Purpose Islamic Regiment (SPIR) and Riyadus-Salikhin Reconnaissance and Sabotage Battalion of Chechen Martyrs.
- **Southern Somalia**—Al-Shabaab and numerous pirates.
- **Northern Iraq**—Al Qaeda in Iraq (AQI).
- **Yemen Northern Border**—Al Qaeda in the Arabian Peninsula (AQAP) and Al Houthi.

MALI'S MILITANTS
- **Ansar Dine**—"Movement of defenders of the faith" is dominated by the Tuareg, including many who fought for Muammar Gaddafi in Libya; emerged after the Algerian Salafist Group for Preaching and Combat (GSPC) aligned with Al Qaeda; has members from Mauritania, Morocco, Mali, Niger and Senegal; seeks Sharia law for Mali.
- **Al Qaeda in the Islamic Maghreb (AQIM)**—Al Qaeda's North African wing, it took the AQIM name after Al Qaeda announced allegiance to Algerian GSPC. Mostly foreign fighters; wants Sharia law and to cleanse Mali of French colonial legacy; kidnaps Westerners; has close ties with Ansar Dine and MUJAO; trained

Boko Haram to execute bombings and assassinations in Nigeria.

- **Movement for Unity and Jihad in West Africa (MUJAO)**—AQIM offshoot seeks spreading jihad and Sharia law throughout West Africa; attacked Tuareg separatists and took control of northern Mali's major cities following the Bamako coup; destroyed sacred Sufi shrines and applied Sharia law (amputated thieves' hands, stoned adulterers and enforced the veil); sphere of influence is northeastern Mali (in towns such as Kidal and Gao, Mali's drug center).

- **Signed-in-Blood Battalion**—AQIM offshoot committed to a global jihad. Launched the January 2013 Amenas Algerian gas facility attack/hostage crisis to make its mark.

- **National Movement for the Liberation of Azawad (MNLA)**—Tuareg seeking Azawad (their name for Northern Mali) independence; cause dates back to Mali independence; many fought alongside Gaddafi's forces and brought back weapons, including surface-to-air missiles; spearheaded uprising in alliance with former allies Ansar Dine and MUJAO but now oppose Islamists.

- **Islamic Movement for Azawad (IMA)**—Broke from Ansar Dine after the French intervention, rejecting "all forms of extremism and terrorism;" claims to champion the people of northern Mali who have been marginalized by Mali's government.

All of Mali's Islamist groups follow Saudi-inspired *Wahhabi/Salafi* Islam making them unpopular with Mali's Sufi Muslim majority.

Ataturk Dies Again

... *should we care?*

"The mosques are our barracks, the domes our helmets, the minarets our bayonets and the faithful our soldiers..."
—recited by Recep Tayyip Erdogan at a public gathering in 1998

Harbinger? The quote above comes from an Islamic poem. Erdogan quoted the above publically and earned himself a jail term for inciting religious hatred and threatening secularism.

A Turn for the Worst. The first warning shot came during the run-up to Operation Iraqi Freedom when the newly elected Turkish government denied the US led coalition permission to move through their territory. The decision prevented the coalition from getting into northern Iraq early on, leaving Tikrit (Saddam Hussein's hometown and Baathist strongpoint) untouched until after the fall of Bagdad. This delay created a safe haven for former regime elements (FRE) to rally and organize the 'Party of Return' resistance—enter the 2003—2007 counterinsurgency campaign.

The world seemed to overlook the relevance of this surprising break in US-Turkish cooperation. The issue was clouded by the European anti-war movement which interpreted the fissure as an extension of global angst. It wasn't—instead, it may well have been the beginning of the end of secularism in Turkey.

It would be helpful to take a whirlwind tour of Turkey's path from the Ottoman Caliphate to pro western secular partner and NATO ally to today's pro Palestinian, pro Iranian, ruling Islamist Party. We haven't come full circle just yet, but how close are we?

Ataturk kills the 'Sick Man of Europe.' The Turks became the de-facto rulers of the Islamic world in 1517 when the Ottoman Empire became the Ottoman Caliphate, supplanting the Egyptian Mamlukes. The Caliphate challenged Europe for the next 400 years; almost conquering Vienna in 1529 with its fearsome Janissaries. The Ottomans ossified and began to falter in the early 1900's. They sealed their fate when they joined the wrong side in WWI. As they witnessed the dissolution of the empire, the Turks attempted to purify their homeland by launching the first genocide of the century—the 1915 Armenian Genocide. The failure of the Caliphate became inevitable following the war and it was laid to rest in 1923 when Mustapha Kemal Ataturk killed it.

- Ottoman Empire became the Ottoman Caliphate in 1517
- Mustapha Kemal Ataturk led the move to secularize (Kemalism)
- He banned the fez and head scarves in public buildings and schools and encouraged western dress
- The Caliphate became a Republic in 1922
- Ataturk dissolved the Caliphate in 1923 following a slow decline culminating in WWI
- He removed the constitutional clause naming Islam the official religion in 1928
- The prominent Jihadist, Sayaad Qutb, declared the dissolution of the Caliphate a catastrophe and a crime

Muslim Secular Stronghold / Bulwark. The new Turkey became a key US ally during the Cold War and the War on Terror. They also became a valuable Muslim ally to Israel.

- The Atatutk legacy charged the military to be the guarantor of Turkish secularism
- Turkey was the second Muslim state, after Iran, to recognize Israel in 1949
- They joined NATO in 1952
- Turkey provided the fifth-largest UN military contingent (5,453 soldiers) at the peak of the Korean War
- Military coups stopped sectarian revivals five times; 1960, 1971, 1980, 1997
- In 2006 Tzipi Livni declared Israeli-Turkish, "bilateral relations are excellent"

Aspirations and Frustrations (the Turkish Dilemma): Secular Turkey suffers from an identity crises—neither fully European nor fully Muslim. They can become part of the former by being accepted into the European Union (EU); an event they can influence but cannot control. They can become the latter by restoring sectarianism; an event they fully control and one that conforms to the current regional trends dating back to the 1979 Iranian Revolution and 1980 Soviet-Afghan War.

- Turkish attempts to join the ECC and EU have been repeatedly rebuffed
- Turkish attempts to tamp down the Kurdistan Workers' Party (PKK) insurgency have repeatedly inflamed EU human rights advocates
- France recognized the Armenian Genocide in 2001—an event secular Turkey has repeatedly denied as being genocide
- The European Court of Human Rights found Turkey guilty of violating Cypriot rights in 2001—another sore point for the Turks
- The Turkish Parliament passed reforms in 2002 and passed laws easing pressure on the Kurds in 2003 to placate the EU
- In response to the above, the EU in 2004 agreed to begin EU talks in 2005
- The 2005 EU talks resulted in a statement that Turkey's penal code violated human rights
- In 2006 Turkeys anti terror laws were criticized by the EU Turkey closes ports/airports to Cyprus in 2006—the EU halts EU talks in response
- In 2007, the US House or Representatives passed a resolution recognizing Armenian Genocide

The Anti-Ataturk (Enter Erdogan and the AKP Islamist Party): Erdogan is an Islamist. He was jailed for inciting religious hatred and was banned from politics for being a threat to secularism. After serving a fraction of his prison sentence he was released. When he returned to society, he did what all good politicians do—he pretended to move to the political center by claiming to embrace secularism.

- Islamists first acquired representation in the '70s under Necmettin Erbakan
- Erdogan becomes mayor of Istanbul in 1994
- Convicted of inciting religious hatred, sentenced to 10 months and serves 4 in 1998
- Erdogan, an Erbakan lieutenant, led the 2001 formation a new Islamist AKP party
- In 2002, the Justice and Development Party's (AKP) wins the majority in the parliament with only 36% of the votes due to rules that deny representation to small parties
- On 14 March 2003, Erdogan becomes prime minister
- He blocks US ground forces from moving though Turkey in 2003 The Erdogan government condemns Israeli Operation Cast Lead 2008-2009
- Turkey goes on joint exercises with Syria in 2009
- Turkey joins Brazil in brokering a deal that allows Iran to sidestep UN sanctions in 2010
- Turkey backs an Al Qaeda affiliated charity and its Free Gaza Flotilla in 2010
- Turkey votes against U.S. backed UNSC sanctions on Iran's nuke program in 2010
- Ehud Barak voices concern that Turkey could share Israeli intelligence secrets with Iran

Sectarian Pressure (Boiling the Frog): Secular Turkey has always been looked upon with suspicion in the west given its sectarian history. As the former leader of the Muslim Nation and its Jihad, they have met repeated frustration in trying to become full partners in the west and the European Union. Latent Islamic sectarianism has always lurked below the surface in secular Turkey. The regional Islamist resurgence appears to have brought it to the surface, pushing Turkey away from secularism and towards a new, Islamically based, strategic position.

- The 1979 Iranian Revolution and 1980 Soviet invasion of Afghanistan incite Islamism
- Multiple Intifada's and two invasions of Lebanon give birth to Hizballah and Hamas
- Kurdish nationalist terrorists (PKK) continue to plague Turkey
- An autonomous Kurdish region in Northern Iraq is established following Operation Desert Storm—an unsettling development for Turkey
- Sanctions against Saddam Hussein hinder Turkish-Iraqi trade and spawns illicit oil trafficking and dealing
- 2003 Operation Iraqi Freedom forces Erdogan and his Islamist AKP party to make their new orientation clear
- Feb 2006: Italian Catholic priest Andrea Santoro is murdered by a killer shouting "Allah Akbar" as reprisal for Dutch Cartoon incident
- 2007: Three members of a Bible publishing company are tortured and killed
- Dec 2009: Bartholomew, the Archbishop of Constantinople, New Rome, and Ecumenical Patriarch, states that Orthodox Christians in Turkey are treated as second-class citizens don't enjoy our full rights in a 60 Minutes Interview
- June 2010: Roman Catholic Bishop and apostolic vicar of Anatolia, Luigi Padovese, is stabbed to death in eastern Turkey
  In 2010 the government announced the discovery of a military coup in the making against the AKP (the Sledgehammer Plot) leading to the arrest of over 100 high ranking officers

Sectarian Turkey—Caliphate Redux?: Recep Tayyip Erdogan's actions are leaning towards the transformation of the Republic of Turkey back into the Caliphate of Turkey. He has begun relaxing sectarian restrictions such as the wearing of headscarves in school. He has drifted away from the west, the EU, the U.S. and Israel. The AKP has purged the Turkish Army Officer Corps as part of its response to the Sledgehammer Plot thus emasculating Ataturk's secular guarantor. Erdogan has cozied up to Syria, Iran, Sudan, Hamas, and Hizballah. He even called Hizballah boss Hasan Nasrallah to send his regrets on the death of Hizballah terrorist leader Muhammad Hussein Fadlallah.

He has also proposed the creation of 'professional military brigades' to fight against terrorists and secure the border. The latter move has generated fears that the new 'professional' force could become a Turkish version of the Iranian Qods Force—an ideological special forces entity that directly challenges the rank and file military; sort of an SS to the Wehrmacht. The question is how far this will go? Is Turkey simply launching a secular bid for regional hegemony and influence or is this a potential bid to reclaim the mantle of leader of the Ummah? Will the Turks actually ally with their ancient rivals the Persians (Iran) or is this an attempt to re-enter the region as a precursor to challenging for its leadership? Worrisome indicators of sectarian drift are listed below:

- Drop their bid for acceptance into the European Union
- Cooperate with non-NATO militaries (already begun in limited fashion)
- Initiate tight restrictions on U.S. basing in Turkey
- Deny U.S. basing in Turkey
- Leave NATO
- Join the Shanghai Cooperation Organization (SCO)
- Become part of a new triad (Iran-Syria-Turkey)

Reference

Al Qaeda Timeline

1957—USAMA BIN LADEN: UBL is born in Jeddah, Saudi Arabia, although his family originates from Yemen.

1984—OFFICE OF SERVICES ESTABLISHED: Sheik Abdullah Azzam, a Palestinian religious scholar, establishes the Makhtab al Khadimat—the Office of Services—in Peshawar, Pakistan to recruit an Islamic army to fight the Soviets in Afghanistan. UBL provides financial support to the organization.

1986 —UBL SETS UP CAMP & BUILDS TIES: UBL establishes the Al Masadah ("The Lion's Den") training camp for Persian Gulf Arabs and begins associating with Egyptian radicals—who, unlike Azzam, advocate a global jihad—he befriends Dr. Ayman al-Zawahiri of the Egyptian Islamic Jihad.

1986—OFFICE OF SERVICES REACHES THE U.S.: The Office of Services journal is distributed in the US by the Islamic Center of Tucson, Arizona.

1989—AL QAEDA ESTABLISHED: UBL, Muhammad Atef, and Abu Ubaidah al Banshiri found Al Qaeda ("The Base") in Afghanistan and Peshawar, Pakistan.

Nov. 1989—POWER STRUGGLE OVER OFFICE OF SERVICES: After a car bomb kills Sheik Abdullah Azzam, a power struggle over the Office of Services breaks out between Azzam's followers who want to focus on the creation of an Islamic state in Afghanistan, and UBL followers who want to expand the struggle worldwide. UBL's faction wins.

Dec. 1989—OK MEETING OF FUTURE TERRORISTS: Wadih el-Hage, a U.S. citizen convicted in the '98 U.S embassy bombings, meets with Egyptian Mahmud Abuhalima, convicted in the '93 World Trade Center Bombing, at a conference of Muslims held in Oklahoma City. Abuhalima tries to buy guns from el-Hage.

Feb. 1989—SOVIETS PULL OUT OF AFGHANISTAN: The Soviet humiliating defeat by mujahedeen forces inspires UBL and other Islamic radicals to believe their victory in Afghanistan can be replicated around the world. At the end of the war, many of the "Afghan Arabs" returned home and UBL returns to Saudi Arabia.

Nov. 1990—BOMB MANUALS, PHOTOS DISCOVERED: During an investigation into the assassination of the right-wing rabbi Meir Kahane, authorities discover bomb manuals and photographs of the World Trade Center and the Empire State Building in the apartment of an Egyptian, El-Sayyid Nosair. Nosair is an associate of Wadih el-Hage. It is learned that Nosair's legal bills were paid for by UBL. This is the earliest known intelligence linking UBL to terrorists.

1991—UBL FLEES TO SUDAN: UBL had offerd to defend Saudi Arabia from Iraq and protested the Kingdom's acceptance of US forces for Desert Storm. Under pressure, he leaves Saudi Arabia and travels to Afghanistan. He eventually settles in Khartoum, Sudan, in 1992.

1992—UBL ORGANIZES ATTACKS ON UN FORCES IN SOMALIA: Egyptian Mohammed Atef travels to Somalia to organize attacks on US and UN troops. He reports to bin Laden in Khartoum.

1992—THE TERROR NETWORK EXPANDS: Al Qaeda makes overtures to Iran and Hezbollah to take part in a global war against the U.S.. Al Qaeda officials meet with Iranian officials and Al Qaeda members go to Lebanon to get training from Hezbollah. Efforts to secure components for chemical and nuclear weapons begin.

Dec. 29, 1992—AL QAEDA'S FIRST ATTACK: A bomb explodes at a hotel in Aden, Yemen, that is intended to kill U.S. servicemen headed to Somalia. It kills two Austrian tourists. Two Afghanistan trained Yemeni Muslims are injured and later arrested. Intelligence officials believe this is Al Qaeda's first attack. The Associated Press reports that two of the Yemenis detained for the 2000 attack on the USS Cole were involved both in this 1992 Aden bombing, and a series of other attacks in 1993.

Feb. 26, 1993—WORLD TRADE CENTER BOMBING: A truck bomb explodes in the parking garage of the World Trade Center (WTC) killing six and injuring hundreds. Investigators discover the suspects have links to a network of Islamic extremists. Several people convicted in the bombing are linked to the Office of Service's Al Kifah Center in Brooklyn. Four are connected to Sheik Omar Abdel Rahman, a blind Egyptian cleric who was the spiritual leader of the Egyptian Islamic Jihad. He is convicted of conspiracy for his involvement in a plot to blow up New York City landmarks and is sentenced to life in prison. Investigators charge Ramzi Yousef as the mastermind behind the WTC bombing and begin a worldwide manhunt. UBL's name surfaces as a financier of the Office of Services. His name is also found on a list of individuals who was called from a safe house used by the conspirators. During the WTC bombing trial, bin Laden's name appears on a list of potential unindicted co-conspirators but Al Qaeda is not mentioned.

April 1993—FINAL TRAINING OF SOMALIS: Muhammad Atef and other members of Al Qaeda return to Somalia to train Somali forces to attack UN troops.

July 1993—BOJINKA CONSPIRATORS MEET: Pakistani Abdul Hakim Murad, later convicted for his role in the 1995 Bojinka ("Big Bang") plot to blow up twelve airliners, meets Khalid Shaikh Mohammed (KSM) in Karachi, Pakistan while visiting with Ramzi Yousef. Murad tells investigators that KSM had an "intense" interest in pilot training.

Oct. 3-4, 1993—BLACK HAWK DOWN INCIDENT: Eighteen U.S. soldiers are killed in Mogadishu, Somalia, by Al Qaeda trained attackers.

Late 1993—AL QAEDA CONTEMPLATES NAIROBI ATTACK: An Al Qaeda cell in Kenya discuss attacking the U.S. embassy. Ali

Mohamed, a US citizen, admits that he took photographs and sketches of the embassy and presented them to UBL in the Sudan.

1994—AIR FRANCE FLIGHT HIJACKED: Algerian hijackers seize an Air France flight headed for Paris. The crisis ends after French commandos storm the plane. According to French investigators, the hijackers planned to blow up the plane above Paris or crash it into the Eiffel Tower.

1994-1995—RAMZI YOUSEF HIDES: Ramzi Yousef, mastermind of the 1993 WTC attack, hides out in the Philippines with his uncle, KSM. The two plan a number of potential terrorist attacks.

Jan. 1994—UBL FUNDS SUDAN TERRORIST CAMPS: UBL supports at least three Sudanese training camps.

July 11, 1994—AL QAEDA'S LONDON OFFICE: UBL opens a media office in London which will serve as a message center and provides cover for Al Qaeda operations.

Aug. 1994—MARRAKESH HOTEL ATTACK: Two Spaniards are killed when three French Muslims open fire on tourists in a hotel lobby in Marrakesh, Morocco. European investigators discover phone calls between the suspects and the Office of Services. They also uncover a network of Afghan jihad war veterans in Europe.

Dec. 1994—KONSOJAYA ESTABLISHED IN MALAYSIA: A front company named Konsojaya funnels money from UBL to regional operatives. Phone calls are made from Konsojoya offices to Mohammed Khalifa, UBL's brother-in-law who allegedly ran a charity front for Al Qaeda.

Dec. 1994—BOJINKA TEST RUN: Ramzi Yousef plants a small bomb on a Philippine Airlines plane that explodes and kills a Japanese businessman. Authorities discover the bombing is a test run for the Bojinka attack.

Jan. 1995—BOJINKA PLOT UNCOVERED: Following an explosion in a Manila apartment the Philippine police uncover the Bojinka or "Big Bang" plot to blow up 12 airplanes bound for the U.S. Authorities arrest Abdul Hakim Murad, a Pakistani associate of Ramzi Yousef. Yousef flees to Pakistan. Investigators also discover that KSM had visited the apartment frequently. His name is found on documents on a computer that contains details of the Bojinka plot.

Jan. 20, 1995—PLANES AS WEAPONS: In the Bojinka investigation, Manila police interview Abdul Hakim Murad who describes his discussions with Ramzi Yousef about hijacking a commercial aircraft and flying it into the headquarters of the CIA. Yousef and Murad discuss the idea of using a small airplane loaded with explosives to bomb targets in the U.S.

Feb. 5, 1995—YOUSEF CAPTURED: Just as FBI Agent John O'Neill begins his new job as section chief of the FBI's Counterterrorism Section, Ramzi Yousef is located in Pakistan. O'Neill helps coordinate his capture. Afterwards, authorities learn Yousef spent part of the previous three years living in a UBL funded guesthouse.

Aug. 1995—UBL'S LETTER TO KING FAHD: UBL sends an open letter to King Fahd of Saudi Arabia calling for a campaign to eject U.S. forces from Saudi Arabia.

Dec. 1995—BOJINKA PLOTTER ARRESTED: Wali Khan Amin Shah is arrested in Malaysia and handed over to the U.S. He is convicted for his role in the Bojinka plot.

1996—FOCUS IN ON BIN LADEN: The U.S. State Department issues a dossier on bin Laden that claims he is a financier of radical Islamic causes and connects him to the 1992 hotel bombing in Aden, Yemen and the training of the Somalis who attacked U.S. troops in Mogadishu. A grand jury investigation of UBL is initiated in New York.

Jan. 1996—"ALEX" STATION CONFIRMS SCALE OF AL QAEDA: The FBI and CIA create a joint station, code-named "Alex," to track down UBL. Alex Station identifies the UBL network in 56 countries.

May 1996—SUDAN EXPELS UBL: Sudan expels bin Laden under international pressure. He returns to Afghanistan.

Spring 1996—AN AL QAEDA INFORMER: Jamal Ahmed al-Fadl leaves Al Qaeda after he's discovered embezzling money. He claims his theft is due to poor pay. Al-Fadl claims to be a charter member of Al Qaeda and he cooperates with the U.S. by providing detailed information on Al Qaeda's organization and operation.

June 25, 1996—KHOBAR TOWERS BOMBING: Nineteen American soldiers are killed and 500 people injured in the Khobar Tower bombing in Dhahran, Saudi Arabia. Investigators conclude that the Iranian government commissioned Saudi Hezbollah terrorists to carry out the attack. Some allege that UBL played some role in the attack.

Sep. 5, 1996—BOJINKA CONVICTIONS: Ramzi Ahmed Yousef, Abdul Hakim Murad, and Wali Khan Amin Shah are convicted for their roles in the Bojinka plot.

May 22, 1997—TERRORISTS REPORTED IN U.S.: John O'Neill, special agent in charge of the national security division in New York, states, "Almost every one of these groups has a presence in the United States today. A lot of these groups now have the capacity and the support infrastructure in the United States to attack us here if they choose to."

Aug. 21, 1997—A NAIROBI AL QAEDA CELL: Police search Wadih el-Hage's home in Nairobi, Kenya and discover documents on his computer that describe an Al Qaeda cell in Nairobi. He is questioned but not detained and he returns to America.

Feb. 23, 1998—AL QAEDA CALLS FOR KILLING AMERICANS: UBL and Dr. Ayman al-Zawahiri issue a declaration calling on Muslims to kill Americans anywhere in the world.

June 8, 1998—UBL INDICTED: A U.S. grand jury issues a sealed indictment charging bin Laden with conspiracy to attack "defense utilities of the United States" and alleges his involvement in the Oct 1993 attack on US soldiers in Somalia.

June 10, 1998—BIN LADEN INTERVIEW: John Miller of ABC News interviews bin Laden in his mountaintop camp in Afghanistan. During the interview bin Laden admits to knowing Wali Khan Amin Shah, one of the Bojinka plotters, but denies having met Ramzi Yousef. He also denies knowledge of the "Bojinka plot" or of a related plot to assassinate President Clinton.

Aug. 1998—FAA WARNS OF HIJACKINGS: The Federal Aviation Administration warns airlines to be on a "high degree of alertness" for possible hijackings by Al Qaeda.

Aug. 6, 1998—EGYPTIAN JIHAD'S WARNING: Ayman al-Zawahiri's Egyptian group warns of a "message" they will be sending to the Americans, "which we hope they read with care, because we will write it, with God's help, in a language they will understand."

Aug. 7, 1998—US EMBASSY BOMBINGS: U.S. embassies in Nairobi, Kenya and Dar es Salaam, Tanzania are bombed almost simultaneously. The Kenya bomb kills 213 and injures 4,500; the Dar es Salaam bomb kills 11 and injures 85. Bomber Mohamed Al-'Owhali of Saudi Arabia flees the scene.

THE EMBASSY INVESTIGATION:
- A search of the apartment of Khalid al-Fawwaz, head of Al Qaeda's London office, finds manuals similar to those found in the luggage of Ahmad Ajaj, a Yousef confidant.
- Mohamed Sadeek Odeh, a Jordanian who later convicted in the embassy bombings, is arrested in Pakistan when he tries to enter from Kenya with a fake passport.
- A group calling itself the Islamic Army for the Liberation of the Holy Places faxes claims of responsibility to news outlets in France, Qatar, and the UAE. It is revealed that the fax was sent from a phone number linked to UBL.
- Mohamed al-'Owhali is arrested by Kenyan detectives and confesses to his role in the embassy bombing.

- Intelligence officials intercept calls between two bin Laden lieutenants implicating them in the embassy bombing.
  Advisors warn President Clinton that they have evidence that bin
- Laden is attempting to purchase weapons of mass destruction.

Aug. 20, 1998—TOMAHAWK ATTACK: President Clinton orders Tomahawk missiles fired at a suspected Al Qaeda camp in Afghanistan and a pharmaceutical plant in Sudan, which was suspected of producing chemical weapons for UBL.

Sep. 1998—ALI MOHAMED ARRESTED: U.S. citizen and Al Qaeda member Ali Mohamed is arrested in the U.S. He admits to taking pictures of the Nairobi embassy that he showed to UBL. Mohamed told the judge that "Bin Laden looked at the picture of the American embassy and pointed to where a truck could go as a suicide bomber."

Sep. 23, 1998—EAST AFRICA AND '93 WTC BOMBING LINKED: At a bail hearing for Wadih el-Hage, the US Attorney claims el-Hage had links to El Sayyid Nosair and Mahmud Abouhalima, both convicted in the 1993 World Trade Center bombing.

Nov. 4 1998—UBL INDICTMENT RELEASED: The U.S. government releases its indictment against bin Laden, Muhammad Atef and other members of Al Qaeda.

1999—KHALID MOHAMMED VISITS GERMANY: KSM visits Hamburg, Germany and is suspected to have met with an Al Qaeda cell in Hamburg.

June 7, 1999—UBL ADDED TO FBI'S "TEN MOST WANTED" LIST: UBL is wanted for murder of U.S. nationals; conspiracy to murder U.S. nationals; and attack on a federal facility resulting in death.

Nov. 30, 1999—JORDAN MILLENNIUM PLOT DISCOVERED: Jordanian officials intercept a phone conversation between Abu Zubaydah, a senior Al Qaeda lieutenant, and members of a Jordanian cell planning a plot referred to as "the day of the millennium." Jordanian raids and discover explosives and a plan to blow up the Radisson Hotel in Amman and other sites.

Dec. 1999—MALAYSIA MEETING: The CIA intercepts phone calls at a Yemeni house and Al Qaeda logistics center which they had learned about from Mohamed al-'Owhali of the embassy bombing. Ahmed Al-Hada, a Yemeni citizen, owned the house. The callers discuss a January 2000 meeting in Kuala Lumpur that Khalid Almidhar, a Yemeni citizen and son-in-law of Al-Hada, and Nawaf Alhazmi, a Saudi national, were to attend the meeting. Almidhar and Alhazmi later became 9-11 hijackers of American Airlines Flight 77.

Dec. 14, 1999—RESSAM INTERCEPTED AT CANADIAN BOARDER: Algerian native Ahmed Ressam is caught entering the U.S. with 130 pounds of explosives at the Canadian border at Port Angeles, Washington. Ressam had links to Al Qaeda militants and trained in an Afghanistan. His was Los Angeles International Airport.

Jan. 2000—MALAYSIA MEETING: An Al Qaeda meeting occurs in Kuala Lumpur, Malaysia. Malaysian agents photograph the meeting. Nawaf Alhazmi and Khalid Almidhar (both 9-11 hijackers) attend. Tawfiq bin-Atash, once the head of UBL's bodyguards and suspect in the Cole attack also attends. Riduan Isamuddin, a militant Islamic preacher, suspected of having had a role in the "Bojinka" plot, also attends. Ramzi bin al-Shibh, a former roommate of 9-11 hijacker Mohamed Atta, also attends. Fahad al-Quso, who is later arrested for his role in the Cole attack, is a "bag man" who carried money to finance the meeting. The importance of the Malaysia meeting would not be known until after the Cole investigation.

Jan. 3, 2000—USS SULLIVANS ATTACK FAILS: A cell of Yemeni terrorists try bombing the USS Sullivans in Yemen's Aden Harbor but fail when their overloaded skiff sinks. Investigators do not discover the attempt until after the USS Cole is successfully attacked by the same cell in October of 2000.

Jan. 15, 2000—ALHAZMI AND ALMIDHAR ENTER THE U.S.: Nawaf Alhazmi and Khalid Almidhar fly into Los Angeles from Bangkok. Neither individual is tracked once they enter the U.S. Both become 9-11 suicide hijackers.

April 17, 2000—FBI INVESTIGATES A FLIGHT SCHOOL: The Phoenix office of the FBI begins to investigate Zakaria Mustapha Soubra, a Phoenix flight school student suspected of having ties to Al Qaeda.

Aug. 2000—ITALY HEARS ABOUT PLANES AS WEAPONS: Italian investigators record the conversations of Abdulsalam Ali Ali Abdulrahman who tells Abdelkader Moahmoud Es Sayad, a suspected Egyptian terrorist, that planes could be used as weapons against the US.

Fall 2000—BIN AL-SHIBH DENIED VISA: Ramzi bin al-Shibh from Yemen and Mohamed Atta's former roommate, applies for a U.S. Visa but is denied. He was supposed to take part in the 9-11 plot but was replaced by Zacarias Moussaoui at the last minute.

Oct. 2000—MOUSSAOUI VISITS MALAYSIA: Zacarias Moussaoui, a French national, visits Malaysia. Moussaoui attains fake identification papers. At the time explosives are purchased for an attack on foreign embassies and other targets in Southeast Asia. The plot is foiled after 9-11 when a videotape of potential targets is found in Afghanistan.

Oct. 12, 2000—REVELATIONS ON THE USS COLE: Two men in a skiff pull alongside the USS *Cole* and detonate an explosive that rips through the hull and kills 17 sailors. Yemeni authorities several capture suspects; among them is Tawfiq bin-Atash, former head of UBL's bodyguards. Authorities realize that bin-Atash was photographed at the Malaysia meeting.

Dec. 8, 2000—COLE LINKS TO BIN LADEN: ABC News' John Miller reports authorities have found connections between the *Cole* attack and UBL including phone records of calls between the bombers of the *Cole* and an Al Qaeda cell in East Africa. Yemeni officials arrest Gamal Al Badawi, who admits he fought with Al Qaeda in Bosnia. Fahad al-Quso, in custody carried $5,000 to Cole conspirators. Miller reports Yemeni authorities suspect Abdul Al-Nassir organized the *Cole* attack and recruited bombers for the attack on the embassies in East Africa in 1998.

Jan. 2001 —FAA WARNS OF HIJACKINGS: Between January and August of 2001, the Federal Aviation Administration issues 15 advisories to airlines and airports warning that terrorists could try to hijack or destroy American aircraft.

Jan. 24, 2001—"THE BROTHERS GOING TO AMERICA:" Italian authorities record Abdelkader Mahmoud Es Sayed, an imam in Italy, talking about forged documents for "the brothers going to America."

Jan. 27, 2001—*COLE* LINKS TO AL QAEDA CONFIRMED: Investigators in Yemen believe that the people in custody are tied closely to Al Qaeda.

Feb. 2001—SUSPICIOUS FLIGHT SCHOOL STUDENT: Instructors at an Arizona flight school becomes suspicious about a student who speaks English poorly and has limited flying skills who wants to learn how to take off but not how to land. The student is the Suaid, Hani Hanjour, who pilots the plane that crashes into the Pentagon on 9-11.

April 2001—THREAT ON U.S. TARGETS: Washington receives a "specific threat" that Al Qaeda may attempt to attack US targets in the Middle East or Europe.

April 18, 2001—ANOTHER FAA WARNING: Another warning to airlines states that: "The FAA does not have any credible information regarding specific plans by terrorist groups to attack U.S. civil aviation interests... Nevertheless some of the current active groups are known to plan and train for hijackings... The FAA encourages U.S. carriers to demonstrate a high degree of alertness."

May 11, 2001—STATE DEPT WARNS AMERICANS OVERSEAS: The DoS warns that American citizens overseas may be targeted by Al Qaeda.

May 29, 2001—EAST AFRICA CONVICTIONS: Mohamed al-'Owhali, Khalfan Khamis Mohamed, Mohammed Saddiq Odeh, and

Wadih el-Hage are convicted on charges including conspiracy to kill Americans stemming from the 1998 embassy bombings.

June 2001—VISA ISSUED TO ALMIDHAR: The State Department re-issues a visa to Khalid Almidhar, a 9-11 hijacker who attended the Jan 2000 Malaysia meeting.

June 2001—FBI LEAVES YEMEN / MORE FAA WARNINGS: The FBI pulls out of Yemen citing security threats. In the same month the FAA issues another warning to airlines. Intelligence experts are concerned that an attack is imminent.

June 2001—EMBASSIES CLOSE: U.S. embassies in Senegal and Bahrain are shut down and the DoS issues a worldwide caution.

Mid-June—YEMEN ATTACK THWARTED: Yemeni authorities thwart an attack on the U.S. embassy in Sana.

June 28, 2001—ATTACK "HIGHLY LIKELY:" Intelligence officials brief National Security Adviser Condoleezza Rice that an Al Qaeda attack is "highly likely."

Summer 2001—FBI IDS *COLE* SUSPECTS AT MALAYSIA MEETING: The CIA informs the FBI about the Malaysia meeting and shows them a pictures of *Cole* suspects. The FBI identifies Cole suspects Tawfiq bin-Atash and Fahad al-Quso.

July 4, 2001—ALMIDHAR RE-ENTERS U.S.: Khalid Almidhar re-enters the US through JFK airport. He meets with Mohamed Atta.

July 10, 2001—SPAIN MEETING: Mohamed Atta meets with his former roommate Ramzi bin al-Shibh in Spain along with a number of other Arab men.

July 10, 2001—REQUEST FLIGHT SCHOOL INVESTIGATION: The FBI's Phoenix office sends a memo to FBI headquarters requesting officials initiate a nationwide investigation of flight schools. The memo warns that UBL operatives may be attending flight schools in the U.S.

July 18, 2001—RESSAM CONVICTED: The FBI warns that the conviction of Ahmed Ressam for the millennium plot to detonate a bomb at Los Angeles airport could lead to retaliatory terrorist attacks.

July 31, 2001—ANOTHER FAA ALERT: The FAA issues another warning to airlines that terrorists could be planning to hijack American airlines.

Aug. 2001—UBL OPERATIVES RETURN TO AFGHANISTAN: In August and early September 2001, close associates of bin Laden were warned to return to Afghanistan from other parts of the world by Sep 10.

Aug. 16, 2001—FAA WARNS OF WEAPONS FROM EVERYDAY OBJECTS: The FAA warns airlines that terrorists may use weapons modified from everyday objects.

Aug. 16, 2001—MOUSSAOUI ARRESTED: Minneapolis FBI arrests Zacarias Moussaoui on immigration charges for overstaying his Visa. The Minneapolis office tries unsuccessfully to secure either a criminal or intelligence warrant to search Moussaoui's belongings, particularly his personal computer, but are denied. After 9-11, a federal indictment shows that Moussaoui was in possession of two knives, a flight manual for a 747-400, fighting gloves and shin guards, and an aviation radio.

Aug. 27, 2001—CIA NAMES ALMIDHAR AND ALHAZMI: The CIA cables the FBI a warning that Khalid Almidhar and Nawaf Alhazmi are in the US and are suspected terrorists because of their presence at the January 2000 Malaysia meeting.

Aug. 28, 2001—FRENCH BRIEF ON MOUSSAOUI: Moussaoui is linked to Al Qaeda.

Sep. 5, 2001—BIN AL-SHIBH LEAVES FOR AFGHANISTAN: Ramzi bin al-Shibh, the former roommate of Mohamed Atta, who had attended both the July meeting in Spain and the January 2000 Malaysia meeting, leaves Germany for Afghanistan.

Sep. 10, 2001—TAJIK LEADER AHMED SHAH MASOUD IS ASSASSINATED: UBL's most dangerous rival in Afghanistan is assassinated by a team of Al Qaeda terrorists posing as a news reporter and a cameramen. The camera was a bomb.

9-11—ATTACK: Hijackers alleged to be members of Al Qaeda take control of four airliners and crash two into the World Trade Center, and one into the Pentagon. A fourth hijacked plane crashes into the Pennsylvania countryside. The attacks kill more than 3,000 people.

Khalid Shaikh Mohammed, wanted for the 1995 Bojinka plot, is linked to 9-11. KSM is ID'ed as Al Qaeda operations chief. Phone conversations between Mohamed Atta and KSM are intercepted before 9-11 but are not translated in time. On Sep 11, 2002, Ramzi bin al-Shibh is captured in Karachi, Pakistan.

http://www.pbs.org/wgbh/pages/frontline/shows/knew/etc/cron.html

This chronology is drawn from news and government information that came out prior to, and after, the 9-11 attacks.

OVERSEAS CONTINGENCY OPERATIONS (OCO)

Countdown

1983 Bombing of US Embassy in Beirut

1986 CIA Counterterrorism Center established

1988 USG terrorism responsibility assigned to DOJ

1993 Bombing of World Trade Center, NYC

1994 Four convicted of WTC bombing

1995 Tokyo Subway Sarin Gas Attack

1995 PDD 39 U.S. Policy on Counter-Terrorism

1996 Bombing of Khobar Towers, Saudi Arabia

1996 Anti-terrorism and effective death penalty act passed

1997 Terrorism Coordination Unit created by FEMA

1998 PDD 62 Combating Terrorism

1998 US Embassy bombings, Kenya and Tanzania

1998 Five Year Plan on Combating Terrorism Prepared

1998 National Domestic Preparedness Office (NDPO) created

1998 CT Coordination Unit created in NSC

2000 Bombing of USS Cole in Yemen

2001 Interagency Domestic Terrorism Concept of Operations Plan

2001 9/11 Attacks

2001 Homeland Security Council formed

2001 Patriot Act passed

2002 Department of Homeland Security Formed

2002 National Strategy for Combating Terrorism

2002 NORTHCOM established

2002 National Military Strategic Plan for the War on Terror

2003 Terrorist Threat Integration Center created

2004 9/11 Commission Report

2004 National Counterterrorism Center (NCTC) established

2004 Intelligence Reform and Terrorist Prevention Act

2005 WMD Commission Report

2006 National Strategy for Combating Terrorism

2006 National Implementation Plan written by NCTC

2006 State Counter Terrorism Office develops Regional Strategic Initiative

2008 Mumbai

2009 Close Gitmo

2009 GWOT name abolished

2010 Al Qaeda *Inspire* Magazine debut 2011Muammar Gaddafi killed and Libya becomes Islamist basket case

2012 Islamists attack the American diplomatic compound in Benghazi resulting in the first murder of a U.S. Ambassador in the line of duty since 1979

2013 ISIL raids on Taji and Abu Ghraib prisons freeing more than 500 terrorists

2014 Islamic State of Iraq and the Levant declares itself a Caliphate / The Islamic State

2015 AlHouthi Rebels seize Sana'a—the Sunni/Shia Civil War begins

Guerrilla warfare: hard to identify terrorists from civilians/noncombatants

Human shields: terrorists will not hesitate to endanger civilians for their own ends

Super-empowerment: advanced technology results in an individual or small group able to achieve mass effects.

Information: The burden of proof is on us, not terrorists.

Religious vs Secular Ideology: We are taking a secular approach to fighting a religious war.

"Know the enemy and your yourself, and you need not fear in a hundred battles"
—Sun Tsu

"Battle between these two centers for command of world (economy) will decide fate of- (capitalism) and (communism) in the entire world."
-—Project X", Kennan, 1946.

"Allah has blessed a group of Vanguard Muslims, the forefront of Islam, to destroy America."
—Osama Bin Laden.

"Policy and academic elites are blinded by their bias against qualitative analysis and especially against the study of religion."
—Y. S. P. Lambert, 2005

"Policy makers have not developed clear guidance from addressing religion abroad, and U.S. efforts have not managed to fully reduce religious risks, account for religious dynamics, and energize religious partners effectively."
—Mixed Blessings, CSIS report, 2007.

Terms and Definitions
for the Long War

•From 1870 to 1945 global conflict was based on multi-polar competition between three socio-economic state models; democracy, fascism, and communism.

•• From 1945 to 1990 global conflict was based on bi-polar competition between two socio-economic state models; democracy and communism. This struggle was called the Cold War and was characterized by proxy war and insurgency. Open warfare between the contending states was repressed by nuclear deterrence.

• The inability to confront the enemy directly transformed the struggle to one of contending ideals instead of contending armies. The opposing ideal had to be defined in order to provide understanding, motivation, and purpose to the struggle. The definition came in a diplomatic telegram titled "The Sources of Soviet Conduct" written by 'X' (George Kennan). This became the framework for understanding the Cold War.

•• Today's Long War prevents direct confrontation between antagonists for very different reasons thus it is also a war of ideals. The opposing ideal is not defined in a manner that offers understanding, motivation, and purpose. The war can't be a 'war on terror' since terrorism is a tactic and not an ideal.

•State—a group of governing and legal principals and mechanisms usually defined by recognized borders and accepted sovereignty

•• Nation—a self conscious ethnic community bound by a common heritage, history, and faith

•• Terrorism—the systematic use of violence for the purpose of coercion of an existing government in order to de-legitimize the target state and bring about social and political change

•• Insurgency—a condition of revolt against a government that is less than an organized revolution and that is not recognized as belligerency that often forms a shadow government to challenge the targeted state's legitimacy.

303

- Forces weakening the sovereignty of the state:
- Imposition of human rights by external organizations
- WMD proliferation rendering borders relatively defenseless
- Transnational, non state, threats
- Transnational markets (Globalization)
- Global communications (Internet)

•Irregular Warfare (IW)—a violent struggle among state and non-state actors for legitimacy and influence over the relevant populations. It is inherently a protracted conflict that will test the resolve of our Nation and our partners.

•IW at the different levels of war. The IW definition takes on different meanings at each level of war because:

At the **Strategic Level**, the focus of the definition is likely that of control and influence over a relevant population.

At the **Operational Level**, the focus may be on indirect approaches for planning and conducting operations and campaigns.

At the **Tactical Level**, the focus is probably on asymmetric applications of tactics, techniques, and procedures (TTP) that may be applied differently in an IW operation than it would under a conventional operation.

•**Militant Sectarianism**—the utopian goal of creating a closed, sectarian, ethno-centric, socio-economic system; the consolidation and segregation of a select sectarian group from all other sectarian groups with the goal of domination or expulsion of non members; not wedded to a conventional state system

•**Opposes** the existing western open, multi-cultural, secular, globalist socio-economic system (both US style democracy and EU style liberal socialism)

•**Strategic Level**—reestablishment of the Caliphate / Ottoman Empire in the middle east; an Abbasid model (Sunni) or a Safavid model (Shia); control global oil market

•**Operational Level**—asymmetric war avoiding open conflict; insurgency and proxy war; create Shia states; generate permanent revolution (jihad)

•**Tactical Level**—employ terrorism; suicide / homicide bombers, and borderline criminal activities

•**The Transnational Terrorist (TNT)** – an independent actor that may receive some state support while retaining ideological, tactical and operational independence

•• **Techno-Guerilla (TG)** – a state sponsored, well equipped, paramilitary combatant that acts in concert with the goals and objectives of its state sponsor(s)

• **Advisors** – Embedded sponsors that augment and support the TNT and TG in the conduct of a proxy war

2nd Lebanon Timeline

Hell's Kitchen.   The problem with the Middle East is that there are too many chefs tending to too many boiling pots. The Middle eastern fever swamp is more Balkanized than the Balkans. Its factions are religious, nationalist, cultural and ethnic and its history is that of a powder keg where civilizations clash (Huntington).

Religion.   It is the birthplace of the world's three dominant monotheistic faiths; Judaism first followed by Christianity and finally by Islam. The first two are interrelated and mutually reinforcing. The oldest faith attempted to establish God's Kingdom on Earth on several occasions only to be ruthlessly rebuffed by the dominant pagans of the times; Rome. The younger faith did, at times, persecute its elder when led by ambitious and misguided fanatics resulting in decidedly un-Christian acts such as the Spanish Inquisition. The youngest faith set its course to not only supplant the elders, but to eliminate them as corruptions and heresies and to finally deliver Gods Kingdom on Earth. The elder two learned that human induced utopia resembles hell rather than heaven. Never the less, the three continue to battle for relevance and influence in the region.

Middle Eastern sectarianism colors all political interaction. The competition and animosity between Islam and its competitors is palpable in all the states. The classic, poster boy, conflict that defines the region swirls around the Palestinian question. Most of the regions Muslims secretly long for the destruction of Israel—they loath the Palestinians yet they hold them up as their cause célèbre. The regions secular governments love Israel for its ability to distract the people from their abject failure to compete in the modern world. For its part, Israel has tried to build and maintain a buffer zone around itself that includes; the Golan Heights, the area south of the Litani River, the Western Sinai, and the fences that trap suicide bombers within Gaza and the West Bank.

In Turkey, the faith struggle is between the new Islamist government and its indigenous Christian population—Greek Orthodox and Roman Catholic. In spite of Ataturk's secular declaration, Turkey has maintained its gradual pressure on its Christians. The latter groups preceded the Turks by a millennia and didn't relinquish primacy until the very walls of Constantinople were breached Mehmed's siege guns, sold to him by a Christian who couldn't get the right price from the Byzantines for the same guns. The current Islamist ruling party is stepping up pressure and harassment on the Christians, is backing Islamist initiatives, and is distancing itself from the Jews of Israel.

Islamic intramurals aggravate the situation as Sunni's and Shia's jockey for leadership of the faithful while Sufi's quietly huddle in the corner suffering sporadic outbursts from their sectarian brethren. From the Wahabbi Ikwan who slaughtered Shia toJindallah who kill the today to Shia death squads killing Sunni's in 2006 Iraq—the struggle is raging. Sure, there's been a temporary alliance of convenience as evidenced by the Hamas-Hizballah coalition, spurred on by Israels decision to drop several hundred Hamas off on the Lebanese Border in the heart of Hizballah-land!

Nationalism. The argument over who should be the regional hegemon (self aggrandizing):

Egypt—first regional Empire, leader in 67 and 73, Nasser Arab secular nationalism
Syria—home to the ancient Assyrian Empire and one of the regions oldest cities (Damascus)
Iraq—home of ancient Babylon and most recent Arab state to flex its muscle (8yr War, ODS, OIF)
Iran—home of the ancient Persian Empire and Shia Caliphate, erstwhile U.S. / UK ally
KSA—Islamic COG as home to Medina and Mecca and global boss of black gold
Turkey—masters of the last, and most menacing, Islamic Caliphate

Culture. The totality of socially transmitted behavior patterns, arts, beliefs, institutions, and all other products of human work and thought:

Western Secular—including democracy, women's rights, free markets and religious tolerance.

Tribalism—adherence to small group loyalty based on geography and local tradition

Arabization—transformation of other cultures into an Arab-centric culture using Islam as the catalyst

Ethnic. Group who identify with each other, through a common heritage, consisting of a common language, a shared religion and common ancestry:

Turkish—the last great leaders of the Muslim world
Arab—the founders of Islam and its first carriers
Persian—the most ancient, continuously extant, and distinct Middle Easterners

Lebanon 2006 Timeline (LH **Bold** and IDF Normal)

12 July: LH rocket attack and ambush of IDF patrol kidnaps two IDF soldiers
13 July: IAF bombs Lebanon infrastructure; Hariri International Airport, Beirut–Damascus highway, and imposes air and sea blockade
13 July: LH fires rockets at Haifa
14 July: IAF bombs Nasrallah's offices in Beirut
14 July: LH attacked the INS Ship with a C802 anti-ship missile
18 July: LH rockets hit a hospital in Safed
23 July: IDF land forces cross into Lebanon
25 July: The Battle of Bint Jbeil.
27 July: LH IDF ambush in Bint Jbeil
28 July: Israeli paratroopers kill 20+ in Bint Jbeil.
30 July: IAF strikes apartment building in Qana killing 28 civilians
31 July: Battle of Ayta ash-Shab.
3 August: Nasrallah warns against Beirut strikes stating LH will stop rocket campaign if Israel ceases air and artillery strikes
4 August: IAF targets southern Beirut
5 August: Israeli commandos execute nighttime Tyre raid
6 August: Rockets kill 12 IDF reservists; kills three civilians at the port of Haifa.
7 August: IAF attacks Shiyyah suburb in Beirut

9 August: Nine IDF soldiers killed when the building they were in collapsed after being struck by AT missiles
12 August: Litani offensive in South Lebanon
12 August: 24 IDF killed; five when LH shoots down a helicopter
14 August: IAF reportedly kills Sajed Dewayer, head of LH Special Forces; LH denies the claim, IDF targets Palestinian faction in Ain al-Hilweh refugee camp 80 minutes prior to cessation of hostilities
25 August: 63% of Israelis polled want Olmert to resign
27 August: Nasrallah apologizes to the Lebanese people; *"Had we known that the capture of the soldiers would have led to this, we would definitely not have done it."*
22 September: Nasrallah calls for LH to celebrate their "divine and strategic victory" at victory rally in Beirut
April 30, 2007: The Israeli Winograd Commission released its preliminary report stating that the Second Lebanon War was a "missed opportunity"; that a semi-military organization of a few thousand men resisted the strongest army in the Middle East which enjoyed full air superiority, size and technology advantages; Hizballah rocket attacks continued throughout the war and the IDF did not provide an effective response; the IDF offensive did not result in military gains

Definitions
Towards a New Lexicon

"But in war more than in any other subject we must begin by looking at the nature of the whole; for here more than elsewhere the part and the whole must always be thought of together."

"Principles and rules are intended to provide a thinking man with a frame of reference."

"Everything in war is very simple. But the simplest thing is difficult."
—Karl Von Clausewitz

THEORY. Theories are models / paradigms that are substituted for actual experience. They are constructed, and when possible, tested for validity. According to the dictionary, a theory is a coherent group of tested general propositions, commonly regarded as correct, that can be used as principles of explanation and prediction for a class of phenomena. It is a proposed explanation whose status is still conjectural and subject to experimentation, in contrast to well-established propositions that are regarded as reporting matters of actual fact. The following theories apply in this work.

Complexity Theory is the study of complicated and chaotic systems and how order and structure arise from them. Processes having a large number of independent agents can spontaneously order themselves into a coherent system. Complexity is non-deterministic, and cannot predict future outcomes although it can imply potential outcomes. [281] [282]

Butterfly effect—The idea that within complex systems a small event can produce a large effect over time. It is the notion that the fluttering of a butterfly's wings may trigger a hurricane half way around

---

[281] *Complexity: The Emerging Science at the Edge of Order and Chaos,* by M. Mitchell Waldrop; Simon & Schuster Adult Publishing Group, September 1993.

[282] *The Logic of Failure; Recognizing and Avoiding Error in Complex Situations,* by Dietrich Dorner, Perseus Books, August 1997.

the world. The military analogue might be Henry Heth's search for shoes in a small town called Gettysburg—the second order effect was a sharp engagement with the Buford's Cavalry while the third order effect was the convergence of the Army of Northern Virginia and the Army of the Potomac on ground neither chose.

Chaos – Systems span a range of possibilities. A closed system that ignores external input is static and will ossify, decline, and fail. An unregulated open system prone to complete randomness will disintegrate. The optimal system is one in between—one that is non-linear yet is deterministic. Such a system is said to be on the edge of chaos. It operate between order and complete randomness where the complexity is high enough to generate dynamic results without blowing apart, where the rate of adaptation approaches chaos.

Systems Theory is the study of complex systems. It serves as the framework for the analysis of groups of objects that interact towards a result.

Open system is a state in which the system continuously interacts with its environment. Its basic characteristics are the environment, inputs, throughput and outputs, and feedback.

Closed system is a system isolated from the surrounding environment. Closed systems are theoretical since no system can be completely closed. There are only varying degrees of closure. Most systems are neither completely open or closed; they are open to some influences and closed to other influences.

Steady State System is one with numerous properties that are unchanging over time. In a steady state system the recently observed behavior will continue into the future. Steady state is not achieved until sometime after the system is initiated.

Complex Adaptive Systems are complex systems that are diverse and made up of multiple interconnected elements that are adaptive in that they have the capacity to change and learn from experience.

System Dynamics is an approach to understanding the behavior of complex systems over time. It deals with internal feedback loops and time delays that affect the behavior of the system. These elements describe how simple systems display nonlinearity. Key is the recognition that the structure of the system is as important in determining its behavior as its individual components. In some cases the behavior of the whole cannot be explained by the behavior of the parts.

A nonlinear system is a system whose output is not proportional to its input. In a nonlinear system the variable to be solved cannot be written as a linear combination of independent components. Most physical systems are nonlinear. Nonlinear equations give rise to chaos. The weather is famously nonlinear, where simple changes in one part of the system produce complex effects.

STATECRAFT. This is the art of leading a country, conducting public affairs, or statesmanship.[283]

Peace of Westphalia is a treaty signed in 1648 to end the Thirty Years' War. It altered religious and political affairs of Europe. The negotiations took place in the German province of Westphalia and the principals were France and Sweden and their opponents Spain and the Holy Roman Empire. The treaty specified that the sovereignty and independence of each state within the Holy Roman Empire were fully recognized making the Holy Roman emperor powerless. Westphalia ended religious (Sectarian) warfare in Europe. Thereafter, armed struggles were waged for political ends. Westphalia supplanted the Church and established the nation-state as the legitimate institution for governance and war.

Thirty Years' War was a series related European conflicts lasting from 1618 to 1648 that were based on the religious antagonism inflamed by the Protestant Reformation. It was primarily fought in Germany. States aligned with and fought for uncompromising sectarian interests. It was a brutal series of conflicts that resulted in the exhaustion and devastation of much of Europe.[284]

State—a group of governing and legal principals and mechanisms usually defined by recognized borders and accepted sovereignty. A state is a political entity (a government)—the USA, Canada or Mexico.[285]

---

[283] *Diplomacy*, by Henry Kissinger, Simon & Schuster, April 1995.

[284] *The Thirty Years War*, by CV Wedgwood, Anchor Books, Doubleday & Company Inc, 1968.

[285] *The Soldier and the State: The Theory and Politics of Civil-Military Relations*, by Samuel P. Huntington, Harvard University Press, August 2008.

Nation—a self-conscious ethnic community bound by a common heritage, history, language, and faith. A nation is a cultural entity (a people)—Jews, Kurds, or Germans.

Nation-State—the convergence of a government and a people into a singular entity. The Nation-State arose in Napoleon's France where the people and the state unified in defense of the Republic against the combined powers of Europe. The people mobilized in support of (as part of) the state thus allowing the levee en-masse. War was now a matter of the people rather than being a dynastic interest conducted by mercenaries. Napoleon could now build mass armies devoted to a singular goal.

Globalization is the tendency of business to move beyond national markets to global markets, thereby increasing the interconnectedness and interdependence of the worlds markets. While globalization provides developing nations with access to technology, it also dislocates 'traditional societies' and erodes sovereignty. Closed societies and traditional states are threatened by globalizations egalitarianism.[286]

Terrorism—the systematic use of violence for the purpose of coercion of an existing state in order to de-legitimize its governance and bring about social and/or political change.

Insurgency—a condition of revolt against a state that is less than an organized revolution and that is not recognized as belligerency; the insurgents often form a shadow government to challenge state legitimacy.[287]

Challenges to State Sovereignty:

- Imposition of human rights by external (international) organizations
- WMD proliferation rendering borders defenseless
- Transnational, non state, threats
- Transnational markets (Globalization)
- Global communications (Internet)

[286]*Terror and Consent: The Wars for the Twenty-first Century,* by Philip Bobbitt, Knopf Doubleday Publishing Group, May 2009.

[287] *Resisting Rebellion: The History and Politics of Counterinsurgency,* by Anthony James Joes, University Press of Kentucky, September 2004.

Irregular Warfare (IW)—a violent struggle between state and non-state actors for influence over the relevant populations. IW is inherently protracted.

Militant Sectarianism—the religious utopian goal of creating a sectarian, ethno-centric, socio-economic sectarian system; the consolidation and segregation of a select sectarian group from all other groups with the goal of domination or expulsion of non members:

- **opposes** the existing egalitarian, multi-cultural, secular, and globalist socio-economic systems
- **Strategic Level**—reestablishment of the Caliphate / Ottoman Empire in the middle east; an Abbasid model (Sunni) or a Safavid model (Shia); control global oil
- **Operational Level**—asymmetric warfare avoiding open conflict; insurgency and proxy war; permanent sectarian revolution (jihad)
- **Tactical Level**—terrorism; homicide bombers, borderline criminal activities

The Transnational Terrorist (TNT)—an independent actor that may receive some state support while retaining ideological, tactical and operational independence

Techno-Guerilla (TG)—a state sponsored, well equipped, paramilitary combatant that acts in concert with the goals and objectives of its state sponsor(s):

- Advisors: Embedded sponsors that augment and support the conduct of a proxy war
- Strengths: Indirect action, Difficult to identify, Cheap, Target will through population
- Weaknesses: Sectarian schism, Ethnic division, Indecisive, 9-11 'high bar'.

iGuerilla (iG) —Tech saavy, fully equipped, terrorist or insurgent trained in and equipped with top of the line off the shelf technology; capable of SOF like precision operations.

Cold War II?
The more things change...

COMINTERN to ISLAMINTERN (Caliphate)
Secular Utopia to Sectarian Utopia
Communism to Islamism
Sino–Soviet Split to Sunni–Shia schism
Che Quevera to Al Zarqawi
Soviet backed to Iranian backed
Angola to Afghanistan
Khruschev to Ahmadinejad

Deniable state sponsorship
Domino Theory (Vietnam in Asia // Iraq in the Middle East)
Professionalization of the guerilla
Proxy Wars
Opposing worldviews
Full DIME

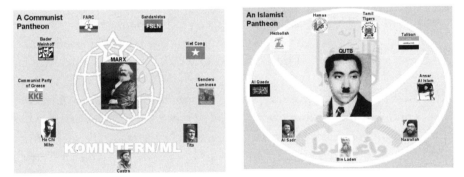

NON-STATE ACTORS...NOT NECESSARILY NEW...

The Red Army Faction (RAF) aka The Baader-Meinhof Gang

*"If one sets a car on fire; that is a criminal offence. If one sets
hundreds of cars on fire; that is political action."*
—Ulrike Meinhof

The Red Army Faction (RAF), more commonly known as Baader-Meinhof Gang, was founded in 1970 to join the chorus of radical socialist groups that had proliferated throughout Europe. They trained in the West Bank and Gaza under the Popular Front for the Liberation of Palestine (PFLP) embracing the Palestinian cause. They partially modeled themselves after the Uruguayan Tupamaro movement. The Tupamaros flipped Che Guevara's concept of a rural guerrilla war upside down by converting it into urban guerrilla war. They also endorsed Brazilian revolutionary, Carlos Marighella's, Mini-manual of the Urban Guerrilla which stated the urban guerrilla's purpose to: *"... fight the military dictatorship with weapons, using unconventional methods. ...The urban guerrilla follows a political goal, and only attacks the government, the big businesses and the foreign imperialists."* [288]

The Base (Al Qaeda)

"We—with God's help—call on every Muslim who believes in God and wishes to be rewarded to comply with God's order to kill the Americans and plunder their money wherever and whenever they find it. We also call on Muslim ulema, leaders, youths, and soldiers to launch the raid on Satan's U.S. troops and the devil's supporters allying with them, and to displace those who are behind them so that they may learn a lesson."
—Usama Bin Ladens 2nd Al Qaeda Fatwah
declaring war on the United States.[289]

---

[288]*Blood and Rage: History of Terrorism,* by Michael Burleigh, HarperCollins Publishers, February 2011.

[289]*Al Qaeda in its Own Words,* by Gilles Kepel (Editor), Jean-Pierre Milelli (Editor), Pascale Ghazaleh (Translator); Harvard University Press, April 2008.

The Story of Islamism

Failure of Secularism
- Nasser
- The Shah
- The Baathists

Autocracies / Theocracies appease or oppress radicals
- Sadat and Mubarak
- The Saudi's
- The Islamic Republic of Iran

Misdirection
- Israel (the little Satan)
- The U.S. (the big Satan)
- Democracy (anti Islamic)

Virulence
- Founder—Al Banna (Marx)
- Catalyst—Qutb (Lenin)
- Revolutionary—Bin Laden (Trotsky)
- Tyrant—Khomeini (Stalin)

Muslim Purist
- Shia Hashishins (Assassins)
- Sunni Ikhwan "The White Terror"
- Egyptian Sunni Muslim Brotherhood
- Iranian Shia Twelvers

Arab failure is due to lack of piety

Western success is due to evil

Women are threatening

The path to Glory is through Islam

Extremism is actuality literalism

Sunni / Shia Split

Post WWII National Liberation
- New Arab States choose autocracy
- Petro-dollars serve as economy
- Profound socio-economic failure

Palestine cause celebre
- Scapegoat for regional cultural failure
- Distraction from dictatorship
- Outlet for Muslim Arab frustration – mimic's Czarist Russia

Egypt breaks up the Brotherhood
- Leaders executed
- Followers exiled
- A revolutionary Diaspora goes global / goes viral

The End of the Cold War
- USSR Collapses
- Cold War imposed restraint is gone
- Hyper-Power = Hyper-Target

Preference for Autocracy

Tendency for intolerance

Proprietary organizing principals

Sectarian rule

Acceptance of extremism

Repression of women

Myths: defeated US in Iran and USSR in Afghanistan

Stray Voltage

WILDCARDS

Terror Trajectory
and
New World Insurgency

Terrorism isn't new—it isn't even novel. State and non-state terror have been with us since the dawn of civilization. The state terrorists came with names and faces like Sulla, Tamerlane, Hitler, Mao, and Stalin and their handiwork included concentration camps, gulags, the Cultural Revolution and the killing fields. The non-state players were known by gang monikers like the Sicarri, Assassins, Thugees, and Fenians and their work includes '72 Munich, 9-11, Beslan, and Mumbai.

Terrorism isn't a movement or an ideology—it's a tactic. By the book, it is the use or threatened use of indiscriminate violence against unprepared and defenseless targets in order to coerce an alteration in state behavior. State terrorists target their people while stateless terrorists target their states. Both seek to convert the uncommitted while coercing the committed.

It may be counterintuitive in today's world but state terrorism has outstripped the non-state freelancers by a long shot. In fact, state terrors' only redeeming quality is its tendency to turn inward since terrorizing outsider's risks war. The stateless need not worry about war. Cloaked in anonymity, they can hit anyone, anywhere, and their lack of sovereign real estate gives them an international free pass. If anyone pays for their crimes, it will be their host country, not them. The stateless actor's relative dearth of body count is made by deniability and superior strategic mobility. Usama Bin Laden could kill thousands of Americans within the Continental United States. Khruschev would never have dared such an act. On the flip side, UBL couldn't dream of matching Mao body count.

The day is looming when non-state actors will achieve the destructive power of states while retaining their stateless immunity. When that day arrives we'd all better take cover.

319

State terror is conducted from a position of strength and is designed to reinforce government omnipotence. The state resorts to terror because of its lack of consent and legitimacy. Their techniques include show trials, public executions, midnight disappearances and random arrests. Question the above and risk your own personal descent into the abyss.

Stateless terror is conducted from a position of weakness and is designed to convince the population that the government is unable or unwilling to protect them. They generate insecurity in order to validate their promise to restore security when their demands are met. They use dramatic media friendly methods. They substitute visibility to substitute for body count. Massacres like Luxor and Mumbai are made to order mayhem designed to attract journalists, terrorize neutrals, and recruit malcontents.

Unfortunately for the terrorists, they are suffering from over exposure and rising expectations. People are getting used to mass murder and none of the post 9-11 extravaganzas has risen to its level of carnage. As spectacular as Mumbai was, its visuals and death toll pales in comparison. Mumbai lent itself to the sound bites and video clips that are the lifeblood of the 'if it bleeds it leads' media.

The state used its monopoly on coercive power to perfect its terror methods from ethnic cleansing to involuntary relocation and indiscriminate imprisonment. Non-State actors have to resort to more modest means. Their methods come from antiquity and include assassination of public officials and intimidation of private citizens.

The lid blew off when the Fenian's discovered dynamite in the early 1800's. Suddenly terrorists could easily kill and maim large numbers of folks in a visibly public setting. Unlike the Guy Fawkes attempt to blow up the Parliament, it was now easy to do.

The next terrorist leap forward came with consumer air travel. The airliner offered a pre-packaged group of hostages riding in a multi-million dollar conveyance. Unlike a train, planes could be redirected to terror friendly destinations and unlike a passenger ship, planes can't be boarded while in transit. Planes became a readymade media drama guaranteed to garner the attention terrorist crave. Terror is a psychological phenomenon best when shared.

Why use terror in pursuit of political, theological, social or cultural goals given the plethora of successful non-violent movements around the world? The answer is simple—terrorists are weak and, like their state counterparts, lack mass support and military power. If they had support or power, they would march on the capital at the head of a mob or at the head of an army.

Then came 9-11. Everything changed. The stateless terror bar got raised. Post 9-11 terrorists seek to equal or surpass the 'Magnificent 19' in order to woo the growing audience of bloodthirsty spectators. The push for more impressive voyeuristic violence (terrorvangelism) has become an end in itself.

The race is on for stateless terror to get more death for the dollar and more exposure per event. Islamists are in the lead given their sectarian drive to kill. Their utopianism provides behavioral resolve towards mass murder. Their *operational practicality* is growing thru virtual recruiting and cyber incitement and the *technical feasibility* of their goals is improving given dual use commercial technology and public access to critical information.

Emergent capabilities are dependent on group dynamics like motivation, organization, and generation. Motivation addresses behavioral resolve (willingness to strike). Organization addresses operational practicality (ability to strike). Generation addresses technical feasibility (ability of succeed).

More small groups and individuals are becoming capable of disrupting an entire society with the Internet transforming local events into global events. These "super empowered" threats are inspired by successful attacks, are empowered by advanced technology and sophisticated tactics, and are enabled by the commodification of goods and services enhanced by associations with criminal networks.

Guerillas and Terrorists. Guerillas and terrorists are flip sides of the same non-state coin. Guerillas are non-state warriors. Terrorists are guerillas who use terror as their tactic. In the ends – ways – means construct, the *ends* are the guerillas purpose. The ways are the methods used to achieve the ends and the *means* are the resources that enable the ways. For the transnational Islamist insurgency the '**ends**' might be re-establishment of the Caliphate (Sunni) or the Imamate (Shia). The 'ways' for might be non-state terrorism (Sunni) or state terrorism (Shia). The 'means' might include IED's (Sunni) or nukes (Shia).

Guerillas are members of irregular paramilitary groups that typically operate in small bands. They harass state armies using irregular warfare while avoiding direct combat. Irregular warfare is used to offset quantitative and qualitative shortfalls. Guerillas use small, non-uniform wearing, units that rely on mobility to conduct hit and run raids and ambushes. Terrorists are individuals, usually part of a paramilitary group, who use or advocate the use of terrorism. So, what guerilla / terrorists are able and willing to 'go the extra mile'? Who will seek and use WMD? The answer lies in group motivation, organization and generation.

Motivation. What drives these groups? Are their goals flexible? Motivation defines the willingness of a group to negotiate on the one hand or the willingness to massacre on the other.

- Pragmatic: goals are not absolute and partial redress of grievance is possible
- Secular: goals are material, political, ethnic or nationalist and are negotiable
- Utopian: goals are idealistic and uncompromising
  Sectarian: goals are spiritual and uncompromising
- Apocalyptic: goals are millennial and require massive upheaval

The traits travel in pairs. The IRA was sectarian pragmatic in that they desired an independent state but would probably settle for autonomy. The Earth Liberation Front (ELF) and the Animal Liberation Front (ALF) are secular utopian in that they seek a vegetarian envirocentric world. Al Qaeda is sectarian utopian in that they seek the recreation of the theological Muslim Caliphate. Apocalyptic groups stand alone and include folks like Aum Shinrikyo, the Manson Family, and Iranian Twelvers—groups that seek global conflagration to trigger their goals.

Organization. How does the group arrange command and control between the leaders, planners and operators? The traditional model consists of a vertical hierarchy that oversees purposeful but isolated cells. Newer groups are horizontal and cellular and the most advanced groups are distributed or wiki networks.

- Vertical cellular: a distinct chain of command directs numerous isolated subunits
- Horizontal cellular: a collaborative team of leaders run parallel isolated subunits
- Distributed network: leaders and cells seldom meet and are united by a shared vision
- Wiki network: an inspirational center motivates autonomous actors to strike at random

Generation. How capable is the group in terms of scope, scale and complexity? I define the modern start point as Generation 1 (G1), the model from the Boer War through the WWII partisans to the late Tamil Tigers. Remember terrorists and guerillas are interchangeable.

G1 Terrorist (T): The G1 is the threat we grew up with. T includes the Viet Cong, the IRA, the PLO, and the 60's freelance groups like the Red Brigades and the Red Army Faction. The T is local to regional; totes small arms; and engages in bombings, hostage taking, and irregular warfare. The T is not going away. It will persist where insurgents lack support, money, know-how, and lack the ability to move up the spectrum.

G2 Techno-Terrorist (TT): The TT emerged during Operation Cyclone in opposition to the Soviet invasion of Afghanistan. The Mujahideen TT were equipped with top of the line weapons (Stingers) and sophisticated techniques that allowed them to conduct operations nearly on par with state armies. The TT could shoot down modern rotary and fixed wing aircraft—a task beyond G1. The TT will morph into G3 threats. The proliferation of first world capabilities has a momentum of its own as we will see in the G3 discussion.

G3 iTerrorist (iT): The iT can match the conventional capabilities of most third world state armies. The guerilla version is embodied by the Lebanese Hizballah as demonstrated during the 2nd Lebanon War which saw the threat equipped with night vision devices, advanced communications, missiles, rocket artillery, and anti ship missiles. Such systems are beyond the G1 and G2 threats. The terrorist version is the convergence of civilian technology, commando techniques, and terrorism. Lashkar e-Tayyiba's (LeT) Mumbai attack embodies the terrorist version where attackers used special operations and exploitation of off the shelf technologies to execute a lengthy made for media bloodbath. The iT will continue to grow. It seeks new state sponsors and new ways to exploit commercial technology.

G4 Super-empowered Terrorist (SeT): The SeT is striving to emerge. SeT aspirants are studying, recruiting, and experimenting with weapons of mass destruction (WMD) and weapons of mass effect (WME). The SeT aspires to use nuclear, biological, chemical (NBC) weapons and cyber attacks to deliver death, destruction, and disruption on a scale on par with the destructive power of nation-states. Although they have failed thus far, we have seen proto SeT variants such as Aum Shinrikyo and the preempted 'dirty bomber', Jose Padilla.

The Proto G4. On 20 March 1995, Aum Shinrikyo released sarin gas on five Tokyo subway trains. The attack killed 12, injured 54, and sickened 980. Thousands more complained of adverse effects following the attack. Police raids on Aum's Mount Fuji headquarters revealed a vigorous WMD effort including chemical weapons and biological agents including anthrax and Ebola. They found chemical stockpiles, drug labs, prison cells, and millions in cash and gold. Aum had overseas test sites and a nuclear weapons research program. Exposed Aum operations included a failed cyanide attack and a failed biological (anthrax) attack. The latter used the right delivery system but the wrong agent while the subway attack used the right agent but the wrong delivery system.

On 8 May 2002 Jose Padilla was arrested at O'Hare International Airport after returning from travels in Egypt, Saudi Arabia, Afghanistan, Pakistan, and Iraq. Padilla grew up in New York, moved to Chicago and joined the Maniac Latin Disciples gang. He was jailed for manslaughter after a gang member he kicked in the head died. He converted to Islam in his prison and attended the Masjid Al-Iman mosque in Florida. He was recruited and trained by Al Qaeda to detonate a radiological dispersal device (RDD) or 'dirty bomb' in the U.S. The RDD was not included in Padilla's indictment, he was indicted in relation to operations in Chechnya, Bosnia, Somalia, and Kosovo. Padilla was found guilty and was sentenced to 17 years in the Florence "Supermax" in Colorado. His projected release date is 28 March 2021.

The proto SeG/T above represent a few abortive attempts that foreshadow a devastating potential. The Internet has made access to once closely held, state controlled, knowledge easy. Rogue state sponsors are willing to provide WMD components, raw materials, and expertise to non-state actors who can employ them as deniable surrogates while black market networks like AQ Khan's nuke superstore stand willing to sell to anyone with the money. A GX super-empowered guerilla / terrorist attack is only a matter of time.

GY: Super-empowered Individual Terrorist (SeIT): As problematic as the GX threat may be – the GY threat will be much worse and is right ion the heels of its predecessor. GY represents the destructive powe of GX embodied in a single, self motivated, self tasking, self trained and equipped, individual. As with GX, the proto SeIT has made its first few attempts with Amerithrax and the DC Sniper.

In the wake of 9-11, a G3 attack, came a proto-GY attack that came to be known as Amerithrax. It came in two waves. The first set of anthrax letters, postmarked 18 September 2001, were mailed to ABC, CBS, NBC and the New York Post in NYC with another sent to the National Enquirer at American Media, Inc. (AMI) in Boca Raton, Florida. Two more Trenton postmarked letters were mailed on 9 October to Senators Tom Daschle and Patrick Leahy. These letters were more potent that the first wave, containing a gram refined dry powder described by researchers as "weaponized" or "weapons grade" anthrax. At least 22 people developed anthrax infections – 11 of whom contracted the dangerous inhalational variety. Five died. The anthrax attacks paralyzed the nation, making it afraid of the mail and generated a cost in the millions to decontaminate. After years of investigation, Bruce Edwards Ivins, a microbiologist, vaccinologist, and senior biodefense researcher at the United States Army Medical Research Institute of Infectious Diseases (USAMRIID) in Fort Detrick, Maryland became the prime suspect. He committed suicide before charges could be filed. On the morning of 27 July 2008, Ivins was found unconscious at his home. He died two days later from an overdose of Tylenol, an apparent suicide. On 6 August 2008 the Department of Justice (DOJ) and FBI announced that that Ivins was solely responsible for the mailing of the letters containing Bacillus anthracis and the five deaths they caused.

The Beltway sniper attacks took place during three weeks in October 2002 in Washington, D.C., Maryland, and Virginia. Ten people were killed and three were critically injured throughout the Washington Metropolitan Area and along Interstate 95 in Virginia. It was later learned that the rampage was perpetrated by one man, John Allen Muhammad, and one minor, Lee Boyd Malvo, driving a blue 1990 Chevrolet Caprice sedan. In September 2003, Muhammad was sentenced to death. One month later, Malvo was sentenced to six consecutive life sentences without the possibility of parole. On 10 November 2009, Muhammad was executed by lethal injection. In each shooting, the victims were killed by a single bullet fired from some distance. Fear quickly spread throughout the community as news of the shootings spread. At this point Malvo and Muhammad started covering a wider area and taking more time between shootings. On October 4, 43-year-old Caroline Seawell was wounded at 2:30 p.m. in the parking lot of a Michaels Craft Store at Spotsylvania Mall in Spotsylvania County, Virginia, just outside the city of Fredericksburg. On October 7, at 8:09 a.m., Iran Brown, a 13-year-old boy, was shot—At this crime scene the authorities discovered a shell casing as well as a Tarot card (the Death card) inscribed with the phrase, "Call me God" on the front and, on three separate lines on the back, "For you mr. Police." "Code: 'Call me God.'" and "Do not release to the press." Two days later, on October 9 at 8:18 p.m., 53-year-old Dean Harold Meyers was shot dead while pumping gasoline at a Sunoco gas station on Sudley Road in Prince William County, Virginia, near the city of Manassas. The incident came to a close on October 24, when Muhammad and Malvo were found sleeping in their car, a blue 1990 Chevrolet Caprice, at a rest stop off of Interstate 70 near Myersville, Maryland, and arrested on federal weapons charges. Police were tipped off by Ron Lantz, who noticed the parked car. Lantz used his truck to block the exit from the rest stop while he alerted police. A Bushmaster .223-caliber weapon and bipod were found in a bag in Muhammad's car. Ballistics tests later conclusively linked the seized rifle to 11 of the 14 shootings, including one in which no one was injured. The attacks were carried out with the firearm found in the vehicle, a stolen Bushmaster XM-15 semiautomatic .223 caliber rifle equipped with a red-dot sight at ranges of between 50 and over 100 yards. The sniper shots were taken from the trunk of the car through a small hole created for that purpose. Investigators and the prosecution suggested during pre-trial motions that Muhammad intended to kill his ex-wife Mildred, who had estranged him from his children. While imprisoned, Malvo wrote a number of erratic diatribes about what he termed "jihad" against the United States. "I have been accused on my mission. Allah knows I'm gonna suffer now," he wrote. Because his rants and drawings featured not only such figures as Osama Bin Laden and Saddam Hussein, but also characters from the film series The Matrix, these musings were dismissed as immaterial. At the 2006 trial of Muhammad, Malvo testified that the aim of the killing spree was to kidnap children for the purpose of extorting money from the government and to "set up a camp to train children how to terrorize cities," with the ultimate goal being to "shut things down" across the United States.

Small groups or individuals that are capable of causing disruption to an entire society with a global effect
These emerging "super empowered" threats are:
- **inspired** by examples of successful small group attacks,
- **empowered** by advanced technologies and sophisticated tactics, and
- **enabled** by the commodification of goods and services and opportunistic associations with transnational crime

Scenarios:
- Chem
- Bio
- Nuke: RDD, Weapon, SADM, loose nukes, Improvised Nuclear
- Device (IND)
- Cyber
- Kinetic

Civil Defense against the GX and GY Threats
Mission Sets: C-WMD, C-SeT, CT, CP, Border Control, Immigration
Monitoring, transportation security, commerce security
Deter: Counter Proliferation—IC, DoS, DoD, DHS, DHHS

Detect: Homeland and international intelligence fusion to include
immigration oversight and border control—IC, DoD, DoS, DoE

Interdict: International National Mission Force—IC, DoD, CIA, Intl
LEA
React: Homeland National Mission Force—IC, Domestic LEA, local
(city, county, state)

QRF

Mitigate: DART, NEST, Decon, Disinfect, Quarantine.

Border Wars.
The Lebanese militia may be using Chavez's ties with its ally Iran
to expand its network, terrorism officials say.[290]
Agents of Iran's Revolutionary Guard and Hezbollah have alleged-
ly set up a special force to attempt to kidnap Jewish businesspeople in
Latin America and spirit them away to Lebanon.
In March 2007, the intensified ties between Venezuela and Iran led
to the start of weekly IranAir flights from Tehran to Caracas, the
Venezuelan capital, that stop in Damascus.
Hezbollah has long operated in the Lebanese communities of Latin
America.[291]
Hezbollah has had a presence in Latin America since the late
1980's, particularly in the Tri-Border Region, where Brazil, Paraguay
and Argentina meet. But since Hugo Chavez's ascension to power in

[290] The Lebanese militia may be using Chavez's ties with its ally Iran to expand its network, terrorism officials say.
http://articles.latimes.com/2008/aug/27/world/fg-venezterror27

[291]*Chavez Provides Fertile Soil for Hezbollah, Hamas, al-Qaeda,* Posted by Nicole Ferrand
July 13, 2010, *Foreign Policy* at 2:47 am in Foreign Policy, Iran, Islamic extremism,
Terrorism.
http://bigpeace.com/nferrand/2010/07/13/chavez-provides-fertile-soil-for-hezbollah-
hamas-al-qaeda/

Venezuela in 1999, Hezbollah and Hamas' activities have increased in the region. Hezbollah, Hamas and al-Qaeda are using Venezuela as their bridge to other Latin American countries.

Training camps are located in the states of Monagas, Miranda, el Páramo, Falcon, Yaracuy, Yumare, and Trujillo and the districts of Maturin, Los Teques, El Jari, Churuguara and Sierra de San Luis. These groups and individuals are supervised by the Hezbollah Organization in Venezuela, along with al-Qaeda Iraqis currently living in the country and by the Palestinian Democratic Front, headed by Salid Ahmed Rahman, whose office is located in Caracas's Central Park.[292]

> *"Today, Chavez is at least as dangerous as Bin Laden..."*
> —Otto Reich, former U.S. Ambassador to Venezuela

Chavez is using his petrodollars just like Ahmadinejad is; to arm and equip his military in preparation to destabilize the region—his first target being the U.S.'s closest ally; Columbia.

Purchases run the gamut from small arms to MANPADs to tanks to Su-35 Fighter Jets to diesel submarines and Russia has not put any restrictions on the re-sale of any of these systems—say, to Iran, for example.

Venezuela is also fulfilling its role as a toadie and troublemaker by building terrorist training camps. One such camp resides outside Caracas and is manned by Cubans and hoists such notables as VZH and FARC among others. Hugo is a big believer in asymmetric warfare.

Iran has decided that since the U. S. is in their backyard they should be in the U.S.'s backyard and Venezuela is the entry point with Cuba, Bolivia, and Brazil following close behind. Iran and Venezuela now have a direct air-link that bypasses any adult oversight.

Venezuela also serves as a conduit to the international banking system for Iran and Syria thus helping them move funds globally through channels that are otherwise closed to them.

They are aiding the Iran nuke program and overall nuclear prolif-

---

[292]*Venezuela: The Unrecognized Threat* by Danny A. Dickerson, Counter Terrorism Journal of Counterterrorism and Homeland Security International, Vol. 15, No 4, Winter 2009.

eration—in 2008 a Colombian raid on a FARC camp found 66lbs of uranium.

Founded a biotech lab in San Antonio Los Altos with partners from IRN and Cuba.

Copying Iran partners 'swift boat swarming tactic'.

VH base in La Guarijira desert with a half dozen or more training camps dotted thought the state—the western version of pre 9-11 AFG. Traffic is two way as Arab-Venezuela are being sent to LH camps in Lebanon to train for g-war in the western hemisphere.

Co-opted criminal gangs like MS-13 and M-18 while aiding Mexican Drug Lords, introducing Muslim Jihadi's into the mix.

Helping FARC destabilize Colombia, and transition to drug smuggling army—submersibles (70) or more. Multi-ton cocaine smuggling capability with 3000 mile range. Fully capable of supporting terror and WMD smuggling.

"The next attack in America could well have fingerprints that point to Latin America."

Triborder Insanity.   The Triborder Zone including Paraguay, Brazil, Argentina is a safe haven for terror funding and is home to support networks for Islamic groups.

The capture of a key member of the Islamic militant group Hezbollah in Paraguay last month and intensified leftist activity in the Triborder zone of Paraguay, Brazil and Argentina highlight the region long known as a terrorist hub.

Paraguayan authorities arrested Moussa Ali Hamdan in Cuidad del Este on June 15. Hamdan is accused of trafficking stolen goods in order to finance Hezbollah money and document counterfeiting.

Hamdan was hiding in the Paraguayan sector of the porous Triborder area among tens of thousands of Lebanese, Syrian and other Middle Easterners who live and conduct cross-border commerce.

U.S. officials have expressed concern about a growing Middle Eastern presence throughout Latin America, where members of Hezbollah and other groups have been detected in several countries, including Venezuela and Mexico.

The former commander of Southern Command, Adm. Stavridis, testified before Congress stating, "Islamic terrorist networks are present in the Triborder area, as well as other countries in the region," and "A robust Hezbollah financial support network exists in the region, as well as active sympathizers and supporters of Hezbollah. Also present are Sunni groups like Hamas. Known al Qaeda members have journeyed to Latin America and the Caribbean, and other terrorist-inspired Islamic radicals have been arrested in the region."

In 2006 Hezbollah was accused of carrying out the 1994 bombing of a Jewish community center in Buenos Aires that killed 85 people. U.S. intelligence officials have uncovered links between Mexican drug cartels and Hamas and other Islamic groups in the Triborder zone.

Authorities in several Latin American countries have reported expanded activity by local leftist groups linked with Colombia's main insurgent group, the Revolutionary Armed Forces of Colombia (FARC).

While FARC has been weakened inside Colombia, other leftist groups adopting FARC's tactics, operational methods and strategy are proliferating everywhere else.

Peru's Shining Path guerrillas have made a comeback in the central Andean region where they have taken control of coca leaf plantations in remote valleys.

The Paraguayan government was forced to declare a siege in half the country to counter a terrorist campaign waged by the Paraguayan Peoples' Army (EPP). The EPP is a small but dangerous and has links to FARC.

Messages between Paraguayan and Colombian guerrillas were uncovered when top FARC commander was killed in a 2008 Colombian government raid on a FARC camp in Ecuador.

Coded e-mails were also intercepted between EPP and FARC. The EPP was getting advice from FARC on managing kidnappings. A key FARC leader was snatched from his Venezuelan hide-out in 2005 and was sent back to Columbia to face charges.

The EPP has collected an estimated $6 million through kidnappings conducted over recent years targeting prominent members of Paraguay's business community. They are also drawing revenues from local marijuana production and cocaine smuggling from Bolivia.

"If the EPP starts coordinating with international terrorist networks, as well as organized crime and powerful Brazilian narco-trafficking syndicates like the Capital Command of Sao Paolo, the situation could get out of control. Three EPP fugitives sought by Paraguay for the kidnapping of a senator's wife have recently taken asylum in Brazil.

Modern Terrorism Milestones: **Terrorists are innovators. Each** successive generation seeks new methods of mass murder that not only escalate the body count but that capture the attention of the 'if it bleeds it leads' media.

- Dynamite patented in 1867: the Fenians launch the London Dynamite Outrage in 1884
- First car bomb: 1905, assassination attempt against Ottoman Sultan Hamid II
- First successful Transportation Hijacking of a U.S. airliner: 1961, Antuilo Ramierez Ortiz
- First Extortion Hijacking was the seizure of an Israeli El Al aircraft in 1968
- First global media terror event: 1972, Black September takes the Israeli Olympic team
- First suicide bombing: 1980, a 13-year old detonated himself by an Iraqi tank in Iran
- First large scale terror attack with chemical weapon: 1995, sarin attack on Tokyo subway
- First airliner suicide mission: 1999, Egypt Air pilot intentionally crashes flight off Mass
- First use of hijacked airliners as weapons: 2001, 9-11 Al Qaeda attack
- First terror/guerilla suicide attack: 2008 Mumbai attack

* * * Insurgency also made a post Cold War transition. * * *

During the Cold War the super powers could not engage in direct conflict given the threat of nuclear holocaust. Potential annihilation eliminated direct competition. In its place came proxy war. The Soviets used the COMINTERN and the KGB to fuel communist insurgencies the world over. The US was forced to back some pretty unsavory characters in the name of containment.

America's new Post Cold War enemies can't directly confront America any more than the Soviets could only this time it's not due to the threat of mutual annihilation. Today, the fear is self annihilation. This was a real dilemma until the Iraq War.

A sectarian animosity towards the U.S. came with the ascension of the Ayatollah Khomeini. The Islamic State cut its teeth on the hostage crises and immediately invested in terrorism. They became victims of their own success when they drove Jimmy Carter out of office. They shied away from direct confrontation when Ronald Reagan took office. Reagan was tough on America's enemies as evidenced by the bombing of Libya, walking out of talks in Iceland and Operation Urgent Fury. His successor, George H.W. Bush, kept up the pressure after the fall of the USSR with Just Cause and Desert Storm. The latter operation would have been impossible during the Cold War. Many predicted another Vietnam. What they got was the defeat of the world's fourth largest army in 100 hours. The post Cold War United States was a hyper-power that could not be challenged directly.

It took Iran a decade to find a way to fight the U.S.—the Great Satan. The opportunity came in 2006 and 2007 when U.S. public opinion turned against the Iraq war. Just as during the Tet Offensive, the press and the Democrats turned on the Republican president's foreign policy and public will faded. The Iranians began to use Hizballah and the IRGC to support the Sunni insurgency in Iraq. They trained insurgents and provided them with advanced IEDs. Iranians could now kill America soldiers on their borders knowing that the liberals in America would prevent the president from effectively responding.

With the election of a pacifist president, the threat saw an opportunity. Today Iran supports Islamists the world over whether they are Sunni or Shia. They backed Hamas (Sunni's), Al Qaeda (also Sunni's) and the Afghan Taliban—a regime they despised. Iran so hated the Taliban that they even helped us fight them during Operation Enduring Freedom in 2002. Now they're allies. Today, Iran is backing the Huthi insurgency in Yemen, promoting instability along Saudi Arabia's border—a critical US ally. The Lebanese Hizballah and IRGC Qods Force have replaced the COMINTERN and KGB as proxies and

Iran has replaced the USSR as the sponsor. Both sought and now seek the reduction of American influence.

Islamic domination of the world is foreordained by Allah in Quranic Sura 24:52 ("It is they that obey Allah and His Messenger, and fear Allah and do right [spreading Islam], that will triumph.")

The humbling of the superpowers, beginning with the 1979 occupation of the American embassy in Tehran (an unanswered act of war), coupled with the 1989 withdrawal of Soviet forces from Afghanistan in defeat, convinced the Islamic jihadis in both the Shia and Sunni sects that the time was right to renew with a vigor the 1,400-year old jihad against the non-Muslim world. The Shia Khomeinist Hezb'allah and the Sunni Salafist al-Qaeda are two of the most prominent jihadi organizations that were launched as a consequence of these superpower humiliations. They began their jihadi terror against the Western world in the 1980s, and it continues to this day.

The lesson learned from history must be to do what we know to be doable and to avoid what we have learned is not. Thus, in place of nation-building in the Muslim world, the U.S. must switch to an aggressive counterterror (CT) strategy that makes maximum use of CIA/military special operations forces, increased air strikes, and even more hunter-killer drones to eradicate the jihadi leadership. These CT operations should be combined with unconventional warfare (UW) to promote civil wars that exploit the tribal, ethnic, and Sunni-Shia cleavages in Afghanistan. The British successfully blunted Islam in the Asian subcontinent through "divide and conquer." The same grievances the British exploited are still there and on display daily.

The change in mission from COIN to CT/UW would significantly reduce the number of U.S. casualties by taking U.S. forces out of the high-risk task of population protection (with its rules of engagement that seem to sacrifice U.S. soldiers on the altar of "hearts-and-minds" that reach out in peace one day only to strap a bomb on the next) to one of our choosing when and where to fight without the need to hold static positions. The objective would change from "winning" (whatever that would mean in Afghanistan) or "building a stable Afghan nation" (an even more uncertain objective) to continually keeping al-Qaeda and the Pashtun Taliban off-balance by assisting the Tajiks, Uzbeks,

Hazaras, Turkmenis, and Baluchis to make war on al-Qaeda and the Pashtun Taliban. Such a war is something they will have to do even without us. None of these ethnic groups want to again be dominated by al-Qaeda and the Pashtun Taliban.

While this strategy objective lacks the clarity of a date certain for departure and a defined end state, it can be maintained as long as conditions warrant, which is what is required to fight our Islamic jihadi enemy, who is in it for the long haul. It would also add what is currently lacking in our strategy (which dooms it to fail): evidence to our "allies" in Afghanistan that we are not cutting and running on them. Therefore, we will demonstrate that we all share a common commitment to a long-term objective—prohibiting the return of al-Qaeda and Pashtun Taliban domination of Afghanistan. A "stable" Afghan government under Hamid Karzai is a losing proposition that should be carefully abandoned as inconspicuously and quickly as possible.

Terrorist Milestones

1. In **1867**, Nobel received U.S. patent number 78,317 for dynamite. The Fenians launch the London dynamite outrages in **1884**.
2. The first car bomb is used for the attempted assassination of Ottoman Sultan Abdul Hamid II in **1905** in Istanbul by Armenian separatists
3. The first successful Transportation Hijacking of a U.S. airliner: May 1, **1961**: Puerto Rican born Antuilo Ramierez Ortiz forced at gunpoint a National Airlines plane to fly to Havana, Cuba, where he was given asylum.
4. The first Extortion Hijacking by guerrillas or terrorists seeking to draw international attention was the seizure of an Israeli El Al aircraft in July **1968**. Hijackers from the Palestinian Front for the Liberation of Palestine (PFLP) seeking to draw attention to their cause diverted a flight originating in Rome to land in Algeria.
5. The first global media terror event occurred when Black September takes the Israeli Olympic team hostage and massacres them 5-6 Sep **1972**.
6. The first modern suicide bombing occurred in Iran in **1980** when 13-year old Hossein Fahmideh detonated himself as he ran up to an Iraqi tank at a key point in a battle of the Iran-Iraq War.
7. On the morning of 20 March **1995**, Aum members released sarin in a co-ordinated attack on five trains in the Tokyo subway system, killing 12, injuring 54 and affecting 980.
8. Al Qaeda uses hijacked airliners as weapons on 11 September **2001**.
9. LeT launches Mumbai attack consisting of ten coordinated shooting and bombing attacks on 26-29 November **2008**, killing 173 people and wounding at 308.

Terrorisms Ten Benchmarks

Terrorism has evolved over the years and that evolution has escalated along with technology—almost in accordance with Moore's Law. I've attempted to capture the top developments that revolutionized 20th Century terrorism and have projected the coming wave of 21st Century innovation. My interpretation is arguable but it is my assessment of what mattered.

1. Dynamite Patent (1867): remote and massive destruction becomes possible
2. First Successful Transportation Hijacking (1961): cross border vulnerability
3. First Successful Extortion Hijacking (1968): global visibility
4. First Global Terror Event (1972): the Munich Olympics garners world attention
5. First Mass use of the Car Bomb (1979): mobile bomb emplacement replaces the assassin
6. First Suicide Bombing (1980): Iranian revolutionaries introduce human precision guided munitions
7. New York Cell (1993): First twin towers attack is done by U.S. based Islamic Terror Cell
8. First Weapon of Mass Effect (1995): chem attack in Tokyo
9. Theatrical Mass Murder (2001): Al Qaeda conducts media fueled mass murder
10. Berg Video (2004): first genuine global terrorvangelism
11. Terror Raid: Mumbai commando style terror raid
12. USA Terror Raid: Mumbai Amcrica

The Impact of Post Cold War Liberalism in the West

Multiculturalism: reduces assimilation and encourages Balkinization
Declining Birth Rate: reduced manpower, reduced tax revenue for entitlements, increased reliance on immigrants to reinvigorate the workforce
Suicidal Self Criticism: narcissistic tendency to blame the world travails on the west

Pacifism: declining will to defend western culture

Disunity: the lack of a common existential threat fragments western unity against post Cold War emergent threats

Legal Dissonance: inability to define terrorism as criminal or an act of war

Bibliography

REFERENCES

The Harper Encyclopedia of Military History Fourth Edition by R. Ernest Dupuy and Trevor N. Dupuy; Harper Collins, 1993

The Harper Encyclopedia of Military Biography by Trevor N. Dupuy; Harper Collins, 1992

Taliban: Militant Islam, Oil and Fundamentalism in Central Asia by Ahmed Rashid; Yale University Press, February 2001

Inside Al Qaeda: Global Network of Terror by Rohan Gunaratna; Penguin Group (USA), June 2003

Al Qaeda in its Own Words by Gilles Kepel (Editor), Jean-Pierre Milelli (Editor), Pascale Ghazaleh (Translator); Harvard University Press, April 2008

Hamas: Politics, Charity, and Terrorism in the Service of Jihad by M. Levitt; Yale University Press, May 2006

Terror and Consent: The Wars for the Twenty-First Century by P. Bobbitt; Random House Inc, April 2008

Hezbollah: A Short History by A. R. Norton; Princeton University Press, March 2007

The True Believer by E. Hoffer; HarperCollins Publishers, September 2002

The Anatomy of a Revolution by C. Brinton; Knopf Doubleday Publishing Group, January 1965

Law and the Long War: The Future of Justice in the Age of Terror by B. Wittes; Penguin Group (USA) Incorporated, Pub. Date: June 2008

Not a Suicide Pact: The Constitution in a Time of National Emergency by Richard A. Posner, Oxford University Press, USA: September 2006

Perfect Soldiers: The 9/11 Hijackers: Who They Were, Why They Did It by T. McDermott; HarperCollins Publishers, August 2006

Complexity: The Emerging Science at the Edge of Order and Chaos by M. Mitchell Waldrop; Simon & Schuster Adult Publishing Group, September 1993

Apocalyptic Politics: On the Rationality of Iranian Policy by Mehdi Khalaji, Policy Focus #79, Washington Institute for Near East Policy, Published in 2008 in the United States of America by the Washington Institute for Near East Policy

The Looming Tower: Al-Qaeda and the Road to 9/11 by Lawrence Wright; Random House Inc, August 2007

Beyond Baghdad: Postmodern War and Peace by Ralph Peters; Stackpole Books, October 2003

Wars of Blood and Faith: The Conflicts That Will Shape The Twenty-first Century by Ralph Peters; Stackpole Books, February 2009

Empires of Trust: How Rome Built—and America is Building—A New World by Thomas Madden, Penguin Group (USA), July 2008

The Cell: Inside the 9/11 Plot, and Why the FBI and CIA Failed to Stop It by John Miller, Chris Mitchell, and Michael Stone; Hyperion, May 2003

Cobra II: The Inside Story of the Invasion and Occupation of Iraq by Michael Gordon, Bernard Trainor; Random House Inc, February 2007

On War by Karl von Clausewitz, Howard Michael and Peter Paret editors and translators; Princeton University Press, 1984

Brave New War: The Next Stage of Terrorism and the End of Globalization by John Robb; Wiley, John & Sons, Incorporated, April 2008

Out of Control: The New Biology of Machines, Social Systems and the Economic World by Kevin Kelly, Basic Books, March 1995

Jihad in the West: Muslim Conquests from the 7th to the 21st Centuries by Paul Fregosi; Prometheus Books, October 1998

The Truth About Muhammad: Founder of the World's Most Intolerant Religion by Robert Spencer; Regnery Publishing Inc, August 2007

Terror in the Name of God: Why Religious Militants Kill by Jessica Stern; HarperCollins Publishers, August 2004

Ultimate Terrorists by Jessica Stern; Harvard University Press, October 2000

Islamic Imperialism: A History by Efraim Karsh; Yale University Press, May 2007

Knowing the Enemy: Jihadist Ideology and the War on Terror by Mary Habeck; Yale University Press, January 2006

The Terrorist Perspectives Project: Strategic and Operational views of Al Qaida and Associated Movements by Stoudt, Schindler, Lacey, and Huckabey; Naval Institute Press, 2008

The Canons of Jihad by Jim Lacey; Naval Institute Press, 2008

A Terrorist Call to Global Jihad by Jim Lacey; Naval Institute Press, 2008

Bracing for Armageddon: The Science and Politics of Bioterrorism in America by William Clark; Oxford University Press, May 2008

The Al Qaeda Reader by Raymond Ibrahim; Bantam Books, August 2007

7 Deadly Scenarios: A Military Futurist Explores the Changing Face of War in the 21st Century by Andrew Krepinevich; Bantam Books, January 2009

The Clash of Civilizations and the Remaking of World Order by Samuel Huntington; Simon & Schuster Adult Publishing Group, January 1998

Islam Unveiled: Disturbing Questions About the World's Fastest-Growing Faith by Robert Spencer; Human Events Publishing, Inc. Nov 18, 2002

The Myth of Islamic Tolerance: How Islamic Law Treats Non-Muslims by Robert Spencer; Prometheus Books, February 2005

In the Path of Hizbullah by A. Nizar Hamzeh; Syracuse University Press, November 2004

When Religion Becomes Evil by Charles Kimball; HarperCollins Publishers, September 2002

The Shahids: Islam and Suicide Attacks by Shaul Shay; Transaction Publishers, July 2004

Voices of Terror: Manifestos, Writings and Manuals of Al Qaeda, Hamas, and other Terrorists from around the World and Throughout the Ages by Walter Laquer; Reed Press, 2004

A History of the Twentieth Century Volume Three: 1952—1999 by Martin Gilbert, Perennial an Imprint of Harper Collins Publishers, 2000

Who becomes a Terrorist and Why: The 1999 Government Report on Profiling Terrorists by Rex A. Hudson and the Staff of the Federal Research Division of the Library of Congress; The Lyons Press, 1999

Jihad Incorporated: A Guide to Militant Islam in the U.S. by Steven Emerson; Prometheus Books, October 2006

Blood and Rage: A Cultural History of Terrorism by Michael Burleigh; HarperCollins Publishers, March 2009

History in Quotations by M.J. Cohen and John Major; Cassell, 2004

The Jews Against Rome: War in Palestine AD 66-73 by Susan Sorek, Continuum September 2008

Bartlett's Familiar Quotations 17th Edition by John Bertlett; Little, Brown and Company, 2002

Asymmetric Warfare by Rod Thorton; Polity Press, 2008

What Went Wrong? by Bernard Lewis; Perennial, 2003

The Middle East: A Brief History of the Last 2,000 Years by Bernard Lewis, Scribner, August 1997

No True Glory: A Frontline Account of the battle for Fallujah by Bing West, Bantam Books, 2005

The Crises of Islam; Holy War and Unholy Terror by Bernard Lewis; Random House, 2003

Jihadis and the Internet Translation by Amstelveens Vertaalburo B.V., Amstelveen; The National Coordinator for Counterterrorism (NCTb) of the Netherlands; 2007

A High Price: The Triumphs and Failures of Israeli Counterterrorism by Daniel Byman, Oxford University Press, June 2011

The End of History and the Last Man by Francis Fukuyama, Free Press, February 2006

Russia Under the Bolshevik Regime by Richard Pipes, Knopf Doubleday Publishing Group, April 1995

Red Holocaust / Edition 1 by Steven Rosefielde, December 2009, Routledge

Humanity: A Moral History of the Twentieth Century by Jonathan Glover, Yale University Press, August 2001

Insurgent Leader Al-Zarqawi Killed in Iraq by Ellen Knickmeyer and Jonathan Finer Washington Post Foreign Service, June 8, 2006

The Grand Strategy of the Byzantine Empire by Edward Luttwak, Harvard University Press, November 2011

Fears of a Hezbollah presence in Venezuela: the World The Lebanese militia may be using Chavez's ties with its ally Iran to expand its network, terrorism officials say by Chris Kraul and Sebastian Rotella, LA Times, August 27, 2008

Strategy in the Missile Age by Bernard Brodie, Princeton University Press, February 1965

Violent Islamist Extremism, The Internet, and the Homegrown Terrorist Threat, United States Senate Committee on Homeland Security and Governmental Affairs, Majority & Minority Staff Report; Joseph Lieberman, Chairman, Susan Collins, Ranking Minority Member, May 8, 2008

Y The Sources of Islamic Revolutionary Conduct by Major Stephen P. Lambert, U.S. Air Force Research Fellow with the cooperation and support of the Institute for National Security Studies (INSS) USAF Academy, Colorado Springs, Washington DC, April 2005

The Soldier and the State: The Theory and Politics of Civil-Military Relations by Samuel P. Huntington, Harvard University Press, August 2008

Who Are We: The Challenges to America's National Identity by Samuel P. Huntington, Simon & Schuster, November 2005

The Last days of Europe; an Epitaph for an Old Continent by Walter Laqueur, Thomas Dunn Books / St. Martin's, 2007

The Thirty Years War by CV Wedgwood, Anchor Books, Doubleday & Company Inc, 1968

The Lessons of Terror; A History of Warfare Against Civilians Why it has Always Failed and Will Fail Again by Caleb Carr, Random House, 2002

Duel: Alexander Hamilton, Aaron Burr, and the Future of America by Thomas Fleming, Basic Books, September 2000

Lebanon, Joint Center for Operational Analysis Journal, Volume X, Issue 1, December 2007

The Evolving Nature of Warfare, Joint Center for Operational Analysis Journal, Volume X, Issue 3, Fall 2008

Consequence Management, Joint Center for Operational Analysis Journal, Volume XI, Issue 1, Winter 2008-2009

Operation Enduring Freedom, Joint Center for Operational Analysis Journal, Volume XI, Issue 3, Fall 2009

Comprehensive Approach Iraq: An Iraq Case Study, Joint Center for Operational Analysis Journal, Volume XII, Issue 3, Winter 2010-2011

This Kind of War: The Classic Korean War History by T.R. Fehrenbach, Potomac Books, Inc., January 1995

The Reuters Photo Scandal, A Taxonomy of Fraud, http://www.zombietime.com/reuters_photo_fraud/

Reuters Admits Cropping Photos of Ship Clash, http://www.foxnews.com/world/2010/06/08/reuters-fake-photos-ihh-gaza-blockade-commandos/, Jun 8, 2010

Hard Fighting, Israel in Lebanon and Gaza, David E. Johnson, For the United States Army and the United States Air Force, RAND Corporation: ARROYO CENTER and PROJECT AIR FORCE, 2011

The Israeli-Hezbollah War of 2006: The Media As A Weapon in Asymmetrical Conflict, by Marvin Kalb Senior Fellow, Shorenstein Center, and Carol Saivetz, Harvard University, Joan Shorenstein Center on the Press, Politics and Public Policy Research Harvard University, February 2007

Hezbollah as a case study of the battle for hearts and minds, by Dr Reuven Erlich and Dr Yoram Kahati, Intelligence and Terrorism Information Center at the Israel Intelligence Heritage & Commemoration Center (IICC), June 2007

Seeds of Terror: How Heroin Is Bankrolling the Taliban and Al Qaeda by Gretchen Peters, St. Martin's Press, May 2009

Terrorist and Organized Crime Groups in the Tri-border area (TBA) of South America, by Rex Hudson, a report prepared by the Federal Research Division, Library of Congress under an Interagency Agreement with the United States Government, July 2003

Charlie Wilson's War: The Extraordinary Story of the Largest Covert Operation in History by George Crile, Grove/Atlantic, Inc., March 2003

Technology of Improvised Explosive Devices by Dr. Carlo Kopp, Land Warfare Conference, Defense Today, January 2008

Resisting Rebellion: The History and Politics of Counterinsurgency by Anthony James Joes, University Press of Kentucky, September 2004

Urban Guerrilla Warfare by Anthony James Joes, University Press of Kentucky, April 2007

War for the Union, The Organized War to Victory by Allan Nevins, Konecky and Konecky, 1971

Think Again: Failed States, by James Traub, Foreign Policy, June 2011

Conflict after the Cold War: Arguments on the Causes of War and Peace by Richard Betts, Longman Publishers, Columbia University, 2001

Living Weapons: Biological Warfare and International Security, by Gregory D. Koblentz, Cornell University Press, August 2011

Jefferson's War: America's First War on Terror 1801 to 1805, by Joseph Wheelan, Public Affairs, August 2004

39 Terrorist Plots Against the U.S. Foiled Since 9/11, research by Jena Baker McNeill, James Jay Carafano, and Jessica Zuckerman, Heritage Foundation, May 2011

Twelve Monkeys written by Chris Marker and David Webb Peoples and directed by Terry Gilliam, Mystery, Sci-Fi, Thriller, January 1996

Columbine by Dave Cullen, Grand Central Publishing, April 2009

Another look at Egypt Air crash by Joseph Farah, WND Commentary, http://www.wnd.com/2001/12/11863/, December 2001

On War by Carl von Clausewitz; Michael Eliot Howard (Translator), Peter Paret (Translator), Princeton University Press, June 1989

Masters of War: Classical Strategic Thought by Michael I. Handel, Taylor & Francis, Inc., September 2000

The Coming Anarchy; Shattering the Dreams of the Post-Cold War World by Robert Kaplan, Random House, August 2000

The Logic of Failure; Recognizing and Avoiding Error in Complex Situations by Dietrich Dorner, Perseus Books, August 1997

In Pursuit of Military Excellence; the Evolution of Operational Theory by Shimon Naveh, Frank Cass Publishers, 1997

The Dynamics of Military Revolution 1300-2050 by MacGregor Knox and Williamson Muray, Cambridge University Press, August 2001

The Last Nazis; SS Werewolf Guerilla Resistance in Europe 1944-1947 by Perry Biddiscombe, Tempus Publishing Limited, 2000

Endless War: Middle-Eastern Islam vs. Western Civilization by Ralph Peters, Stackpole Books, March 2010

Diplomacy by Henry Kissinger, Simon & Schuster, April 1995

Holy Madness: Romantics, Patriots, and Revolutionaries, 1776 - 1871 by Adam Zamoyski, Penguin Books, 1999

Shariah Law and American Courts: An Assessment of State Appellate Court Cases, Center For Security Policy; The Center For Security Policy Occasional Paper Series, 20 May 2011

RIP: Free Speech about Islam by Adam Turner, American Thinker, 8 July 2012, http://www.americanthinker.com/articles/../2012/07/rip_free_speech_about_islam.html

Shariaphobia by Richard Butrick, American Thinker, 25June 2012, www.americanthinker.com/articles/../2012/06/shariaphobia.html

Islamic Extremism: Common Concern for Muslim and Western Publics by Pew Research Center; Pew Global Attitudes Project, July 14, 2005

British Muslims Urged to Reject Democracy, Embrace Shari'a-Ruled 'Emirates,' by Patrick Goodenough, CNS News.com, http://cnsnews.com/news/article/british-muslims-urged-reject-democracy-embrace-shari-ruled-emirates, July 15, 2011

Learning About Lawfare, Nathaniel Burney, November 2010, The Burney Law Firm, LLC, http://burneylawfirm.com/blog/tag/lawfare/, 2008

Counter Terrorism: The Journal of Counterterrorism and Homeland Security International, Volume 15, No. 2 Summer 2009, published by SecureWorldnet Ltd; - *Twitter.com and Coordinated Mayhem* by Lance Lamoreaux

- *How Critical Infrastructure is at Risk of Cyber Attack* by David Gerwitz
- *Piracy in the Gulf of Aden* by Stefan H. Leader, Ph.D.

Armchair General (ACG) and ACG online, the Weider History Group
  - iGuerilla: The New Model Techno-Insurgent by John R. Sutherland, May 2008
  - iGuerrilla Version 2.0 - The Terrorist and the Guerrilla Converge at Mumbai by John R. Sutherland, December 2008
  - Global Terror Assessment; Where We Are, Where We're Headed by John Sutherland, May 2010
  - The Way Ahead in Afghanistan, online debate between Ralph Peters and John Sutherland
  - Persian Arrows: America's Winning Iran Strategy by John Sutherland, March 2011
  - Learning from History's Turning Points by John Sutherland, March 2012
As Posted on Armchair General online 12/9/2008

Unleashing the Devils; The Ottoman collapse still creates crises today by Ralph Peters, ARMCHAIR General Magazine, April / May 2010

LAWFARE, The Burney Law Firm, LLC, online, 2008

The Muslim Brotherhood in the United States by Steven Merley, Research Monograph on the Muslim world Series No. 2, Paper No 3, Hudson Institute, April 2009

Radicalization in the West: The Homegrown Threat prepared by Mithcell D. Silber and Arvin Bhatt, Senior Intelligence Analysts NYPD Intelligence Division, NYPD, 2007

Cairo Declaration on Human Rights in Islam, August 5 1990, UN GAOR, World Conf on Human Rights, 4th Session, Agenda Item 5, UN Doc A/CONF.157/PC/62/Add.18 (1993) {English Translation}

Islamic Extremism: A Viable Threat to US National Security, an open forum at the US State Department, Transcript of a presentation by Shakyh Muhammad Hisham Kabbani, January 1999

Muslim Public Opinion on US Policy, Attacks on Civilians and al Qaeda, Principal Investigator Steven Kull, WORLDPUBLICOPINION.ORG, International Policy Attitudes at the University of Maryland, April 2007

DOOM, America in the Dark: an EP attack could plunge the United States into chaos, outing the country at the mercy of its enemies by Cynthia E. Ayers and Sarah J.M. Kolberg, Armchair General, July 2011

Shari'a and Violence in American Mosques by Mordechai Kedar and david Yerushalmi, Middle East Quarterly, Summer 2011

The Next Middle East War by Chuck DeVore, HUMAN EVENTS, Eagle Publishing, 2011

Islam in the Classroom; What Textbooks Tell Us by Gilbert T. Sewall, American Textbook Council, 2008

The New Wars of Religion, The Economist, November 2007

Columbine, by Dave Cullen, Grand Central Publishing, April 2009

Department of Homeland Security Bioterrorism Risk Assessment: A Call for Change by the Committee on Methodological Improvements to the Department of Homeland Security's Biological Agent Risk Analysis, National Research Council, DHS 2006

The Great Influenza: The Epic Story of the Deadliest Plague In History by John M. Barry, Viking Penguin, February 2004

Al Qaeda Manual Drives Detainee Behavior at Guantanamo Bay by Donna Miles, American Forces Press Service, June 29, 2005, http://www.defense.gov/news/newsarticle.aspx?id=16270

Terror and Consent: The Wars for the Twenty-first Century by Philip Bobbitt, Knopf Doubleday Publishing Group, May 2009

Blood and Rage: History of Terrorism, by Michael Burleigh, HarperCollins Publishers, February 2011

Why Terrorism Works: Understanding the Threat, Responding to the Challenge by Alan M. Dershowitz, Yale University Press, August 2002

It's Logical to Be 'Islamophobic' by R.C. Marsh, American Thinker, October 18, 2010, http://www.americanthinker.com/archived-articles/../2010/10/its_logical_to_be_islamophobic.html

Islamic Supremacism Trumps Christianity at Ground Zero by Pamela Geller, American Thinker, July 21, 2011, http://www.americanthinker.com/2011/07/islamic_supremacism_trumps_christianity_at_ground_zero.html#ixzz1zUbw6jVl

Undercover Mosque, a Documentary by Hardcash Productions, British public-service television Channel 4, September 2008, www.hardcashproductions.com/recent29.html

Army Chief Of Staff Worried About Anti-Muslim Backlash by Sam Stein, Huffingtonpost.com, March 18, 2010

Lawmakers Blast Administration For Calling Fort Hood Massacre 'Workplace Violence' by Catherine Herridge, FoxNews.com, December 07, 2011

America Alone: The End of the World as We Know It by Mark Steyn, Regnery Publishing, Inc., An Eagle Publishing Company, April 8, 2008

The 'Istanbul Process': A Success for Muslim Diplomacy by David Pryce-Jones, National Review Online, March 12, 2012

Shariah: The Threat To America, An Exercise In Competitive Analysis Report Of Team B II, Center for Security Policy, October 2010 Edition

Britain to Seek Curbs to 'Libel Tourism' by Eric Pfanner, New York Times, May 9, 2012

Hatred's Kingdom: How Saudi Arabia Supports the New Global Terrorism by Dore Gold, Regnery Publishing, Inc., An Eagle Publishing Company, February 15, 2003

Pakistanis Kill Man Accused of Insulting Quran by Munir Ahmed, Associated Press, Islamabad July 4, 2012

Female activist: Muslim men need sex slaves to keep from committing adultery, Acharya Murdock, From the Kuwait Times, 08 June 2011, http://www.freethoughtnation.com/contributing-writers/63-acharya-s/541-female-activist-muslim-men-need-sex-slaves-to-keep-from-committing-adultery.html

Saudi Arabia execution of 'sorcery' woman condemned, The UK Telegraph, December 13, 2011

Insurgency & Terrorism: Inside Modern Revolutionary Warfare by Bard E. O'Neill, Brassey's (UK) Ltd, November 1990

Swiss Ban Building of Minarets on Mosques by Nick Cumming-Bruce and Steven Erlanger, New York Times, November 29, 2009, http://www.nytimes.com/2009/11/30/world/europe/30swiss.html

Unholy Alliance: Radical Islam and the American Left by David Horowitz, Regnery Publishing, Inc., an Eagle Publishing Company, March 2006

Yale press passes on showing Muhammad cartoons, The Grand Scheme, http://eileenflynn.wordpress.com/2009/09/10/yale-press-passes-on-showing-muhammad-cartoons/, September 10, 2009

South Park's Mohammed Episode Censored By Comedy Central by Jon Bershad, Mediaite, http://www.mediaite.com/online/south-parks-mohammed-episode-censored-by-comedy-central/, April 22nd, 2010

Muslim Brothers; Muslim Brotherhood; al-Ikhwan al-Muslimin; Jama'at al-Ikhwan al-Muslimun; Hizb Al-Ikhwan Al-Muslimoon; al-Ikhwan ("The Brothers") prepared by Prepared by Julie Spears and maintained by Steven Aftergood, Updated January 8, 2002, http://www.fas.org/irp/world/para/mb.htm

Soldiers of God: With Islamic Warriors in Afghanistan and Pakistan by Robert D. Kaplan, Knopf Doubleday Publishing Group, November 2001

My Turn to Speak: Iran, the Revolution and Secret Deals With the U.S. by Abu Al-Hasan Bani Sadr (Author), Abol Hassan Bani-Sadr (Author), Jean-Charles Deniau, Brassey's Inc, April 1991

Persian Puzzle: The Conflict Between Iran and America by Kenneth Pollack, Random House Publishing Group, November 2004

Y, The Sources of Islamic Revolutionary Conduct by Maj Stephen P. Lambert USAF, Joint Military Intelligence College, Center for Strategic Intelligence Research, Institute for National Security Studies (INSS), Washington D.C., April 2005

Iranian Video Says Mahdi is 'Near' by Erick Stakelbeck, CBN News Terrorism Analyst, http://www.cbn.com/cbnnews/world/2011/March/Iranian-Regime-Video-Says-Mahdi-is-Near-/, April 03, 2011

Iran: President Says Light Surrounded Him During UN Speech by Golnaz Esfandiari, Radio Free Europe Radio Liberty, http://www.rferl.org/content/article/1063353.html, November 29, 2005

Ahmadinejad Promoted Shrine Draws Millions by Ali Reza Eshraghi and Raha Tahami, Mianeh, http://mianeh.net/article/ahmadinejad-promoted-shrine-draws-millions, May 4, 2010

Mesbah-Yazdi: The Regime Ayatullah by By Michael Theodoulou, The National [United Arab Emirates], Views from the Occident, http://occident.blogspot.com/2009/09/mesbah-yazdi-regime-ayatullah.html, August 23, 2009

Iran's President and the Politics of the Twelfth Imam by John von Heyking, Ashbrook, Ashland University, http://ashbrook.org/publications/guest-05-vonheyking-twelfthimam/, November 2005

Persian Fire: The First World Empire and the Battle for the West by Tom Holland, Doubleday, May 2006

Immortal: A Military History of Iran and Its Armed Forces by Steven R. Ward, Georgetown University Press, March 2009

A Time to Betray: The Astonishing Double Life of a CIA Agent Inside the Revolutionary Guards of Iran by Reza Kahlili, Threshold Editions, April 2010

Son of Hamas: A Gripping Account of Terror, Betrayal, Political Intrigue, and Unthinkable Choices by Mosab Hassan Yousef, SaltRiver, March 2010

Hezbollah adopts new manifesto, United Press International, Nov. 19, 2009 at 12:05 PM http://www.upi.com/Top_News/Special/2009/11/19/Hezbollah-adopts-new-manifesto/UPI-88531258650312/#ixzz22KB3riFN:

To read the actual Manifesto go to For a Better Lebanon, http://forabetter-lebanon.blogspot.com/2008/02/hizbollahs-manifesto-english-version.html

The Grand Jihad: How Islam and the Left Sabotage America by Andrew C McCarthy, Encounter Books, May 2010

2006 Lebanon War: An Operational Analysis, by Major Sharon Tosi Moore, Joint Center for Operational Analysis Journal, Volume X; Issue 1, December 2007

Winograd Report: English Summary, Joint Center for Operational Analysis Journal, Volume X; Issue 1, December 2007

Terrorist to Techno-Guerilla: The Changing Face of Asymmetric Warfare, by Clyde Royston, Joint Center for Operational Analysis Journal, Volume X; Issue 1, December 2007

Super Terrorism; Biological, Chemical, and Nuclear, by Yonah Alexander and Milton Hoenig, Transnational Publishers, 2001

The Last Great Revolution: Turmoil and Transformation in Iran, by Robin Wright, Vintage, February 2001

Atomic Iran: How the Terrorist Regime Bought the Bomb and American Politicians, by Jerome R. Corsi, Cumberland House Publishing, April 2005

God's Terrorists; the Wahhabi Cult and the Hidden Roots of Modern Jihad, by Charles Allen, Da Capo Press, August 2006

The Russian Revolution by Richard Pipes, Vintage, November 1991

Al-Qaeda's Growing Online Offensive by Craig Whitlock, Washington Post Foreign Service, June 24, 2008, http://www.washingtonpost.com/wp-dyn/content/article/2008/06/23/AR2008062302135.html?sid=ST2008062302295

The rise of al-Qaeda's franchises by Sreeram Chaulia, Asia Times Online, January 6, 2012, http://www.atimes.com/atimes/Middle_East/NA06Ak03.html

Al Qaeda's Most Dangerous Franchise, by Alexander Meleagrou-Hitchens and Peter R. Neumann, The Wall Street Journal, May 10, 2012, http://online.wsj.com/article/SB100014240527023042036045773956110144 67928.html

Ghost Wars: The Secret History of the CIA, Afghanistan, and Bin Laden, from the Soviet Invasion to September 10, 2001, by Steve Coll, Penguin Press HC, February 2004

The Islamist ascendancy by Charles Krauthammer, The Washington Post, July 12, 2012, http://www.washingtonpost.com/opinions/charles-krauthammer-the-islamist-ascendancy/2012/07/12/gJQArj9PgW_story.html

Military Adaptation in War: With Fear of Change by Williamson Murray, Cambridge University Press, October 2011

A Revolution in Military Adaptation: The US Army in the Iraq War by Chad C. Serena, Georgetown University Press, September 2011

Military Misfortunes: The Anatomy of Failure in War, by Eliot A. Cohen and John Gooch, Free Press NY, 1990

Decade of War, Volume I; Enduring Lessons from the Past Decade of Operations, Joint and Coalition Operational Analysis, June 15, 2015

Prodigal Soldiers: How the Generation of Officers Born of Vietnam Revolutionized the American Style of War by James Kitfield, Simon & Schuster, February 1995

America's First Battles,1776-1965 by Charles E. Heller and William A. Stofft, University Press of Kansas, December 1986

SEAL Target Geronimo: The Inside Story of the Mission to Kill Osama bin Laden by Chuck Pfarrer, St. Martin's Press, November 2011

Carnage and Culture: Landmark Battles in the Rise of Western Power by Victor Hanson, Doubleday, August 2001

Jawbreaker: The Attack on Bin Laden and Al-Qaeda: A Personal Account by the CIA's Key Field Commander by Gary Berntsen and Ralph Pezzullo, Crown, December 2005

Why Benghazi is a Crucial Strategic Moment by James Lewis, American Thinker, americanthinker.com/2012/10/why_benghazi_is_a_crucial_strategic_moment .html#ixzz29laGVK8Z, October 2012

Grant Wins the War: Decision at Vicksburg by James R. Arnold, Wiley, October 1997

The Strategic Corporal: Leadership in the Three Block War by Gen. Charles C. Krulak, Marines Magazine, January 1999

The Joint Operating Environment 2010, US Joint Forces Command Joint Futures Group, 18 Feb 2010

Strategic Trends 2012, Center for Strategic Studies, 12 March 2012

Global Trends 2030: Alternate Worlds, The National Intelligence Council, December 2012

U.S. Army Counterinsurgency and Contingency Operations Doctrine 1860-1941 by Andrew J. Birtle, Center of Military History, United States Army, Washington DC, 1998

The Dynamics of Doctrine: The Changes in German Tactical Doctrine During the First World War by Tomothy T. Lupfer, US Army Command and General Staff College, Fort Leavenworth Kansas, July 1981

The Dictator's Learning Curve, Inside the Global Battle for Democracy by William Dobson, Doubleday, New York 2012

Why Nations Fail: The Origins of Power, Prosperity, and Poverty by Daron Acemoglu James Robinson, Crown Business, March 2012

Civilization: The West and the Rest by Niall Ferguson, The Penguin Press, November 2011

The American Way of War: A History of United States Military Strategy and Policy by Russell F. Weigley, Indiana University Press, January 1960

Makers of Modern Strategy from Machiavelli to the Nuclear Age by Peter Paret, Princeton University Press, March 1986

Invisible Armies: An Epic History of Guerrilla Warfare from Ancient Times to the Present by Max Boot, Liveright Publishing, January 2013

Index

Theocracy, 101
Third Wave Insurgency (New Model Insurgents), 65-66
Thirty Years War, xv, 2, 12, 26, 43, 66, 72, 102, 218, 312
Torture, 34, 112, 122-124, 140, 147, 205-206, 244
Thuraya Phone, 198-201
Twelvers, 83-84, 93, 228; Hidden Imam, 265-267
Twitter, vii, xix, xxi, xxx, 12, 16, 50-51, 189, 214
Transnational insurgency, 38, 51, 63, 68, 80
Trotsky, Leon, 66, 118, 156, 237,
Truman, Harry President, 132; establishment of Control of Electromagnetic Radiation (CONELRAD), 194
Tsarnaev, Dzhokhar and Tamerlan, vii-viii, 211
Turkey, 11, 23, 39, 106-107, 221, 223, 229, 235, 238, 253, 257, 259, 268, 280-286, 306-307,

Ummah, the Muslim Nation, 28, 33, 39, 80-83, 96, 124, 219-220, 225, 229, 235, 285
Umayyad Dynasty, 81, 235
United Arab Emirates, 105

Van Gogh, Theo, 152
Varus, 30, 170
Velayat-e Faqih (Guardianship of the Jurist), 84, 92
Vendee Uprising (1793-95), 66, 170, 242
Vicksburg, 166-167
Viet Cong, 6, 60-61, 323
Village Stability Operations (VSO), 160
Violent Extremist Organizations (VEO's), 45, 98, 163, 218, 223, 228
Virtual Organizations and States, 28-29, 46, 68-69

Wahabbi, Sunni, 62, 75, 77, 79-80, 94, 105, 218, 307
Weaponization, 47
Weapons of Mass Destruction (WMD), xxv, 7, 22, 25, 57-58, 201, 301, 304, 313, 322, 324-325, 328, 330
West Bank, 42, 107, 268, 306, 316
Western Civilization, 109, 141-144, 148, 227, 229-230
Westphalia, Treaty, xv, xxiv, xxx, 3, 4, 6, 10, 12, 22, 25, 101, 228, 312
Wiki War, viii, xxvii-xxviii, xxix, 10-12, 46, 53, 67
Wireless Application Protocol (WAP), 200
Woolsey, James, xiii, 30
World Trade Center 1993 bombing, xiii, 54, 64, 74, 133, 287-288, 293, 299-300

Admiral Yamamoto, 151
Yakuza (Organized Crime, Japan), 23
Yazdi, Ayatollah Mesbah, 84-85, 267
Yemen, 8, 35, 85, 98, 104, 106-108, 140, 148, 212, 218, 226, 253, 270, 278, 284, 287, 290
Yousef, Mosab Hassan (the Green Prince), 7
YouTube, vii, xix, xxi-xxii, xxx, 16, 50, 216, 245

Zarqawi, Abu Musab, xxi, xxii, 34, 98, 120, 205-207, 211, 315
Zawahiri, Ayman al, Leader of Al Qaeda after Bin Laden, 23, 33, 68, 98, 113, 206-207, 286, 291-292